A YEAR IN MUDVILLE:

**AN ORAL HISTORY OF CASEY STENGEL
AND THE ORIGINAL METS**

By **DAVID BAGDADE**

© Copyright 2010 David Bagdade. All rights reserved.

No part of this book may be reproduced, stored in a retrieval system, or transmitted by any means without the written permission of the author.

First published by Fortnight Publications in November 2010.

Printed in the United States of America.

First Edition

Manufacturing by CreateSpace

Book design by David Bagdade

ISBN-13: 978-1456342456 (CreateSpace Assigned)
ISBN-10: 1456342452
BISAC: Sports & Recreation / Baseball / History

A YEAR IN MUDVILLE

This title is also available as an e-book. For more information, visit www.smashwords.com/books/view/11400.

ACKNOWLEDGMENTS

This book has taken me nearly eight years to write, and it and I have both been through many twists and turns during that time. I would first like to thank my father and mother, Dr. Al and the late Susan Bagdade, accomplished writers themselves, for obvious reasons. My father and I were originally going to write this book together, and although his many other obligations prevented him from joining me in this endeavor, he has been a constant source of support and encouragement. Although I have been a fan of Casey Stengel since reading his biography as a child, it was Steve Rushin's 1992 anniversary piece in *Sports Illustrated* which truly sparked my interest in the Original Mets. It was after reading that article for the forty second time that I thought that someone should get it all down on paper, and why not me? Someday I hope to have a beer with Mr. Rushin and tell him thanks. I would especially like to thank Craig Anderson, Jay Hook, the late Rod Kanehl, Frank Thomas, the late Leonard Koppett, Walter Pullis, Ed Wolff, Jim Fertitta Sr., Jim Fertitta Jr. and John MacMaster, for allowing me to draw on their time and recollections, and Brian Heyman, Stan Isaacs and Rich Williams, with whom I corresponded by email. Rich, in particular, responded to my query with an essay which ran to five printed pages. Thanks, man . . . I really appreciate that. The Koppett interview was especially memorable too, in that it was one of the few times in my life where I felt that I was in the presence of actual genius. Finally, I would especially like to thank Linda Talley, my partner in life's journey, who has constantly inspired and encouraged me in this and in all things, and to whom I dedicate this book.

This book is also dedicated to the memories of Rod Kanehl and Leonard Koppett.

PROLOGUE	ix
CHAPTER ONE – The Void and the Idea	1
CHAPTER TWO – The Organization	20
CHAPTER THREE – Casey at the Helm	38
CHAPTER FOUR – Assembling the Team	53
CHAPTER FIVE – Spring Training	82
CHAPTER SIX – The First Month	108
CHAPTER SEVEN – Being Embalmed	129
CHAPTER EIGHT – The Players	155
CHAPTER NINE – The Manager	175
CHAPTER TEN – The Fans	199
CHAPTER ELEVEN – The Media	222
CHAPTER TWELVE – The Season Continues	236
CHAPTER THIRTEEN – Journey's End	260
CHAPTER FOURTEEN – The Aftermath	278
CHAPTER FIFTEEN – The Legend	321
AFTERWARD	340
BIBLIOGRAPHY	345
NOTES ON QUOTATIONS	362

PROLOGUE

"I been in this game a hundred years but I see new ways to lose I never knew existed before." – Casey Stengel, manager of the New York Mets

June 17, 1962, the Polo Grounds, New York: Marv Throneberry, first baseman for the New York Mets, steps into the batter's box to face Chicago Cubs starter Glen Hobbie. It's the bottom of the first inning, and Throneberry is in the unaccustomed position of having two runners on base and a run across the plate. More familiar, though, is the fact that the Mets are already behind 4-1. This deficit is substantially due to Throneberry; while the Cubs were batting in the top of the inning, he was called for interference with a Cubs base runner caught in a rundown. Having been given an extra out because of Throneberry's gaffe, the Cubs took advantage, scoring four times. Now, in an effort to atone for his mistake, Throneberry drives Hobbie's pitch into right center field for a triple, scoring the two runners ahead of him. The Cubs' lead has been cut to one and the Mets are back in the game with a runner on third – or so it would seem. Before the home crowd has had a chance to celebrate, Ernie Banks, the Cubs' star first baseman, calls for the ball. Hobbie dutifully tosses it to Banks, who steps on the bag. Tom Gorman, the first base umpire, has seen what Banks has seen – Throneberry clearly failed to touch first base on his way to third. He didn't even come close. Gorman calls Throneberry out on the appeal. Casey Stengel, the Mets' seventy-one year-old manager, instantly charges out of the dugout to challenge the call, moving as fast as his knobby legs will carry him, only to be intercepted by second base umpire Dusty Boggess. "Don't bother, Casey," says Boggess. "He didn't touch second base either." Stengel, in a line preserved for the ages, replies, "Well, I know damn well he touched third, because he's standing on it!"

Like the tales of Casey Jones and Davy Crockett, the story of this particular Throneberry misadventure has become legendary, and like these and other legends, the actual details have become blurred over the forty-eight years which have passed since the event took place. For example, some versions have Mets coaches Solly Hemus or Cookie Lavagetto or umpire Gorman delivering the setup line preceding Stengel's immortal reply. Other versions have Throneberry being called out at second, rather than first, with second baseman Ken Hubbs filling the role normally attributed to Banks. But the details really don't matter. Rather, the story exemplifies the travails of the 1962 New York Mets, the worst baseball team of the twentieth century.

Throughout baseball history, some players have been remembered only for a single moment of tragedy or misfortune which obscures any memory of the rest of their careers. Al Smith, the Chicago White Sox outfielder who had beer poured on his head by a fan during the 1959 World Series, is one example. When he died in 2002, *Sports Illustrated* even included in his obituary the famous picture of beer splashing onto the top of his cap. Another is Ralph Branca, the Dodger pitcher who threw the pitch which Bobby Thomson hit for the winning homer in the final inning of the last game of a playoff, thus sending the New York Giants to the 1951 World Series. Almost nobody remembers that Branca had been a very good pitcher prior to that moment, a three-time All-Star who had won 21 games only four years earlier.

The Original Mets, however, are different. Created as the result of substantial effort after the New York Giants and Brooklyn Dodgers fled for the West Coast in 1957, the Mets debuted in 1962 with a collection of over-the-hill veterans and unproven youngsters. Rather than a single moment of calamity or ineptitude, the has-beens and never-weres comprising the '62 Mets are remembered for an entire season in which the fine line between tragedy and comedy was repeatedly trampled on to the point of obliteration. With few notable exceptions, the players on the '62 Mets are known or recalled publicly for little else.

It seems every baseball aficionado over the age of 35 – Mets fan or otherwise – has his or her favorite story about the Original Mets. Some are clearly nonsense or intentionally exaggerated hokum, while others, having been related fifth-hand by a cousin's friend whose brother knew a guy whose barber claimed to have been there and witnessed the event, have had the details substantially rewritten over time (such as the passage leading off this prologue). Beyond dispute, however, are the facts and the statistics. The 1962 Mets batted .240 as a team, with only one regular hitting over .275, and they committed 210 errors (28 by their first basemen and 32 by a single utility player). They were eliminated from playoff contention on August 7, at which point they had won 29 games and lost 82 on their way to finishing 40-120 – 60 ½ games out of first place (and eighteen games behind the next-worst team). In setting a record for losses, they endured losing streaks of nine, eleven, thirteen and seventeen games. The pitching staff had a collective earned run average of 5.04, gave up 948 runs (147 unearned) and threw 71 wild pitches and 192 home run balls, and the ace of the staff, Roger Craig, not only led the team with ten wins but also with twenty-four defeats. He was one of four Mets pitchers who lost at least seventeen decisions (with two losing at least twenty), and Ken MacKenzie, the only hurler with a winning record, finished 5-4 with an ERA of 4.95.

In addition to the statistics, though, there are other historical curiosities which have contributed to the legend surrounding the 1962 team, as will be shown throughout this book. For example, after their first nine games, all losses, they found themselves nine-and-a-half games out of first. Also, due to a playoff resulting from the regular-season tie between the Dodgers and Giants, the Mets continued to drop in the standings even after the season had ended. The Mets were 0-15 on games played on Thursday. No other baseball team has ever traded a ballplayer for himself or hosted an

Old Timers' Game in its inaugural season. The Mets, of course, did both. No other club's roster likely contained a pitcher who won both games of a doubleheader and then never won another major league decision. The Mets had two. Nor did any other team have two players with the same first and last name – both pitchers – and assign them to be roommates. Indeed, the legend of their futility preceded their first game, as several of the players they acquired prior to their debut season chose to retire rather than play for the Mets. Of the forty-five who did play at some point during that first year, nearly half never appeared in another major league game after 1962. Finally, the Mets were probably the only team ever to be insulted by their patron at their coming-out party.

In sum, the '62 Mets' status as the worst baseball team of the modern era is beyond dispute. At the same time, though, they also were – and remain – one of the most beloved teams of any era. For better or worse, they were, in the immortal words of their equally immortal manager, "amazin'." The Mets drew over 900,000 fans to the decrepit Polo Grounds in 1962, paltry attendance by today's standards but good enough for sixth in the National League that season. More important, the Mets gave the hated Yankees stiff competition for attention and headline space in New York even as the Yanks were in the process of winning their third consecutive pennant and second World Series in a row. Met fan traditions, such as the "Let's Go Mets" chant and the displaying of banners, began that season, and some of these continued for decades and even to the present day. In addition, Stengel and others achieved folk hero status, while some ballplayers parlayed their membership on the Worst Baseball Team Ever into lucrative careers later in life (most notably Throneberry, who appeared in a dozen Miller Lite beer commercials in the 1980s). Eight people associated with the club are in the Baseball Hall of Fame (albeit not for anything they did that season), and its alumni have gone on to subsequent careers as successful businessmen, coaches, managers and broadcasters, and even a U.S. Congressman and a state senator. Through it all, interest in the team has never abated. In fact, Hall of Fame centerfielder

Richie Ashburn, best known for his stellar tenure with the Phillies before finishing up with the Original Mets, said in 1992 that he got more mail as the result of the 1962 season than he did for the previous fourteen years of his career.

In light of all this, it is hard to believe that there has never been a single comprehensive literary work focused on the events of the '62 season and the personalities of those involved. Sure, there was Jimmy Breslin's *Can't Anybody Here Play This Game?*, written in 1963 (and recently reissued), and Leonard Shecter's *Once Upon The Polo Grounds*, which appeared in the wake of the Mets' improbable 1969 World Series victory. These books, though thoroughly entertaining and highly recommended by the author, differ significantly from this text. Breslin and Shecter, both excellent writers, were newspapermen who covered the story with the veneer of their own personalities, even occasionally ignoring facts which did not fit the myth they wished to convey. With this book, though, it is the author's belief that no such treatment is necessary. Any strong story, and the saga of the Original Mets is no exception, should be allowed to tell itself; failing that, it should be told through the actual words of those who participated in, or at least witnessed, the events on which the story is based. With all due respect to Messrs. Breslin and Shecter, this text goes well beyond their earlier works not only in scope and in attention to the details of the events, but also based on the simple fact that the story is largely told herein by those who played a part. In fact, pitcher Jay Hook, who recorded the team's first win on April 23, 1962, told the author that this text will be the ultimate clearinghouse for information about the Original Mets – everything you ever wanted to know, and more.

Therefore, in addition to just telling what happened, this book will provide insights into the fascinating characters involved, and it will also explore the reasons for the team's legendary status even today. So pour yourself a cold Rheingold Extra Dry Lager and come examine what it was like to have spent a year in Mudville with the Original Mets.

CHAPTER ONE –
THE VOID AND THE IDEA

> "There are some things in baseball 35 to 50 years ago that are better now than they were in those days . . . How could you transfer a ball club when you did not have a highway? How could you transfer a ball club when the railroads then would take you to a town, you got off and then had to wait and sit up five hours to go to another ball club?" – *Casey Stengel, manager of the New York Yankees, testifying before the Senate Subcommittee on Antitrust and Monopoly on July 9, 1958*

The story of the Original Mets begins with a notice on a bulletin board. The notice was posted by Arthur E. Patterson, an aide to Brooklyn Dodger owner Walter F. O'Malley in the World Series press headquarters on October 8, 1957, during the Series between the New York Yankees and the Milwaukee Braves. The note succinctly informed the world that the Dodgers were moving to Los Angeles. They were joined by the former New York Giants, who had announced their own relocation to the West Coast seven weeks earlier.

The departures came as a shock to New York baseball fans, but they had been in the works for several years. Although both teams had been staggeringly successful on the field (in fact, the Series that fall was the first since 1950 in which the National League was represented by neither the Dodgers nor Giants), the neighborhoods in which their pre-First World War ballparks were situated were changing. Each had lobbied for new parks in better parts of town, and both had hinted that relocation was a possibility if their demands were not met.

The Giants clearly had a valid argument. For years, they had been third in a three-team city. Having to play their home games at the decaying Polo Grounds, the eighty-year-old ballpark located in Manhattan adjacent to Harlem, certainly did not help. The Giants had enjoyed considerable success in the early fifties, winning pennants in 1951 and 1954. However, despite these triumphs and the presence of exciting players such as Willie Mays, the team's attendance had plummeted by mid-decade, from 1.6 million in 1954, when they swept the World Series over the Cleveland Indians, to half that number the following year, to 630,000 in 1956, to 600,000 in 1957, when they finished sixth for the second year in a row. Of that paltry figure, a huge chunk came from eleven home dates with the Dodgers, without which the Giants' attendance would have been downright embarrassing. For unlike Dodger fans, who went to games regardless of how the team performed, Giant fans went to the Polo Grounds only when the Giants were winning.

Thus, while suffering through hard times on the field, the Giants were being abandoned by their fan base. A low-income housing project had been erected near the Polo Grounds, which had little on-site parking, and a trip to the ballpark was increasingly seen as a dangerous proposition.

In 1956, Giants chairman Horace Stoneham proposed an ultra-modern roofed stadium in Manhattan on a tract owned by the New York Central Railroad. Nothing came of this idea, and the next year, Stoneham raised the idea of an arena in Queens near the Bronx-Whitestone Bridge. For the first time, he made references to looking outside the city if he did not get his new facility.

The transformation of the Dodgers from the most beloved team to the most hated was very different. The Dodgers were the most successful National League club of the era, with six pennants in the eleven years after World War II. In the five years they didn't win, they had three near-misses, losing playoffs in 1946 and 1951 and being eliminated in extra innings on the final day of the 1950 season. Attendance at Ebbets Field was second in the league in 1956. In fact, they drew over a million fans every year between 1950 and 1957, a remarkable showing considering the ballpark's capacity was only 33,000. Moreover, Walter O'Malley owned Ebbets Field and thus did not have to pay rent. However, O'Malley still claimed the Dodgers were at a competitive disadvantage compared with teams with larger facilities, and beginning in 1951, shortly after assuming control of the Dodgers, he began asking the city for a new stadium. He was particularly envious of the former Boston Braves, who in 1953 had moved to Milwaukee and a modern stadium with parking for ten thousand cars. At that time, O'Malley had prophetically noted that the move could set off a chain reaction.

The Braves presented a tantalizing example of the potential of relocation. In 1952, their last year in Boston, their attendance was an unbelievable 280,000. The following season, their first in Milwaukee, they drew over 1.8 million, more than a six-fold increase. From 1954 through 1957, they topped two million a season, the first time a National League team had managed this. O'Malley drooled over these accomplishments, especially when the Braves defeated the Dodgers for the pennant in 1957 and then beat the hated Yankees in the Series – something the Dodgers had managed only once in seven tries since 1941.

O'Malley also worried about the changing complexion of his fan base. For decades, the Dodgers had drawn from the white middle-class communities surrounding the ballpark. Now, many lower-income African-American and Hispanic families were moving in, causing the whites to flee. Going to Ebbets Field was now viewed as a riskier venture, and the poor parking facilities didn't help, especially with more night games. While O'Malley certainly capitalized on this sentiment for his own purposes, the problem did exist.

Not everyone shared O'Malley's assessment of Dodgers' economics, though. Irving Rudd, the Dodgers' promotions director, pointed out years later that the Brooklyn ballclub made more money than any other in baseball, even the Yankees. O'Malley, he claimed, was just engaging in typical posturing; if the team drew two million, he would claim this was the minimum he needed to stay afloat.

In fact, attendance was the main factor distinguishing the Dodgers from the three teams which had moved earlier in the decade (the first teams to change addresses in five decades) – the Boston Braves, the St. Louis Browns and the Philadelphia Athletics. In fact, the Dodgers brought in over a million fans in 1957 – almost 100,000 more than the combined total the Braves, Browns and Athletics had drawn in their final seasons before moving.

The city moved fitfully in response to the Dodgers' request and took no action at all for the Giants. Mayor Robert Wagner proposed a new Dodgers stadium on the 1939 World's Fair site in Flushing, but O'Malley wanted a ballpark in Brooklyn. However, the location he chose – the end of the Long Island Railroad Line at Flatbush and Atlantic Avenues – met with the city's disapproval. Rumors continued afterward that O'Malley, having made up his mind to move, insisted on this site, knowing the city would not go along. In any event, his demands grew increasingly strident, and his threats to move grew louder and more ominous. The gulf between O'Malley and Mayor Wagner and Parks Commissioner Robert Moses grew wider.

When it became clear to O'Malley and Stoneham that their demands would not be met, they prepared to move. O'Malley got things rolling in August 1955 by demanding that the city seize the Flatbush site by eminent domain. When Moses refused, as expected, O'Malley announced that the Dodgers would play fourteen "home" games in Jersey City over the next two seasons, one game per year against each National League team. In doing so, he agreed to assume the expense of rehabbing dilapidated Roosevelt Stadium, an even smaller facility than Ebbets Field.

Red Smith, the venerable *Herald Tribune* columnist, saw the flaws in O'Malley's reasoning, which he demonstrated with amazing foresight in a piece he wrote in 1956, a year before the cataclysm. Smith pointed out first that O'Malley owned Ebbets Field free and clear, and yet, he was willing to embark on what Smith called "the New Jersey caper." Did O'Malley "have his eye on some distant city?" Smith postulated, identifying Minneapolis and Los Angeles as likely candidates. Clearly, said Smith, the "New Jersey caper" was merely part of a larger campaign on the part of the Dodger owner to convince the other National League owners to authorize a move.

Smith, though, was a voice in the wilderness at that stage. O'Malley's maneuvers then caused puzzlement and amusement, rather than anger. In their annual show that fall, the New York Baseball Writers referred to Walter's "Oldest Established Permanent Floating Franchise in New York." Few saw the irony at the time.

Then, in a move clearly intended to force the city's hand, O'Malley sold Ebbets Field to housing developer Marvin Kratter and took only a three-year lease in return. Wagner and Moses now had only a few months to get a stadium package approved so that it could be built in time for the 1960 season. O'Malley rammed this point home early in 1957, proclaiming that "unless something is done within six months, I will have to make other arrangements."

In the meantime, a secret courtship was taking place with the city of Los Angeles, which had been trying to attract a major league team since the late 1940s. Kenneth Hahn, Los Angeles County Supervisor, was in Brooklyn for the 1956 World Series with instructions to find a team – any team – willing to move to the west coast. While at the Series, he met with Calvin Griffith, owner of the Washington Senators, who was anxious to pull up stakes. As Hahn sat watching the game after meeting with Griffith, he was handed a note from O'Malley, which contained three words: "Don't sign anything."

Thereafter, O'Malley engaged in cloak-and-dagger maneuvers with Hahn while Griffith dallied. He soon hammered out a deal which gave him everything he could possibly have wanted. The concessions began with a modern new stadium with plenty of parking, to be built on 300 acres at Chavez Ravine and then handed over to him. The Dodgers' moneymaking capability was about to go into hyperdrive.

At the moment, though, the territorial rights to Los Angeles were controlled by Chicago Cubs owner Phillip Wrigley. O'Malley knew that Wrigley was disgruntled as the result of a disagreement with the city over his Pacific Coast League franchise. During the Baseball Writers Association's meeting in February 1957, O'Malley passed a note to Wrigley, offering the Dodgers' farm team in Fort Worth in return for the Cubs' Los Angeles minor league franchise. Wrigley agreed, and thus O'Malley acquired the right to put a baseball team into the city. It was quite a coup, considering that the Dodgers had paid $75,000 for the Forth Worth club ten years earlier and had put $500,000 into a new stadium. One commentator noted that it was "slicker than a Reese-to-Robinson-to-Hodges double play . . . along the lines of the Dutch buying Manhattan for twenty-four dollars."

Meanwhile, Stoneham had originally intended to move the Giants to Minneapolis, where he controlled the territorial rights and had a stadium deal. O'Malley, though, having worked out his coup in Los Angeles, knew it would be advantageous to have another National League ballclub in California, since the other teams could play them in succession, thus easing the expense of travel. Therefore, O'Malley convinced Stoneham that San Francisco would be a better option. On May 28, 1957, the league's other owners gave their blessing to O'Malley's and Stoneham's attempts to negotiate deals to move their respective clubs to California, provided the two announce their intentions by October 1. Both men denied that there was any significance to these events other than their desire to explore all options. On June 4, Mayor Wagner met with O'Malley and Stoneham and urged either owner to consider the Flushing Meadows site. Both refused, and the die was cast.

In the face of official ineffectiveness, some citizens were prepared to take action to either prevent the Dodgers and Giants from leaving, or, if they left, to replace them. George V. McLaughlin, the man responsible for bringing O'Malley into the Dodger organization as a young lawyer in the 1930s, first tried to buy the Giants from Stoneham. After being turned down, he then discussed forming an organization to lure an existing National League team to New York, or, failing that, to convince the League's owners to expand. The League, and its president, Warren Giles, rejected this latter idea on the grounds that the Giants and Dodgers were still in New York – for the time being, anyway.

On August 19, 1957, the Giants' board of directors, with one dissenting vote, approved the move to San Francisco. Stoneham made the announcement at a press conference. When asked if he felt any guilt about taking National League ball away from New York children, Stoneham pointed out that he hadn't seen many of their fathers at the Polo Grounds of late.

The lone dissenter on the nine-man board (which included Stoneham's son, nephew and brother-in-law) was M. Donald Grant, a long-time Giants fan who sat on the board as a proxy to Joan Whitney Payson, also a long-time fan and a minority shareholder. Mrs. Payson had been attending games at the Polo Grounds since 1910 (the same year a ballplayer named Charles Dillon "Dutch" Stengel signed with the Kansas City Blues of the American Association) and throughout the fifties, she had acquired a ten-percent ownership interest. Only Stoneham had a larger individual share. As a means of forestalling the move to the West Coast, Mrs. Payson even offered to buy the franchise from Stoneham, who turned her down as he had George McLaughlin. The Giants were going, and that was all there was to it.

On September 29, 1957, the Giants played their last game at the Polo Grounds in front of fewer than 12,000 fans. Attendance had been terrible all year – about 600,000 came to witness the long goodbye. As soon as the game – a 9-1 pounding by the Pittsburgh Pirates – was over, the players fled to the safety of the clubhouse, while the fans swarmed the field, taking the bases, bits of turf, anything that wasn't nailed down, along with some things which were. Many called for Stoneham's neck, but he wisely stayed away. Someone on the Giants' staff removed a two-foot square section of the center field sod, which the team took to San Francisco. One of the last to leave the ballpark was the widow of John J. McGraw, the tough-as-nails manager who led the Giants to ten pennants between 1902 and 1932. The loss was the eighty-fifth of the season against only sixty-nine wins, which ensured a sixth-place finish, only three years removed from their World Series sweep of the Indians.

Walter Pullis, a future Met fan, attended the final game. Ten years old at the time, he went with his mother; his father was too angry to go. They were approached by fans who had come with saws so they could remove the seats and take them home as souvenirs. Pullis' mother declined the offer to have their seats sawed, to their subsequent regret.

Five days earlier, the Dodgers had played their Ebbets Field finale, a 2-0 victory, in front of less than 7,000 fans. The team had still made no announcement, but everyone knew. House organist Gladys Gooding, acting on her own, acknowledged the occasion by playing "Am I Blue," "How Can You Say We're Through," "After You've Gone," "Don't Ask Me Why I'm Leaving" and "Thanks For The Memories" during the game. After the final out, she let loose with "May the Good Lord Bless You and Keep You" and "Auld Lang Syne," while some fans helped themselves to souvenirs and others simply stood and wept. Only the groundskeepers seemed not to have heard. After the last out, they raked the infield and covered it with a tarp, readying the field for the next game which would never occur.

O'Malley continued to play all the angles before finally posting his notice on the World Series press board on October 8. Of course, this was after the October 1 deadline imposed by the other owners. As the deadline approached, though, O'Malley suddenly faced a revolt among some Los Angeles officials who knew the value of what was being given away. For a heart-stopping moment, it looked as though the deal might fall through. On the eve of the deadline, though, Los Angeles mayor Norris Poulson, a staunch supporter of the pact, notified league president Warren Giles, untruthfully, that the deal was all but done, thus convincing the owners to grant a brief extension to take care of a few remaining details. O'Malley, Kenneth Hahn and Poulson used the time to mount a major PR blitz which carried the day. Therefore, Arthur Patterson was able to post O'Malley's notice, which read as follows:

> "In view of the action of the Los Angeles City Council yesterday and in accordance with the resolution of the National League made Oct. 1, the stockholders and directors of the Brooklyn Baseball Club have today met and unanimously agreed that necessary steps be taken to draft the Los Angeles territory."

Without fanfare or farewell, there was now no National League team in New York for the first time in 75 years. It was as unthinkable as it was unbelievable. For the overwhelming majority of Dodger and Giant backers, many of whom were second- or third-generation fans, there was no question of transferring their loyalty to the Yankees. Some became followers of other National League teams, while many others simply gave up on baseball.

Jim Fertitta grew up in Brooklyn and was a typical Dodger backer. He was born in 1931 and became a fan following the team's heartbreaking loss to the Yankees in the 1941 World Series. By 1957, he was married and living in Brooklyn with his wife and two children. Like many others, he heard the rumors but did not believe them. He felt the Dodgers were too much of an entrenched tradition to ever leave. After all, weren't the "Bums" even mentioned frequently in Hollywood movies? What bothered him most when the team did leave was what he saw as O'Malley's abandonment of that history.

Presidential biographer Doris Kearns Goodwin grew up in Rockville Centre, Long Island, and she became a rabid Dodger fan at a tender age. She was fourteen when the team left, and forty years later, she recalled the effect of the departures on her neighborhood in her touching personal memoir, *Wait Till Next Year*. It was, she stated, truly the end of an era, the end of rivalries, the end of arguments in the street over which team had the best center fielder, the end of tradition.

Although the city had dragged its heels in responding to the Dodgers' and Giants' threats to leave, it is also possible that the move westward was going to happen regardless of what the city did. Certainly there were many people who felt that way. Whereas former Dodger presidents Larry MacPhail and Branch Rickey pushed hard for increased attendance, O'Malley never did, and many observers theorized that he refrained from doing so in order to use the perceived turnstile decline as justification for his later actions. Maverick baseball owner Bill Veeck was only one of many who posited that O'Malley would have kept raising his demands on the city until they couldn't be met.

In his well-researched 1987 book, *The Dodgers Move West*, Neil J. Sullivan attempts to portray O'Malley in a positive light, with, it must be said, some success. Among other things, Sullivan posits that O'Malley was at all times prepared to bear the cost of building the new stadium and only wanted the city to assist in the process of obtaining the land. However accurate Sullivan's arguments may be, though, they do not alter the traumatic effect of the Dodgers' defection on Brooklyn fans.

Once the teams had actually moved, though, the city woke up. As Leonard Koppett noted, "A vacuum had been created. And if nature abhors a vacuum, a politician who may be blamed for its creation abhors it even more." The mayor immediately began to feel the heat from hotel owners and others who feared losses from an expected decline in tourism. Mayor Wagner, who was up for re-election the following month, knew he had to do something.

Within days of O'Malley's announcement, Wagner, with George McLaughlin's help, appointed a "Mayor's Baseball Committee" consisting of former Postmaster General James A. Farley; magnate Bernard Gimbel (father-in-law of Hall of Famer Hank Greenberg); Clint Blume, a prominent real estate developer and former Giants pitcher; and William A. Shea, a politically-connected attorney who had once owned a Long Island semi-pro football team. In subsequent years, Shea would also be instrumental in bringing the New York Titans pro football team (later the Jets) to town, as well as the New York (New Jersey) Nets basketball club and the New York Islanders hockey franchise. Although Shea was the least-publicly known member of the committee, he brought with him a number of important relationships as well as a reputation for getting things done, and he emerged as the chair.

The committee's mandate was clear: get a National League baseball team into New York as quickly as possible, by any means necessary. While the mandate may have been clear, the means by which to accomplish it were not. Shea immediately contacted the other National League clubs in an attempt to convince one to relocate to New York. This was a daunting concept, due in no small part to the lack of a place to play. The Yankees were not going to share Yankee Stadium, and the housing developer to whom O'Malley had sold Ebbets Field planned to demolish it. This left the ancient Polo Grounds as the only option, at least until a new stadium could be built.

Nonetheless, Shea forged ahead and was quickly stymied. Indeed, it is hard to see how he might have convinced another team to move to New York. The Phillies and Cardinals had just become the only teams in former two-club towns; moreover, Cardinals owner August Busch was not likely to abandon the Anheuser Busch brewery, which he also owned. The Braves had led the league in attendance for four years running in Milwaukee. The Cubs were staying in Chicago, the Pirates declined Shea's overtures, and the Giants and Dodgers were not coming back. The Pirates had also already turned down George McLaughlin's idea for the sale of the team to a New York owner. While Reds owner Powel Crosley showed initial interest, it soon became apparent this was just a tactic to extract a new ballpark from the city of Cincinnati. Nor was an American League team an option. Under Rule 1(c) of the rules of major league baseball, the Yankees had a territorial monopoly which would prevent another American League team from relocating into the city without the unanimous consent of all the clubs in both leagues, which was not going to happen. Dan Topping, co-owner of the Yankees, made it clear that he would personally veto any such move.

Expansion appeared to be another dead end. Although the number of major league teams had remained at sixteen since 1903, and although the league owners had been talking about expanding for at least ten years, there had been no action to further these discussions. As Veeck pointed out, if the major leagues ran Congress, "Kansas and Nebraska would still be trying to get into the union."

Shea soon realized that despite the desire of cities such as Atlanta, Denver, Houston and Minneapolis to host a baseball team, the major leagues were disinclined to expand, and certainly not into New York. In fact, the trend was for clubs to move away from cities in which there was already a team in the opposite league. Of the six franchise shifts between 1953 and the end of the decade (counting the Dodgers and Giants), five involved teams moving from a situation in which they had local competition to one where they were the only game in town. The Braves got the ball rolling, thus becoming the first major league team to relocate since fifty years before, when the Baltimore Orioles became the New York Highlanders (and, ten years later, the Yankees). Their departure from Boston got them out of the wake of the Red Sox. The Athletics then left Philadelphia to the Phillies and fled to Kansas City, and the St. Louis Browns emerged from under the shadow of the Cardinals (having drawn under 300,000 in four of their last five seasons in St. Louis) and reappeared in Baltimore as the Orioles. The Braves, Athletics and Orioles each posted attendance figures exceeding one million their first season after relocating, and the baseball owners believed that these franchise moves represented quite enough expansion. Even the sixth team was arguable. Although the Washington Senators did not have another team pressing them within the nation's capital, they were feeling the heat from the nearby Orioles to the extent where they found the environment of Minneapolis (recently spurned by Stoneham's Giants) much more inviting.

Now Shea was trying to convince baseball to put a team back into New York, where it would compete against the Yankees, the most dominant team ever. Moreover, he was doing so in a climate of heightened tensions resulting from his perceived efforts to "kidnap" a team. In the bad blood which followed, National League President Warren Giles was quoted as asking, "Who needs New York?" Of course, Giles' salary was paid by the league's owners, and he was known throughout the league as "Walter O'Malley's dancing bear."

Therefore, the only foreseeable solution besides giving up was to create a third major league with a franchise in New York, and the committee soon embarked on this path. Shea, who was nobody's fool, realized that he needed an experienced baseball hand to guide him. At George McLaughlin's suggestion, Shea formed a partnership with Branch Rickey, the most esteemed baseball executive of his time. In the 1930s, Rickey had created the minor league farm system, which he used to build the downtrodden Cardinals into a consistent contender well into the 1940s. In 1942, he moved to the Dodgers as part owner and turned the former Bums, the laughingstock of the league, into the powerhouse which dominated the circuit in the decade after World War II. Along the way he broke baseball's long-entrenched color barrier by signing Jackie Robinson. At the end of the decade, he sold out to O'Malley and joined another loser, the Pirates. In Pittsburgh, he demonstrated he had not lost his touch, assembling the nucleus of the team which would defeat the Yankees in the 1960 World Series.

Now, Shea reached out to Rickey, still employed as a consultant with the Pirates at a salary of $50,000 per year. Unbeknownst to either Shea or Pirates general manager Tom Johnson, Rickey had already been considering the idea of a third league as a counterweight to baseball's monopolistic behavior. Although Rickey was almost eighty, he still had energy and ingenuity. He agreed to serve as commissioner of the new league, thus giving Shea's enterprise instant credibility. When Johnson heard the news, he flew into a rage and terminated Rickey's consulting contract, at which point attorney Shea stepped in and negotiated a settlement for the remaining years of the agreement.

The two joined forces with a number of wealthy would-be owners and consulted with influential figures inside and outside of baseball. On July 25, 1959, in front of hordes of reporters at the Biltmore Hotel, Shea announced the formation of the Continental League. Five initial franchises were announced: Denver, Houston, Minneapolis, Toronto, and, of course, New York. Later to follow were Atlanta, Buffalo and Dallas, with play to begin in 1961. The owners of each franchise paid a $50,000 entry fee, giving the new venture a substantial war chest that would soon come in handy (and giving these owners attractive tax write-offs in the highly likely event that the league cratered). Looking ahead, Shea and Rickey also secured investors for possible future clubs in Honolulu, Indianapolis, Miami, Montreal, New Orleans, Portland, San Diego, San Juan and Seattle. Shortly after the announcement, the owners convened and elected Rickey president of the new league. Shea and Rickey made it clear they intended to compete with the established leagues for the same ballplayers and fans. First, though, they attempted to convince the existing owners to recognize their league on an equal footing, even addressing a group of them and Commissioner Ford Frick within hours of Rickey's election. Their message was couched in conciliatory terms, but it contained a barely-veiled threat to wage a no-holds-barred baseball war if the need arose.

In prior years, the major leagues had unmercifully crushed similar ventures, but the landscape in the fifties was different. Baseball had enjoyed an exemption from antitrust laws due to a curious 1922 Supreme Court decision stating that baseball did not qualify as interstate commerce since it could not be considered a "business." This had allowed baseball to act, in effect, as a legally-sanctioned monopoly. However, when Shea and Rickey commenced operations, the continued existence of the exemption was no longer a sure thing. In early 1957, the Court rejected professional football's attempt by to secure a similar exemption, holding that the matter should be decided by Congress. The Court's decision clearly stated that, but for its 1922 ruling, baseball's exemption would also be treated as a matter for Capitol Hill rather than the courts. The following year, the Senate Subcommittee on Antitrust and Monopoly held public hearings on competing bills concerning baseball's attempt to legislatively formalize the exemption. During these hearings, Yankee manager Casey Stengel stole the show with his testimony, delivered without a script or notes, reducing all present to helpless laughter.

At the time Shea and Rickey launched their new league, the legislature had still not acted. However, Senator Estes Kefauver, the chair of the subcommittee and a fervent trust-buster, had by then introduced a bill countering baseball's proposed exemption by placing the major leagues within the reach of the Federal Trade Commission. He also scheduled hearings on the bill to begin the day following Shea's rollout announcement. As a result, the owners had to act carefully, for if they destroyed the Continentals as they had previous ventures, this would prove they were acting in an anti-competitive manner, thus arousing the ire of fence-sitting Senators whose votes they needed. Shea and Rickey also kept the heat on by spending three weeks in the fall of 1959 visiting every member of the Senate subcommittee, especially those whose constituencies included the proposed Continental franchises. They also issued the following statement:

> "The present major league franchise-owners apparently have a total lack of loyalty to the communities which support their enterprises. The major league owner today refers to the 'national pastime' with great reverence. And, when it suits him, he behaves as if he were operating a quasi-public trust. But let a better 'deal' be offered in another city and he reverts instantaneously to the hundred percent businessman whose only guide is the earnings statement. The men who would hold franchises in the Continental League are local, civic-minded, financially sound baseball fans of excellent reputation. They pray for legislation which will permit them to exercise their franchises."

Not coincidentally, Senator Kefauver's bill would have made illegal any actions "preventing, hindering, obstructing, or adversely affecting the formation and operation of a new major league." It also would have drastically reduced the number of players each team could have under contract, thus making hundreds available to the Continental teams. The bill was supported by Senate Majority Leader (and future President) Lyndon Johnson and former Colorado Senator Edwin Johnson, former minor league president and father-in-law of Continental franchise owner Bob Howsam. The failure of the bill by only four votes gave the owners a wake-up call. If that were not enough, Shea also established a direct relationship with Senator Kefauver, and he made it clear that, regardless of whatever the legislature did, he was willing to test the strength of baseball's antitrust exemption in court.

In the face of these facts, the major league owners came to understand that the best way of killing the Continental League was to expand into its charter cities. Not only would this tactic undercut much of the logical argument on which the new league was based, it would also provide a pool of wealthy new owners from amongst the Continental backers. In addition, it would eliminate the need for a rematch on Kefauver's bill. New York reporter George Vecsey wrote that "expansion suddenly seemed such a good idea that the owners began to think they dreamed it up themselves."

Thereafter, a complicated dance ensued in which the two sides negotiated the Continental League out of existence before it ever got going. They reached an agreement in Chicago in July 1960, a short time after the narrow defeat of the Kefauver bill. In return for the Continental League falling on its sword, the National and American Leagues would each absorb two of the proposed Continental franchises. Once Commissioner Ford Frick got around Rule 1(c) by declaring Los Angeles and New York "open cities," it was decided that the AL teams would be based in Washington (with the existing Senators departing for Minneapolis, one of the Continental cities) and Los Angeles, to O'Malley's chagrin, and would take part in the 1961 season, while the NL clubs would be located in Houston and New York but would not begin play until 1962. The deal almost fell apart because the other owners wanted New York to guarantee the construction of a new stadium. At

Shea's request, Mayor Wagner sent telegrams to each owner containing such a guarantee. Shortly thereafter, the city and state began to cooperate on legislation designed to build the new team a municipally-owned stadium on the Queens site O'Malley and Stoneham had rejected. Shea and his backers formed a corporation called the Metropolitan Baseball Club of New York, which was awarded the franchise on October 17, 1960 – slightly more than three years after O'Malley's notice had been pinned to the bulletin board. They issued the following press release:

> "We have been officially notified of our acceptance into the National League, and we are justifiably proud that the National League has entrusted our group, the Metropolitan Baseball Club of New York, Inc., with the franchise awarded New York City. We accept this as an obligation to baseball followers the world over; to Organized Baseball; to the National League; and particularly to the people of the New York City metropolitan area whose needed support we are confident we will earn."

To this day, it remains unclear to what extent the Continental League masters ever actually intended to compete with the established leagues. Shea and Rickey made public pronouncements to this effect, asserting that a nation of 160 million people could certainly produce 200 more big-league ballplayers. Rickey worked especially hard, both publicly and behind the scenes, to secure baseball's blessing as well as passage of the Kefauver bill, and he was bitterly disappointed when the league was negotiated out of existence. However, while the Continentals assembled backers, hired administrators and, to varying degrees, went about organizing baseball operations, the fact remains that in over a year of existence, the league never signed one player (although other sources dispute this, maintaining that one team signed one infielder), much less played a single game. Moreover, Shea was at all times aware that his mandate, first and foremost, was to bring a team back to New York. Thus, it is possible, if not probable, that the entire enterprise was intended simply to force baseball to expand. One of the Continental backers, Craig Cullinan of the Houston franchise, summed up the venture as "an enormous success because it ran what became the biggest bluff in the history of professional sports." Baseball was frightened of losing its monopoly in the legislature or the courts. Knowing this, Shea kept hammering at the doors until they opened.

In any event, Shea had accomplished his mission, though it had taken three years, and it would be another year and a half before the unnamed team took the field. At this point, he went back to his long-neglected law practice, leaving others to get on with the business of building a baseball team literally from scratch.

CHAPTER TWO – THE ORGANIZATION

> "Resigned, fired, quit, discharged, use whatever you damn please. I'll never make the mistake of being seventy again." – *Casey Stengel, announcing his "resignation" as manager of the New York Yankees, October 18, 1960*

Once the National League awarded the franchise to Bill Shea's Metropolitan Baseball Club of New York, the group set about constructing a complete organization from the ground up. They needed a place to play, ballplayers, a manager and someone to run the entire operation. The first problem would be solved as the result of considerable finagling between the team, the city and the state. The second was resolved, after a fashion, by means of a player draft. The third and fourth issues were taken care of with help from an unlikely source – the mighty Yankees, fresh off their tenth American League pennant in twelve years.

The preliminary step, though, was to determine the ownership group. The prime money behind the late and unlamented Continental franchise had been Dwight F. "Pete" Davis, a sportsman from Long Island, whose family who had originated the Davis Cup in tennis. Bill Shea, also from Long Island, recruited Davis based on his ties to other wealthy aficionados.

Among the investors Davis recruited was Dorothy J. Killam, a wealthy Brooklyn Dodger fan from Canada. Whenever the Dodgers played in the World Series, she traveled to New York in her private railroad car to attend the games. She was the widow of Isaak Killam, a Canadian lumber magnate who had also owned part of the *Brooklyn Eagle*, the demise of which in the late 1950s had led one commentator to note that Brooklyn had become the only American city of at least two million residents which had neither a daily newspaper nor a major league baseball team. Mrs. Killam had once offered to buy the Dodgers from Walter O'Malley for five million dollars; he was so stunned that he reportedly spilled his drink on her, but he maintained enough of his composure to decline the offer.

The third member was Mrs. Joan Payson, who still held a ten-percent interest in what were now the San Francisco Giants. Mrs. Payson owned the famed Greentree racing stable with her brother, John Hay Whitney, who additionally owned the *New York Herald Tribune* and served as the Ambassador to the Court of St. James. She was an heir to the substantial Whitney family fortune, valued at $200 million at the time of the elder Whitney's passing in 1929. She was married to Charles Shipman Payson, a multi-millionaire in his own right.

Mrs. Payson was one of the richest women in the country, but she seemed an unlikely person to own a baseball team. However, she had been a staunch Giants fan for almost five decades, regularly attending games at the Polo Grounds. Before the team's departure in 1957, she could frequently be seen sitting in a box near the home dugout wearing a Giant cap. She was present when Bobby Thomson hit his legendary home run in the ninth inning of the third game of a playoff with the Dodgers to determine the winner of the 1951 pennant. Her loyalty to the Giants and National League ball was so great that, like many fans after 1957, she stopped going to games rather than visit Yankee Stadium.

Even so, when Pete Davis traveled to Florida to convince Mrs. Payson to back the Continental League team, she was initially not interested. Then Branch Rickey went to see her himself, and he persuaded her to change her mind. Mrs. Payson agreed to bankroll the enterprise, and she once again designated M. Donald Grant, her long-time investment counselor, as her proxy. Grant, a senior partner in Wall Street's Fahnestock & Co., had formerly served on the Giants' board of directors at Mrs. Payson's behest, where he had cast the lone dissenting vote against the move to San Francisco.

Also in the picture was Jack Kent Cooke, the wealthy trial lawyer who had been one of the principal backers of the Continental League. Branch Rickey saw Cooke as a potential ally and solicited his involvement.

Originally, Davis, Mrs. Killam and Mrs. Payson each owned thirty percent of the Continental League franchise. However, when Mrs. Killam expressed her intent to be president of the venture, the others bought her out. Davis also wanted to run the team, and once he realized this was not going to happen, he sold his stock to Mrs. Payson, who ultimately ended up with almost all but the five percent held by Grant and the six percent owned by stockbroker G. Herbert Walker (uncle of President George Bush and great-uncle of President George W. Bush). She paid about three million dollars for her share. Afterwards, she maintained some vague officership; when questioned, she would say, "I think I'm some kind of a vice-president or something."

After the National League awarded the franchise, Mrs. Payson found that league rules prevented her from owning stock in more than one team at a time. She solved her dilemma by donating her Giants shares to New York Hospital (which thus became the team's largest minority owner) rather than sell them back to Stoneham. After this reorganization, Grant was named president of the Metropolitan Baseball Club. Despite having spent so much time bringing the franchise into existence, Bill Shea did not own any portion of the team.

This left the issue of what to do about Branch Rickey, co-founder of the Continental League. He had originally brought in his son-in-law, Charles Hurth, to serve as general manager of the New York Continental franchise. Although Hurth had years of minor league experience, including a stint as president of the Southern Association, the ownership group wanted someone with solid major league credentials and designated Grant to conduct a search. At first, Rickey himself seemed the obvious choice, since he was familiar to all involved and no one could question his track record. On February 15, 1961, Grant formally offered Rickey a contract to become general manager, but Rickey demurred, apparently hoping that Cooke would be able to buy a larger share of the enterprise and support Rickey in his bid to become chairman. He also alienated the others, especially Mrs. Payson, with his terms. He insisted on a budget of five million dollars to sign and develop talent as well as an unfettered hand in spending that money. He also wanted to continue living in Pittsburgh while running the New York operation. His demands were more than Mrs. Payson was willing to meet. Cooke had no appetite for the resulting conflict and sold his interest, thus depriving Rickey of his one ally, and Grant notified Rickey that the contract offer was withdrawn. Thus was Rickey eased aside, although Hurth remained on the payroll for most of the year.

The problem was soon solved by, of all people, the Yankees. On October 18, 1960, the day after the League awarded the franchise to Shea's group, a most unusual press conference took place at the Le Salon Bleu room in the Savoy Hilton Hotel on Fifth Avenue. The Yankees had called the conference to announce the "resignation" of their seventy-year-old manager, Casey Stengel. However, they miscalculated by having Stengel show up, believing he would simply acknowledge the move and share some memories with the press corps. With the help of some alcoholic lubrication, though, Stengel made it abundantly clear that if he had "retired," it was not by his choice. He accused the club of starting a "youth program" as a "solution as to when to discharge a man on account of age." The reporters immediately figured out that things were not as they seemed, and someone asked Stengel if he had been fired, to which he responded that they could call it what they wanted. With that, Stengel simply took over the press conference and badly embarrassed the organization in the process.

The press and public were stunned by the abrupt removal of Stengel, whose Yankees had spent the preceding twelve years making the American League an amazingly dull place. Unlike the National League, where the pennant was often decided on the last day of the season or even by a playoff, the issue in the junior circuit was not whether the Yanks would win the pennant, but on what date they would clinch. Indeed, Stengel's players soon came to depend on their anticipated World Series shares as part of their compensation (a sentiment on which the Yankees' notoriously cheap general manager, George Weiss, relied in order to keep salaries low) and would even begin discussing how they would spend the money in spring training. In his dozen years at the helm of the most storied franchise in baseball, Stengel had brought ten pennants (including a record-setting five in a row in his first five seasons) and seven World Series championships to New York. Fifty years after Stengel's removal, these records have still not been equaled. In the two other years, the team had finished second; in fact, in 1954, the Yankees had won 103 games – their best showing under Stengel – but still couldn't catch the Cleveland Indians, who finished with an unbelievable 111 victories. Only once had Stengel's team won less than ninety games, and his record in pinstripes was 1,149-696, a winning percentage of .623. In fact, the Yankees had just been to the Series, although they had lost in seven games to the Branch Rickey-constructed Pirates. However, there was a barely-veiled sentiment that despite Stengel's success, the game was passing him by. In addition, there was a ready successor in Ralph Houk, a former Marine officer and third string catcher who had risen through the Yankees' ranks during the previous decade. There was a clear concern that Houk would soon be enticed by another team's managerial vacancy, and the Yankees, having an investment in Houk, did not wish to lose him. Therefore, Stengel was gone.

But there was more to come. Two weeks later, on November 2, the Yankees called another press conference to announce that George Weiss, who had built the teams that Stengel so successfully managed, had also "retired." The Yankees explained, belatedly, that they had adopted a mandatory retirement age of sixty-five, and therefore, Weiss, who was sixty-six, had to go. Weiss had been with the team since 1932, when he was hired to run the farm system, and he ascended through the hierarchy to become general manager in 1947, hiring Stengel as manager two years later. He kept the roster filled with outstanding players, keenly anticipating when an aging luminary would break down or retire and having another budding star waiting. In doing so, he achieved renown for his skills as a talent evaluator and master manipulator, for his attention to detail and for his penurious nature. Unlike Stengel, though, Weiss went quietly, as a reward for which he was allowed to continue in an advisory role, for which he was to be paid $35,000 per year for five years as long as he did not become general manager of any other ballclub.

Don Grant could scarcely believe his luck. Here he was looking for someone with the ability to build a major league team from scratch – not a common skill set – and the best man had just become available. Grant had not become a successful businessman by passing up opportunities such as the one the Yankees had just dropped into his lap. Two opportunities, actually – first, to hire an extremely successful and experienced baseball man, and second, to make the Yankees look bad in the process. As he said later, "Acting more or less on my own, I turned to the most obvious man in the world who might be available – to George Weiss, of course."

In February, he reached out to Weiss. Although Weiss had planned to wallow in nostalgia in Florida during spring training, he agreed to meet Grant for dinner at the Savoy Hilton that night. This was followed by further discussions, both before and after Weiss traveled south, and a March 1 meeting at Mrs. Payson's Florida mansion to discuss terms. Although Weiss was happy to be back in the game he loved, his wife was at least as thrilled to have him out of the house again, as she told columnist Red Smith while Weiss was still out of work: "I married George for richer or poorer, for better or worse. But for heaven's sakes, I didn't marry him for lunch."

On March 14, 1961, Weiss was hired to construct and run the new team. His terms were in the neighborhood of five years at $100,000 per year – more than he ever earned with the Yankees. This enabled him to have lunch downtown near the team's offices on Fifth Avenue, leaving him to Hazel for breakfast and dinner. In an effort to get around the restrictive clause in Weiss' Yankee contract, Don Grant promoted himself to chairman of the board and was "succeeded" by Weiss as president. Charles Hurth remained as general manager, at least in name, until November. Although the Yankees grumbled, they had to keep paying Weiss, even as he began to lure the press and the public away from his former employer. He kept his title of president, and Grant conveniently forgot to hire another general manager once Hurth was gone.

Ever prepared for any eventuality, Weiss had started scouting National League teams even before he joined the new franchise. By the time he signed his contract, he had seen every National League team in action except the Giants and the Cubs, who were training in Arizona.

Weiss was immediately presented with five principal problems, the most immediate of which was where the team would play its home games in 1962. Obviously, a new facility could not be built in a year. The Yankees had already rejected any idea of sharing their stadium in the Bronx, and Ebbets Field had been demolished the year before. This, unfortunately, left only the Polo Grounds, situated at 155th Street and 8th Avenue in Manhattan.

The Polo Grounds sat on land which had originally been given to John Lion Gardiner by the King of England in the 17th century, and it had indeed hosted polo matches in the 1800s. The park had been in use for baseball since the early 1880s; the Giants had played there for sixty-seven years, and the Yankees had used it while waiting for Yankee Stadium to be completed. Although the park had a storied history, the words most often used to describe itby the time the Giants left were "decrepit" and "crumbling."

It was an odd place. The ballpark was horseshoe-shaped, and it featured ludicrously short right- and left field lines (257 and 279 feet, respectively) and a cavernous centerfield which stretched 483 feet from home plate. A team without a fast centerfielder could be in for a long afternoon. The Giants, of course, had had Willie Mays, and his exploits in the Polo Grounds were legendary (including the historic snagging of a ball off the bat of Cleveland's Vic Wertz in the 1954 World Series which would have been a home run anywhere else). Only one batter, Braves first baseman Joe Adcock, had ever hit a ball into the centerfield bleachers in a regular season game. The short porches, though, meant that pull hitters could pad their power stats hitting "Chinese home runs," and more than a few games were decided by a lazy 260 foot fly ball, indeed, Bobby Thomson's famous home run had traveled only 300 feet to left. Also, the clubhouses were located behind the wall in straightaway centerfield. This meant that a pitcher sent to the showers had a seemingly endless walk to the clubhouse, having to endure jeering fans the entire way. The bullpens were also located in center field, and Met pitcher Roger Craig remembered that "they had this little awning over the bench to keep the fans from spilling beer on you." The layout of the facility was also conducive to all sorts of sideshows and other distractions which gave the ballpark a carnival midway feel. Hitting in the Polo Grounds, according to columnist Murray Kempton, was like "playing a pinball machine."

The Polo Grounds had stood unused for baseball since the final Giants home game on September 29, 1957, and it had been in bad shape then. Since that time, it had hosted stock car races, soccer matches and, beginning in 1960, the New York Titans of the American Football League. Having no alternative, though, Weiss and Grant began negotiating with the City Housing Authority for use of the facility. In fact, the Board of Estimate had already decided to demolish the Polo Grounds to allow the Housing Authority to build a housing project. Realizing the predicament, though, the Authority put its plans on hold until a new stadium could be completed in time for the 1963 season. In return, the team agreed to spend $300,000 putting up new lights and an electronic scoreboard, building a private club and restaurant, preparing the playing field and painting the place. The club also had to assume the cost of dismantling the tower lights, seats and turnstiles when the park was ultimately torn down. Considering the team only intended to use the Polo Grounds for one season, this was an exorbitant investment, but there were no options.

In order to get the park into usable condition, Weiss hired James K. "Big Jim" Thomson, who had just resigned as the Yankees' stadium manager. Thomson, who had also previously managed Ebbets Field, was deputized to do whatever he could to get the Polo Grounds ready in time for the 1962 season. The field was in such poor shape that the crew ended up plowing the entire grounds and re-planting fresh sod imported from Long Island. Unfortunately, though, about the only other improvement which could be done in time for play to begin was a fresh coat of white paint.

The next area of concern for Weiss was to find a permanent home for the team, an endeavor he later described as "my biggest problem and headache." However, Weiss quickly proved that he could spread the problems and headaches around. Unfortunately, the day after Weiss took the job, the State Assembly voted down the city's plans to build the new ballpark in Flushing Meadow, the site Walter O'Malley had previously rejected. Ironically, Weiss, while with the Yankees, had vociferously opposed the city's request for state stadium funds, submitting detailed reasons why the concept was unworthy of approval. Now that his allegiance had changed, he was able to see the merits of the plan which had previously eluded him, stating that "I have a different picture now . . . with the additional information I have received, I think the new stadium is a good deal for both the city and the club."

Now, the city and the team pulled out all the stops, with Mayor Wagner, Robert Moses and Bill Shea joining the effort, and they convinced several dozen legislators to change their minds. The Assembly soon took a second vote and granted the funding.

Once the money was approved, the wrangling over the stadium itself could begin. This process involved protracted negotiations between Don Grant, representing the principal tenant, and Newbold Morris, City Parks Commissioner, on behalf of the owner. Once they reached a consensus, the Board of Estimate had to sign off on the plan. The Board was comprised of the mayor, the president of the city council and the comptroller (each of whom had two votes) and the five borough presidents (with one vote each). Two board members opposed the measure – both from the Bronx.

After Grant and Morris reviewed the plans, reached an agreement and secured the blessing of the Board of Estimate, they ran into an unexpected obstacle – George Weiss. The meticulous Weiss had assembled a list of over two hundred defects he had found in the proposed plan, and he wanted each addressed. This took six months of daily – and sometimes nightly – meetings, since the alternative was to go back before the Board of Estimate, which nobody wanted. Morris employed all sorts of diversionary tactics, including taking everyone to Tavern on the Green; however, the group spent six hours at the restaurant that night trying to resolve the issue of where three clocks were to be placed and what kind of signs should go with them. Another struggle involved the number of toilets; although the plans called for 329, Weiss wanted 600, remembering a shortage of these at Yankee Stadium, especially for women. Morris got so exasperated that he went to Yankee Stadium, counted the toilets and called Joan Payson to ask whether she intended that fans would watch baseball or go to the bathroom. This resulted in a compromise figure of 526.

On October 28, ground was broken on the stadium, which still didn't have a name. A massive letter-writing campaign resulted in the facility being named for Bill Shea, who by now was not involved with the team in any capacity. Still, it was hard to argue with the choice, since it had been Shea's monumental effort which had brought the team into existence. Branch Rickey threw his own influence into the campaign, even writing a letter to the mayor and the City Council warmly praising his former partner, comparing Shea to "a turkey in a tobacco patch, not caring if he knocked down the stalks to get the worm" and stating that "the responsibility for the result is his and his alone." Mayor Wagner agreed, stating that "there never would have been a stadium if it hadn't been for Bill . . . it would probably still be a parking lot." Thus, the Mets were to play in what was probably the only baseball park named for a lawyer.

Another order of business was to come up with a nickname for the team. This turned out to be easier than anything else so far. Writers such as Dan Parker of the *New York Mirror* had already been referring to the team as the "Mets," an abbreviation of the corporate name, the Metropolitan Baseball Club. Even before the National League had officially awarded the franchise, Mrs. Payson had organized a committee consisting of herself and the wives of her compatriots. The committee asked for suggestions through the local papers, and the public responded with over five hundred different names, which included such offerings as the Dwarfs, Ex-Isles, Gashouses, Kangaroos, Knights of the Diamond, Molars, Mother-in-Laws, Muggers, Rickey-Rockets, Rickey-Sheas, Shea-Rickeys, Slumlords and Wigwams. The Mets name was one of the finalists resulting from a cocktail party Mrs. Payson held in her Manhattan apartment in which she presented a number of sportswriters with a list of proposed nicknames and asked them to narrow the list down to ten. She preferred this name all along, although she reportedly also favored the Meadowlarks, a reference to the team's future home in Flushing Meadow. The other eight were the Avengers, Burros, Continentals, Jets, NYBs, Rebels, Skyliners and Skyscrapers. The Mets nickname had numerous advantages. It was short, punchy and easily employed by copywriters. It also signified that, unlike the

Yankees and especially the Dodgers, the team would draw its base from the entire metropolitan area, rather than being identified with a single borough. Plus, of course, there was the fact that people were already using it. "Mets" was announced as the winner on May 8, 1961. Of course, the name had actually been in use since the previous fall.

In fact, it was far older than that. By 1961, few remembered that there had already been a baseball team called the New York Metropolitans, or "Mets." It had been brought forth in 1883 by John Day and Jim Mutrie to join the American Association, which had been created to compete with the National League. Day appointed Mutrie manager, and with players such as Hall of Fame pitcher Tim Keefe, the team won the AA title in 1884 with a record of 75-32. An estimated hundred thousand New Yorkers celebrated the pennant with a torchlight parade. The Mets then participated in baseball's first-ever postseason event, being swept by the National League champion Providence Grays. Day also owned the New York Gothams of the National League, and despite the Metropolitans' accomplishments, he was convinced the Gothams had a better chance of long-term success. Therefore, he raided the Metropolitans' roster, transferring most of the best players to the Gothams along with manager Mutrie. Both teams continued to play their games at the Polo Grounds, which at the time was divided into two parks. After a predictably disastrous 1885 campaign, Day then sold the remnants of the Metropolitans to Long Island businessman Erastus Wiman. Wiman tried to make the franchise a go, enduring two horrendous seasons before selling the few quality players he had left to Charlie Byrne, owner of the National League's Brooklyn Bridegrooms (later the Trolley Dodgers, later still the Dodgers) in 1887. The AA moved what remained of the Metropolitans to Kansas City, where they became the Cowboys and folded after two more horrible seasons. In the meantime, Mutrie managed the Gothams, by now renamed the "Giants" because of their stable of tall players, to NL pennants in 1888 and 1889. The Metropolitans, having thus contributed to the development of both the Giants and

Dodgers, disappeared into baseball history and were forgotten by the dawn of the new century.

Once the Mets name was made official, a logo was created, although it was not formally approved until November 16, 1961. The logo, which was designed by sports cartoonist Ray Gatto, has remained virtually the same ever since. The circular shape and overall theme of the logo, as well as its orange stitching, were all intended to resemble a baseball. The team's colors were blue (from the Dodgers) and orange (from the Giants), again dramatizing the return of National League baseball to New York; blue and orange are also the official state colors of New York. The bridge in the front of the logo and the skyline in the background were meant to symbolize that the Mets represented all five boroughs, in contrast to their predecessors and the Yankees. The church spire on the left of the skyline honored Brooklyn, the borough of churches. Then was the Williamsburg Savings Bank, the tallest building in Brooklyn, followed by the Woolworth Building. After a broad view of Midtown, next came the Empire State Building and, at the far right, the United Nations building.

The logo was well-received by fans of the new club, including Jim Fertitta, who was especially pleased with the colors. "It was exciting how the Mets took their uniform colors from both teams. A little orange, a little blue, the white . . . and I says, 'They're making this here team like the two [departed] teams combined together.'"

The next order of business was for Weiss to assemble his troops, a mix of capable foot soldiers and solid baseball men. He kept Rickey's son-in-law, Charles Hurth, and Wid Matthews from the staff of the Continental League franchise, although Hurth was gone by November. Weiss added Lou Niss, chief of publicity for the Continentals and former sports editor of the late *Brooklyn Eagle*, as traveling secretary. Also retained from the Continental organization was Matt Burns, a former assistant of Rickey's when both were with the Dodgers. Burns was to earn notoriety during the banner craze which swept the Polo Grounds during the Mets' first season.

Tom Meany, who had written about New York baseball for years, became the publicity director. This turned out to be a curious choice, since Meany was not interested in assisting the press. While he was happy to regale a barroom full of reporters until all hours, he had no desire to help them learn things they actually wanted or needed to know. Leonard Shecter recalled when a *Times* reporter asked Meany for a press brochure; Meany replied that he didn't have enough for himself and walked away. Meany had also attracted notoriety during Mrs. Payson's team-naming cocktail party by reportedly spilling a drink onto her $50,000 Persian rug.

Weiss then tabbed Bill Boylan, another New Yorker popular in baseball circles, to run the press lounge at the Polo Grounds. Boylan had been a former minor league pitcher before becoming a mailman in Brooklyn. For years, following the completion of his route, Boylan would park his mail truck outside Ebbets Field, go inside and put on a Brooklyn uniform and pitch batting practice.

Weiss also brought in more than twenty scouts, including ex-Yankee Gil McDougald; Hall of Fame second baseman Rogers Hornsby; former Brooklyn star Babe Herman; and Johnny Murphy, a veteran Yankee relief pitcher who had also run the Red Sox' farm system. Murphy and Matthews soon became Weiss' right-hand men, and Murphy, given the unwieldy title of "New England and New York Metropolitan Area Supervisor," rose through the ranks to become general manager in 1968. Meanwhile, Hornsby became the team's batting coach in time for the 1962 season. In addition, Bill Bergesch, the head of the farm system, soon set up a network of over thirty full- and part-time scouts and several dozen "bird dogs" – fans who recommended local players in return for various considerations. Matthews was immediately dispatched to Arizona to watch the players training there, while Murphy did the same in Florida.

Of course, Weiss' efforts were defined by the penny-pinching nature which had been widely reported during his tenure with the Yankees. Described by *Sports Illustrated*'s Steve Rushin as "tighter than a Speedo two sizes too small," Weiss was said to have justified an extremely low salary offer to traveling secretary Lou Niss by pointing out, with a conspiratorial wink, that "traveling secretaries are usually voted a full World Series share."

This was not entirely true, though. On his first day in the Mets' office, he assembled all the holdover Continental employees and announced that not only would they all keep their jobs, but they would also receive the same medical and pension plans Weiss had instituted with the Yankees, widely regarded as the best in baseball.

For all of Weiss' attempts to draw order from chaos, the enterprise had a certain pulled-together charm. This was partly because Jim Thomson's crew was revamping the Polo Grounds, meaning that the Mets' offices had to be set up in other places. Bob Mandt, who was hired by Thomson and remained with the team more than four decades later as vice president of special projects, worked a variety of jobs in the early days. Mandt first found himself working out of a basement at Howard Clothing Store, a company which was to earn its own place in Mets lore at the end of the first season, doing clerical work in preparation for the opening of the team's ticket office at Penn Station. Mandt assumed responsibility for responding to an enormous amount of ticket requests, despite never having sold a ticket previously. This led to him being asked to take over the task of actually opening and running the Penn Station office.

The first ticket office, though, was set up in November 1961 at the Martinique Hotel under the auspices of Bill Gibson, who had run the former Dodger ticket office at Ebbets Field. The Martinique was seven blocks from the Metropolitan Opera House, or Met, as it was known. The sign Gibson put up – METS TICKET OFFICE– was bound to cause confusion between the Met's ticket office and the Mets' ticket office. In a well-known story, possibly apocryphal, a patron appeared one day and asked Gibson for "two for Traviata." Gibson is reputed to have replied, "Where would you like them? On the first- or third-base side?"

Even if office space was a problem, money was not, thanks to Mrs. Payson. In an additional *coup de grace*, Brooklyn-based Liebmann Breweries, whose Rheingold products were hugely popular in the boroughs, bought heavily into the excitement surrounding the return of National League baseball. Phillip Liebmann himself, a longtime fan who read *The Sporting News* as a boy, led the company's charge. Rheingold paid six million dollars, the biggest deal of its kind at the time, in return for the radio and television rights to 126 Mets games per year for five years. This sum was roughly double what the franchise and all its first-season players would cost. The brewery also agreed to purchase thousands of dollars worth of tickets each season. Cigarette manufacturer Brown & Williamson bought the rights to the remaining games. The games were to be televised on WOR Channel 9, and aired on the radio at WABC 770.

Meany and Niss, among many others, then reviewed over a thousand applications for radio and television broadcasters. One memorable contribution came from a gentleman who called himself "the voice of the Black Hills of South Dakota." After listening to 160 audition tapes, they selected Lindsey Nelson, who had years of experience broadcasting both baseball and football.

Nelson was a solid choice. He first achieved prominence re-creating games over the radio for the Liberty Broadcasting Network and quickly rose to become NBC's sports director in the early 1950s at the tender age of 33. In addition to broadcasting many baseball games, he also announced for the fledgling National Basketball Association and called many college and pro football contests as well. As if this were not enough, he had served alongside Leo

Durocher on NBC's Saturday Game of the Week telecasts for the previous five seasons.

Selected to join Nelson were Bob Murphy, who had announced for Boston and Baltimore and had done college football play-by-play, and Ralph Kiner, the former Pirates slugger who had also broadcasted games for the White Sox. Murphy auditioned with a tape of his call of Roger Maris' sixtieth home run the season before off Oriole pitcher (and future Met) Jack Fisher. Kiner, one of the most feared power hitters of his day, then ranked tenth on the career home run list, and his total of one homer every 14.1 at-bats has to this day only been exceeded by seven other players. After his playing days, he served as general manager of the minor-league San Diego Padres before going into broadcasting with the White Sox in 1961. This was one area in which the Mets organization made excellent choices. Nelson remained at his post for seventeen years, retiring in 1979. Murphy called his last game in September 2003, a few months before his death, and Kiner has been with the team ever since the 1962 season.

The new triumvirate wasted little time in establishing their personalities. Nelson developed the habit of wearing the most bizarre sports jackets he could find. Murphy, like any sportscaster, had his stable of recognizable phrases, and Kiner delighted fans with his occasional verbal missteps in the booth. Kiner's interview show, "Kiner's Korner," provided quite a few memorable moments during the 1962 season, and since.

In addition, former Dodger pitcher Ralph Branca, who had served up Bobby Thomson's legendary home run, was tabbed to do the pre-game radio show. One can only imagine how Branca, who was never the same following the event, felt about spending so much time at the Polo Grounds. He reportedly knew the exact section number of the seats into which Thomson's "shot heard round the world" had traveled.

Weiss also established a working relationship with the Mets' first farm team, Class B Raleigh of the Carolina League, and he entered into an agreement to share the Triple-A Syracuse franchise of the International League with the Minnesota Twins. In addition, he started to accumulate the first batch of players, signing whatever college or high school athletes (the major league amateur draft did not begin until 1965) and free agents he could find. Almost none of the dozens of players who entered the system during this time ever cracked the big league roster. Among the first of these was Mark Hoy, who had been throwing against a wall before being selected in an open tryout at the Polo Grounds.

Finally, Weiss signed a pact securing the Yankees' old spring training facilities in St. Petersburg, Florida, which the Yankees had abandoned in favor of Ft. Lauderdale. The St. Pete facilities were among the best in baseball, and even before Weiss returned with the Mets, he had his eye on them. He asked Elen C. Robison, chairman of the Florida Baseball Commission in St. Petersburg, to hold the site for him. Robison was good as his word, and the Mets, whoever they would turn out to be, were set for spring training.

The Mets also acquired a mascot, a beagle named Homer. Homer resided in luxury at the Waldorf-Astoria on Park Avenue, and he was trained by Rudd Weatherwax, who had also schooled Lassie. Eventually, Homer learned to perform tricks like barking on cue and holding a small "Let's Go Mets" banner in his teeth. Unfortunately, despite Weatherwax's efforts, Homer never quite learned to run the basepaths at the Polo Grounds, which was to be his signature stunt. Many commentators were soon to point out that this gave him something in common with certain Mets players.

Finally, only two significant steps remained. One of these, the accumulation of major league players (some actual, most merely alleged), would take place by means of an expansion draft following the 1961 World Series. The other was to hire a manager.

CHAPTER THREE – CASEY AT THE HELM

"A lot of people my age are dead at the present time, and if you ain't, it ain't bad." – *Casey Stengel, manager of the New York Mets*

By the spring of 1961, Charles Dillon Stengel had spent half a century as a ballplayer, manager and even a team president. He was born on July 30, 1890, one of three children. As a player, he appeared in almost 1300 games with the Brooklyn Dodgers, Pittsburgh Pirates, Philadelphia Phillies, New York Giants (for whom he hit two game-winning home runs in the 1923 World Series) and Boston Braves, finishing with a career .284 average. In the twelve years between 1949 and 1960, the Yankees he managed had made a joke of the American League, winning ten pennants and seven World Series. He had won the Series in each of his first five seasons in New York, setting a record which still stands. His rosters had boasted players such as Mickey Mantle, Whitey Ford and Yogi Berra, and he had done what any manager is supposed to do when provided with such an embarrassment of riches –win big.

In the process of becoming baseball's most successful and highly-paid manager, he had also become a national hero, speaking in a baffling style known as "Stengelese" and providing New York columnists and national writers with daily reams of lively copy. Leonard Shecter has provided as good a definition of Stengelese as exists: "He would refer to 'he' and 'the fella' and 'the left-hander' and 'their second baseman' and 'my outfielder' and while his logic was at all times impeccable, his arguments always entirely lucid, one had to be *en courant* with his team, all other teams in the league and his problems of the moment and the past, to understand his references. This is why wretches all over the country have written that Casey Stengel spoke a species of double-talk. They just didn't know enough about the game of baseball. About that, Stengel knew everything."

Leonard Koppett, who described Stengel as "very much my baseball guru" and who wrote about him in a series of books, listed Stengel's recurrent phrases as "'why wouldn't ya . . .' and 'you're fulla bull and I'll tell ya why . . .' and 'now wait a minute, that's what I been tryin' to tell ya,' and 'what's wrong with . . .' followed by some unorthodox suggestion." Robert Lipsyte, another young writer unofficially mentored by Stengel, observed that "the columnists who drifted in and out would get chunks of what sounded like gibberish repeated as Stengelese and then leave, but if you stayed there long enough, you got to know who the pronouns were about, and then you could follow the course of the conversation and you'd have very interesting stories about baseball, and great discussions of strategy and technique, none of which I remember, because I was drunk. I really thought he was a genius."

To the uninitiated, Stengel's manner of speech did sound like doubletalk. Indeed, he was often criticized for doing so as a means of avoiding questions he didn't want to answer. Those who dealt with Stengel all the time felt differently. Maury Allen, who covered the early Mets and later wrote a Stengel biography, believed that the doubletalking was mostly for public consumption, since Stengel would often talk in a more straightforward manner privately. As far as public remarks were concerned, it just took a bit of deduction. Allen cited one particular example from Stengel's days with the Yankees. Stengel was generally loathe to reveal his lineups too far in advance, preferring to do it minutes before delivering the lineup card to the umpire. If someone asked him who he intended to start at second, he would dance around the question rather than be rude or offer a simple "no comment." As Allen pointed out, though, the beat writers learned to read between the lines of supposed doubletalk. "If he veered off into talking about Rogers Hornsby, you knew he wanted an offensive second baseman for a high-scoring game," wrote Allen. "That meant Billy Martin. If he mentioned a good defensive player from years past, he wanted one for a low-scoring game. That meant Jerry Coleman, who could field better than Martin."

Other observers from other cities were less inclined to engage in the deductive exercise. "Stengelese made you swear English was Casey's only foreign language," said Indians broadcaster Jimmy Dudley. Columnist Jim Murray of the *Los Angeles Times*, who wrote a wonderful obituary on Stengel's death, stated that "Casey Stengel is a white American male with a speech pattern that ranges somewhere between the sound a porpoise makes underwater and an Abyssinian rug merchant."

Some of those around the Mets quickly came to understand how Stengel operated. "I think Casey was a very bright, quick guy," said pitcher Jay Hook. "My interpretation of Stengelese – and he didn't always speak in Stengelese – is that Casey was thinking about what he was saying, then he'd think about what he wanted to say next. Now he'd still be talking about the first subject, but he'd be thinking about the second one. Well, then, he'd jump to the second one, and then while he was in the second one, he'd remember he didn't finish the first one." Lindsey Nelson, despite being a veteran broadcaster, quickly became aware that in order to have a relationship with Stengel, one had to surrender one's identity. Stengel, he learned, was meant to be listened to rather than talked with, and if he happened to assign to you a name other than your own, that became your name.

In the period following Stengel's firing by the Yankees, he was offered $150,000 by the *Saturday Evening Post* for his views on life and baseball. In the story, serialized in five parts beginning in September 1961, Stengel summed up his own career as follows: "When I was signed to manage the Yankees after the 1948 season, many of the writers couldn't understand why I was brought in to handle such a big job. They had watched some of my work evidently, as a manager at Brooklyn in the '30s and at Boston later on. They thought that I wasn't very serious, and that I never cared very much about winning games, and that I was too easy to get along with, and so forth. But if you think you're going to do better just by being serious all the time and never telling any stories or doing any kidding around – why, you're a little mistaken. Some people never could understand that. At the time the Yankee job came up I was managing at Oakland in the Pacific Coast League. We had just won the pennant out there. Edna, who is Mrs. Stengel, enjoyed the Coast league very much, and she thought possibly I wasn't going back to the big leagues. And there was a question that I wouldn't too. There were half a dozen times before then that I was going to quit baseball altogether. I'd been a ballplayer and manager for thirty-eight years. I didn't care much whether I went back up. Of course, I'm glad I did go with the Yankees. We started off by winning five straight pennants, which was a record, and five straight World Series, which naturally was also a record. By the end of my twelve years there we'd won ten pennants and seven world championships, which I guess is as much success as a manager ever had over that span."

One of Stengel's most legendary features was the humor he employed to deal with trying situations. In 1918, during the First World War, he was playing for the Pirates and had a salary dispute with the club's owner. He left the team and, at the age of twenty-eight, enlisted in the Navy. His brief wartime service involved managing the Brooklyn Navy Yard's baseball team, and he developed the habit of scheduling games against teams of sailors who had just returned from months at sea. In 1925, while serving as player-manager and team president of minor league Worcester, he received a better offer to manage Toledo of the American Association. However, Judge Emil Fuchs, the owner of the Worcester club, was unwilling to let him go. Stengel then took three more actions in his capacity as club president. The first was to give rightfielder Casey Stengel his unconditional release. The second was to fire his manager, Casey Stengel, which he did in accordance with the rules of the Eastern League in a letter also forwarded to the

Commissioner of Baseball. The letter read: "Manager Casey Stengel is hereby and as of this date dismissed as manager of the Worcester Eastern League club. Signed: Charles Dillon Stengel, President, Worcester Baseball Club." His final action was to resign as president, after which he led Toledo to the AA pennant, the first in franchise history, in 1927.

When the Toledo club went bankrupt, he was hired to manage the Brooklyn Dodgers on a four-year contract, serving threeyears before being fired. After using the buyout of his Dodgers deal to make a killing in the oil business, he then managed the Boston Braves, this time lasting six years. In his nine seasons with Brooklyn and Boston, his teams never finished higher than fifth, and he developed a reputation as a buffoon who never took his job seriously enough to win. After leaving Boston, though, he managed minor league Milwaukee to the American Association pennant in 1944 and was asked by George Weiss, head of the Yankee farm system, to take over its Kansas City minor league affiliate. He then went to Oakland in the Pacific Coast League, winning the pennant in 1948. His timing couldn't have been better. Weiss was now New York's general manager and had just fired skipper Bucky Harris after the Yankees lost the 1948 pennant to Cleveland. Overcoming substantial resistance within the organization, Weiss brought in Stengel, who, after years of losing, now had the premier job in baseball – managing the New York Yankees.

Through his tenure in New York, he never lost his sense of humor, as noted by *Sports Illustrated* in 1956, when Stengel was still with the Yankees: "Casey is a clown; not a buffoon, but an authentic clown, a skilled practitioner of an ancient art who can calculate a comic effect as accurately as he can sense a pitcher's fading stuff." Stengel biographer David Cataneo posited that "Stengel used humor the way some people use a Swiss army knife – for many, many purposes." Veteran columnist Jack Lang noted that Stengel "had a reputation as a clown, and he didn't do anything to deny it . . . baseball to him was fun," while the venerable Red Smith wrote that "it is erroneous and unjust to conceive of Casey Stengel merely as a clown. He is something else entirely – a competitor who has always had fun competing, a fighter with the gift of laughter. There is wisdom in comedy." If Stengel was a clown, wrote Maury Allen, then "you need a new dictionary."

Others outside baseball noted his abilities, comic and otherwise. George Gobel, the famed comedian and after-dinner speaker, said that if Stengel "turned pro, he'd put us all out of business." Former president Richard Nixon, speaking in 1992, had this to say: "If I had it to do over again, I'd name Casey secretary of state. The essence of diplomacy is to confuse the opposition. The opposition never knew what Casey was talking about. Stengel always knew."

Humor aside, though, no one could doubt Stengel's knowledge of the game, a subject he took very seriously indeed. Hobie Landrith, the Mets' first draft pick, said that "Casey was always known as a storyteller and kind of a jokester. He had players on the Yankees, you know, you felt like he'd push some buttons and they're gonna win. When I got over to the Mets and observed and listened to Casey, I appreciated the fact that he had something to do with those world champion teams because he was just an encyclopedia of baseball." Veteran outfielder Richie Ashburn was more succinct in his view: "I never knew a man could know so much about the game."

After the Yankees stunned the baseball world by firing Stengel within days of another Series appearance, he returned to the West Coast. Before leaving, he commented on his dismissal: "I commenced winning pennants as soon as I got here, but I did not commence getting any younger. If we'd been a little luckier and won that last World Series game from the Pirates I don't think it would have made any difference. They'd made up their minds and explained it as puttin' a new program in which it said your time was up at sixty-five. The last month of that 1960 season I knew I was through because the attitude of the people in the front office, outside of Mr. Weiss, was different. It was as though they had heard the word. Then, after the Series I was asked to meet Dan Topping and Del Webb at the Waldorf Astoria. I was pretty sure what was going to happen. There wasn't any contract on the table for me to sign. When you don't see that paper anywhere in sight you just know they're gonna lower the boom on you."

As Weiss put his Met organization together in the spring of 1961, Stengel was enjoying semi-retirement at the age of 71 in Glendale, California, with Edna, his wife of almost four decades. He and Edna lived in an eleven-room house with an enclosed tennis court, and he was working as a vice president at the Valley National Bank. The bank, formed in 1957 by Edna's brother, Jack Lawson, named Stengel a stockholder and director even before he left the Yankees. The operations expanded to Toluca Lake in 1961 and then merged with four other banks. In Stengel's autobiography, published the following year, he stated that "I have a nice office in the Toluca Lake branch. I'm a vice-president, although I'm still not what you'd call a full-time banker. I tell people my job is to stand in front of the vaults." His brother-in-law offered a differing view: "Casey was an important investor in the bank and a serious vice-president. He talked to customers, he worked with the staff, he interested people in investment, he helped generate new business."

His desk at the bank was adorned with a sign reading "Stengelese Spoken Here." He was in good spirits, and while he kept in contact with baseball people, he had no thought of returning to managing. In fact, he turned down a formal offer to manage the Detroit Tigers, and he declined to respond to several other feelers. He acted as an advisor to Gene Autry and Bob Reynolds, the owners of the new Los Angeles Angels, but he declined to formalize his role. "When he turned down Detroit and other offers to manage in the majors," said Edna the following year, "I was sure he would not take another baseball position." "I had some amazing offers," confirmed Stengel. "Some of them involved more than just managing. I was to get a piece of the ball club, and possibly a piece of an outside business, and perhaps end up making more money than I ever did before. Actually the propositions started even before I left the Yankees. During the 1960 season a group that hoped to acquire the ownership of the Kansas City ballclub – but didn't succeed in getting it – asked if I'd be interested in going in with them. Then I was approached about the new Continental League that Branch Rickey was trying to start. As it turned out, the new league fell through, with some of its franchises being taken over by the present major leagues. There were numerous other propositions after the Yankees let me go. But all these people wanted to get somebody as soon as possible, and I wasn't ready to commit myself to a new baseball job just then. I finally decided I'd sit out a season and then see how I felt about it."

At the same time, the game had not left him. He attended most Yankee-Angel games as Autry's guest, and he also saw a number of Dodger games as Walter O'Malley's guest. When the reporters asked him, as they often did, whether he would ever manage again, he would answer elliptically: "I'm outta baseball and I was in it for a long time and it don't have to be forever. By the time the season's over, I'll know what's going to happen to myself in baseball or whether I don't want to go back into baseball. Right now, I can't tell you just what I'm going to do. I can't just take baseball and cast it away."

On the opposite coast, George Weiss needed a manager, and he knew from his first day on the job who he wanted. So, apparently, did everyone else, including Jimmy Cannon of the *New York Journal American*. Immediately following Stengel's firing by the Yankees, Cannon had published an open letter to Joan Payson: "I am not asking you to engage Casey for sentimental reasons. Most of your players will be obscure kids or used-up old timers. Casey's the most famous man in baseball. He's the only box office manager in the game." Now, as Weiss got his ducks in a row, Cannon wrote that "The type of team the Mets assemble will decide whether Casey

Stengel manages them or remains in the banking business. The old Yankee manager, who is stalling George Weiss, president of New York's new National League franchise, would be agreeable to a one-year contract if he believes he has a respectable team to run. Otherwise, the *Journal American* was informed, he will remain out of baseball forever."

The chase began on an April morning, when Weiss telephoned the Stengel household. He called to get Stengel's telephone number at the bank and told him that a fellow named "Don Grant" would be calling later that day. This, of course, was M. Donald Grant, chairman of the Metropolitan Baseball Club of New York. When Grant called, the two men discussed Stengel becoming the new team's first manager. Stengel thanked Grant for the call and wished him luck with his endeavor while stating emphatically that he was happy in his present capacity.

This, of course, was merely a softening-up process, as Weiss was not content to take no for an answer. He traveled to San Francisco ostensibly to go to the All-Star game, but actually to confer with Stengel, who also attended. Weiss also made three trips to Los Angeles, ostensibly for scouting purposes, but he met with Stengel on each visit. The two spoke earnestly about the manager position. After Stengel again said no, Weiss kept after him for the rest of the summer until Stengel finally said he would think about it. Meanwhile, the press kept the pot boiling with endless speculation. "When we were seen together at Dodger games in the Los Angeles Coliseum," recalled Stengel the following year, "many of the newspapermen and broadcaster immediately thought that I had already been signed up by Mr. Weiss. But the truth of the fact was that I had not agreed to take any position." George Weiss confirmed this. "He couldn't make up his mind," Weiss told *Sports Illustrated* the following year. "My impression was that his wife was encouraging him not to return."

As a fallback, Weiss took the precaution of hiring two former managers, Solly Hemus and Cookie Lavagetto, as coaches as the 1961 season wore on. Both had had just been fired from their clubs during the season, Lavagetto from the Twins in June and Hemus in July from the Cardinals. Weiss promised each of them that if Stengel declined the job, they would be considered for the position, and that if Stengel did come aboard, they might have the chance to succeed him when he retired.

However, Weiss was determined to have his man. He called Stengel again in late September and formally offered him the job. He told Stengel that he had to have a manager in place by the expansion draft the following month. By this time, Stengel was wavering. He told Weiss to call him back in a couple of days. Instead, Weiss played his trump card, arranging for Joan Payson to call Stengel herself. Stengel was clearly flattered by having the team's charming multi-millionaire owner tell him that she needed him. In the end, that did the trick. Weiss and Stengel soon agreed on a one-year contract which would pay Stengel $100,000. Rumors of Stengel's return had coursed through the city as soon as Weiss was hired, and it had taken more than six months, but Weiss finally had the manager he wanted. "His wife, Edna, later told us that he had really wanted to come and how glad she was we had called him again," said Weiss. "He flew East right away." Weiss "had the idea that I was the best man for the job," recalled Stengel, "because he knew I could handle the playing end of things to his satisfaction, and leave him free to concentrate on the office end, where there was so much to be done. Finally I began to feel that if Mr. Weiss wanted me that much, maybe I owed it to him, after his many years of getting me good ballplayers on the Yankees. So on September 28, I said perhaps I'd accept, after all. He told me he'd announce it at ten o'clock the next morning. Later on that day I began to change my mind again. I was going to call him back and tell him so. But before I could do it he had some of his owners on the Mets talk to me. He put Mrs. Joan Payson on the phone, and she said, 'My goodness, we're enthused about having you come here, and we're honestly ready to go to considerable expense to build up the club.' Then Don Grant came on, and he told me the same thing. And I said to myself, 'Well, these are nice people to work for.' And good owners are very important in baseball."

Before flying back east, Stengel held a press conference in his bank office in Glendale: "I guess they want high-class people back there. You can say I'm happy to be joining the Knickerbockers and going back to the Polar Grounds and the salary – well, it's wonderful. I was pleased to think they wanted me over so many men now available in baseball. You're gonna have troubles in the baseball business every day, no matter who you're with. Myself, I'll expect to win every day. I hope not to get sick worrying about it if I don't. The main thing is to keep up the spirit of your men. Keep your head up and feel you're gonna win the next one." Leonard Shecter also recorded the event: "He leaned back into the deep swivel chair in the office of his bank and talked about how happy he was to be running the New York Knickerbockers. It was a half hour at least before he realized they were the Mets. And a week at least before he began calling them amazing."

In his reference to the "Knickerbockers," Stengel apparently confused his new club with New York's professional basketball team. Or did he? Few baseball fans remembered that there had been a New York Knickerbockers baseball team formed by Alexander Cartwright in 1845 (commonly acknowledged as the first organized club), but Stengel, a master of baseball history, probably did; a few wags remarked that Stengel had probably played for the team. For neither the first time nor the last, Stengel left everyone wondering whether he was mistakenly befuddled or exceedingly clever. Only the old man himself knew what he meant – assuming even he did.

When asked later why he had agreed to return, Stengel explained that it was to "assist Mr. Weiss and see if I can't start and rebuild this thing in a hurry. Mr. Weiss influenced me by getting on the phone too often. I talked to the ownership and the first thing you know I changed my mind and said 'yes.'"

In his autobiography, he expanded on his reasons: "A lot of people thought I was wrong [to come back]. I'd gone out of baseball with a pretty good record, and they thought I should stand on it. But I believe that baseball is larger than Casey Stengel's record. I couldn't turn down this group that is sincerely out to give New York City another fine major-league ball club. I know that this city needs more than just the one team, for the benefit of the people that live there and for the many visitors that come to town."

In what was to become a pattern, the Mets trumped the Yankees at the PR game. On October 2, 1961, two days before the start of the World Series between the Yankees and the Reds, the Mets introduced Stengel as their new manager in the same room, Le Salon Bleu of the Savoy Hilton, in which the Yankees had held Stengel's farewell almost a year to the day earlier. He was in classic form as he bantered freely with "his" writers. He also introduced his coaches, Hemus and Lavagetto, each of whom was sure he would be manager within a year. Stengel, in a playful mood, spied a broom, retrieved it, and, with his coaches, held it up so the photographers could capture their intent to make a "clean sweep" of the league. The World Series was forgotten for the moment, the Yankees simply couldn't compete with the return of the Old Perfesser to New York. When asked about his health, Stengel responded, "I didn't say I'd stay fifty years or five and my health is good enough above the shoulders." When reporters inquired soon afterward as to how the team would be run, Stengel answered, "Can't say how the Mets will be run. They never been run yet."

It was clear that Stengel was back where he belonged – in charge of a ballclub. This opinion was shared even by Edna Stengel, who, ten years earlier, had complained, tongue in check, to Joe Williams about her husband's obsession with the game in which he had spent his adult life: "'If he does not quit baseball this year I'm going to leave him,' insisted Mrs. Casey Stengel yesterday [February 21, 1952], 'and I want you to put that in the paper too . . . For 27 years all I've heard is baseball talk. This boy can't go to his right. That boy can't hit a curve ball. You can run on this fellow. You can pitch to that fellow. One man is a Kraut Head, another is a Road Apple, and another is a Fancy Dan and last year I heard all about switch hitters because Mickey Mantle was on the team. If just once in a while we had some other topic of conversation around the house. Even a good messy ax murder.'" Now, as her man was about to get back into the game he loved, she told Mrs. Payson, "Thank God you didn't take his no. He's been miserable without baseball."

However, Jack Lawson, Edna's brother, didn't seem so sure. "I don't think she was terribly excited about getting back into baseball again at that stage," he said. "I think she would have preferred it if Casey stayed away. I can tell you this. Casey would not have gone back if she had made a strong stand against it. They always made decisions together. Casey knew baseball. Edna knew business and she knew Casey."

Mrs. Stengel also related a touching anecdote. The advertising agency representing Rheingold, the Mets' media sponsor, had sent a camera crew and Miss Rheingold herself to the Stengel household in Glendale to film a number of print and billboard ads before Stengel left for spring training in Florida. Stengel appeared in these ads in his new Mets uniform (which, as will be seen, got him in trouble with commissioner Ford Frick), and simply did not wish to take it off afterward. "He kept the uniform on after they'd all left the house. When it came time for dinner he arrived at the table still wearing the suit with the word METS scrawled in orange and blue script across the front. Later in the evening, when I happened to go into his den, there was Casey sprawled out with a book in his favorite arm-chair sound asleep still wearing the uniform. He did everything but wear it to bed instead of his pajamas – that's how glad he was to be in a baseball suit again."

Leonard Koppett offered an additional explanation for why Stengel re-entered the fray: "Casey felt very deeply that he owed baseball something. Here was a team that had been set up in New York and couldn't possibly be competitive. His motivation was, 'I want to make this franchise viable. I can't turn a sow's ear into a silk purse and win games with these guys, but I can make some of them better players, I can fascinate the public, I can sell tickets, I can promote, I can be out front, available to everybody.' That's how he looked upon his position." After all, as Stengel himself put it, "What difference does it make if the monuments they built for you when you are a king lean a little bit after you've gone?"

The public relations windfall to the Mets cannot be overestimated. Although it remained to be seen how Stengel would deal with young players on a team guaranteed to lose, one thing was certain: when he spoke, people paid attention, and attention was something the Mets badly needed. With Casey at the helm, they would never suffer from a shortage of news coverage. This turned out to be a good thing, because Tom Meany, the Mets' publicity director and former newspaperman, didn't care about helping the media publicize the team. Stengel, naturally, leapt into the breach. "When he wasn't at the ball park, he wanted to talk about the game," said Lindsey Nelson, "so he could always be found where people gathered – in lobbies, in restaurants, in bars, in press rooms. You never had to go looking for Casey. He was always right at hand."

Stengel also filled a role for which Weiss was particularly ill-suited – the focal point for the team. Although Weiss was well-respected, he was not well-liked, certainly not as Stengel was. As Leonard Shecter wrote later, "The personality of George Weiss was such that he always held back something. He was a stiff, cold man who brought with him from his days with the Yankees an unfriendliness that might have destroyed the good will which fell so easily to the Mets, had it not been for his old friend Casey Stengel. One of the great wonders of the world is that Stengel and Weiss were able to remain friends through the years. Perhaps it was that they were such different men."

In seven months, Weiss had succeeded in finding a place to play in 1962; ensuring that the team would have a new stadium; hiring competent administrators, scouts and coaches; and securing the most recognizable manager in the game – all while garnering maximum publicity every step of the way. Now it was time to get some players, and Weiss' hitherto unbroken string of successes was about to end.

CHAPTER FOUR – ASSEMBLING THE TEAM

"I want to thank all those generous owners for giving us those great players they did not want. Those lovely generous owners." – Casey Stengel, manager of the New York Mets

The Mets' first defeat came before they even played their first game. The coin flip which would decide who would select first in the expansion draft was won by the Houston Colt 45s.

The expansion procedure was curious. Baseball's later expansions resulted in the entries having to pay fees in the tens of millions of dollars. The Mets and Colt 45s, however, had to pay only $50,000 each. The real cost of admission would come in the form of payments to the other National League teams as compensation for the 22 players drafted by each expansion club.

The three-round draft took place in at league headquarters in Cincinnati on October 10, 1961, the day after the Yankees won the World Series over the Reds. Each of the other eight teams had contributed fifteen names, with seven to be players who were on the club's active roster as of August 31, 1961, and the other eight to be drawn from elsewhere within the team's system. In the first round, New York and Houston would each select sixteen players – two from each of the existing clubs – at $75,000 per player. In the second, they would then pick two more players at $50,000 each. Finally, each would take four players from the "premium list" at $125,000 per player. Thus, Houston and New York would each pay close to two million dollars, with the proceeds to be divided *pro rata* among the eight existing teams.

The year before, the American League had also conducted a draft in order to populate its Los Angeles and Washington expansion franchises. The league froze the established teams' forty-man rosters at a fixed point during the season, and any player not on the rosters as of that date was deemed available. As a result, the Senators and Angels were able to acquire some quality players, and the Angels actually finished third in their second season.

The National League, though, was not about to let such a thing happen, despite Walter O'Malley's assertions that the National League would use the same system as the American League. They treated the expansion pool as a dumping ground for players they didn't want, thus ensuring that the new teams would remain in the second division for years to come. This was not a prospect designed to cheer the front offices of the expansion clubs. Reportedly, when Houston general manager Paul Richards left the owners' meeting in which the draft framework was announced, he walked up to a group of reporters and stated, "Gentlemen, we've just been fucked." In fact, Richards complained so loudly that league president Warren Giles felt obliged to call him in and silence him. But the bitterness remained.

Even the timing of the NL draft was an indication as to how things would go. It was scheduled to proceed before October 16, 1961 – the date on which minor league players could be called up by the senior club and put on the forty-man roster, thus making them ineligible to be raided by another ballclub. The club would often have to release veterans to make room for the callups on the roster. In the American League draft, this wasn't an issue, since rosters were frozen during the season, precisely to remove the potential for wrongful gamesmanship. What this distinction meant was that the NL teams could take players they were going to release anyway, designate them as draft-eligible, and if they were selected, pocket an amount far in excess of their worth as compensation for their "loss." This was a sure sign that while the league's owners had agreed to expand after being backed into a corner, they didn't like it. Their apparent intent was to ensure that the two new franchises, stocked with the older clubs' roster jetsam, would remain noncompetitive, while at the same time recouping handsome sums as compensation for the loss of players they hadn't wanted anyway.

The draft format produced some bizarre results. During the 1961 season, the Phillies lost an unbelievable 23 games in a row. It was widely speculated after the draft that the slump had occurred because the Phillies intentionally loaded up their roster with mediocre players to keep their best prospects off the draft list. As the result of this strategy, an obscure young catcher named Clarence "Choo Choo" Coleman was able to remain on the big league roster long enough to appear in 34 games, despite hitting .128. He was drafted by the Mets.

The quality of the players on the draft list was quite underwhelming, as noted by Jimmy Breslin in *Sports Illustrated*: "The list was carefully prepared and checked and rechecked by the club owners. This was to make certain that no bona fide ballplayers were on it."

Stengel, in typical form, offered his thoughts: "It was so thoughtful of them. I want to thank all of them owners who loved us to have those men and picked them for us. It was very generous of them. We are damn lucky they didn't expand to 12 teams."

As expected, the draftees were either youngsters of dubious potential or veterans who would soon have been released anyway to clear roster space. In fact, many of the available veterans who were not drafted were indeed released shortly thereafter. Nonetheless, the Mets had done their homework in an effort to make the best of a bad situation. During the 1961 season, Weiss assigned Rogers Hornsby to scout the National League rosters to determine who might be available and worth pursuing. Hornsby, who filed reports on 450 players, delivered the following assessment that summer: "They say we're going to get players out of a grab bag. From what I see, it's going to be a garbage bag. Ain't nobody got fat on eating out of the garbage, and that's just what the Mets is going to have to be doing. This is terrible. I mean, this is really going to be bad."

He certainly didn't get any argument from Houston's Paul Richards. Reportedly, when Richards saw the list of available players, he threatened to boycott the draft entirely.

Richards and Hornsby, however accurately assessing the talent, missed the point. By having to draft unwanted players at an extravagant cost, the two new teams were paying the cover charge to get into the party. The amounts they paid for these men were not intended to reflect their actual value, and no one pretended otherwise. There is no better proof of this than the fact that, while the Mets' twenty-two selections cost $1.8 million in compensation to the other clubs, the team's actual payroll for the 1962 season was about a third of this amount.

At least no one could accuse Weiss of being unprepared. In addition to Hornsby's reports, he also tabbed coaches Cookie Lavagetto and Solly Hemus to perform similar services. The three men kept a close eye on players throughout the league, especially second-stringers, to get an idea as to who might be made available and what their potential might be. Weiss himself went to several games in nearby Philadelphia to scout talent, and Met scouts Johnny Murphy and Wid Matthews reviewed the minor league teams for likely prospects.

However, the basic underlying problem was that the system was rigged from the start, as Hornsby quickly determined. Met broadcaster Lindsey Nelson, writing after the fact, put it another way: "A man goes into this pool only after his talents have been thoroughly discussed and evaluated by a staff of baseball men more closely associated with him than anybody else – and they have found him wanting. There is something wrong with him, or they wouldn't be willing to give him up."

In fact, the two new teams pursued very different draft strategies. Weiss felt he was under pressure to draw people to the ballpark immediately. Therefore, he sought older players who would be familiar to Mets fans, especially former Brooklyn Dodgers or New York Giants, even if they were past their prime. He told Don Grant that "we've got to draft two things – nostalgia and young pitchers. Nostalgia to bring people into the ball park – Duke Snider [who didn't join the Mets until 1963], Gil Hodges, the old names of New York. After that, we need young pitchers." Solly Hemus noted that Weiss also felt that another team in the middle of a pennant race might want one of the Mets' veterans later in the season, a hope which did not materialize. During the 1962 season, when many of the old familiars had been traded or simply broken down, Stengel offered an after-the-fact assessment of this strategy: "We took too many names. Wonderful fellows, but at the end of their string."

Houston, by contrast, did not have to contend with a legacy. Since the city had never hosted major league ball, the enterprise would be a novelty for the fans, who would accept whatever team was put in front of them. As a result, Richards was able to build for the future by selecting what passed for prospects. Stengel similarly wanted to draw from what he referred to as "the youth of America," but Weiss had the final say, just as when Stengel previously worked for him across town. In fact, Weiss' opinion trumped that of even Mrs. Payson, although she was reportedly behind the drafting of former Dodgers star Gil Hodges and the deal for ex-Giant pitcher Johnny Antonelli. Weiss, she said, "would shoot me if I interfered."

With the dubious honor of having won the coin toss, Houston selected Ed Bressoud, a shortstop from the Giants (who later wound up with the Mets). The Mets also drew from the Giants and picked Hobie Landrith, a thirty-one-year-old journeyman catcher from Strawberry Plains, Tennessee, who had also played for the Reds, Cubs and Cardinals. Landrith was a career .237 hitter who had been in the majors for twelve years without a lengthy stint as a starter, having batted over 300 times in a season only once. The year before, he hit .239 in limited action with the Giants. Stengel's well-known justification for this unexpected choice was, "ya gotta start with a catcher, 'cause if you don't you'll have all passed balls."

Landrith was born on March 15, 1930, in Decatur, Illinois, but he grew up in Detroit. As a teenaged Tigers fan, he got into the ballpark and volunteered to shag fly balls for Hank Greenberg, just returned from World War II. He was so persistent that the Tigers allowed him to stay and run errands, and Tigers Hall of Fame catcher Mickey Cochrane gave Landrith a pair of his old shoes – Landrith's first spikes. After catching batting practice for the Tigers, Landrith was signed by the Reds at the age of eighteen. He made his big-league debut two years later, just four years removed from being a Tiger errand boy. However, he was never able to see any consistent, much less regular, duty.

At the time of the draft, Landrith was golfing at the Los Altos Country Club, oddly enough, with Ed Bressoud and Giant manager Alvin Dark. One of the club managers came to greet them on the course and told Landrith and Bressoud that they were, respectively, the first Met and the first Colt .45.

After Landrith, the Mets made the following selections in the first round of the draft:

2. Elio Chacon, infielder, Reds;
3. Roger Craig, pitcher, Dodgers;
4. Gus Bell, outfielder, Reds;
5. Joe Christopher, outfielder, Pirates;
6. Felix Mantilla, infielder, Braves;
7. Gil Hodges, infielder, Dodgers;
8. Craig Anderson, pitcher, Cardinals;
9. Ray Daviault, pitcher, Giants;
10. John DeMerit, outfielder, Braves;
11. Al Jackson, pitcher, Pirates;
12. Sammy Drake, infielder, Cubs;

13. Chris Cannizzaro, catcher, Cardinals;
14. Clarence "Choo Choo" Coleman, catcher, Phillies;
15. Ed Bouchee, infielder, Cubs; and
16. Bobby Gene Smith, outfielder, Phillies.

The two $50,000 picks in the second round were Cardinal outfielder Jim Hickman and pitcher Sherman Jones from the Reds. The third round netted four so-called "premium" $125,000 players: pitcher Bob Miller from the Cardinals, pitcher Jay Hook from the Reds, infielder Don Zimmer from the Cubs, and outfielder Lee Walls from the Phillies.

This was not an awe-inspiring group. *Sports Illustrated* barely covered the draft, giving the event only a few agate-type sentences in its "For the Record" section. Reportedly, Weiss got about two-thirds of the players he sought, and while it is easy to criticize his choices with the benefit of hindsight, many of his selections made some kind of sense at the time. Hodges, Bell, Zimmer, Bouchee and Christopher were all pull hitters who could conceivably reach the short fences in the Polo Grounds. He could not have known that the five would hit a combined nineteen homers in 1962 or that only Christopher would finish the season with the team. In addition, while observers have focused on half of Weiss' strategy as expressed to Don Grant, namely, the selection of familiar players, they missed the other half. By taking Hook, Anderson, Miller, Daviault and, most notably, Jackson, Weiss assembled the nucleus of young pitchers he needed. Daviault, the oldest, was twenty-seven when the 1962 season opened, and Anderson and Miller were each twenty-three. Although Miller and Daviault lasted just the first year and Anderson only slightly longer, Jackson was the Mets' most effective starter in the early years, and Hook contributed some significant wins, including the team's first victory.

Clearly, though, the attention was on the veterans, especially former Brooklynites such as Hodges, Craig and Zimmer. Although Zimmer was drafted from the Cubs, he was best known for his years with the Dodgers. He came up in 1953 as Pee Wee Reese's backup at shortstop, and he played on several pennant-winning teams before being traded to Chicago in 1960. He had his best year in 1961, serving as team captain and being named to the All-Star team (the only Original Met to have been an All-Star the season before). However, Zimmer made the mistake of criticizing the Cubs' "College of Coaches," a revolving-door management scheme which called for nine coaches to manage for ten games each before being rotated to other coaching positions in the organization. The scheme had predictably disastrous results, as the Cubs lost 100 games; however, management, in its infinite wisdom, decided to try it again in 1962. After Zimmer blasted the implementation of such a stupid idea on Lou Boudreau's postgame radio show, he knew his days in Chicago were numbered. He found out later that he had not originally been part of the expansion pool, but the day after his comments were broadcast, the club removed relief pitcher Barney Schultz from the $125,000 "premium" list and replaced him with Zimmer.

Hodges, the long-time Dodger first baseman and perennial All-Star, would be 38 years old by Opening Day and had such bad knees that he could barely run. Although he was a fan favorite throughout his brief Mets career, Hodges was only able to appear in 54 games in 1962, batting just 127 times with nine home runs, before his season was effectively ended in July by a kidney stone. In addition, Bell was thirty-three, and Zimmer and Landrith were over thirty. Craig, who was to become the "ace" of the pitching staff, in a manner of speaking, was thirty and not far removed from shoulder problems. Although Bell had once hit thirty home runs and batted .308, he had hit just .255 for Cincinnati in 1961 with three homers in 103 games, and his best days were clearly behind him.

Few of the remaining players had accomplished much, and not many improved their lot with the Mets. Sammy Drake, John DeMerit (a former "bonus baby" who had signed with Milwaukee for $100,000) and Bobby Gene Smith appeared in 47 Met games between them, with 90 total at bats. Walls was traded immediately after the draft, and Zimmer, Landrith and Bell were dealt after appearing in fourteen, twenty-three and thirty games, respectively. Of all the position players selected, only Felix Mantilla, Jim Hickman, Elio Chacon and Joe Christopher appeared in more than 100 games in 1962, and Mantilla and Chacon were gone after the season. The pitchers fared somewhat better, as Stengel's five principal starters (one of whom, Craig Anderson, would also be his most-used reliever) were all acquired via the draft. Of the twenty-two draftees, over half had been traded, released or demoted for good by the time the 1963 season began, and just Jackson, Christopher, Cannizzaro and Hickman were still with the team by the beginning of 1965. By the following year, only Hickman remained, and he was traded after the season.

First baseman Ed Bouchee was in the middle of the pack. He played in every game as a rookie with the Phillies in 1957, batting .293 with seventeen homers and seventy-eight runs batted in and finishing second to teammate Jack Sanford in the balloting for Rookie of the Year. He would never equal those numbers, though, suffering through emotional problems and a brush with the law, and the Phillies sent him to the Cubs during the 1960 season. With Chicago, Bouchee was initially able to play regularly; however, by 1961, Ernie Banks, the Cubs' future Hall-of-Famer, was beginning his transition from shortstop to first base, and Bouchee knew his time was about to drop significantly. He and Hodges were the only first basemen taken in the expansion draft, and Hodges' bad knees were no secret. Therefore, Bouchee was initially glad to go to New York, figuring he'd get to play. After his opportunity failed to materialize, though, Bouchee became bitter. He quickly found himself out of favor with Stengel, who used him only nineteen times at first base. He appeared in 50 games, primarily as a pinch hitter, batting just 87 times with an average of .161. When the season ended, so had his major league career, even though he was only 29 years old.

One of the more intriguing selections was Elio Chacon, who became the Mets' second pick just before his twenty-fifth birthday. Chacon had starred for the Havana Sugar Kings of the International League, winners of the 1959 Junior World Series. A favorite of Mrs. Payson's, Chacon had appeared in 61 games with the NL champion Reds in 1961, batting .265. He attracted attention during the 1961 World Series, when he dashed in to score from third on a passed ball. The Mets had high hopes for Chacon.

One of the youngest picks was pitcher Craig Anderson, who had several months of big league experience. Anderson had been born in Washington, D.C., and played in the boys' clubs as a youth. After having success as a high school pitcher, he was pressured by major league scouts to sign upon his graduation. His father, though, wanted Anderson to go to college. Baseball rules then provided that a prospect could not sign for more than $4,000 except in rare cases. In fact, any player signed for more than $4,000 had to be put on the major league 40-man roster and remain there for two years, failing which he could be drafted by any other club. Anderson's father reasoned that his son's college education was worth a lot more than $4,000, so Anderson went to Lehigh University in Pennsylvania and continued to play baseball.

While in school, Anderson tried out for the Yankees at Griffith Stadium in Washington while the team was in town to play the Senators. This gave him the chance to meet Stengel. The scout who had brought Anderson introduced him to Stengel, who responded, "Ohhhhh yeah, I've heard a lot about you," Anderson remembers. "I didn't think too much about that then, but then I realized that was Casey for you."

During his college career, Anderson continued to receive attention from the scouts. The rules by that time had changed, allowing players to receive signing bonuses of $50,000 or even $100,000. He received two more offers while in school, but each time, his father told him his college education was still worth more.

As it happened, though, Anderson suffered an injury his senior year, and by the time the season ended, only the Cardinals were still interested. He signed with St. Louis ten days before graduating in June 1960. He did not receive a bonus.

Anderson rose quickly through the Cardinal system. He was soon pitching for Double-A Tulsa in the Texas League. "I proceeded to have an excellent year," he recalls. "I didn't think I'd do that well." Tulsa won the Texas League playoff and then defeated the winner of the Mexican League. That winter, St. Louis put him on the forty-man roster, even though Anderson was by that time in the Army. In 1961, they sent him to Triple-A Portland of the Pacific Coast League, where he continued his success. "The Cardinals weren't doing quite that well, so I was able to get to the big leagues a year and a week from the day I graduated, in June of '61." He was 6-3 as a short reliever when he was called up. He appeared in 25 games with the Cardinals, all in relief, and went 4-3. Before the season ended, Vern Benson, who had been his manager at Tulsa and Portland and was by then a Cardinal coach, asked him to pitch for San Torsi of the Puerto Rican Winter League. Also making the trip were future stars Bob Gibson and Juan Pizarro. Anderson accepted, pitched well and contributed to another minor league pennant winner. "It was a thrill being in the same rotation with Gibson and Pizarro," he recalled four decades later. "I got tremendous experience there, and that was starting experience that I didn't have with St. Louis."

By the time he went to Puerto Rico, though, he had already been drafted by the Mets. He had met his wife during a whirlwind courtship after he was called up by St. Louis in June. They planned to be married on October 14th, two days after the draft and two days before Anderson was due to leave for Puerto Rico. Unlike most clubs, the Cardinals chose to protect their veterans and instead made their young players available. As a result, Weiss took Anderson, along with Jim Hickman, Bob Miller and Chris Cannizzaro. In an odd twist, one of which the penurious Weiss would surely have approved, Anderson now had the opportunity to continue his education at his old club's expense. "I had no clue I was going to be on the Mets," he says. "We knew we were going to Puerto Rico on the 16th, so I still ended up being with Benson and Gibson, but when I came back from Puerto Rico I was property of the Mets."

Another of the young pitchers taken was twenty-four-year-old Jay Hook, originally from Grayslake, Illinois. Hook, a Cubs fan, started playing baseball with his father, a White Sox fan, at age four. He was quite an athlete by the time he started high school, and he played football, basketball and baseball all four years. He started as a shortstop, since he was 5'3 and 107 pounds as a freshman. By the time he was a senior, though, he'd grown to 6'1 and weighed 180 pounds and had become a hard-throwing pitcher. Hook's uncle managed a lumberyard in Grayslake, and Hook and his cousin worked there, unloading sheet rock and cement off of railroad cars and delivering it to homes and businesses. This, of course, contributed to his growth: "It was really good for me, because a lot of kids nowadays do a lot of physical conditioning and weight training; I was really doing weight training without even knowing it."

Hook graduated in 1954 and went to Northwestern on an academic scholarship to study engineering. While in college, he played baseball and basketball, and in his sophomore year, he was granted an athletic scholarship. Former major leaguer Fred Lindstrom was the baseball coach, and his son Chuck was a catcher on the team. "We had a good baseball team," Hook recalls. "You know, Northwestern isn't necessarily known for its sporting events." He enjoyed success as a pitcher for Northwestern. In fact, almost fifty years later, he is still tied for the school's eighth-best career earned run average.

Even as he pursued his engineering degree, he continued to hone his skills. Every summer, he went up to Wisconsin to play semi-pro baseball. One year he stayed in Oconomowoc, working in the Carnation Can Company's machine shop and playing baseball for a bar team. The Braves had recently come to Milwaukee, and baseball was extremely popular in many a small Wisconsin town. "We'd get a thousand people coming to watch a semi-pro team," Hook states. "I could throw very hard and had a pretty good curve ball, so I struck out a lot of guys." The following year he worked for a lithographing company in Milwaukee while playing for the Shallard's Liquor team on the north side of town. Shallard's son also went to Northwestern, where he was a catcher, and he caught for his dad's team in the summer. Hook continued to strike out a lot of batters there, often aided by the poor lighting at many of the fields. He began to attract attention as a hard-throwing pitcher, a process which was helped by Mr. Shallard, who would call up the scouts and tell them to come and watch.

One of these scouts was Dale McReynolds, who covered southern Wisconsin for the Cincinnati Reds. Things began to happen quickly for Hook. "Near the end of the 1957 season, in August, Dale McReynolds asked if I would come and throw to a guy the Reds were looking at. So I went out to one of their tryouts and pitched against this guy, and he didn't hit me at all." McReynolds, impressed, asked Hook to come throw on the sidelines before an upcoming Braves-Reds game in Milwaukee. He did, and he was then asked to fly back to Cincinnati on the charter that same night. After calling his boss to get the next day off, he traveled with the team that night. He was told to come out to the park at 2:00 the next day, as they had a night game that evening. When he arrived, "they had Frank Robinson and Ted Kluzewski and all these guys, and they wanted me to throw to them. They didn't hit the ball very well that afternoon, and after I'd worked out with them, they said, 'Gee, do you think your dad would fly down to Cincinnati?'" Hook called his father, who had a small drugstore in Grayslake. Mr. Hook quickly came to Cincinnati and met with general manager Gabe Paul, after which Hook agreed to sign with the Reds for a bonus. He was not concerned when Paul told him the sum he received represented not only his bonus but his first two years' salary; "I wanted to play ball;

I'd have played for a couple of old gloves." Paul and an entourage came to Grayslake two weeks later for the signing, which the elder Hook had to do because Jay was 20.

As soon as the contract was signed, Hook packed up and went to Cincinnati, having been playing sandlot ball only a few weeks earlier. He ended up starting the last game of the season against the Milwaukee Braves. "I had a no-hitter going for five innings, and Birdie Tebbetts took me out of the game," Hook said later. "'Hey, kid,' he said, 'you're too young to pitch a no-hitter.' The reality was he wanted to look at somebody else – you know, it was the end of the season."

Hook got into three games with the Reds without ever having played in the minors. Over the winter, though, the rule requiring bonus players to be kept on the major league roster was changed to allow clubs to farm them out. From the beginning of his relationship with the Reds, though, Hook showed he was not a typical ballplayer. He had gotten Paul to agree to allow him to report late for spring training the first two years of his contract, by March 6 instead of February 20, to allow him to finish the winter quarter at Northwestern. In 1958, he went to spring training and came back north with the Reds. After staying in Cincinnati a week, just long enough for him and his wife to have signed an apartment lease, he was farmed out to Nashville. He spent the summer there and was called up in September. In 1959, he was farmed out to Seattle right away, early enough to join the Seattle club at its own spring training facility in El Centro, California, in the middle of the Mojave Desert. "I thought I was in good shape when I left Florida, but in El Centro, you get in shape," Hook relates. Hook was with Seattle till the middle of July, managed by Fred Hutchinson. Then Reds manager Mayo Smith was fired, and Hutchinson became his replacement. After week, Hutchinson called up Hook, and he was a starter for the rest of the year.

Following the 1959 season, Hook had another memorable encounter with Gabe Paul. Hook had gotten married in December 1957, a few months after signing, and the couple's first son was born in March of 1959. He was paid $7,000 per season under his original contract. When Hook, who had by then earned his degree in mechanical engineering and had just started graduate school, received his new contract that winter, he saw that it was for $7,000 again even though he was now one of the Reds' starting pitchers. He went to see Paul, explaining that he now was married and had a son, and unlike many other players, he could not work in the offseason because of graduate school. He asked for $10,400, explaining that he had reached this sum after figuring out his expenses. When Paul held firm at $7,000, Hook agreed to sign but he asked Paul for permission to take a second job *during the season*. As Hook relates: "He looked at me and said, 'You mean you'd get a second job so you can play ball?' And I said, 'Yeah, I want to make this come out right.' He said, 'Well, what would you be doing?' I said, 'I don't know. I know a lot about car engines and transmissions, I might be working on cars, I might be doing lube jobs, I might be pumping gas, whatever I can get a job doing.' He said, 'I've negotiated thousands of contracts. Nobody has ever said they'd get a second job so they could play baseball. Can you imagine what the press would do to me if one of my starting pitchers is down on the corner doing lube jobs or pumping gas? I won't pay you $10,400, but I'll pay you $9,600 if you don't get a second job.' It was a little different negotiating then."

Hook spent the entire 1960 season with the Reds, going 11-18 with a 4.50 earned run average. The next year, though, saw a considerable drop in his production, as he went from 222 innings pitched in 1960 to 62 in 1961. This was due to the mumps, which he likely contracted during an appearance at a school in California. He laughingly remembers that "when they wanted someone to speak at schools or somewhere where they weren't paying, they called me." The team returned to Cincinnati and then went on to Philadelphia. Hook, who did not know he was sick, continued to work out, and his jaw started swelling. By the time the team got back to Cincinnati, Hook "was really puffed up. All the guys had to go get gamma globulin shots, which was a real headache." By that point, he was very sick. The doctor let him stay at home, fearing that if they put him in a hospital, even in a quarantined area, he might contract something else. Although he recovered before the end of the 1961 season, "I was so weak that I was completely ineffective."

The Reds went to the World Series that season, and while Hook got to go with them and dress, he didn't pitch. After the Yankees' five-game triumph, Hook and his wife Joanne headed back to Chicago in their Austin-Healy so he could resume his graduate studies at Northwestern. While they were traveling, they heard on the radio that Hook had been drafted by the Mets.

Alvin Jackson, another of Weiss' young pitchers, turned out to be one of the finds of the draft. Born on Christmas Day 1935 in Waco, Texas, Jackson was the thirteenth child of a sharecropper. The family members all farmed, raising their own food, and there was always enough to eat. "We had a big family but that was not something that anybody really noticed," he told Maury Allen later. "Most of the families in the black areas of Waco were big families. You needed a lot of kids to work those farms."

Although diminutive in stature (he was 5'10 and 170 pounds), Jackson was a fine athlete, having starred as a pitcher and quarterback in high school. In fact, it was his football skills which first drew attention, and he accepted a scholarship to Wiley College in Marshall, Texas. He also pitched for the semipro Waco Pirates and then traveled with the all-black Jasper Steers through small towns all over Texas, Alabama, Mississippi, Arkansas and Kansas. "Those were tough places in those old days," he recalled. "You ate where you could and slept where you could. Lots of times it was in the bus or somebody's old jalopy. I don't know how those old cars made it on those dusty roads but we never missed a game."

In 1955, at age 19, he signed with the Pirates for a $4,000 bonus but then spent years stuck in the minors. He appeared in eleven big league games in 1959 and 1961 (before and after, but not during, the Pirates' 1960 championship season), totaling 42 innings, but it seemed clear he was not going to get anywhere in the Pittsburgh organization despite several fine minor-league seasons. He was continually told that he had the makings of a good pitcher but needed more "seasoning."

After Pittsburgh called him up in late 1961, he confronted Branch Rickey, back with the Pirates as a consultant, and demanded to know his future with the club. Rickey reminded him that expansion was coming and predicted Jackson would be pitching somewhere in the majors the following season. Soon after, he was selected by the Mets. This was the opportunity he had been waiting for. During the first spring training, he also found that he was a rare commodity. "I was doing my laps with Ken MacKenzie and after three or four laps we paused to catch a breath. Mac suddenly looked over at me and asked, 'Do you know how many lefthanders there are in this camp?' I told him I didn't think there were too many. He said there were only two and he pointed at me and then at himself. Then he said, 'Don't say anything about it.'"

Jackson became the only Mets lefthanded pitcher to start more than half a dozen games in 1962, and his four shutouts were the only ones thrown by any pitcher on the staff.

At least publicly, Weiss and Stengel lauded their draft picks, although Branch Rickey described the draftees as players who "are about to climb down the other side of the hill." Stengel, though, asserted that with Bell, Hodges, Walls and Zimmer, "we're going to hit the ball out of the Polo Grounds once in a while." Weiss added that, "while there now remains a tremendous lot of work to be done, I honestly believe we have the nucleus around which we can build an interesting ball club."

Immediately thereafter, Weiss set out to do so, filling out the roster by making trades and acquiring free agents. Although Landrith was the first player drafted, he was not the first major leaguer to sign a Met contract. That honor went to infielder Ted Lepcio, who signed on October 25, 1961, having just been released by the Twins. During the preceding season, he had batted .183 with minor-league Syracuse and a combined .167 in short stints with the White Sox and Twins. Lepcio, who first signed with the Red Sox ten years earlier when Johnny Murphy ran Boston's farm system, was the first major leaguer to join and one of the final players to be cut from the 1962 squad.

The day after the draft, Weiss purchased pitcher Johnny Antonelli from Milwaukee, another familiar name. He originally signed as a "bonus baby" with the Boston Braves in the late 1940s. He was a bust with the Braves, but he won 21 games for the Giants in 1954, helping New York win the World Series. The Braves acquired him again on his way down, having missed the productive middle part of his career in which he won at least 19 games three times for the Giants. Also from Milwaukee came pitchers Ken MacKenzie and Bob "Butterball" Botz and outfielder Neil Chrisley. Weiss then turned his attention to the Giants, picking up Giant and former Dodger pitcher Billy Loes, who claimed to have lost a ground ball in the sun in the 1952 World Series, and first baseman Jim Marshall.

Next, Weiss also sent "premium" draft pick Lee Walls and $100,000 to the Dodgers for second baseman Charlie Neal (thus, in effect, making Neal a $225,000 infielder, something he quickly proved he was not). Neal had enjoyed some good seasons with the Dodgers but was clearly on the decline. In 1958, he hit 22 home runs, and the following year, he hit 19 more, along with 30 doubles, 11 triples and 83 RBIs, making the All-Star team and starring for the Dodgers in their 1959 World Series win over the White Sox with two homers in game two. He also led the league in several fielding categories during this period, winning a Gold Glove in 1959. After these successes, though, Neal's skills mysteriously abandoned him, and he spent more and more time on the bench.

Other than Neal, McKenzie and Marshall, none of these early acquisitions ever played a game for the Mets, and Marshall was traded in early May. Antonelli chose to retire and go into the tire business, although Milwaukee kept the money Weiss had spent for him. Loes, too, went off to run a restaurant instead of joining the Mets. Botz and Chrisley were cut during spring training (though Chrisley appeared on a 1962 Topps baseball card), as were most of the other nonentities acquired during this period, such as Bruce Fitzpatrick, Dawes Hamilt and Aubrey Gatewood, names which are now nothing more than trivia answers.

However, Weiss did make two deals which bore fruit. The first came in November, when he again tapped Milwaukee, acquiring veteran power-hitter Frank Thomas for $125,000 and a player to be named later (who ultimately turned out to be Gus Bell; considering that Bell had been a $75,000 draft pick, this meant Weiss had paid $200,000 for Thomas). Originally from Pittsburgh, Thomas had just homered 27 times for the Cubs and Braves, and Weiss and Stengel were counting on him to do the same for them. In fact, he did better, leading the '62 Mets in home runs and runs batted in, both by sizable margins, and his 34 homers were not exceeded by another Met until Dave Kingman thirteen years later. His status as the Mets' only legitimate power threat overshadowed the fact that his defense in the outfield and at third base was rather suspect.

Like most players of his era, Thomas, who was born in Pittsburgh on June 11, 1929, pursued his early interest in baseball as industriously as he could. He told the author that "my mom and dad said I never went to bed unless I had a baseball and bat in my hand." At the age of twelve, he would get up every Saturday morning and walk to the Shindley Oval, about three-and-a-half miles away. He would go to one end and play ball with a group of people, and once they were finished, he'd go to the other end and play with another group, not returning home until 9:30 at night, most likely with his pants torn and incurring his father's wrath for having missed supper. His mother, though, would sneak him up a plate. He spent his high school years at the seminary at Mount Carmel College in Niagara Falls, Ontario. By then his abilities were blossoming, and soon he found himself prohibited from batting right-handed because he hit the ball too far, and from pitching because he threw the ball too hard.

Such talent did not go unnoticed for long, and Thomas had the good fortune of landing with his hometown team, the Pirates, in July 1947, having just turned eighteen. He reported the following year to Tallahassee of the Class D Georgia-Florida League, and in 1949, he split his time between Davenport, Iowa, Waco and Tallahassee. While at Class B Waco, where he was hitting .352, manager Buddy Hanken held a meeting in which he stated that every player should have the desire to succeed and move to a higher classification each year. During the meeting, the phone rang. As Thomas turned to go, Hanken called him back and told him the front office wanted him to return to Tallahassee. Thomas reminded the manager that this contradicted the lecture he'd just received. Thomas recalls Hanken's response: "'Well, they feel you were the fair-haired boy there in '48, and possibly you'll be able to bring some fans into the ballpark.' And I said, 'If that's the way baseball is gonna be, I don't want any part of it.'" His girlfriend – later his wife – talked him out of quitting, though, and in 1950, he went to spring training with the Pirates before being farmed out to Charleston of the Sally League. In 1951, he went to spring training with the Pirates again, expecting to have a shot. He went north with the Pirates, stopping in New Orleans, where Pittsburgh had its Class A team, for some exhibition games. Lester Biederman, a writer for the *Pittsburgh Press*, asked Thomas how he felt about staying in New Orleans. It was the first Thomas had heard of it, and once he learned it was true, "I went into the clubhouse, took off my uniform, went out to the airport, caught a plane and flew back home. Joe

Brown and Joe O'Toole, the general manager and assistant general manager, kept calling me, and finally I relented and went back down." He played at New Orleans in 1951 and 1952 and was called up to Pittsburgh at the end of the 1952 season.

Thomas got his opportunity after the Pirates traded Hall of Fame slugger (and future Mets broadcaster) Ralph Kiner on June 4, 1953. He hit 30 home runs and drove in 102 that season, establishing Pittsburgh rookie records which still stand. Between 1953 and 1958, he never hit less than 23 homers or drove in fewer than 72 runs. Although initially an outfielder, he began to see increased time at first and third as the decade went on. He made the All-Star team as an outfielder in 1954 and 1955 and as a third baseman in 1958. That was his best year as a pro. He batted .281 and finished second to Ernie Banks with 35 homers and 109 runs batted in, and he came in fourth in the voting for the Most Valuable Player award. However, it was also his last season in Pittsburgh.

Thomas hurt his hand near the end of the season, and when it would still not heal after the season, he went and saw the team doctor, Joseph Feingold, who operated on Thomas' thumb in his office. Six weeks later, the injury still had not healed, and shortly thereafter, Thomas was traded to Cincinnati. He told general manager Gabe Paul before signing his contract that the Reds had gotten "damaged goods." The following year, Thomas remembers, "proved to be the worst year of my career. You saw the movie *The Lost Weekend* with Ray Milland – well, I had the lost year. I only hit twelve home runs, and you don't go from thirty-five home runs to twelve in the prime of your career unless there's something radically wrong with you. After the season, the Cubs wanted their doctor to examine me. He put me to sleep. When I came through the anesthesia, he said, 'I think there's going to be a lot of red faces. I don't know how you even hit twelve home runs with that type of hand.' I had tumors going around my nerve. After he took all of those out, I went back to hitting again."

Although Thomas batted only .238 with the Cubs in 1960, he rediscovered his power stroke, knocking out 21 home runs. After only fifteen games with the Cubs in 1961, though, he was sent to Milwaukee, where he hit 25 homers and drove in 67 runs in 124 games, setting a record for homers by a Braves leftfielder. He played so well that in June, Braves general manager John McHale called Thomas in to discuss a contract for 1962. Thomas responded, "John, this is June. I may go good, and I'll be sorry. I may go bad, and you'll be sorry. But I'll sign before I go home." In September, he saw McHale again, asking what the team's intentions were for him in 1962. McHale stated that Thomas would be the Braves' leftfielder. Thomas, in turn, offered to sign whatever contract the team wanted, since he was grateful for the opportunity to play regularly again. But, "I said, 'If you do have intentions of trading me, please do not sign me. Let me dicker with the new club I'm going to.' In November, I'm up hunting with some friends, and my wife calls me. She says, 'You just got sold to the Mets.' I called John McHale four times. He never did return my calls. I felt bad about it because I trusted him. But when I saw him in spring training, I just went by him and said, 'Thanks.' You don't burn your bridges behind you. You might need them sometime."

After his initial shock, though, Thomas saw the situation more optimistically based upon the players the Mets had acquired. "You know, we're going to have a pretty good little ballclub," he recalled thinking at the time. "We're going to score a lot of runs. I knew we were going back into the Polo Grounds, which was a pretty good hitting park for me. I was strictly a pull hitter."

Soon after, Weiss purchased thirty-four-year-old centerfielder Richie Ashburn from the Cubs for $100,000. Born March 19, 1927, in Tilden, Nebraska, Ashburn made his debut with the Phillies in 1948, batting over .300 that year, and he became one of the mainstays of Philadelphia's 1950 "Whiz Kids" pennant-winning team. In fact, it was his throw which gunned down Brooklyn's Cal Abrams at home plate on the last day of the season, helping win the game, and thus the pennant, for the Phillies. He won batting titles in 1955 and 1958 and finished second twice, and he led the league in on-base percentage, walks and singles four times (the latter a record), in hits on three occasions, in triples and games played twice, and once in stolen bases. In addition, he was regarded as one of the best defensive centerfielders ever to play the game. In an era dominated by the Giants' Willie Mays and Brooklyn's Duke Snider, he set records for the most years leading his league in chances (nine), the most seasons with at least 500 putouts (five – no other outfielder before or since has ever done it more than once), and most seasons with at least 400 putouts (nine). He also batted an astounding .556 in four All-Star games. A gritty but classy player, he was also the prototypical leadoff hitter, as his new teammate Roger Craig recalled, "You could throw him a perfect pitch. He'd foul it off and laugh at you until you made a mistake and he got a hit."

In 1961, Ashburn had hit only .257 with the Cubs and was thought to be nearing the end of his stellar career. With the Mets, though, Ashburn showed he could still play, becoming the team's only .300 hitter in 1962 and being chosen as their sole representative on the All-Star team. Fiercely competitive, he also emerged as a clubhouse leader.

The Mets also filled their ranks via the Rule 5 minor league draft, by which a club could select any player who had been in the minors for at least three years without being on the forty-man roster of the big league club which held his rights. One player tabbed by Weiss was a utility infielder named Rod Kanehl, who had been in the Yankee farm system for eight years without ever coming close to making the big-league roster.

Kanehl was originally born in Wichita, where his father was a physical education teacher and track coach. His first baseball experience was in Lawrence, Kansas, at the age of twelve, in a Little League precursor known as the C.C. Karl League, named for a

Lawrence clothier. When Kanehl was fourteen, the family moved to Springfield, Missouri, which he recalls "was a hotbed of baseball players – Bill Virdon, Sherm Lollar, Roy Smalley, Preacher Roe." Yankee scout Tom Greenwade also lived there. During summers in Springfield, Kanehl and his friends played what was known as "Indian ball," a pickup game that could be played with five or six players. He and his running mates were all Cardinal fans, and when Harry Caray would come on, everything stopped.

Kanehl did not play high school baseball. Since his dad was a track coach, that was where his interest lay. He won state medals as a high jumper and pole vaulter. As a freshman at Drury College in Springfield, he competed in decathlon as well. "I could throw the javelin 190 [feet], high jump 6'2, pole vault thirteen [feet] with a bamboo pole, and I took fifth in the Kansas Relays as a freshman." He also played American Legion baseball in the summer, and his team went to State both years that he played. After that, he played semi-pro baseball. Tom Greenwade had begun watching Kanehl since his sophomore year in high school, and he told Kanehl to get in touch if the baseball bug bit. Eventually, it did. "I called Mr. Greenwade, and he signed me in January of '54. He knew I could run and throw and field, but he wasn't sure I could hit. He knew my determination and desire was there. So he took a chance on me and signed me with the Yankees."

Under the then-prevailing rules, Kanehl received the standard $4,000 bonus. However, even this meager sum wasn't all it was cracked up to be. "You got $4,000, and that included your salary," he explained. "I got a $2,750 bonus and I played for $225 a month at McAlester, Oklahoma."

Soon after signing, Kanehl, who described himself as "green as a gourd," found himself at the Yankees' rookie instructional school in St. Petersburg, and an event occurred which played a huge role later in his career. Yankee manager Stengel was there, and Kanehl remembered him being quite involved. "It was a great honor," said Kanehl. "I was lucky enough to room with Tom Hamilton, a first baseman that they'd got from Philadelphia in some trade that winter. He'd been around some and took me under his wing – you know, showed me how to get to the chow line."

It was during this camp that the nineteen-year-old Kanehl endeared himself to Stengel by leaping over a low outfield fence. Kanehl was in the outfield at Miller Huggins Field. The fence was made of barbed wire rather than chain link, which allowed balls to roll under and through it, and there were frequently a number of ball-hungry kids stationed nearby. Kanehl chased a ball which rolled up to and then under the barbed wire. "Being a high jumper," Kanehl related, "I hopped this five-foot fence. No big deal for me. I beat a kid to the ball, then hopped back over and threw the ball in. I was just trying to beat the kids to the ball. When you're used to playing in a one-ball league, why, you ran down the ball. I didn't hear that Casey had noticed until the next winter at the Hot Stove League dinner in Springfield. Tom Greenwade came over to me and said, 'You know, you really impressed Casey with that.' Nobody made anything of it at the time, but Stengel remembered it." Indeed he did, and he often related the story, telling listeners that "anybody can save the club $2.50 on a baseball like that can play for me."

The camp itself, and the experiences which followed, made up a crucial part of Kanehl's then-incomplete baseball education. To begin with, the coaches were all experienced, including former Hall of Fame catcher Bill Dickey, longtime Yankee third base coach Frank Crosetti, ex-Yankee pitcher Jim Turner and past and future big league managers Johnny Neun, Harry Craft and Mayo Smith. The Yankees' bonus players were all there as well – Bob Bonebrake, Frank Leja, Gus Triandos, John Blanchard, Bob Grim, Bobby Richardson, Tony Kubek, and a recently-signed first baseman named Marv Throneberry. The focus was on the fundamentals. Kanehl, like many others, found that he had holes in his game. "My American Legion and semi-pro stuff was, you know, you throw a ball and you hit it and you run," said Kanehl. "I went to spring training then with Birmingham over at Ocala, Florida. Mayo Smith was the manager. That's where you learned things. I remember missing a bunt sign. You miss one for Mayo Smith, and you learned *right away*." After a short time in Florida, Kanehl was sent to McAlester, where he played every game of the season in the outfield. The climate was stiflingly hot. In those days before air conditioning, the rooms were fitted with overhead fans, and the players learned to wet their sheets and sleep in them. At the end of the season, Kanehl remembered that "Stengel put down the dictate that anyone playing centerfield would be moved to shortstop. Phil Rizzuto was retiring, and they were looking for a shortstop. A lot of these things you take for granted with Stengel. He started platooning and specializing relievers and all that. He'd take centerfielders and play 'em at shortstop. If you could play shortstop you could play anywhere on the field. He wanted the guys with the arm and the range."

After that, though, Kanehl bounced around the lower rungs of the Yankee system, even being loaned out to the Cincinnati chain (while remaining Yankee property), and winding up in Loredo, Texas. Eventually, though, he started to rise through the ranks and was even invited to spring training with the Yankees for the first time in 1959. Although Bill McCorry, the Yankees' curmudgeonly traveling secretary, had prohibited rookies from bringing their spouses and families, Kanehl turned up in his station wagon with his wife and four children. He told the furious McCorry, "I could leave her at home and make her mad or bring her and make you mad, and I have to live with her." Stengel eventually interceded to allow Kanehl to keep his family there. Kanehl lived out on Madero Beach and would commute with Bobby Shantz, Ralph Houk and Gil McDougald, alternating cars. The group preferred Kanehl's Ford Ranch Wagon rather than the others' Cadillacs, since that meant they could pull right into Miller Huggins Field without being stopped for autographs. Kanehl learned one more important lesson while in camp. "I went down unsigned, which was against the rules," he recalled. "No rookie comes to camp unsigned, and I was unsigned and also had my wife." Spring training was half over before they realized that Kanehl had no contract. Jack White, general manager of the Yankees' Richmond farm club, began hounding Kanehl. "He offered me $700 a month, and I was holding out for nine. One day driving in, Houk said, 'Stengel said don't sign until you get what you want.' Then Jack White called me back in the equipment room, and he gave me this contract for $800. I said, 'Well, that's not what I want.' And he said, 'Goddamn it, I knew that.' He had the other contract for $900 already made out. He was just trying to buffalo me one more time."

Having signed with Richmond, Kanehl was soon sent down to Houston. The discussion among Kanehl's teammates often involved the Continental League. Among his Houston teammates was Roy Smalley, one of Kanehl's boyhood idols. Smalley was 33 years old with eleven big league seasons under his belt, and he was hanging on trying to draw the attention of Continental League scouts. In 1960, Kanehl again went to spring training with Richmond and was then farmed out to Amarillo of the Texas League. "They told me to get off to a good start and they'd get me out of there," said Kanehl. "Well, they were 2-12 when I left. But Dallas wanted me, so I went there for a month. That didn't pan out, so I went to [AA] Nashville. I had a good half season there. I went back to spring training with Richmond in 1961, and at the end they said, 'Nashville wants you back and the season starts tomorrow.' I was ready to go. I was kind of on my last try. I had to talk my wife into it . . . you know, 'If I don't have a good year, I'm gonna quit.' So '61 was gonna be it."

As it happened, Kanehl had his best year in 1961, playing in every game for Nashville and batting .304. Although expansion was in the air, giving hope to hundreds of minor leaguers, Kanehl was not thinking along those lines. "I was oblivious to expansion," he said. "I had no conception of what it was about. I know other players on that Nashville ballclub were trying to have good years so they might be picked up by an expansion team. I'd just go out and play, and that was it. The Yankees left me on a Double-A roster, and Syracuse drafted me on behalf of the Mets. Syracuse was owned by the Mets and by Minnesota, and Minnesota thought they were drafting me. The commissioner had to make a ruling. So I became a Met. I went to St. Petersburg now aware that I had a chance to be on a big league roster."

Stengel had not forgotten Kanehl, and when he learned that Kanehl was available, he demanded that Weiss select him in the minor league draft. "I remembered him," said Stengel. "He climbed a fence for me once."

In the midst of all this, the Macy's Thanksgiving Day parade took place. The Mets had a float in the parade, on which rode Stengel, Gil Hodges, Billy Loes (who probably decided right then that this wasn't for him), and Monte Irvin, the former Giant star now employed by Rheingold, the Mets' principal sponsor. The temperature was below freezing and a bitter wind was blowing, and everyone stood on the float and shivered. All except Stengel, who had just flown in from California. He stood without an overcoat or hat, oblivious to the weather, yelling enthusiastically to the crowd and pressing whatever flesh was presented to him. He then made a speech to the assembled masses, including a lengthy dissertation on the history of the spitball. Over and over he referred to the team as his "amazin' Mets," a phrase which quickly caught on.

Lindsey Nelson was there too, part of the NBC crew covering the parade along with Ed Herlihy and Buster Crabbe. Herlihy, who had known Nelson for years, was supposed to introduce him when the Met float went past the cameras. "He introduced me all right," remembered Nelson, "but the words didn't come out the way either of us expected. 'And now,' he said, to describe the baseball float for you, here is NBC's ace sports announcer, Leslie Nelson.'"

Besides the signings, purchases and trades he engineered, Weiss also worked on developing the farm system. Besides Syracuse, he established working agreements with Class C Santa Barbara (of the California League) and Auburn, New York (New York-Pennsylvania League), Quincy, Illinois (Midwest League) and Salisbury (Western Carolina League), all Class D teams. By year's end, he had over one hundred players under contract. He signed six of these to agreements paying bonuses totaling $70,000, as well as allocating over $500,000 to fund scouting operations and to pay the minor league players and managers. This, of course, was in addition to the $1.8 million he had spent on draft day and the hundreds of thousands used to purchase Neal, Ashburn, Thomas, Antonelli and others. As he told *Sports Illustrated* the following spring, Weiss was not unmindful of the substantial sums being expended: "This is a tremendous amount of money, of course. It means a lot to know that Mrs. Payson is willing to spend what we deem necessary to produce a respectable team, but that doesn't mean the ceiling is unlimited. It will take time and patience, and there's a lot of luck as well as skill involved, but with any sensible management the future ought to justify itself financially. We may not have a winner for a while, but I don't think we'll have anything to be ashamed of."

Unfortunately, history does not record whether he still felt that way at the end of the season.

CHAPTER FIVE – SPRING TRAINING

"Look at that guy. He can't hit, he can't run, and he can't throw. Of course, that's why they gave him to us." – *Casey Stengel, manager of the New York Mets*

When the Mets assembled for spring training in St. Petersburg in February 1962, it seemed the entire New York press corps was with them. The Yankees were still successful, but they were an old story. The Mets were new, exciting, amazin', and managed by the Old Perfesser himself, hand-picked by his former and present boss, George Weiss. This was paying immediate dividends, as Don Zimmer noticed the first time he pulled up to Miller Huggins Field. There were dozens of camera crews, not only from New York but also from all three networks and outlets all over the country, as well as over 100 newspapermen. "You'd have thought the Mets had won four straight world championships, not starting out their first year," Zimmer wrote in his autobiography. "It was like that every morning. All these TV crews and sportswriters, waiting to talk to Casey. We'd watch in amazement as Casey would do one interview after another, all the while selling the ballclub, not just to New York but to the whole country." Pitcher Craig Anderson remembered that "Stengel was just a magnet for all these guys, and we kinda sat back and did our job and watched him operate with these writers and manipulate the names of all these players, young players, old players . . . I'll never forget it."

Stan Isaacs, writing for *Newsday*, issued one of the earliest bulletins. He recalled that about twenty players, mostly pitchers and catchers who reported first, took an amble around the field, and then took another one for the benefit of the photographers. This caused the hundred or so spectators in attendance to give a subdued but noticeable standing ovation.

Until recently, the facilities had belonged to the Yankees, who had just moved to Ft. Lauderdale, where Dan Topping, the Yankees' principal owner, lived. Upon taking over the Mets, Weiss immediately signed a contract for his team to train at Miller Huggins Field in St. Pete, named for the Yankees' manager of the Ruth-Gehrig era, and play its games at Al Lang Field, eighteen blocks away.

Even further away was the Colonial Inn, where the team was staying. It was a poorly-kept secret that the Colonial Inn had been chosen because it was the only hotel in that area of segregated Florida which would accept both white and black players. This required a long bus trip each day to Huggins or Lang Fields and another long trip back at the end of the day.

Later, Miller Huggins Field was renamed Stengel Huggins Field. Craig Anderson visited the facilities in 2001, and he found that "it's in exactly the same condition as when we were there in 1962. I couldn't believe it. The locker room is exactly the same. It hasn't changed."

The ex-Yankee presence was everywhere. Weiss had hired trainer Gus Mauch, who had been with the Yankees since 1944, and he brought in ex-Yankee hurler Red Ruffing as the pitching coach. Ruffing, who would later be inducted into the Hall of Fame, had interesting ideas on how to condition his staff. Central among these was to run his pitchers until they vomited; when they stopped vomiting, they were in shape.

As with his manager, though, Ruffing's attitude seemed to have softened. Anderson described Ruffing as "a gentleman. He was easygoing and didn't push you very hard. We ran, but it was pretty much the same as it was with the Cardinals [the year before]. But he liked me and I liked him. I think that was kind of the way it was there; if you got to be friendly with certain coaches, you might get into games more often." Jay Hook agreed: "Ruffing was a good guy. I don't know that I learned a lot, but he certainly oversaw all the stuff we had to do."

Physical fitness was a concept which applied differently to some players. This, of course, was an era where year-round conditioning did not occur. Indeed, many players still had off-season jobs and had little time or inclination for exercise. Anderson was an exception. "I was in excellent shape," he recalled. "Winter ball was an advantage for me. Some of the players were not in good shape. You know, players used to come down there to get in shape. Now they come in good shape and they train for a week or so and then they start playing games. We trained maybe two to three weeks before we started playing. But these guys were not in shape. They hadn't done anything all winter."

Rogers Hornsby was there too, now as the team's batting coach. "A lot of players hadn't gotten along with Hornsby over the years, but I liked him," said Frank Thomas. "He was always nice to me and willing to talk. I'd pick his brain. He'd say, 'Just swing and hit the ball hard.' That was his theory. Let the chips fall where they may." Pitcher Jay Hook also found Hornsby to be helpful. Ever the student, Hook was looking for ways to improve his game. Although he was a righthanded pitcher, he batted lefthanded, and he reasoned that if he became a better hitter, he might be able to stay in games longer instead of being lifted for a pinch hitter. "I got Hornsby to come out to the batting cage with me after practice every day," he stated. "They had a pitching machine, and I'd spend a half hour getting him to help me with my hitting and my bunting. And it was helpful."

The remaining coaches quickly fell into their roles. Red Kress threw batting practice all day. Cookie Lavagetto and Solly Hemus devoted most of their time to infield instruction. However, as Thomas recalled, most of the players, particularly the veterans, "just went about their business and knew what they had to do to get themselves in shape for the season."

Assembled by Weiss in somewhat desperate fashion, the Mets were an interesting mix. There were the old Dodgers, Gil Hodges, Don Zimmer, Roger Craig and Charlie Neal, as well as coach Lavagetto, a former Brooklyn infielder.

Zimmer, in fact, had the honor of becoming the Mets' first pinup star. He was the only Met player who lived in the vicinity in the offseason. Over the winter, before spring training began, he got a call asking him to come to Huggins Field to model the team's new uniform. With his son Tommy sitting on his shoulders, Zimmer spent the afternoon being photographed as the first player to wear a Mets uniform.

In addition to the sizable Dodger contingent, there were also four ex-Cardinals in camp: Anderson, Bob Miller, Jim Hickman and Chris Cannizzaro. Of course, Hemus, who had been the Cardinals' manager for part of the previous season, was at least partially responsible for that, since the players were known to him.

There were also the other familiar veterans, Richie Ashburn, Frank Thomas and Gus Bell. Ashburn set the tone right away, showing up in Bermuda shorts and parking his borrowed antique car in George Weiss' spot on the first day, a habit he continued. Robert Lipsyte, then a neophyte baseball writer for the *Times*, found Ashburn to be warm, friendly, and above all, accessible. These traits were not shared by all the veterans. Lipsyte found Gus Bell to be "grumpy" and Frank Thomas to be grumpier still, but Ashburn "seemed happy to be alive. Richie was an enthusiast, and he just lifted everybody's spirits. If he thought it was appropriate for him to be there, then hardly anyone else could complain. Gil Hodges didn't talk a lot, and you remember Casey's famous line about him, 'Be careful. He can tear your earbrows off. He's that strong.' We thought he might have meant 'eyebrows,' but he said 'earbrows.'

Gil was solid, pleasant enough. There was no sense of circus about this. These were solid ball players. I don't think they were happy to be there, but it was great fun."

Then there were Ray Apple, Bruce Fitzpatrick, Bill Whalen and dozens of others destined never to appear on a major league roster. "The Mets were signing every prospect who could move," wrote Lindsey Nelson. "They had a stream of players coming and going. It appeared that nobody really knew who all of them were." Since the Mets had no minor-league system to speak of and there was not yet an amateur draft, they grabbed whoever they could find in hopes of discovering an unknown gem. Billy Loes, the ex-Dodger pitcher who signed and then failed to report, put it another way: "The Mets is a very good thing. They give everybody a job, just like the WPA." Anderson described the camp as "guys from seven different teams, all ages, all backgrounds, and nobody was quite sure what it was all about."

On the first day, Stengel gathered all of his would-be amazin' Mets and gave a pep talk, telling them, in essence, that nobody had a job won and that everybody had a chance to make the team and make some money in the process. He then delivered a walking monologue that literally took him around the basepaths and left few subjects unaddressed, which was thankfully recorded for posterity by Maury Allen: "'Now if you get to first base you can make a living in New York, because everybody wants to support a new team and the public expects their best and the Polo Grounds is an old field but a new one is being built.' The players nodded that they understood (they didn't) and Stengel moved on to second base. 'And if you play hard and good they give you jobs in the winter and your family can get all set to stay in New York in one of them big buildings and I'll rent you my room in the Essex House 'cause me and Edna go home to California.' They all marched toward third. 'If you can make a living with the club, why wouldn't you want to do it in New York which is the biggest city and you can do lots of things and go to the theaters and be stars and all and why wouldn't you want to play for the Mets.' Now they were closing in on home plate, all forty of them, watching Casey's face, listening to his words, studying his pointing fingers. 'This is where you make your living when you score, and they tell you that the distance is the same but you will find out that it is not so 'cause it's longer to get here. Everybody got it? Let's commence playing.'"

Hobie Landrith, the Mets' first draft choice, remembered Stengel coming into the clubhouse looking like a Normal Rockwell character and starting to talk. "That was very revealing to me as to the wealth of baseball knowledge that he had," said Landrith. Stengel spoke of the virtues of reading newspaper box scores to learn which opposing players were hot, preferably before they faced the Mets. He then discussed training, telling the players that "you do it on your time, you don't do it on my time." He then instructed Landrith and the others to follow him to the dugout. "So we go and he explains everything you should be doing in the dugout. You don't sit there and play jokes on each other, you observe the players as they're swinging and taking their infield drills and so forth. We went to the on-deck circle, and he says, 'In the on-deck circle, this is what you do.' You anticipate what the possibilities are, and mentally go through the signs. What's the steal sign? What's the take sign? What's the squeeze sign? You do that so that when you get up to home plate and you get a sign, you don't step back in amazement . . . 'what was that?' You can just imagine Casey with all of his gyrations and everything. Then he took us up to home plate, and you should recognize that the rightfielder is a right-hand thrower. You hit the ball down the line, he's got to turn all the way around to make that throw to second base, whereas if he's a left-hand thrower, he doesn't have to do that. That could be the difference of you being safe or out at second base. Bunting situations – you know, who's the guy who can handle the ball the best? Stay away from him. Well, he took us from home plate to first base to second base to third base to home. We got to third and he finished talking there, and he says, 'And then we go home, and that's when we win, win WIN!'"

Reactions among the players were many and varied. "He came walking out and the room got silent," recalled Anderson. "The old man came out and addressed us for a few minutes and kinda welcomed us to New York in his own intriguing language. None of us can remember anything he said, then or now." Joe Ginsberg said, "We all looked at each other and said, 'Oh, my God.' That had never happened to us before. We said, 'What a year this is going to be.'"

Among the more interesting players who had failed to establish themselves elsewhere was Rod Kanehl, the former Yankee. Now a twenty-eight year-old rookie, Kanehl was in a make-or-break situation. Although never much of a hitter or fielder, Kanehl was a scrappy, determined ballplayer who, as "Hot Rod" Kanehl, became a favorite of both his manager and the fans. Leonard Shecter described the "immediate affinity between Kanehl and the Mets. They were both losers. But with the Mets, Kanehl managed to attain a fame of sorts. To this day [1970], at the drop of a suggestion he'll play a game of baseball trivia. Who was Marvelous Marv Throneberry's roommate on the Mets? What Met was removed for a pinch hitter in the second inning of their historic 23-inning game? Who got the last pinch hit in the Polo Grounds before it was torn down? Who was the first man to hit a grand-slam homer for the Mets? The answer to all is Rod Kanehl."

"Kanehl was the soul of the Mets, their living symbol of mediocrity," Mel Allen wrote. "He knew he was getting a chance because of expansion and like the Mets, he knew he was lucky to be in the league. He would play it for all it was worth." Stengel's friend Bob Sales recalled that the manager "loved Rod Kanehl. He was a guy who had a certain amount of baseball sense, and he would do anything for you. He played his ass off." "Casey and I got along very well," said Kanehl shortly before his death. "We talked the same language. I played hard, and that's all he expected from you."

Kanehl was also a point of contention between Stengel and Weiss. Although Weiss gave in to Stengel's demand that he draft Kanehl, he was less than impressed with him. They clashed again over Kanehl at cut-down time. The rules allowed teams to open the season with three extra players before the cut-down occurred in May. Weiss wanted to demote Kanehl and keep outfielder John DeMerit, while Stengel wanted to send DeMerit down. The manager vented his frustration to reporters in vintage Stengelese, without naming names, leaving the writers to work out the pronouns for themselves: "He says I've got to get rid of the guy who busts his ass for me, but the other guy you don't know if he's awake."

Stengel prevailed again on this occasion, and DeMerit was farmed out. Kanehl, for his part, responded warmly to Stengel. Of Stengel's opening monologue, Kanehl remembered it as "a brilliant speech. When it was over and we started working out, I had to translate for a few guys, but they all appreciated the part about making a lot of money."

When Stengel managed the Yankees, he insisted on the standardization of training at all levels of the organization. Thus, any player promoted to the majors would have received the same instruction as his teammates and would know what was expected of him. When Stengel took over the Mets, though, Kanehl was the only ex-Yankee in camp, and with eight years of Stengel-mandated training under his belt, he soon found himself in an unusual role. On the one hand, there were veterans like Hodges, Thomas, Ashburn, and so on, players with long resumes, but unfamiliar with their manager's approach. On the other, here was Kanehl, fresh from Double-A, never having been on a major league roster but who nonetheless was soon Stengel's mouthpiece. "He intended to teach the Mets the Yankee system," explained Kanehl, "and he said, 'Kanehl, go to first base and show them how to lead off.' 'Kanehl, show them how to lead off second.' 'Kanehl, show them how you take the signs.' 'Kanehl, show them how to bunt.' Those guys were veterans. They were thinking, who is this fucking Kanehl? They didn't know me from Adam."

Of course, some of the veterans reacted differently than others to Kanehl's favored status. When Stengel instructed Kanehl to demonstrate the fine art of Yankee bunting, Roger Craig was on the mound with instructions to lob the ball over to facilitate the demonstration. Instead, Craig brought a fastball high and tight that sent Kanehl sprawling. Undeterred, Kanehl picked himself up and hurled the ball back at Craig, yelling, "Get the ball over, Meat!" "You have to know Craig, though," explained Kanehl forty years later. "Craig would do that to anybody. But it finally got to him. Here Ashburn was one of the best bunters in baseball, and Stengel's having me demonstrate bunting."

Kanehl was also the first to collect on a standing offer Stengel promised to the club, namely, that if any player got himself hit by a pitch with the bases loaded, he would earn a fifty-dollar bonus. "I did it in the first week and he went right to his checkbook and gave me a personal check for fifty," said Kanehl in 1970. "I have it still."

Kanehl was as determined with teammates as with opponents. Early in spring training, Ashburn, the venerable center fielder, called for a ball hit to the outfield and then let it drop. Kanehl, the 28-year-old rookie, growled at Ashburn, the 15-year veteran, saying, "If you call for it, goddamn it, catch it!" However, Ashburn soon came to respect the brash Hot Rod. "Casey loved Rod Kanehl," he stated. "He was a guy who never made it until the '62 Mets. He kept grinding it out without a whole lot of ability but with a lot of desire. He could play seven different positions and get himself hit by a pitch with the bases loaded." Kanehl recalled fondly the impression he made on Ashburn: "Later Ashburn told me he was wondering, 'Who is this brash fuck from Double-A ball?' Ashburn was just as brash as anyone. He loved it. I didn't give a shit. I was 28 years old. I either make it, or I go home. He told me later, 'I knew you were gonna make the club after that. Your brashness was enough to convince me.'" My attitude was this was my last go around and I'm not going to be intimidated by anyone."

Every night, Stengel would hold court in the bar of the Colonial Inn's press room. He spent hours talking with "my writers about this here team," and he would often remain until every writer had finished asking questions, however late that turned out to be. His epic monologues involved Yankee stories or tales dating back to his early days as a player and manager. These had differing effects depending on the interests, and in some cases stamina, of the listener. Broadcaster Bob Murphy said later that "Lindsey, Ralph, and I decided that the best thing we could do was get acquainted with Casey. So we start hanging out with him and found that he was indefatigable. After 10 days we're hiding behind potted palms in the hotel lobby. He was over 70 years old and running us into the ground!" Nor were they the only ones. As Craig Anderson explained, "After a couple weeks, we started to notice that the coaches were really dragging. And they told us he would keep them up for very late hours. He'd like to have a couple of drinks and sit up and talk baseball, and if he didn't have writers to talk to, he would have his coaches around him. And these guys started to drag, and they were telling us he was running him down. We laughed about that. And he did it all season, too."

The players quickly learned to watch Stengel's arrival for clues. "If his shoulders were slumped," posited Zimmer, "we knew he'd been out drinking and telling stories to the writers until 4 a.m. Usually when that was the case, Casey would sit on the grass at the far end of the dugout, leaning up against a wire fence." In that case, Anderson remembered that Stengel would sit out there with a writer, coach or someone from the front office while the coaches ran the practices.

More important than Stengel's stories, though, was his continual salesmanship of his new club. Besides the writers, he also addressed the throngs of fans attending the daily workouts. "I'm out to build a good ball club as soon as I can," he told an assembly one day. "This ain't gonna be no five-year plan. Why, this is a great opportunity for a young ballplayer. If he can show me, I'll put him right in that lineup, and I'll get him more money, too. I ain't a banker for nothin', you know."

In a reversal of his earlier practices, Weiss also came out to the park regularly, and his public statements were similar. "I told Casey and the coaches that they have to keep telling these fellows, both the old ones and the youngsters, that they've got a chance, that it doesn't take too much to be a winner in this even-up league," he told *Sports Illustrated*. "Also, that they're in New York, where every ballplayer wants to be, and don't let 'em forget it."

The taciturn Weiss showed that even he had been changed by the aura surrounding the Mets. The change was noted by, among other people, Bill Veeck, the former maverick owner and a staunch Weiss foe, in his outspoken biography, *Veeck – As In Wreck*: "Now that he is with the Mets, he has suddenly become quite promotion-minded and readily available to the press, which shows that George is able to adapt himself to changing conditions. The question is whether he will still be able to come up with all those good young players now that he has neither the Yankee prestige nor the Yankee scouting system going for him. It was interesting to note that he began by signing up scouts the way Huey Long used to sign up bodyguards. Well, each of us to our own dark fears."

Leonard Shecter, too, was stunned when, on one occasion, Weiss invited questions from the assembled reporters. "To the men who knew him when he was general manager of the Yankees," wrote Shecter, "this was like a Burchite inviting a Pravda man to breakfast. 'I want to thank you fellows,' Weiss told reporters. 'You've been very kind.' A year before, Weiss thought all newspaper men should have their glands removed as a condition of employment. But he was changing a lot. He even agreed to have his picture taken with Miss Rheingold and a beagle [Homer, the Mets' mascot]."

Moreover, Stengel's constant teaching was not limited to the "youth of America," the young ballplayers with whom Weiss had provided him. As Shecter pointed out, the Perfesser spent a lot of time that spring educating the writers. This education often took subtle forms. For example, Stengel would tell newly-arrived reporters to keep an eye on one Dawes Hamilt, "who, the old man would say with a serious, intense look on his face, was the greatest prospect since Mickey Mantle. What Stengel wanted them to see, however, was that poor Dawes Hamilt, an extraordinarily amiable young man, was leaden-footed, uranium-assed and titanium-headed and had less chance of playing baseball for a living than he had of dancing on a moonbeam. The very few of those who recognized this were rewarded by one of Casey Stengel's shyest smiles."

The hapless Hamilt (whose real name was Marshall; he'd changed it to Dawes because he liked the way it sounded) did not survive spring training. He later claimed that this was due not to his being "leaden-footed, uranium-assed and titanium-headed," but rather, because he was Jewish. Pitcher Bob "Butterball" Botz failed when even Hamilt proved able to hit him hard. Although Botz pitched well initially, he gave up five runs in an inning against the Senators, including a home run to deep center (leading one reporter to change Butterball's nickname to "Longball"), and he was gone soon after. Similarly, pitcher Evans Killeen, originally considered a possibility to make the club, didn't in the end. Killeen, who was from Long Island and had been signed for a bonus by Kansas City, aroused hopes by pitching four innings of hitless relief. However, on the morning he was supposed to start his first exhibition game, he somehow managed to cut his thumb while shaving. Failing an explanation as to why he was shaving his thumb, he was soon released, never making the majors. Another pitcher, Ray Apple, had even worse luck. On the first day he stepped onto the field, he was hit on his throwing arm by "Iron Mike," the mechanical pitching machine. Although he was not seriously injured, he didn't last long. "You have empathy for them," said Jay Hook, "but, you know, that's kind of the game."

Another was Aubrey Gatewood, signed during Weiss' free agent feeding frenzy the preceding fall. Upon releasing him, Stengel gave an eye-popping justification. "I'd like to keep you," he said. "But I got some experienced pitchers here and we may be fighting for the pennant so I got to go with experience."

Then there was John Pappas, a twenty-one year-old furniture salesman from Queens who showed up in St. Pete and requested a tryout. Although he had no pro experience, he said he'd pitched in the Police Athletic League and had worked himself into shape by throwing a ball against a wall under the Triborough Bridge over the winter. Any other team would have laughed him out of sight. Even the Mets were not interested, but after being pressured by Stan Isaacs of *Newsday* and Bob Lipsyte of the *Times*, Johnny Murphy reluctantly agreed to give the kid a look. However, he refused to allow the tryout to happen at Huggins Field. Instead, Murphy, Pappas and a host of reporters ventured to a local vacant lot, where it took little time to conclude that while Pappas certainly had moxie, he was not a major league pitcher. "It was the perfect story for me," said Lipsyte. "Pappas was another young guy from Queens. And Stan Isaacs and I bedeviled the Mets into giving him a tryout. He threw three or four pitches, and Murphy slapped him on the back and said, 'Nice try, son, but we don't have anything for you.'" "At least I tried," Pappas said afterward. "I'm only sorry they didn't give me a chance to hit. I'm not a bad hitter and I play the outfield, too."

The spring was full of assorted dramas. Hall of Fame broadcaster Ernie Harwell spoke of an incident in which a prospect approached Stengel about the possibility of playing for the Mets. When Stengel asked about his history, he replied, "In my senior year in college, I hit 40 home runs, I knocked in 85 runs. I was a pitcher, threw five no-hitters and won ten games. I had an earned run average of 1.30, and I ran the 100-yard dash in 9.7 [seconds]." When Stengel asked if he had any weaknesses, the youngster said, "Well, I do lie a little."

Another incident occurred when Channel 9 interviewed catcher Hobie Landrith. The problem, as Craig Anderson recalled, was that there was a fifty-mile-an-hour wind blowing. "They were saying, 'Hobie, how's the catching staff looking?' He said, 'The catching staff is working hard, and we got a nice group of guys, and today,' he says, 'we're working on popups, as you can see.' So he's standing there, and [the camera] shows a catcher behind him, and you see the guy circling and running and diving and missing the ball, and these two guys were breaking up laughing."

The wind also plagued Lindsey Nelson and Bob Murphy, who were filming commercials for Rheingold Beer. During one filming, Murphy sat a table with a Rheingold bottle in front of him. He read his way through the scripted virtues of the product, during which he was to reach for the bottle and hold it up for the camera. Just as he did so, though, the wind gusted and blew the bottle just out of his reach. He reached for it again, straining farther, and again the wind blew the bottle away from him. "He just managed to grab it before it slid off the table altogether," wrote Nelson, "but by that time he was sprawled at about a forty-five-degree angle. He looked like a guy trying to pick up a windblown hat that wouldn't stay still." Nelson had his own problems during another shoot. He was stationed in front of a grill wearing a chef's hat, cooking burgers while talking about how well Rheingold would go with those burgers. The wind played havoc, blowing so much grill smoke into Nelson's face that his eyes were streaming as he tried to get through the filming. "We finally got a couple of usable takes out of it," he wrote in his autobiography. "Before we broke camp I had a letter from a friend, saying, 'I thought you'd like to know that you're famous as the worst chef on television.'"

Stengel was also involved in a memorable spring training shoot, this one for Bromo Seltzer. The script called for Richie Ashburn to slide into second base and be called out by umpire Augie Donatelli. Stengel would then charge out of the dugout to argue with Donatelli, during which he would develop a state of upset which would be relieved by Bromo Seltzer. This was during a period in which the Federal Communications Commission was cracking down on commercials featuring celebrities who did not actually use the products they endorsed. In order to avoid trouble, someone from the ad agency asked Stengel whether he actually used Bromo Seltzer. "Why, sure," replied Stengel. "Only I never get sick, so I don't have to." Undeterred, the agency went ahead with the shoot. Ashburn slid into second and Donatelli called him out. So far so good. The problem developed when Stengel overacted his resulting stomach ache to the point where the director told him it was a bit over the top. "You mean you don't want me to die?" asked Stengel. "I'm old enough." Once the commercial was finally done, Stengel kept telling people he had done an ad for Alka Seltzer.

There was also Elio Chacon, who played in the World Series with the Reds the year before and for whom the Mets had paid $75,000 in the expansion draft. Chacon had trouble getting in from Venezuela, where he played winter ball. After several delays for various incomprehensible reasons, Chacon got on a flight which was to have arrived in Tampa at 11:00 p.m. but which did not get there until 5:00 the following morning. Lou Niss, the traveling secretary, had been waiting for Chacon and was not happy. "I asked him what happened to his plane," said Niss afterward. "I still haven't been able to figure out what he said."

Shortly after his arrival, Chacon, who was far from fluent in English, gave a press conference, which contained the following highlights:

Q. During the World Series [which the Reds lost to the Yankees], you said you were going to get married. Did you?

A. I say only if we win the whole thing.
Q. What did you tell your girl friend?
A. I told her take it easy.
Q. Isn't she impatient?
A. No.
Q. Do you know what impatient means?
A. No.

Through it all, Stengel, who knew the value of publicity as well as anyone, demonstrated his understanding of its uses. No one, certainly not Stengel himself, was under any illusions as to the caliber of team the Mets would field in 1962. The writers, many of whom had previously covered the Yankees, Giants and Dodgers, could not have been blind to the team's many shortcomings. By and large, though, this is not what they wrote about. Since everyone knew the team would be bad, they seem to have reasoned, what was the point of writing about that? Stengel, sensing this, made sure to give the reporters something else to talk about. One example was Kanehl, the subject of continual praise despite his limited skills. The writers enjoyed reporting about a failed Yankee who was suddenly a hero across town. "We knew what he was doing," said Dick Young. "He was using diversionary tactics. We did not mind because we knew what the situation was."

Although Stengel was always upbeat in talking about his club with reporters and fans, privately he was less sanguine about the level of talent. Rogers Hornsby, who had scouted many of the players before the draft, reported on Stengel's mood after one particularly grim session. "Casey come back today like a ghost," said the coach. "Like a ghost, I tell you. Don't you know, that man is used to good teams. These fellas here, I tell you they frighten you."

Weiss continued to bring in even more players. Before spring training, he signed reliever Clem Labine, yet another ex-Dodger, and veteran catcher Joe Ginsberg, both 35. Between them, they appeared in only six games with the Mets before both were released on May 1. Still, no one could doubt Weiss was making an effort, and he wasn't getting much cooperation from the other general managers, as he told *Sports Illustrated* that spring: "A year ago, everyone down here was promising me all kinds of help, but now, of course, it's different. We're in the league now and no one wants to give me anything, but I'll keep trying." It must have been difficult for him after his success with the Yankees. He was used to raiding lesser teams whenever he needed a player, not paying exorbitant prices for other teams' castoffs.

The pattern for the season was set in the first intrasquad game. The players were divided into two teams, the Lavagettos and the Hemuses. Infielder Sammy Drake was scheduled to lead off for the Hemuses, but when it was time for him to bat, he could not be found. Stengel sent up Joe Ginsberg to pinch hit for him. With the count at a ball and a strike on Ginsberg, Drake suddenly turned up, having taken a detour to the men's room, and he was immediately sent in to pinch hit for Ginsberg, who, of course, was already pinch hitting for him. Once Drake finally made it to the plate, he hit a triple. "See how smart Casey is?" asked Ginsberg. "Puts a pinch hitter in for the leadoff hitter and he gets a triple. No wonder he won so many pennants."

The pattern continued in the opening exhibition tilt with the Cardinals. Roger Craig had been tabbed to start for the Mets. He declined to throw the day before, saving his arm for the game. Instead, he worked out by practicing sliding, in the unlikely event that he would be called upon to break up a double play. In doing so, he pulled a muscle in his pitching shoulder and had to miss the start. As a result, Jay Hook got the nod instead, and the Mets lost 8-0. During the game, Frank Thomas hit a massive foul blast which everyone present agreed would have stayed fair within the confines of the Polo Grounds.

The next day, the Mets trailed the Cardinals by three runs late, still looking to cross the plate for the first time. Choo Choo Coleman went up to pinch hit and homered with a man on. Another run followed, and the score was tied. In the ninth, Ashburn doubled and then scored on Chacon's single, and the Mets had their first win. They then dropped their next seven in a row before defeating the Tigers 1-0, the only run coming on a Gus Bell triple driven by the wind. Ray Daviault, Herb Moford and Bob Moorhead combined on the shutout.

Having achieved their initial victories, the Mets soon had their first hero. Hot Rod Kanehl was a fan favorite right from the start, exemplified by a banner hung in left field during one of the Mets' first games at the Polo Grounds, reading "WE LOVE THE METS ROD KANEHL." It was the first of many banners to be displayed that year, and every year thereafter. The banner, recalled Kanehl, was on a large window shade, which the artist unwound until the whole message was displayed. "I was on the bench," he stated, "and Ashburn called me over, and he said, 'What did you pay those kids?'"

Kanehl's fame resulted in part from his heroics during a spring game with the Dodgers which was televised back in New York. It was the bottom of the ninth, and Dodger ace Sandy Koufax was on the mound. The Mets were down by two runs, but they had runners on second and third. "Don't ask me how they got there," said Kanehl years later. "I was asleep in the dugout. I'd had a rough night and it was one of those sleepy days in St. Petersburg." He was awakened by Stengel barking his name and asking if Kanehl wanted to win the game. "What could I say? I said, 'Sure.'" He grabbed a bat and headed for the plate. "The first pitch, zap! Strike one," he told Leonard Shecter. "I didn't even see it. The next one was another fast ball, I guess. The umpire said it was a strike. I wouldn't know. Strike two. Now Casey starts hollering from the bench, 'Butcher boy! Butcher boy!' He meant take a short swing, meet the ball, don't strike out. Well, the next pitch I can see. I start going for it, then I realize it's too high, so I pull back. But it turns out to be one of Koufax's big curve balls. I'm pulling back, and the ball is curling down over the plate. It's also curling down into my bat. Damndest thing." Kanehl punched the ball between the first baseman and the bag for a double, scoring both runners. The next batter, Felix Mantilla, hit Koufax's first pitch safely, and Kanehl scored the winning run.

The real highlight of the exhibition schedule, though, was still to come. The Yankees, as they had in so many ways already, provided a huge publicity bonanza when, on March 22, they returned to Al Lang Field, now as the visitors. Over 6,000 spectators jammed the park. Yankee skipper Ralph Houk, beginning his second season as Stengel's successor, treated the game as another spring tune-up. Stengel, though, aware of the opportunity the game afforded, used his regular position players and his number one starter, Roger Craig. When Craig left the game after six innings, Stengel sent in his number two starter, Al Jackson. Jackson was not expecting to pitch that day, and he even had to borrow a glove.

The game was close throughout, and the crowd cheered every Met accomplishment. Mickey Mantle was greeted with polite applause the first time he batted in the second inning, but when Charlie Neal speared his hard grounder and threw him out, the crowd roared. The Yankees pushed a run across the plate on three singles, but the Mets served notice they had come to play when Thomas doubled off Bill Stafford, the first hit off Stafford that spring. The crowd roared again when Hodges and Chacon turned a 3-6-3 double play on a grounder off the bat of Roger Maris.

Unbelievably, the home team took a 3-2 lead into the final inning, having scored on two errors, two walks and a single by Don Zimmer. After the Yankees tied it up in the top of the ninth, the Mets won in the bottom when Joe Christopher tripled and scored on Ashburn's base hit. The winning pitcher was Howie Nunn, who relieved Jackson and got the last batter, Johnny Blanchard, to pop out, and who never appeared in a regular season game as a Met. Stengel and the players took multiple bows before the fans, almost all of whom had stayed till the end of the game and for hours afterward. The team hosted a victory cocktail party at the Soreno Hotel for the many media personalities present, some of whom had traveled from New York for the game. When Stengel walked into the room, dressed in a natty blue serge suit, the reporters broke into applause. Stengel, ever the master of ceremonies, told them that "it shows you how easy this business is." "It meant a lot to him because that was the team that fired him," said Christopher. "You want to come back with some sort of revenge. But at the time, most of us were just trying to save [our] career and make the team. Casey was no fool. He was one of the most astute men that I ever met."

The Mets' victory in what should have been a meaningless exhibition game stunned the fans back in New York. Toots Shor's restaurant, the leading night spot, was jammed with merrymakers. Speaking with Stengel by phone later that night, Shor told him that it was "like New Years Eve in this joint." The *Times* reported the Mets win as the lead sports story the next day, while the *Daily News*, not to be outdone, highlighted its own coverage on the front page. Enthusiasm was dampened only slightly when the Yanks soon beat the Mets in a rematch.

Through it all, the players gradually began to form a cohesive unit. The club had its own ideas on how this should occur, not all of which were well-received. "I had recently gotten married," explained Anderson, "and although my wife was coming, I would have to stay at the Colonial Inn with the players. The only ones they let live out were the ones who had children. Maybe that was their plan to try to pull the team together in there. But I didn't have any choice. Jay Hook and his wife lived out [since they had two children]. A lot of guys didn't bring their wives, so there weren't that many living out. It was a situation that I never experienced any other time, where they brought us in there to try to control us and mold the team using that tactic. The interesting part was that we really did get to know some of the older guys. Judy and I were starting to play bridge a little bit, and Jay and his wife played bridge, so we used to go over to Jay's house and play. Somehow, Lavagetto and Hodges got wind of that. One day we were having dinner at the Colonial Inn, and they said, 'Hey, we hear you guys are really good bridge players, and we'd love to play a couple hands with you.' And they were really good bridge players. A lot of the Dodger players played bridge. We were so nervous going to their room. That was something that my wife never forgot. They were such super guys, and we had a lot of fun."

Rod Kanehl also had fond memories of Hodges that spring. During Kanehl's first Yankee camp in 1954, he remembered Stengel's instruction to always listen to older players when they discussed baseball. He now discovered that Hodges talked shop all the time, usually with Ashburn, Zimmer and Bell. Kanehl began to work his way into their circle, listening at first. "It was a ritual," he said later. "We'd be the last to leave the locker room, and I was part of that crew. I was invited along, and I was flattered to be invited along with these guys. We also did a lot of bowling."

One day the workouts were rained out. Rather than excusing the players, Stengel called a clubhouse meeting to discuss pickoff plays. Stengel tossed a towel onto the floor to represent first base, and he designated catcher Chris Cannizzaro as the baserunner. Cannizzaro dutifully took his lead off first while Stengel, halfway across the clubhouse, pretended to be a pitcher working from the stretch. Cannizzaro got into the swing of it, edging away from the towel and moving back and forth while Stengel spoke. Ten minutes passed, then fifteen, and Cannizzaro began to droop as Stengel's lecture continued. With the catcher practically asleep on his feet, Stengel suddenly whirled toward him, made a pretend pickoff throw and yelled, "Gotcha!" "We were there for two-and-a-half hours listening to him talk about pickoffs," said Anderson. "But he knew what he was talking out, and the players got a big kick out of it."

As the Mets broke camp, they made a final move. Ted Lepcio, the first big-leaguer to sign a Met contract, was expected to be the utility infielder. However, on almost the last day of spring training, Lepcio was cut and Joe Christopher was sent to Syracuse. This meant that Hot Rod Kanehl, who had hit .440 during the exhibition season, would spend Opening Day on a big league roster for the first time. He found out the day before the team was to leave Florida when Solly Hemus asked what number he wanted to wear. This began a pattern which continued the next couple of years. "Stengel probably knew that I was going to make the club from the very beginning," Kanehl recalled. "It was on his mind that at least he wanted me to. He always fought for me. Every time there was a cutdown, he'd fight for me. Solly Hemus told me that many times. He said, 'Jesus, Stengel would fight for you every time, and he'd play you a few days before [the cutdown date].' And I'd always do something. Not that I was aware of the cutdown date – it just happened that way."

After the Mets left St. Pete, they embarked on a barnstorming swing up the East Coast. They were to have played the Orioles in Norfolk, Virginia, but the game was rained out. That morning, though, there was a breakfast at the Norfolk Sports Club honoring the players of both teams. Stengel asked Lindsey Nelson if he would "be interested in introducing our squad to these nice people on account of they are the hosts and we should tell 'em who they are hosting and maybe you could do that." Nelson respectfully demurred on the grounds that he did not yet know all of the players by sight. "Well, that's the problem I got," replied the manager. "I don't know 'em either." In any event, Stengel got up and made a few remarks before introducing his pitchers, catchers and infielders and then the broadcasters. He sat down without mentioning any of his outfielders. "Well," recalled Anderson, "whenever Casey made a mistake, it wasn't like there was just one reporter to catch it. When I had been with St. Louis, there were two guys from the two major newspapers in St. Louis. In New York, we had 24. So whenever he made a mistake, they were all over him. So they said to him, 'Hey, Casey, you forgot to introduce any of your outfielders.' Well, he never wanted to admit he'd made a mistake, so he said, 'Gentlemen, I have some big trades pending, and I didn't want to mention any names.'"

Pitcher Jay Hook also found himself in an unexpected role. "I don't know how this happened, but I got voted player rep, and I ended up having to negotiate with Casey," he explained. "There were a number of us who had never lived in New York before. We didn't know how to go about finding a place for our families. It's a huge area. So I went to Lindsey Nelson, Bob Murphy and Ralph Kiner – this is my fault, I shouldn't have done it this way – and I said, 'Would you guys announce that a number of the players are looking for housing, and if people have apartments or homes that they're going to be away from for the summer, they could let us know?' Well, people started to call in to the park, and the operators refused to take any information. So I went in to see Casey, and I said, 'I don't want to be a pain, but if I don't have a place for my family to move into before we go on the road, I'm not going.' Man, he hit the ceiling. He said, 'Now don't tell me we're gonna have problems with you and your family.' And I said, 'No, I don't want problems, but I think the club should offer some help to the players who've never been here before. I told him what I had done, and he said, 'Well, I'll work on it.' He made sure the operators would take down the information when people called, and did the same thing I had done but did it the right way. Within a week, we had fifty places to look at. So it turned out great."

The Mets wound up the spring with a respectable record of 12-15. This led all sorts of people who should have known better to predict that New York would finish out of the cellar in the new ten-team league. *Sports Illustrated*, in its annual baseball preview, predicted that the Mets "cannot possibly finish higher than seventh." The same article enumerated the team's strengths and weaknesses as follows:

"Strong points: Potential power and the incomparable Casey Stengel. Gil Hodges, Frank Thomas, Gus Bell, Second Baseman Charlie Neal and Third Baseman Don Zimmer can all reach the cozy right- and left-field seats of the Polo Grounds with ease, if they haven't forgotten how. Manager Stengel, bubbling with enthusiasm, carries an 'I'll show 'em' attitude back to the Yankees' hometown.

"Weak spots: Old age and shallow pitching could hurt the most. Of the regulars, only the shortstop candidates – Elio Chacon and Felix Mantilla – are under 30. The outfield, especially in the roomy Polo Grounds, will be porous, if Bell (33) is in right, a slowed-down Ashburn (35) is in center and Thomas (32) is in left. Reserves Joe Christopher and John DeMerit can run but their hitting is questionable. Gil Hodges, at 38, will need frequent help at first. Except for Thomas, who had a big year in 1961 (27 HRs), none of the home run hitters have reached many fences in the last few years. Catcher Hobie Landrith (32) is a good receiver but a light hitter. At short, Chacon is an exciting but undependable fielder, and Mantilla has some glove talent but little with the bat (.215 BA). Roger Craig, with five wins last year for the Dodgers, is the Mets' 'ace' pitcher. After him there is a plethora of inexperience.

"The big ifs: The fate of the Mets depends on how young the old-timers act and how fast the young pitchers develop. Jay Hook (25), Craig Anderson (23), Ken MacKenzie (28), Bob Miller (23) and Sherm Jones (26) all have promise. Herb Moford

(33) will start and Clem Labine (35) will relieve if his arm holds out. This spring the pitching was surprisingly sharp. It could turn out to be the strongest part of the Mets."

A month earlier, SI's Robert Shaplen, in a lengthy piece on the team, was much bolder. "Upon Ashburn and Hodges, who are 34 and 37 years old respectively, as well as on veterans Thomas, Bell, Zimmer and Neal, and on their young and untried pitchers, the Mets' fortunes will depend," wrote Shaplen. "No matter what, Weiss undeniably has succeeded in building an attractive first-year team that, conceivably, could finish as high as sixth."

Roger Angell, writing for *The New Yorker* the day of the improbable victory over the Yankees, summed up the team as follows: "I doubt whether any of the happy six thousand-odd filing out of Al Lang Field after the game were deluding themselves with dreams of a first-division finish for the Mets this year. The team is both too old and too young for sensible hopes. Its pitchers will absorb some fearful punishment this summer, and Chacon and Neal have yet to prove that they can manage the double play with any consistency. Still, though, the Mets will be playing in the same league with the Houston Colt .45s, another newborn team of castoffs, and with the Phillies, who managed to finish forty-six games out of first place last year and will have eight more games this year in which to disimprove that record. The fight for the National League cellar this summer may be as lively as the fight for the pennant."

Even veterans like Ashburn, Zimmer and Thomas, speaking after the fact, professed early optimism. "When I went down to spring training, I knew it was going to be a tough year," Ashburn recalled, "but I didn't think it would be that tough because I was surrounded by a lot of players who were pretty good. Gil Hodges, Gus Bell, Frank Thomas. They could do some damage." "It was hard to tell that first spring we were going to be so bad," wrote

Zimmer in his autobiography. "So much of the spring focused on Casey that nobody paid much attention to the quality of play on the field." "When I arrived at spring training," said Thomas, "I found a lot of other players with high expectations. We all had pride in our abilities and expected to have a fair record. We never expected to have a horrendous year and lose 120 games." "At that time," confirmed Anderson, "I think Stengel felt that the team was gonna be competitive. I thought we were. I played with all these big names in St. Louis, and we had just as many big names in New York. The only difference was they couldn't play like they used to, and that started to show up. I had no clue – and you can underline that – that we would be as poor a team as we turned out." "Everybody was optimistic," added Kanehl. "We had a fair spring, and we were in most of the games. We went north very optimistic. We just didn't realize we didn't have the pitching it took to do it with."

Only Stengel, it seems, was not deluded. "We had a remarkable spring record for the kind of club they say we are," he told the press after breaking camp. "But the record don't fool me. I think I'm gonna win every day, sure, an' I'm mad if I don't win. But I know in a lotta games if the other side put in their regulars we wouldna' beaten them at all."

After a spring training win, he summed up the team's performance: "I'm glad we did good. It's good for the club. But we ain't so great. My pitcher didn't throw the ball over to first base [to hold the runner] so they got down and broke up two double plays. It was a good game, but we still did the same thing [failing to hit] with men on base. I don't know when they're going to learn."

When asked where he thought the team would finish, Stengel responded, "We'll finish in Chicago." This turned out to be the only accurate prediction, as six months later, the Mets lost their 120th game of the season before a handful of fans on a forbiddingly cold day at Wrigley Field.

CHAPTER SIX – THE FIRST MONTH

"Our first Mets game was April 10, 1962. And it was our best game. It was rained out." – Casey Stengel, manager of the New York Mets

In retrospect, it couldn't help but be an omen. On Monday, April 9, 1962, the Mets flew to St. Louis, where they were to begin their first season against the Cardinals the following evening. Immediately upon the team's arrival at the Chase Hotel, there was a memorable incident. There were no hang-ups at the front desk, since the players had all been pre-registered by traveling secretary Lou Niss. They got their keys and then headed *en masse* for the nearest elevator, cramming into every inch of space. The elevator went several feet up and ground to a halt. "That was the highest they got all season," wrote Lindsey Nelson afterward.

In all, sixteen Mets, including Opening Day starter Roger Craig, were stranded in the elevator for half an hour, during which a recorded message repeatedly informed them that "dinner is being served in the Tenderloin Room." Hobie Landrith, the 5'8 catcher, was the butt of inevitable jokes. Craig kept telling the others to "lift Hobie up for air, he's gonna die." Jay Hook remembered, "You can imagine a bunch of guys on an elevator for twenty minutes and all the comments that were made. We were all laughing, and it got a little crude. Later, we found out that this buzzer and the microphone played out right in the lobby of the hotel. Once you pushed that button, the speaker was on, and the people who were down in the lobby could hear all these comments. It was hilarious."

The next day, it rained, and the game was postponed.

Shortly before the first game, Stengel was interviewed by Lindsey Nelson, during which he introduced the starting nine.

Beginning with "the noted Mr. Hodges of the Dodgers," he went through the entire lineup, discussing each player in turn. Nelson, who had budgeted ninety seconds for Stengel's remarks, knew he was in trouble when Stengel went three minutes before even reaching the outfield. The Perfesser spent additional time on Frank Thomas ("who hit 25 home runs last year in Chicago, two in Milwaukee gets him 27, hits balls over buildings, he's got experience and power, very good, we can use him"), some on Richie Ashburn ("one of the Quiz Kids in Philadelphia, gets on base 200 times a year, which is excellent, delighted to have him on our side"), and then ran into a recollective wall when he got to right field. He could not remember Gus Bell's name, but he continued on nonetheless, stating that Bell was "the best of five or six fellas that's doing very good," that Bell had hit .300 for Cincinnati and manager Rogers Hornsby (then the Mets' hitting coach), that he had seven children, and on and on, before concluding as follows: "He's a splendid man and he knows how to do it. He's been around and he swings the bat there in right field and he knows what to do. He's got a big family and he wants to provide for them, and he's a fine outstanding player, the fella in right field. You can be sure he'll be ready when the bell rings, and . . . that's his name, Bell." Stengel's answer to Nelson's question had taken twelve minutes.

Ashburn led off and played center field, followed by shortstop Felix Mantilla. Charlie Neal batted third and played second. Thomas, the left fielder, batted cleanup, then came Bell in right. The noted Mr. Hodges was sixth and played first, after which were third baseman Don Zimmer, catcher Hobie Landrith and Craig, the pitcher.

Stengel's Opening Day outfield probably set a record for fathering children. Ashburn and Thomas each had six kids, and Bell had seven, a fact which inevitably led to wisecracks. Stengel told the press that "if they can produce as well on the field as they do off the field, we'll win the pennant."

Also on the roster were infielders Elio Chacon, Ed Bouchee, Jim Marshall and Rod Kanehl; outfielders Jim Hickman, John DeMerit and Bobby Gene Smith; catchers Chris Cannizzaro and Joe Ginsberg; and pitchers Al Jackson, Jay Hook, Craig Anderson, Bob Miller, Ray Daviault, Ken MacKenzie, Bob Moorhead, Herb Moford, Sherman Jones and Clem Labine.

When the Mets finally began play on Wednesday, April 11, a number of things happened which would become familiar over the course of the season. With one out in the Cardinals' half of the first inning, Julian Javier singled, and Bill White hit a ground ball past Hodges, who would have easily fielded it in his prime. Javier took third on the play and was driven in by Stan Musial. Just like that, in the first inning of their first game, the Mets gave up the first of the 948 runs they would surrender that season. They made three errors, and Craig left in the fourth inning trailing 5-2, on the way to the first of his 24 losses. Gus Bell got the first hit in team history, a single up the middle, and Hodges and Charlie Neal homered, but the Cardinals pounded out sixteen hits off Craig and relievers Bob Moorhead, Herb Moford and Clem Labine and cruised to an easy 11-4 victory behind the pitching of Larry Jackson. Three of the sixteen hits were by the 41-year-old Musial. It was the first of 23 games in which the pitching staff would allow at least ten runs.

It has been widely reported that White scored the first run of the game, and therefore Met history, as the result of a balk by Craig in allowing the ball to drop out of his glove. While the notion that the Mets gave up their first run ever on a balk is certainly attractive, it is pure folklore. After Musial singled, scoring Javier with the first run and moving White to second, Craig turned to throw to first in an attempt to pick off Musial (though where he was expecting Musial to go is unclear, since second base was occupied by White). When he turned to throw, though, he discovered that Hodges was not covering first. The umpire called a balk, advancing White to third and Musial to second. White then scored on Ken Boyer's groundout. Although the balk advanced White into scoring position and White would not otherwise have scored, he did not score on the balk, and, in any event, his run was not the first. However, this did not stop Jimmy Breslin and others from relating what they clearly regarded as the better story. Curiously, the "balked-in-first-run" tale acquired such momentum over the years that when a tribute album entitled *Miracle Mets* was released in 1970, it included what was purported to be Lindsey Nelson's radio call of the play. In fact, Nelson's call was performed in a recording studio over fake crowd noise specifically for the record. Nelson had not even called the play; the first three innings of the game were called by Bob Murphy.

One of the other key plays had been a fly ball which landed between Bell in right and Ashburn in center, leading to a five-run Cardinals rally. "My head knew I had it," said Ashburn after the game, "but my legs forgot to get it."

In addition, Landrith made a bad throw to first on a pitchout, and the Cardinals stole three bases against him. In fact, ten of the first eleven men attempting to steal on Landrith were successful, and his inability to throw out runners soon led to his downfall. After the game, a reporter suggested to Stengel that all he could do was pray for things to get better. Stengel responded that, "Prayers don't win for you. You've got to do it yourself." Stan Isaacs quoted Ashburn's reaction to the loss: "Damn, blankety blank and damn."

The team flew back to New York to be honored a day later with a ticker-tape parade up lower Broadway before 40,000 fans. The parade, the first in New York since that afforded to astronaut John Glenn, was surely a singular event. The players, broadcasters and other officials rode in groups of three and four while seated in fourteen open convertibles onto which were stuck placards bearing their names. They wore their brand new home uniforms. Promotion director Jules Adler had stocked the cars with plastic baseballs, which the players threw to the cheering throngs as they drove by. Stengel, waving like a maniac, and George Weiss were in the lead car. The Mets were serenaded by four brass bands situated at intervals along the way, as well as the delighted crowd. One of these bands, provided by the Department of Sanitation, kicked things off at 12:05 with their rendition of "Hey, Look Me Over." McCandlish Phillips, reporting for the *Times*, noted that the Mets "had done nothing to deserve this tribute except to redeem the city from its bereft estate as a National League widow." "It was a real thrill," remembered Rod Kanehl. "It was something that usually only happens to someone once."

When the procession reached City Hall, the players disembarked and sat on a platform on a stage to be officially welcomed by Mayor Robert Wagner. Stengel introduced each player by his last name ("Mr. Craig, Mr. Hook," and so on), which spared him having to remember their first names, and asked each to stand. Mayor Wagner then presented Stengel with a large golden key to the city, leading Stengel to observe that "I got a lotta keys to a lotta cities, but this is the first one I'm using to open a team."

However, not everyone remembered the event fondly, especially after Bill Shea, who had invested so much time and energy in bringing National League baseball back to New York, spoke. Shea offered what was, in effect, an apology for the quality of the players. "It still sticks in my craw," recalled Ashburn thirty years later. "Before we had played a single home game, Shea told the fans, 'Be patient with us until we can get some real ballplayers in here.' And the players – we were standing right there! I mean, he was probably right, but he didn't have to *say* it." Craig Anderson, reminded of the event, stated, "That doesn't always get you off to the right start."

After the parade, Stengel took his ballplayers for their first workout at the Polo Grounds. The session was delayed for over an hour while they waited for their spikes to be delivered from the Hotel Manhattan. Because the field was still wet with morning rain, Stengel had his team change out of the new home uniforms they'd worn in the parade and into their gray road uniforms. Whatever happened during the opener, the team would at least look good.

One of those most looking forward to the opener was thirty-five year-old Joe Ginsberg, selected by Stengel to catch the game. Ginsberg had never played in the Polo Grounds, having spent his entire career – which extended back to 1948 – in the American League. "He called me into his room," Ginsberg recalled. "'Son' – he called me 'Son' because he couldn't remember my name – 'you're going to get more recognition today than in your 13-year career because you're catching the first game in New York.' And he was right."

The next day – fittingly enough, Friday the thirteenth – the Mets played their home opener against the Pittsburgh Pirates. Also fitting was the opponent, since it had been the Pirates who had last visited the Polo Grounds, pounding the Giants 9-1 on September 29, 1957. The ballpark was indeed the Polar Grounds that day, with the temperature in the low forties and falling, as were occasional snow flurries. Although a number of important people attended, including Shea, Weiss, Mayor Wagner, Mrs. Payson, Edna Stengel and National League president Warren Giles (he who had once asked "Who needs New York?"), not many other people did, as the paid attendance was less than 12,500. There was a guest seated in the owners' box with Mrs. Payson and Don Grant, a seventeen-year-old prospect named Ed Kranepool, who would shortly graduate from James Monroe High School in the Bronx. He had broken all the hitting records set by Monroe's most famous alum, Hall of Famer Hank Greenberg. Less than three months later, Kranepool would receive $85,000 of Mrs. Payson's money for signing a contract with the Mets. His major league career began when he was called up in September, and he played for eighteen seasons before retiring in 1979, having spent his entire career with the Mets.

Plenty of things went wrong that day, even before the game started. Stengel managed to lock himself out of his newly-refurbished office, and when he tried to get back in, it was discovered that no one had a key fitting the lock. Stengel only managed to get back into the room after workmen disassembled the door frame. Then there was the National Anthem. As Leonard Shecter wrote, "Brian Sullivan of the Metropolitan Opera and the St. Camillus Band rendered 'The Star-Spangled Banner.' But not together." Further, there was some doubt that Sherman "Roadblock" Jones, the designated starter, would be able to go that day. During the team's bus sojourn from Norfolk after the conclusion of spring training, Jones lit a cigarette, only to have a piece of the match head break off and lodge in his eye.

Still, by the home opener, the Mets had already sold over 2,000 season tickets, more than twice as many as the Giants managed during their best year at the Polo Grounds. The fans were ready to make their feelings known. Mayor Wagner threw out the first pitch and was roundly booed by those who felt he had not done enough to prevent the Giants and Dodgers from leaving. Don Grant gave a speech in which he puffed up the team's sponsor and encouraged the freezing fans to drink lots of ice-cold Rheingold Beer. Nelson spoke as well, introducing many of the attending dignitaries, including Joan Payson and Mrs. John McGraw, widow of the immortal Giants manager. The loudest cheers were reserved for Stengel and Hodges. However, Hodges had pulled a muscle and could not play. Unfortunately no one told the public address announcer, and the fervent cheers which greeted Hodges' familiar name turned to equally fervent boos as the unfamiliar figure of Jim Marshall trotted out to first base. Ralph Kiner noted in his autobiography that Marshall "is believed to be the first player ever booed while playing for a team that was yet to engage in its first home game." Marshall took it ins stride, noting that Mayor Wagner had also been booed and concluding that he and the Mayor "were in a class by ourselves."

The tone was set right away, as Zimmer fielded the first ground ball and threw it over Marshall's head. In addition, the

Hodges-hungry fans kept booing Marshall even after he doubled and scored the Mets' first run. The crowd also expressed displeasure when Gus Bell misplayed a ball in right field and the next batter hit one which fell between Bell and Ashburn for a triple, scoring the runner whose drive Bell had misplayed. Although Roadblock Jones pitched well enough to keep New York in the game, the Mets lost 4-3 in the ninth inning.

Two of the Pirates' runs scored on wild pitches by Herb Moford and Ray Daviault. With the game tied at three in the eighth, Daviault walked the leadoff man, Dick Groat. Groat quickly advanced to second on Daviault's first wild pitch and to third on an infield out. When Daviault uncorked his second wild pitch of the inning, Groat raced home with what would prove to be the decisive run.

Although the attendance was disappointing, those attending were enthusiastic. Ashburn got a standing ovation for driving in the Mets' first run in the fifth, and although the fans booed Daviault after his wild pitches, they cheered him lustily after he struck out a batter with the bases loaded to end the inning. In fact, the fans were so loud that Yankee officials, listening to the game on the radio on their way back from the airport, accused the Mets of using canned crowd noise to make a better impression.

After the game, Stengel committed a memorable gaffe. In the clubhouse, Stengel talked to reporters while undressing, something he had done frequently throughout his career. He removed his pants to reveal boxer shorts emblazoned with the logo of the New York Yankees.

The close loss was the highlight of Roadblock Jones' season. He was gone by late spring after starting 0-4 and never returned to the majors other than a one-game September call-up. "He was one of the front-line starters coming out of spring training," remembered Craig Anderson. "And then he was gone." "Now what was that all about?" asked Met fan Walter Pullis, still incredulous after forty years. "So what if he lost the first four? If you trot those guys out every four or five days, they're going to lose twenty games with a team like that."

The Pirates went on to sweep the three-game weekend series. Craig Anderson relates that odd things were already happening routinely. In one of the games, Stengel brought in Herb Moford to pitch with Pirates on base. Moford pitched out of the jam, and with the Mets coming to bat in their half of the inning, he was slated to lead off. The coaches asked Stengel who was going to hit for Moford. "In other words, they were trying to dictate to Stengel, 'you're going to pinch-hit,'" explained Anderson. "Well, the old man at times could get his dander up, and he'd say, 'Get out of my way.' He went over to Herb and said, 'Herb, are you a good hitter?' Well, you never ask a pitcher if he's a good hitter. We always said we were good hitters. So Herb says, 'Yeah, I'm a good hitter.' I was in the dugout that day, and the coaches were laughing back and forth. Next thing you know, crack! Herb gets a base hit to left field. So now we're carrying on pretty good in the dugout. You know . . . managerial strategy. We look up, and Stengel has put a pinch-runner in for Moford."

One little-known fact is that the Mets narrowly missed the chance to record their first win on the last day of the series, although, had they done so, it would have been strangely appropriate. Having lost the home opener on Friday and the second game on Saturday, the Mets had a doubleheader scheduled for Sunday, April 15. Walter Pullis, then fifteen, wanted to go, but his father demurred because of the weather. "It was too cold to go," he remembers. "I was disappointed. So the Mets lose the first game, and now they're 0-4. They start the second game, and they take a 2-0 lead into the fourth. Four and a half innings, of course, is an official game if the home team is ahead. So they're batting in the bottom of the fourth, and guess what. It starts to snow. Not rain. Snow. And the game got snowed out. So if they could have gotten past one more inning, part of the Mets lore would have been that they won their first game because the game got snowed out. Since it got snowed out before it was an official game, obviously, it never happened."

Hodges was in and out of the lineup over the next ten games after sitting out the home opener with a sore knee and a pulled leg muscle. He later claimed he had hurt his left knee "falling asleep on a bus." He would clearly need surgery on his knee at some point; in fact, the Mets' team physician, Dr. Peter LaMotte, told Hodges that although he was thirty-eight years old, "that knee looks seventy-six." It was the continued unreliability of Hodges' aching legs which led to the most significant trade of the club's early history within a few weeks.

The other expansion team, the Houston Colt 45s, came to town for the first time. Stengel took advantage of a light (some said nonexistent) rain and had the opener postponed. In addition to Hodges, Charlie Neal was nursing a hand injury. "If I was winning, I'd play five games a day because you tend to keep winning when you're winning," Stengel told the press. "But I had a chance to call this game, so I did. You tend to keep losing when you are losing. The way our luck has been lately, our fellows have been getting hurt on their days off."

The game was played the next day. In the bottom of the ninth, Gus Bell rewarded the faithful – who were already chanting "Let's Go Mets!" – with a home run (his only one as a Met) which tied the game at two apiece. However, the Mets blew a chance to win in the tenth when Felix Mantilla doubled but then got caught in a rundown. In the eleventh, Herb Moford served up a three-run homer to Don Buddin, and Houston won 5-2. It was Moford's only decision of the season, and his only one as a Met. The Mets were already 0-5, and Stengel, the master of the understatement, spoke with Jimmy Breslin about starting off the season this way: "The trouble is, we are in a losing streak at the wrong time. If we was losing like this in the middle of the season, nobody would notice. But we are losing at the beginning of the season and this sets up the possibility of losing 162 games, which would probably be a new record, in the National League at least."

Even the Mets could not be that unfortunate, although they did lose their next four, including consecutive 15-5 and 9-4 decisions to the Cardinals. Thus, the Mets were 0-9, tying the NL record for season-opening futility held by the 1918 Brooklyn Dodgers and the 1919 Boston Braves. Roadblock Jones had been charged with three of those defeats, Roger Craig and Al Jackson had two each, and Moford and Bob Miller had one apiece. Other than Thomas, who had four home runs and six RBIs in the first nine games, Neal and Ashburn, who were batting .318 and .316, respectively, in that same span, and Ed Bouchee (six for twelve with two homers), the team wasn't hitting either. The loss on April 22 to the Pirates was Jones' third and the team's ninth.

After the season started, *Sports Illustrated* sent a reporter to follow the Mets in order to report their first victory. Upon learning that the reporter had recently been married, Stengel told him he might not see his bride again until October.

By one of those curiosities which seemed to continually occur throughout the season, the Mets were already nine-and-a-half games out of first place despite the fact that they had only played nine games. This was because the red-hot Pirates started with a ten-game winning streak, tying the NL record at the other end of the spectrum.

At this point, though, the team was doing its best to keep its collective spirit in good order. "We lost our first nine games, but we were in a lot of them," remembered Rod Kanehl. "Even though we lost, we were still upbeat." Craig Anderson agreed: "Some of those games were close. We just didn't do the right things at the right times. The veteran players were visibly trying to hold it together and get the guys going. Early on, there was a lot more concern about 'let's get this going' and 'we're not this bad.'"

The next day, April 23, the Mets finally registered their first victory, breaking the Pirates' winning streak in Pittsburgh. Stengel sent Jay Hook, the engineering student and "premium" draft pick, to the hill, and he was masterful. He pitched a complete game, scattering five hits and only one walk, and the Mets won 9-1, pounding out 14 hits in the process. Hook also paced a four-run second inning rally with a bases-loaded single, driving in two runs, and he scored twice as well. The Mets pounded starter Tom Sturdivant (a former Yankee and future Met, who retired only three of the eight batters he faced, the other five all scoring) and reliever Diomedes Olivo for six runs in the first two innings. In the second, they batted around for the first time in the team's young history. Hodges went two for three, and Felix Mantilla, leading off that night, added three hits. Rightfielder Bobby Gene Smith drove in the only two runs of his brief Met career with a triple. Elio Chacon, the little Venezuelan shortstop, contributed three hits, two runs and two RBIs and ran the bases with bravado. They also played error-free ball, while the Pirates uncharacteristically committed three miscues.

In the jubilant locker room afterward, catcher Joe Ginsberg hollered "break up the Mets," and Stengel was heard to shout, "Ninety-nine more and we got the pennant. I'm gonna let Hook pitch every day. We shouldna lost the first nine and I don't see how we lost a game. The damn streak cost us the pennant. We might win the next twenty straight!" He told Chacon that "you played shortstop like you owned Venezuela." Chacon himself, whose English was (to put it kindly) idiosyncratic, issued a prediction to a reporter, stating, "Yesterday I say we play better today. Tomorrow, we play more better. You watch."

The reporters were understandably eager to talk with Hook, the hero of the day. He patiently answered their questions, and when they were finally done, he went to get his shower. "By the time I went to take a shower, there was no more hot water," he recalled. "So I ended up jumping in the whirlpool and kinda taking a bath, because at least that was still warm."

Although the team was scheduled to catch a charter flight to Cincinnati immediately after the game, Stengel told Lou Niss to hold the plane until "his" writers had all the information they needed. Stengel pointed out to Niss that, contrary to his own buoyant postgame remarks, they might not get the opportunity to report wins very often.

As if to prove him right, the Mets lost the next three, running their record to 1-12. They dropped two to Cincinnati by scores of 7-3 (in which the Mets lost despite drawing eleven walks) and 7-1. The third loss was to Philadelphia in the first of a three-game series, featuring two Neal errors, two passed balls by Landrith and a dropped fly in left by Thomas. In the second inning, after Neal let a ball get away, pitcher Craig Anderson fielded a routine ground ball, but he could not make the play because first baseman Jim Marshall had also gone for the ball and no one was covering the bag. Then Zimmer misplayed a grounder. The Phillies scored two unearned runs on the way to an 11-9 decision.

However, the Mets then recorded their first two-game winning streak with a pair of wins over those same Phillies. In the first contest, Thomas, Neal and Hodges hit back-to-back-to-back homers in the sixth inning. Rod Kanehl, who was to score the tying or winning runs in many of the Mets' early victories, scored the go-ahead run when he sped all the way home from second on a wild pitch. The next day, Al Jackson pitched the team's first shutout, beating the Phillies 8-0. Thomas also tied an obscure record by being hit by pitches twice in the same inning, first by Art Mahaffey and then by Frank Sullivan, during the Mets' seven-run fourth.

In the midst of these events, there was more tragicomedy. Rheingold, the Mets' sponsor, had been aggressively promoting the new team. The brewery's best-known symbol was its Miss Rheingold campaign, which featured a number of attractive young women in the title role. Stengel appeared with Miss Rheingold in several print and billboard ads for the company's Extra Dry Lager, the ads which had been shot at the Stengel household before he left for spring training. One such ad bore a caption reading, "No, she's not Mr. Stengel's new shortstop; she's Kathy Kersh, our Miss Rheingold 1962." On April 24, commissioner Ford Frick fined Stengel $500 for appearing in his uniform, a "violation of the baseball rules, which prohibit men in uniform from posing for alcoholic beverage ads." Suspicion abounded in the Mets camp that the fine had been the result of a complaint submitted to Frick by an unsuccessful would-be sponsor.

Five days later, Stengel received an award as baseball's "top salesman of the year" (a no-brainer for sure) from the Sales Executive Club of New York. Addressing their banquet, Stengel took the opportunity to hurl another slam at the National League owners for the way the draft had been conducted: "We had to purchase these men from the demon salesmen in baseball to get into business. And sometimes we put these men back up for sale. And those wonderful salesmen, those wonderful people in baseball, would you believe, they don't want those men back. So we can't make the trades we need. We're going to have to go to the farm system and that takes money and time. So I want all you salesmen to go home and sell your boys on playing baseball and when they get older to play for the Mets and only ask for a small bonus." Upon receiving his award, Stengel pointedly rustled the package, telling the meeting that he was looking for home plate, since his players couldn't seem to find it.

Even more ludicrous was the Harry Chiti trade. On April 26, Weiss acquired the veteran catcher from Cleveland for a player to be named later. Authors Brendan C. Boyd and Fred C. Harris summed up Chiti's career, which also included stints with the Cubs, Athletics and Tigers, as follows: "Harry Chiti [was] a reserve catcher with any number of teams over a period of any number of years who looked like everybody's brother-in-law, and played like him too. Fortunately for Harry, his lack of speed was not as noticeable as [that of other slow catchers] because he was such a lousy hitter that he rarely got on base. The only time you really noticed how slow he was was when he was trotting back to the dugout after striking out."

It did not take long for Chiti to run afoul of his new manager. Stengel had instituted a rule against card playing, believing that this would prevent resentments among the players. During a plane trip soon after joining the Mets, Chiti went to Stengel and asked for permission to start a game of gin rummy. Stengel said no and suggested that if Chiti had nothing to do, he should go over the hitters the team would face in upcoming games, since Chiti had come over from the American League. Instead, Chiti took a nap.

As noted, the Mets had acquired Chiti for a player to be named later. The identity of that player was revealed on June 15, when the Mets returned Chiti to the Indians, thus making him the first player ever to be traded for himself. George Vecsey of the *Times* noted that it was hard to tell who got the better of the deal. And this, wrote Steve Rushin thirty years later, "began a Mets tradition that continues to this day, in which fans in the street endlessly second-guess the team's front office. 'Yo, I can't believe Weiss couldn't get more for Harry Chiti than, you know . . . Harry Chiti.'"

Chiti appeared in fifteen games as a Met and batted 41 times, accumulating eight hits, eight strikeouts, no homers or runs batted in, and a batting average of .195, to go with two errors behind the plate. When he was returned to Cleveland, his major league career was over. Although Shecter referred to Chiti in his writings as an "ancient catcher," he was in fact several months short of his thirtieth birthday.

Around the time of the Chiti deal (the first part), Weiss got yet another catcher, Sammy Taylor, from the Cubs, in return for outfielder Bobby Gene Smith, an expansion pick who had barely seen any action -- eight games, 22 at-bats and a .136 average. He soon went from the Cubs to the Cardinals and then did not appear in the majors again until 1965. Taylor became about the closest thing to a regular catcher the Mets had that year; the 50 games he caught were second only to Chris Cannizzaro's 56. Weiss also signed Dave Hillman, a thirty-five year-old pitcher from the Reds. Hillman appeared in 13 games with the Mets, running up an earned run average of 6.32 before being released on June 20; however, he did record one of the team's ten saves in 1962. As with many others, his career ended when he was cut by the Mets.

To make roster space for Chiti and Hillman, the Mets released veterans Clem Labine and Joe Ginsberg, neither having done anything in their brief Met careers. Ginsberg had played in two games behind the plate, the first being the home opener, the second being two days later, going hitless in five at-bats. Labine had thrown a total of four innings in three appearances with an ERA of 11.25. Labine was especially aggrieved by his release. He signed with the Mets when George Weiss promised to equal the salary Labine had made with the Pirates in 1961, although the Pirates had not wanted him back. When he reported to spring training, Stengel told Labine and Ginsberg that they would be working with the young pitchers, which they agreed to do. "What we didn't realize was that we were getting a snow job," stated Labine years later. "I was taking on the pitchers and Joe had the pitchers and catchers, and neither of us was getting into the ballgames. When we asked Casey about it he said, you guys can do anything you want, but we've got to get these kids into the games. Oh, boy. So what happens when the season starts and it's cutdown time? Who do you think went? Joe and I. They cut us and gave us severance pay. I just thought it was a lousy thing to do. They should have told us to come down, set a price, and let us know we were going to be coaches and not players. But that was it for me. I went home." Ginsberg, who hadn't played in more than two weeks, accepted his release with more equanimity. "I thought I had a good chance to stay," he asserted. "But then I got off to a bad start and I knew they had to make a move. It's the perils of the trade." Neither was picked up by another team after being released.

The losing continued. After Jackson's shutout against the Phillies, the team dropped their next four, at which point they were 3-16 and surrendering almost seven runs a game. Nor were they hitting in clutch situations. Against the Phillies on May 4, the Mets trailed by a run in the bottom of the ninth. Against all odds, they managed to load the bases with nobody out and their thumpers, Thomas and Hodges, coming up. Thomas hit a weak popup, and Hodges grounded into a double play, ending the game. The next day, they went into the ninth again trailing the Phillies by a run. They had blown a chance in the seventh, when Jim Hickman and Felix Mantilla struck out with two runners on. After Chacon and Hodges were retired to begin the final frame, Gus Bell hit a two-out double to center. Stengel sent in the speedy Rod Kanehl to run for Bell. Harry Chiti came up next and singled to left. Kanehl attempted to score from second on the play and was gunned down by Johnny Callison's perfect one-hop throw to the plate. The Mets, having held the Phillies to two runs, had managed only one themselves, wasting fine performances by Jackson and Craig Anderson.

Stengel and Weiss, clearly frustrated, continued to re-shape the team. Smith, Ginsberg, Labine, Roadblock Jones and Herb Moford were followed out by Don Zimmer, another "premium" pick. Zimmer was hitting .077 when he was traded to the Reds on May 6. After starting the season three for twelve, he then went hitless in his next 34 at-bats. Two days before he was traded, he finally broke his horror-show slump with a double, and upon reaching second, he bent down and patted the base. On news of the trade, one commentator suggested that the Mets had dealt Zimmer "while he was hot." Shortly before the trade, a reporter asked

Stengel, somewhat tongue in cheek, whether Zimmer was the "guts" of the team, to which the Perfesser responded: "Why, he's beyond that. He's much more. He's the perdotious quotient of the qualificatilus. He's the lower intestine."

In his autobiography, Zimmer recalled how he learned of the deal. He was in the shower after a loss in Philadelphia when Stengel said he wanted to see him. Zimmer emerged from the shower and was treated to a monologue. "I've got something for you," Stengel told him. "You'll love it. That left field fence is just right and your dad is gonna be delighted [Zimmer was from Cincinnati]. They got that little hill out there in center field and the beer tastes good and the people are just great, especially in the summer." After listening without comprehension for while, Zimmer finally felt compelled to ask the manager what the hell he was talking about. "Oh," Stengel responded, "didn't I tell you? We traded you to Cincinnati."

In return for Zimmer, the Mets received third baseman Cliff Cook, who, unbeknownst to Weiss, had such a bad back that he was often unable to bend over to field ground balls. Since this was something of a problem for an infielder, Stengel moved him to the outfield. It hardly mattered, as Stengel barely used him in either spot. The year before, Cook had batted .311 with 32 homers and 119 runs batted in for the minor league Indianapolis Indians, winning the American Association Most Valuable Player Award, but he only appeared in 40 games with the Mets in 1962, coming to bat 112 times and hitting .232 with two home runs and nine RBIs. On May 11, five days after the trade, he showed both his positives and negatives against Milwaukee. He contributed a triple and a single but made two errors and narrowly avoided a third, as the Mets lost 8-5. In only sixteen games at third, he made five errors. Unlike most of Weiss' pickups, though, he lasted not only through the season but through 1963 as well.

The Zimmer deal also brought left-handed pitcher Bob Miller. Of course, the Mets already had a right-handed pitcher named Bob Miller. The team had to refer to them as Robert L. or R.B. ("Righty Bob") Miller and Robert G. or L.B. ("Lefty Bob") Miller. Lefty Bob Miller had received a $50,000 bonus from Detroit as a seventeen-year-old in 1953, but the six games in which he'd appeared with the Reds before the trade (in which he'd given up 13 runs in five-and-a-third innings, an ERA of 21.94) were his first big league action since 1956. When he learned that the Mets wanted to send him to Syracuse, he decided not to report. At age 26, he went home to Illinois to go into the automobile rental business. Chief scout Wid Matthews went to Miller's house and talked him into reporting to Syracuse. After all, Matthews pointed out, Miller only needed 18 days of major league service in order to qualify as a five-year player under baseball's pension plan. That meant Miller would receive $125 per month once he reached the age of fifty. Buoyed by this incentive, and with his boss' promise to hold his job open, Miller reported to Syracuse, posted a 4-1 record and was called up in July.

Once Lefty Bob Miller was brought up, Lou Niss saw to it that the two Bob Millers roomed together on the road. "That way," he reasoned, "if somebody calls for Bob Miller, he's bound to get the right one." In addition, both Bob Millers appeared together on "To Tell the Truth," a TV show which featured three contestants being questioned by a panel to determine which was the person he claimed to be. At the show's climax, the announcer asked, "Will the real Bob Miller please stand up?" Of course, both did.

Also, Stengel, for no apparent reason, referred to Righty Bob Miller as "Nelson." However, while the saga of the two Bob Millers is well-known, few people know that Righty Bob Miller's real last name was Gemeinweiser – a name he ultimately changed because, as he said, "I couldn't pronounce it myself."

The Zimmer trade also had an effect which could not have been known at the time. By starting as the Opening Day third baseman, Zimmer became the first of an endless parade of Mets to play the position. In the first 24 seasons of the franchise, the team used 79 different players at the hot corner. It was a problem that certainly never got solved during 1962, as Stengel tried nine different men at third. Together, they committed a total of 34 errors.

In another May 6 deal, Weiss sent Jim Marshall to Pittsburgh. At the time of the trade, Marshall (to whom Stengel referred as "Blanchard," after the Yankees' super-sub Johnny Blanchard) was batting .344 as a frequent stand-in for the oft-injured Hodges at first. Before one pinch-hit appearance, Stengel imparted some words of wisdom to him: "Hey, Blanchard, there's something you ought to know. Son, you see them foul lines, the ones on first base and third base that run all the way out to the building? You know what they're there for? Those are for the hitters to shoot at. When you get in the batter's box, I want you to try to hit that ball as close to those lines as you can because, you see, all those opposing players are standing in the middle." Armed with such advice, Marshall went to the plate and struck out.

In return for Marshall, the Mets received pitcher Wilmer David "Vinegar Bend" Mizell. Mizell's tenure with Mets, which spanned 17 games over the three months preceding his release on August 1 at the age of 31, was a hiccup in the rest of his life. He had had some prior success pitching for several teams (most notably the Pirates, for whom he appeared in the 1960 World Series against Stengel's Yankees), compiling a career record of 90-86 before coming to New York. He also held a record, albeit an odd one, as the result of his having pitched a shutout while giving up nine walks. After leaving baseball, he entered politics, ultimately serving three terms as a U.S. Congressman from North Carolina beginning in 1968, after which he held positions in the Ford, Reagan and Bush administrations. As a Met, though, he lost his only two decisions and compiled an earned run average of 7.34. Lindsey Nelson watched Mizell warm up in the bullpen one day. He noticed that Mizell's cap came off with every pitch, and that "the cap moves almost as fast as the ball . . . Vinegar Bend has had it."

To make room, Herb Moford was demoted to Syracuse. Like so many others, Moford's departure meant the end of his big league career at the age of 33. He had appeared in only seven games, with a record of 0-1 and an ERA of 7.20. As the Mets began their second month of play, their roster was already drastically different than it had been only four weeks earlier. Zimmer, Marshall, Labine, Ginsberg, Moford and Smith were gone, and Miller, Cook, Taylor, Hillman, Chiti and Mizell had taken their place (none of whom would finish the season with the team except Taylor). The best, however, was yet to come.

CHAPTER SEVEN – BEING EMBALMED

"When you're losin' everyone commences playin' stupid." – Casey Stengel, *manager of the New York Mets*

On May 6, the same day as the Zimmer and Marshall trades, a funny thing happened: the Mets got hot. Over the next two weeks, they won nine out of twelve, three in extra innings and five at the expense of the Braves, from whom the Mets had acquired a number of players.

A season highlight occurred during a May 12 Braves doubleheader visit to the Polo Grounds. In the first game, Milwaukee's legendary Warren Spahn carried a 2-1 lead into the bottom of the ninth. With a runner on, Stengel left Hobie Landrith in the game when most other managers would have pinch hit for him. Stengel called time, walked up to Landrith, whispered something to him and walked away. Landrith then hit Spahn's first pitch curve into the 257-foot right field porch for a game-winning homer. When asked what he had told Landrith, Stengel replied, "I told him to hit a home run." After the game, Spahn, who posted 363 career victories, said he wanted to kill himself. "You almost felt sad for Spahn," remembers Walter Pullis. "It was one of the dinkiest home runs you ever saw."

In the nightcap, Stengel started rookie Bob Moorhead, who would ultimately appear in 47 Met games without earning a victory, against future Met Carl Willey. With the score tied at seven in the bottom of the ninth, Gil Hodges hit a lazy fly which carried into the right field seats just a few feet past where Landrith's had gone. And just like that, the Mets had swept their first doubleheader. Jimmy Breslin, writing for *Sports Illustrated*, opined that "they did it with two home runs that only a Little Leaguer would own up to. And there are smart people today who insist it never happened."

Landrith's and Hodges' homers were two of only four game-winning homers the Mets hit all year, and the third was more than three months away. In another historical curiosity, Craig Anderson, pitching in relief, got the wins in both games, becoming one of the few pitchers of the modern era to register two victories in a day. As he had won another earlier in the week (becoming the only Met pitcher to enjoy such a cluster of wins all season), his record stood at 3-1. "I didn't win another one after that," recalled Anderson ruefully. "I never thought that would happen." Anderson proceeded to lose his next sixteen decisions that season, and three more over the next two years, without recording another win in his major league career.

The home run Landrith hit off Spahn was his only one as a Met. By early June, he was on his way to Baltimore as additional compensation in another of Weiss's cash deals. At the time he learned of the trade, the team was on the road. Landrith was upset because his young son had accompanied him on the trip, and he was unsure how the boy would take the news. His son, though, said he'd known about the trade for three days, having heard Lou Niss discussing the deal on the clubhouse telephone. When Landrith asked why his son hadn't told him, the boy replied, "You always told me not to repeat what I heard in the clubhouse."

The trade which sent Landrith packing brought the Mets a first baseman to stand in for the ailing Gil Hodges, one who could also improve the team's anemic power numbers. "We've tried to make the Mets look better with distance hitting," explained Stengel, "so we brought in this here new fella."

The new fella was Marvin Eugene Throneberry, from Collierville, Tennessee, who had spent seven years in the Yankee system after signing for a $65,000 bonus in 1954. He had some power, having hit 82 homers in two years for the Yankees' Denver club. Throneberry played four seasons with the Yankees before being sent to Kansas City in 1960 as part of the Roger Maris trade. He had even started 1958 as the Yankees' regular first baseman, and he appeared in the World Series that year, striking out in his only plate appearance. During the 1961 season, the Athletics traded him to the Orioles, and while he batted only a composite .226, he hit eleven homers despite seeing only limited action.

Throneberry (whose initials even spelled "MET") was 28 and already balding when he arrived. Leonard Shecter of the *Post* was widely credited with christening him "Marvelous Marv," though Shecter said the name originated when Throneberry had been a Yankee prospect and was called "Marvelous" when he turned out not to be. However, Throneberry's new teammates attributed the origin of the nickname to other sources, including Marvelous Marv himself. Here, for the first time, are the collected theories as to how he got the name:

1. Leonard Shecter; see the preceding paragraph.

2. George Vecsey of the *Times* also believed Throneberry came to the Mets with the nickname already in place, having picked it up as a Tennessee high school football star or as a Denver farmhand when he hit 82 homers in 1956-57.

3. Craig Anderson, and many others, believed that Richie Ashburn was responsible for the name. "Marv was a low-key guy, a real slow-moving boy from Tennessee," says Anderson. "Everybody really liked him. Ashburn took it upon himself to name him 'Marvelous Marv,' and we all thought that was great. It was sort of like a unifying thing to have 'Marvelous Marv' on our team. At that point, he hadn't really done anything unusually bad." Lindsey Nelson was another who believed Ashburn to be responsible. Ashburn, asserted Nelson, "was Marv's straight man, cheering his every move, feeding him his lines, and nursing him

through impromptu locker-room interviews. One day, soon after Marv came to the Mets, his name was gone from his locker, replaced by a card that read Marvelous Marv. This must have been Ashburn's inspiration, although Richie never admitted it."

4. Jay Hook, and not Ashburn, was the person responsible for the card. He said that Throneberry came to him shortly after being traded and asked Hook if he was an engineer. Hook confirmed that he was. "Well, engineers can print real good, can't they?" asked Throneberry. Hook replied that he had taken some drafting classes. Throneberry went over to his locker, took the sign which read "Throneberry" from above it, handed it to Hook, and said, "Write 'Marvelous Marv' on this card, would ya?" Hook wrote "Marvelous Marv" on the blank reverse side of the card, whereupon Throneberry took it and slid it back into the slot above his locker. After the game, in which Throneberry homered, the reporters came into the clubhouse and saw the card, and that was that.

5. Throneberry himself claimed a different source. "Every sportswriter in New York took credit for that, but they didn't do it; Mets owner Joan Payson invented it," he asserted years after the fact. "I hit a home run to win a game and she said, 'Oh, wasn't that marvelous,' and I was called Marvelous Marv from that point on because of her, not some writer." Of course, as we are to see later, Throneberry was prone to revisionist history.

6. Finally, Rod Kanehl believed that Stengel was the one who coined the phrase out of sarcasm, insisting it sounded like something the Perfesser would have said.

Whatever the genesis, he was soon Marvelous Marv, for better, or more usually, for worse. "We had Choo Choo Coleman, and Marvelous Marv, and Hot Rod Kanehl," said Anderson. "That gave our team a personality. Maybe I should have had a nickname too." Of course, Throneberry had an earlier nickname, according to

Hook. "He hit some home runs, but he really wasn't a very good fielder. In fact, some of the veterans called him 'Iron Wrists.'"

Upon arriving in New York, Throneberry expressed optimism, seeing the trade as an opportunity to finally establish himself, telling the press that "wherever I have been, I have played behind an established first baseman; I feel that this is the first time I'm getting a real chance." "The Mets gave him that chance," wrote Shecter. "It revealed him."

Throneberry quickly came to personify the lovable incompetence that marked the team's performance that season. "It was not that he missed thrown balls or threw to the wrong base," columnist Maury Allen pointed out. "All the Mets did that. It was not that he lost pop-ups in the clouds or ran men across home plate with his charge or struck out with three men on. It was that he had the flair for the wrong play at the right time. Marvelous Marv only made bad plays before huge crowds. He only made the bad play in the key moment. Only in a 2-1 game." Lindsey Nelson agreed, noting that "his mistakes were not ordinary mistakes, nor did they come at ordinary times . . . Marvelous Marv saved the worst of them for the best of occasions." At first, Throneberry reacted with bewilderment and even anger at being ridiculed. Soon, though, according to Shecter, "with the help of Richie Ashburn, whose locker was next to his in the clubhouse, he came to understand his special role. There was the rainy night, for example, after he had had one of his routinely terrible games. He sat in his underwear in front of his locker and allowed a leak in the ceiling of the decrepit old clubhouse to drip, drip, drip, directly onto his bald head. 'I deserve it,' he said. 'Yes, you do,' said Richie Ashburn."

Ashburn was certainly responsible for much of the publicity which Throneberry received, regardless of whether he was directly responsible for Marv's sobriquet. He clearly knew something was odd about Throneberry right away. Soon after Throneberry's arrival, Ashburn noticed a photo of a beautiful but scantily-clad woman hanging in Throneberry's locker. A few days later, Ashburn noticed what appeared to be the same woman sitting in the stands, this time dressed more normally. Ashburn naturally asked Throneberry the identity of the near-naked pinup in his locker. "That's my wife," Throneberry responded.

However, the effect of the Throneberry acquisition was not immediately felt. After the May 12 doubleheader sweep against the Braves, they posted consecutive extra-inning 6-5 victories against the Cubs at home. In the first of these, on May 15, the Mets trailed 4-3 in the bottom of the ninth. After catcher Cuno Barragan dropped a Frank Thomas pop foul, Thomas singled and was replaced by Kanehl, who promptly stole second. Gus Bell fouled off several pitches before singling to right, scoring Kanehl. Things looked bad when Billy Williams homered off Anderson in the tenth, but in the bottom of the inning, Jim Hickman doubled and scored the tying run on Charlie Neal's single. Stengel pulled Anderson and put in Roger Craig, who held the Cubs scoreless for three innings. In the bottom of the thirteenth, the Mets loaded the bases, and Stengel sent up Hobie Landrith to hit for Craig. Cub pitcher Cal Koonce walked Landrith on four pitches, forcing in the winning run. The game had lasted almost five hours.

The next day, the Cubs jumped out to a four-run lead, but the Mets tied the score in the fifth. After a late Cliff Cook error led to a Chicago run, Gil Hodges used the cavernous Polo Grounds to his full advantage, hitting a 455-foot inside-the-park home run despite his gimpy legs. "I was at that game and I saw his inside-the-park homer," recalls Walter Pullis. "Boy, was he tired. He crossed home plate and he nearly died. He actually lay at home plate for about five seconds before he got up."

It was the only inside-the-park homer of Hodges' long career. With the score tied, Stengel again tabbed one of his starters, this time Jay Hook, who entered the game in the tenth inning and shut down the Cubs. In the eleventh, Stengel went against the book and let Hook bat for himself, and he responded with a single, sending John DeMerit to second. Hickman moved the runners over with a sacrifice, and the Cubs walked Elio Chacon intentionally, loading the bases. Felix Mantilla then singled to left, driving in DeMerit with the winning run.

The team then traveled to Milwaukee, and after losing to Spahn on Friday, May 18, they beat the Braves 6-5 on Saturday, and then, unbelievably, they swept another doubleheader on Sunday, scoring sixteen runs in the two games. Frank Thomas punished his former team with eight hits in eighteen at-bats in the four games, including three home runs, two doubles, a triple and seven runs batted in. Nor was he alone. Ex-Brave Ken MacKenzie won both the Saturday game and the opener on Sunday, earning his first two big league victories, while ex-Brave Felix Mantilla hit a three-run homer in the second game on Sunday.

At one point, Stengel inserted MacKenzie, a Yale graduate, into a tough situation. Before leaving the mound, Stengel advised MacKenzie to "make like they're the Harvards." MacKenzie later said, "I don't remember if Stengel actually said that to me on the mound or if he told the reporters afterward, but that was typical of him, wasn't it?"

This winning streak improved the Mets' record to 12-19, good enough for eighth in the league. This led many around the club, including the staid Weiss, to conclude that a seventh place finish, ahead of the Colt 45s, Cubs and Phillies, was within the realm of possibility. Craig Anderson remembers that "at that point, it was like, 'okay, now we're coming together.' Things were starting to get a little more reasonable. We were all contributing."

The second doubleheader sweep in nine days served as a prelude to a vintage Stengel performance. After the second game, the team left for the airport to pick up their United Airlines charter to Houston. They arrived only to learn their plane had developed engine trouble, and another plane had to be flown in. In the meantime, United arranged a cocktail party in a private room at the airport. With Stengel as master of ceremonies, the party lasted until the arrival of the replacement plane at about midnight. Stengel kept going on the flight, talking nonstop in his customary front row seat. After all, as sportswriter John Lardner noted, Stengel "could talk all day and all night, on any kind of track, wet or dry." The Mets coaches took turns sitting with him, as if on naval watch, so he would have someone to talk to. At 4:00 in the morning, the pilot announced that due to heavy fog at the Houston airport, they would have to land at Dallas until the fog cleared. The plane arrived in Dallas shortly, and Stengel told Lou Niss to "wake up the writers and tell them I'm buying breakfast." The team got to their hotel in Houston at 8:00 a.m. Stengel had then been awake for more than 24 hours straight, and he told Niss, "if any of my writers come looking for me, tell them I'm being embalmed." Many of the writers went to bed and did not rise until the afternoon. When they did, they were told that Stengel had gone up to his room, showered and come back down to the lobby an hour after the entourage arrived at the hotel.

Unfortunately, May 20 was the season's high-water mark. They spent exactly one day in eighth place, followed by three more in ninth before returning to the cellar for the rest of the year. They lost the two games in Houston, each by a score of 3-2, before leaving for their first-ever West Coast swing for three games against the Dodgers and three more against the Giants. They lost all six, including a doubleheader, giving up 44 runs in the process. Thus, in the seven days after May 20, when they were 12-19 and in eighth place, the Mets had lost eight straight and were once again in last. They had spent a total of seventeen days out of tenth place, but after losing to the Dodgers on May 24, they would remain there for good.

At least the Mets did not go down without a fight – figuratively and literally. In the first Giants game, the Mets went into the bottom of the eighth leading 5-4. Then Willie Mays hit a homer off Jay Hook to tie the score – the first of eight home runs he would hit against the Mets that season. The game was tied until the tenth inning, when Felix Mantilla homered to put the visitors up by a run. However, in the bottom of the tenth, Harvey Kuenn led off with a single and Mays went deep again, giving the Giants a 7-6 victory.

The next day, the Mets dropped a doubleheader to the Giants in grand fashion. The festivities were scheduled to start at noon, leading an unnamed person in the Mets entourage to comment, "Noon? I won't be done throwing up by then." In the seventh inning of game one, with Mays on first, Roger Craig drilled Orlando Cepeda with a pitch. Cepeda barked at Craig all the way down to first, and then walked off the bag and continued his verbal assault. Noticing Cepeda was standing several feet away from first, Craig wheeled and fired a perfect pickoff throw to first baseman Ed Bouchee. Cepeda was not expecting the pickoff move, but unfortunately, neither was Bouchee. He dropped the ball, and Cepeda got back safely. Then Craig attempted to pick Mays off second. The Giants star slid back safely, knocking down Elio Chacon in the process. The shortstop took exception to Mays' hard slide and came up with his fists raised. It wasn't much of a fight; when Chacon charged, the much larger Mays simply picked him up and dropped him on the ground. Nonetheless, with the Mays-Chacon bout serving as a distraction, Cepeda charged the mound, bellowing and throwing punches at Craig. After they were separated and Chacon was ejected, Cepeda retreated in the general direction of first base but never quite got there, as he continued to holler at the pitcher. Craig noticed that Cepeda was once again off the base, and, once again, he fired a perfect pickoff throw to Bouchee, who once again dropped it. The Giants won 7-1, with Mays adding four hits to his two homers the night before.

In the second game, Jim Hickman hit a three-run home run in the seventh to put the Mets up 5-2. However, the Giants tied the score in the eighth after Craig Anderson came in to relieve Al Jackson. Righty Bob Miller relieved Anderson, facing Jim

Davenport with Matty Alou on first. Miller threw a wild pitch, which allowed Alou to advance, and then walked Davenport, Alou stealing third in the process. With Willie McCovey batting, the Giants won the game on a passed ball by Harry Chiti. The next day, Jack Mann led off his story in *Newsday* with the observation that "the Mets can't fight either."

The team returned to New York for seven home games, three with the Dodgers over Memorial Day weekend, followed by four with the Giants. The centerpiece of the Dodger series was a Memorial Day doubleheader, which was attended by 55,000 fans – the largest crowd at the Polo Grounds since September 6, 1942. There were hundreds of standing-room-only attendees behind the lower-deck seats, on the upper-deck ramps and anywhere else that would afford a reasonably unobstructed view. Most cheered rabidly for the home team and booed the visitors lustily. Some fans in the upper right field stands walked to the railing and unrolled seven window shades on which they had printed "OMALLEY GO HOME" in two rows of block letters. They were chased away by security and had their window shades confiscated.

Although the Mets lost both holiday games by scores of 13-6 and 6-5, there were at least some bright spots. In the first game, the Mets had the satisfaction of scoring six runs against Sandy Koufax, pounding out thirteen hits in the losing effort. In addition, Hodges hit three home runs against his former teammates that day to move into a tie with Mets broadcaster Ralph Kiner for tenth place on the all-time list, and he also collaborated with Chacon and Charlie Neal in the second game to turn the Mets' first triple play. However, they lost in the ninth when Willie Davis, who had hit into the triple play, homered off Anderson to give the Dodgers the victory. Dodger star Maury Wills, who would win the National League Most Valuable Player award that year, homered twice in game one, including an inside-the-park job, a performance which accounted for one-third of his season total.

Roger Angell, covering the games for *The New Yorker*, brought his fourteen-year-old daughter to the doubleheader. During the first game, "it first occurred to me that the crowds, rather than the baseball, might be the real news of the two series," he wrote. "The Dodgers ran up twelve runs between the second and the sixth innings. I was keeping score, and after I had jotted down the symbols for their seven singles, two doubles, one triple, three home runs, three bases on balls, and two stolen bases in that span, the Dodger half of my scorecard looked as if a cloud of gnats had settled on it. I was pained for the Mets, and embarrassed as a fan. 'Baseball isn't usually like this,' I explained to my daughter. 'Sometimes it is,' she said. 'This is like the fifth grade against the sixth grade at school.'"

They then proceeded to drop the four games against the Giants while being outscored 31-12. Mays added three more home runs during the series, and McCovey hit two of his own. On June 1, the Giants went up 4-0 on three homers off Roger Craig, two by McCovey and one by Mays. Rod Kanehl hit his first major league home run to cut the Giants' lead to 4-1, but then the Giants put five runs on the board. Trailing 9-1, the Mets rallied in the eighth, scoring five runs of their own and bringing the tying run to the plate. The rally fell short, and the Mets lost 9-6. Kanehl, though, took the opportunity to add to his own legend. Stengel wanted to use a righthanded first baseman against Giants lefty starter Billy Pierce. However, Hodges was injured, and the other first basemen, Throneberry and Bouchee, were both lefthanded batters. "So Stengel asked if I could play first base, and I said sure," stated Kanehl. "Well, I'd never played first base before. He said, 'Get a glove,' and Hodges threw me his. I played first base and hit a home run off of Pierce, and we got beat. Then the second game, I went two for three off [Giants star pitcher Juan] Marichal. And this was just before the cutdown date. We had an off day the next day, so for a day and a half I was the toast of New York. And they couldn't cut me. Things like that seemed to happen."

In all, over 190,000 fans showed up for the seven-game home stand, almost a fifth of the Mets' entire season total attendance. It didn't help. With these seven defeats, the losing streak now stood at fifteen games in the fourteen days since the sublime heights of May 20. The New Yorkers then left for Philadelphia, where they dropped a doubleheader on June 6 for their sixteenth and seventeenth consecutive losses.

After losing the twin bill to the lowly Phillies, the Mets finally ended the seventeen-game skid with a victory against the even more lowly Cubs on June 8. Anderson came on in relief of Hook and got the save when Cub third baseman Ron Santo hit a come-backer to end the game. This led Stengel to exclaim: "Whew! I thought I would have to call in the fire department, my team's so hot!" Walter Pullis, who was home from school with a sprained ankle, remembered Lindsey Nelson's increasingly enthusiastic call as the Mets drew closer to victory. "I'll tell you, it was like D-Day or the seventh game of the World Series in the bottom of the ninth," he remembers.

The streak-breaking win against the Cubs was the first game of a doubleheader, the second of which featured the pinch-hitting debut of Jay Hook, who had already won the opener. Stengel had earlier told Hook to "take some batting practice with the extra men," which Hook would do after shagging flies every day. On that day in Chicago, Hook got a hit during the first game and drove in a run, bringing his season average at the time to .269. After the game, he intended to shower and then watch the second game from the stands, the usual practice after pitching the first game of a twin bill. Stengel told him, "Hook, take a shower, but put on one of your extra uniforms and come back out. I may want to use you." In the eighth inning of game two, with a runner on first, Stengel sent him up to pinch hit. He squared off against hard-throwing Don Elston as dusk began to gather in Wrigley Field, which had no lights. Hook fouled off two pitches and then ducked away from an inside fastball and was rung up by the umpire. Hook went back to the bench to be confronted by an angry Stengel. "Casey chewed me up one side and down the other, and his final comment to me was, 'And you can quit hittin' with the extra men!'" Hook recalled "That was the last time I pinch hit for him."

Thus invigorated, the Mets took three of five from the Cubs and the first of a three-game set with the Colt 45s before losing seven more in a row, including four straight to the very same Cubs. The loss on June 10 was particularly painful for Anderson, who had come on in relief with the Mets leading 4-1 (one of the runs coming on a rare Ashburn homer). He pitched three and two-thirds innings of no-hit ball. "Two outs [in the ninth], and there's a ground ball to Kanehl at third base," Anderson remembered "The game's over, I get the win, I'm walking off the field . . . and he boots the ball. So the next guy up was Bob Will, and I walked him on five pitches or something, which was my mistake. So now they put Ernie Banks in to pinch-hit. I go 0-2 on Ernie and I make a big mistake. He nails it out of the park. So they tie the game. I'm out of there, and I'm pretty upset because I had won the game. We lost in the tenth."

The following day, though, Jackson outdueled Houston's Dick Farrell for a 3-1 win. The Mets took a 2-0 lead on the fifth on a walk, a triple by Sammy Taylor and a single by Jim Hickman, and for once the lead held up. The Mets turned three double plays behind Jackson, who went the distance (as did Farrell). Three days later, though, Hook failed to get out of the first as the same Colt .45s scored seven times in the opening frame on the way to a 10-2 win. Houston starter Bob Bruce pitched in and out of trouble, giving up only two runs despite six hits and five walks in eight innings. In the ninth, Bruce ran into another jam, walking the bases loaded after retiring the first two batters. Throneberry came to the plate, having already homered, singled twice and walked, but he tapped weakly to Norm Larker, ending the game.

In the meantime, George Weiss kept adding players. On May 25, pitcher Willard Hunter arrived from Los Angeles as the player to be named later in the Lee Walls-for-Charlie Neal trade. Hunter, a twenty-eight year-old rookie, had appeared in only one game with the Dodgers that season, giving up six hits, four walks and ten runs in only two innings. With the Mets, he was used as a reliever and spot starter (in fact, he was the only lefty besides Al Jackson to start more than twice), losing six of his seven decisions with the Mets and running up an ERA of 5.57. On June 15, the Mets purchased Gene Woodling, who had hit at least .300 five times in his lengthy career, from Washington for $45,000. Washington had lost 100 games the year before and was well on the way to repeating when Woodling was traded; when asked by a New York reporter how he felt about coming to a loser, Woodling asked, "Where in the world do you think I've been?" Woodling, who was pushing forty and who had been a key member of Stengel's first five pennant-winning Yankee teams, was apparently a sop to the fans. "While this isn't altogether in keeping with our youth movement, our fans have supported us so well that we wanted to do something," admitted George Weiss. "And Woodling can still hit. I think we were lucky to get him."

Woodling had clashed with Stengel over being platooned with Hank Bauer, but with the passage of time, he had come to appreciate Stengel's acumen. Now, in the twilight of his career, he was reunited with his skipper and given a last chance to play. Stengel realized this, telling the media that "I'm having a tough time getting hitters into my lineup, but I just traded for a guy who won't say one damn word because he can't. He gave me hell all those years about wanting to play. Now he can play all he wants." At times when things were going poorly on the field, Stengel would catch Woodling's eye, wink at him, and say, "It wasn't like this over there," nodding at the home of the other New York team just across the river.

Woodling at least contributed some badly-needed experience and depth, batting .274 in 81 games, although his Mets tenure would end abruptly the following spring after he appointed himself as Marv

Throneberry's contract negotiator. To make roster space for Woodling, the Mets returned Harry Chiti to Cleveland, thus completing the unique Chiti-for-Chiti exchange. In another move, Gus Bell was sent to Milwaukee as the player to be named later in the Frank Thomas deal the previous fall. At the time of the trade, Bell had appeared in only thirty games and was hitting .149, with one homer and six runs batted in. Bell's departure cleared the way for Jim Hickman and Joe Christopher, recently called up from Syracuse, who platooned in right field the rest of the year. Hickman and Christopher had both come to the Mets via the expansion draft, and they outlasted all the other draft picks in their longevity with the team.

By this time, the Throneberry Effect was in full force. June 17 marked his real coming-out party, the doubleheader which featured some of his most famous exploits. "There were approximately 13,000 fans on that pleasant Sunday afternoon," wrote George Vecsey. "They were about to see an epic defensive-offensive performance by Throneberry that would live in history. In fact, there are probably 200,000 people who claim to have been in the Polo Grounds that afternoon. This often happens with historic contests."

In the first inning of game one, Chicago's Don Landrum walked on four pitches. With two strikes on Ken Hubbs, Landrum broke for second on a called hit-and-run play. However, Hubbs swung and missed, and catcher Sammy Taylor fired the ball to Charlie Neal, catching Landrum in a rundown. It should have been a classic "strike 'em out, throw 'em out" double play. However, Throneberry had a problem with rundown plays all season, and this one was no exception. With Taylor and Al Jackson covering first, Throneberry threw the ball back to Neal but got in the way as Landrum tried to get back to the base. Since Throneberry did not have the ball, he was called for interference, and the umpire waved Landrum to second. Instead of none on with two outs, Landrum was in scoring position with only one away. Jackson retired the next batter (for what should have been the third out), but he then walked Ernie Banks and gave up a triple to Ron Santo, with Landrum and Banks scoring. Thus, instead of the inning being over, two runs were in, and that doubled when the next batter, Lou Brock, hit a massive shot into the right centerfield bleachers. Brock, the skinny Cub centerfielder not known for his power, was only the second player ever to homer into the centerfield seats at the Polo Grounds in a regular-season game, and the first ever to reach the right centerfield bleachers. "I was sitting right behind home plate in the grandstands," says Walter Pullis. "When he hit the ball, it was like a climbing line drive. But it just kept going. In most stadiums, it would have been long over the fence. It had to go at least 460 feet just to get into the bleachers." In fact, it hit the top of a thirty-foot background 475 feet from home plate and then bounced another twenty feet. It was, according to Lindsey Nelson's play-by-play call, "a *tremendous* wallop." By the time the inning was over, Jackson, who was victimized by this sort of thing all year, had given up four runs, helped in no small part by Throneberry's interference call.

In the bottom of the first, Ashburn bunted for a hit and went to second on Chacon's sacrifice. After Gene Woodling walked in his first Met plate appearance, Thomas singled, scoring Ashburn. Now it was 4-1 and the Mets had runners on first and second with one out. Throneberry came up next and drove the ball deep for an apparent triple, scoring Woodling and Thomas, but was called out on appeal after failing to touch first (and, presumably, second), as recounted in the prologue of this book. Throneberry's baserunning misadventure is one of the best-known of all the stories which made up the Mets saga in 1962, and the facts have been verified by Mets players, Richie Ashburn among them: "We could all see from the dugout that Marv really didn't even come close to touching first base."

Included in this group was Stengel, who nonetheless rushed out of the dugout to challenge the call before being told not to bother. Stengel later offered this explanation to Max Kase of the *New York Journal-American*: "I see where he didn't touch first and I know he's gonna be called out, which he is when he gets to third. So I go out there to see what can be done about it and I says to the umpire, 'He did too touch first base.' And the umpire says to me: 'I don't know about first but I called him out because he didn't touch second.' In that case, I got to admit he didn't touch first, either."

Right after Throneberry's mishap, Neal came up and hit a home run, tying the score. Had Throneberry not been called out, the Mets would have had the lead. Moreover, Throneberry, having blown a chance to redeem his interference call with the apparent triple, then blew a chance to redeem his baserunning gaffe. He came up in the bottom of the ninth with the tying run on base, two out and the Mets down by a run. He struck out, and the Mets lost 8-7. Thus, Marvelous Marv completed the trifecta – a defensive mistake leading to four runs, an error on the basepaths resulting in the potential tying run not scoring, and the failure to drive home the tying run late in the game, all of which added up to a one-run loss to the pitiful Cubs. As if all this were not enough, he rounded off the day with a first-inning error in the second game. Two other miscues by Chacon and Thomas (in his season debut at third base) led to two unearned runs, which ultimately constituted the margin of defeat in the Cubs' second one-run decision of the day. Chacon's two-base error on a Lou Brock grounder led to a run when Brock scored all the way from second on a little dribbler hit in front of the catcher, beating Throneberry's throw to the plate. The game was lost in the ninth inning when Santo hit a two-run shot off of Vinegar Bend Mizell.

At least Stengel was able to maximize the inherent humor potential the situation offered. When Neal homered after Throneberry was called out, Stengel again charged from the dugout, intercepted Neal on his way to first, pointed to the base and stamped his foot. After Neal touched the bag and headed to second, Stengel pointed to that base and stamped again, and then watched closely as

Neal made his way around the basepaths. Once Neal crossed home plate, Stengel nodded in grim satisfaction and went back to the dugout. "That really happened," affirmed Pullis. "I'd like to verify that. Stengel did do that. I remember him coming out of the dugout. If memory serves, though, he pointed to first base and then to second, but then he stopped."

Throneberry, also able to appreciate the humor, explained, "it was so long since I was down there [to first base] that I forgot where it was." Nor was he the only one. "How could he be expected to remember where the bases are?" queried Jack Lang in the *Long Island Press*. "He gets on so infrequently." "I happened to be the official scorer that day, so I had all the details in my scorebook," recalled Leonard Koppett. "It was incredible. That first inning really establishes the persona of Throneberry."

As noted above, Brock's unlikely homer marked only the second time in the Polo Grounds' decades-long history that anyone had deposited a pitch into the centerfield bleachers in a regular season game (the first being the Braves' Joe Adcock nine years earlier; Luke Easter, the Negro League star, hit one there during an exhibition, as did Yankee legend Babe Ruth during a World Series game). The third person to do it was Henry Aaron of the Braves, who hit a Jay Hook pitch into the left-centerfield seats for a grand slam the very next day. Stengel came out to the mound when Aaron stepped into the batter's box with the bases loaded. "He said, 'Okay, perfesser, pitch him outside and make him hit it to centerfield,'" says Hook. "The next pitch, I threw a low outside fastball, and Aaron hit it about six hundred feet."

It wasn't long before Throneberry's misfortunes became a source of humor and began to be reported by the press. While all the Mets made errors, Throneberry had a penchant for the particularly dramatic ones, the miscues which came at especially inopportune times and cost the team games. On any every other team, Throneberry would have been an outcast in the clubhouse and a fan pariah; on the Mets, he achieved a heroic status after being booed initially. It is almost inconceivable that a first baseman who made seventeen errors, in addition to countless mental mistakes not reflected in statistics, in only 97 games would be the subject of an approving fan cheer such as "Cranberry, Strawberry, we love Throneberry!" – particularly in New York. Nonetheless, it happened, as reported by Stan Isaacs in *Newsday*. Isaacs identified the "love affair flowering between the Met fans and Marv Throneberry," and he stated his intention to form "a press-box chapter of the 'I Love Marv Throneberry Club.' I am not disturbed that only one other has agreed to join – as membership secretary, because there would be no work. I can see other potential members whose expressions of exasperation with Marv's work indicate that they are potentially fervent club members."

Although Isaacs' suggestion of a fan club was made with his tongue firmly implanted in his cheek, it wasn't long before such a thing really existed. By season's end, the real-life Marv Throneberry Fan Club boasted over five thousand members. Soon, Maury Allen reported, "there were large banners in the stands saying MARV. Then Marv T-shirts. Then a Marv for President club, a Marv Losers club and the Iron Glove Award for Marv. Each day the volume of mail grew until Throneberry's locker looked like a branch Post Office."

Thus, to say that Marvelous Marv was the embodiment of all that was wrong with the '62 Mets and leave it at that is to miss the point. He certainly was that type of symbol, but he was also a symbol of what made the team lovable, fun and so immensely appealing to both the reporters who covered the team and the fans who attended the games. Indeed, the attention and affection afforded him by the press and the fans elevated him from a bumbling ballplayer, which he certainly was, to a legitimate tragic-comic hero, a label which also fit

Reactions to Throneberry's travails were many and varied. Yankee manager Ralph Houk was certainly familiar with Throneberry and discussed him with Jimmy Breslin during the 1962 season: "I can't understand what's happening to that Throneberry. I had him three years at Denver. He's not that bad a ballplayer at all. Why, he opened the season with the Yankees one year there. [Regular first baseman Moose] Skowron was hurt, I guess. Marv never made plays like they say he makes now. I guarantee you he never did. If he ever played that way for me, I'd of killed him with my bare hands."

Mets owner Joan Payson adored Throneberry. After the season, she received a gift of a large felt turtle. She promptly had a Mets logo sewn onto the turtle's shell and named it Marvelous Marv.

As the legend spread, fans around the league flocked to watch the Mets when they came to town, if for no other reason than to see for themselves. Throneberry, for his part, appeared as mystified as everyone else, saying, "Things just sort of keep on happening to me." This was a common phrase, as Jimmy Breslin wrote, "Throneberry is a serious ballplayer. He tries, and he has some ability. It's just that things happen when he plays." Rod Kanehl, signed to the Yankees around the same time as Throneberry and his roommate on the Mets, recalled that "things just happened around him. Balls would go through his legs with two outs in the ninth inning and that sort of thing, and we'd lose ball games. It was kind of sad, because he was trying so hard. But things would just . . happen around him."

To Throneberry's credit, though, he at least had the ability to laugh at himself and even occasionally participate in the merriment. When the Mets returned home after the first West Coast swing, the Polo Grounds faithful were particularly hard on Ed Bouchee, who had dropped Craig's two pickoff throws in the loss to the Giants. Throneberry confronted Bouchee, asking, "What are you trying to do, steal my fans?" He made the same mock accusation of Stengel when the fans booed the manager as he went to the mound to remove a pitcher. His teammates got in on the fun as well. Ashburn would regularly advise reporters to "go ask Marv if he has oiled his hooks yet." "As long as they pay me," said Throneberry, "they can say what they want."

The Mets broke their latest seven-game losing streak with yet another win against the Braves, the cure for their ills, on June 19, in front of fewer than 4,000 fans at the Polo Grounds. Roger Craig went the distance to earn a rare one-run victory, at one point retiring twelve Braves in a row. Woodling and Joe Christopher homered in support. During the game, the Braves' Eddie Mathews hit a 260-foot "Chinese home run" into the right field seats. The next time Mathews came up, there was a runner on first. Craig threw fourteen pickoff throws to first in an effort to disrupt Mathews' concentration. It worked, as Mathews popped out. However, the Mets then dropped six of the next eight, including a doubleheader against the Braves. The first game featured a three-run homer by former Met Gus Bell, equaling his Met output, as the Braves won 9-4. In the rain-shortened finale, Willard Hunter allowed the Braves only two hits; unfortunately, both were Hank Aaron homers. The resulting three runs were enough for yet another one-run loss.

On June 22, three days later, the Mets split a memorable doubleheader with Houston. In the opener, Al Jackson threw a one-hitter, striking out nine batters, walking only two and earning his second shutout. After Jackson gave up a walk and a cheap hit to Joe Amalfitano in the first, no Houston batter reached again until Pidge Browne drew a leadoff walk the ninth. Chacon and Neal also provided some sparkling defense. With a man on first, Chacon went behind second base to spear a sizzling line drive off the bat of Hal Smith, then made a backward flip to Neal covering second, who threw to first to retire Smith. Ashburn homered again as the Mets won 2-0, despite collecting only three hits off Dick Farrell. It was the second time in twelve days that Jackson had bested Farrell in a complete-game duel. "It was one of the best games you'll ever see pitched," said Stengel afterward. "And one of the players said to me, 'Is Jackson going in the second game?'"

Unfortunately, he wasn't. Righty Bob Miller was, and he got hammered. It seemed the Mets had used up their quota of good pitching and defense in the opener. In surrendering seventeen hits (including two triples and a single by pitcher Jim Golden) and losing 16-3, the Mets made six errors, three by Throneberry. Commenting on the disparity in his club's play in the two games, Stengel asked, "You wouldn't think it was the same team, would you?"

The Mets responded by thrashing Houston 13-2 the next day, with Ashburn hitting two more home runs, one a Polo Grounds inside-the-park specialty. In his previous fourteen years, he had never hit more than four homers in a season, and his lifetime total to that point was 22. After receiving a polio shot with his teammates, he hit four in a single week, three in two days against Houston. His last round-tripper had been in 1959. Now, helped along by the peculiar dimensions of the Polo Grounds, he would finish 1962 with seven. Four days later, he achieved another milestone, recording his 2500th career hit in a 6-5 loss to the Pirates.

The team then headed west again for seven games against the Dodgers and Giants. Although they won the first against the Dodgers, their first win against their predecessors (and their only win in Los Angeles that year), they lost the next two. In the middle game, Sandy Koufax no-hit the Mets, striking out Ashburn, Kanehl and Mantilla, the first three batters, on nine pitches. It was the first of his four no-hitters. After the game, the press corps clustered around the Dodger clubhouse, leaving Stengel alone for once. "Where's all them reporters tonight?" he asked. "Something must be goin' on." Stengel's patented "whommy" (his version of the "whammy," or hex) took the day off, along with the Met bats. He later said, "You put the whommy on him, but when he's pitchin', the whommy tends to go on vacation."

The series-opening win, though, was almost as memorable as the no-hitter. The Mets managed to score ten runs (an event by itself) on only four hits, helped along by a mind-boggling sixteen walks issued by Dodger pitching. Seven of these occurred in a row in the first inning, in which the Mets pushed six runs across the plate in support of Hook. Later, Hook got into a jam, and Stengel told Craig Anderson, his scheduled game two starter, to warm up. Anderson warmed up for two innings while Hook worked out of the jam and finished the game. Stengel then scratched Anderson in favor of Righty Bob Miller, who became Koufax' victim.

After posting their first season win against the Giants, they lost the next three by scores of 10-1, 11-4 and 10-3. In the series finale, Mays continued to terrorize Met pitching, hitting two more homers and driving in seven runs. At one point, Giant third basemen Jim Davenport lifted a high fly ball. Kanehl, playing shortstop, tore into left field, while third baseman Felix Mantilla went the other direction, making the catch just off the pitcher's mound. "I have to think the wind got hold of it," Stengel told the *Times*. "Otherwise, my mind tells me my fielders would have been running towards it instead of away from it." Frank Thomas homered, a meaningless event as it occurred after the game was out of reach. Thomas, though, celebrated into the clubhouse after the game, laughing and joking and drawing the ire of none other than Throneberry. "Some people think losing is funny," said Throneberry. "You'd never hear anybody laugh on the Yankees."

Although most of the fans and media had given the Mets a pass to that point, this sentiment was not unanimous. Columnist Dick Young, a fervent early backer, lambasted what he saw as their lackluster attitude, that they had grown accustomed to losing and were taking it for granted: "The present philosophy seems to be that this is no time to get hurt. Most of the boys are playing as if their Blue Cross has lapsed. Those of the Mets who still hustle resent the quitting attitude of others, but they are helpless to do anything about it."

However, two important events now occurred, although their significance would not become apparent for several years. On June 27, the Mets signed Ed Kranepool, the Bronx high school star who had been Mrs. Payson's guest at the home opener, for an $85,000 bonus. Johnny Murphy and Met scout Bubba Jonnard came to the Kranepool household to meet with his mother and their next door neighbor, Jimmy Schiaffo, Kranepool's Little League coach. Kranepool was supposed to work out with the White Sox and had a meeting scheduled with the Yankees. Murphy convinced him that the Mets were a better opportunity. Two days later, he took the first plane ride of his life, flying to Los Angeles to meet the team and the press. On his first night, Koufax pitched his no-hitter. "What a welcome to the major leagues," Kranepool commented later.

Within a few days, he was sent to Syracuse and then fell as low as Class D Auburn before working his way back up in time for a September callup. It was a difficult adjustment for Kranepool, who was still seventeen and fresh off a staggeringly successful high school career. He found that he had little in common with his teammates, almost all of whom were considerably older than him. This was not helped by the fact that his first roommate was the 35-year-old Frank Thomas. "He did everything he could to help me, but he was old enough to be my father and we had different interests," said Kranepool.

Eight days later, the Mets signed a nineteen-year-old outfielder from Alabama named Cleon Jones. They had been tipped by Clyde Grey, a semi-pro teammate of Jones who had taken the teenager under his wing. When he saw that scouts from five teams were following Jones, along with several football scouts, Grey told the Mets to get someone down to Alabama quickly. Grey convinced Jones that the Mets were offering a better opportunity to play sooner and more, and Jones signed. By 1965, he and Kranepool were in the majors to stay, and they formed the foundation on which the 1969 championship team was built.

A week earlier, Weiss had also signed twenty-year-old Larry Bearnarth, just off a college career at Syracuse in which he had won an astonishing 33 of 35 decisions, including a perfect game against Army. Although Bearnarth did not achieve the success expected, he was a tough, gritty reliever and a favorite of the fans and Stengel during his four years with the Mets.

Following the western trip, the Mets returned home, where they split four games with the Cardinals leading into the All-Star break. The July 6 opener was Mrs. Payson's first opportunity to see her amazin' Mets in several months, as she had just returned from a long trip to Greece. Upon leaving shortly after the home opener, she had instructed her chauffeur to attend all the home games, keep score and retain the scorecards and to cable her the results of each game. After a short while, though, the continuous stream of bad news led her to wire back instructions that she only be informed when the Mets won. "That was about the last word I heard from America," she told Breslin.

Stengel used her presence as a motivator before the July 6 game, telling the team, "she's just back from Europe where she's been hearin' bad things about us. Let's win one for the old girl!" Gil Hodges hit his 370th home run (and the last of his career), moving ahead of Ralph Kiner on the all-time list, and the Mets bunted three times for base hits. Two of those came in the seventh, loading the bases against Cardinal relief ace Barney Schultz, and Kanehl followed with the Mets' first grand slam. As a reward for his feat, Kanehl received 50,000 King Korn trading stamps. "King Korn had a store in Chicago, and I traded the stamps in there," he told *Sports Illustrated*. "I got a living-room suite, a Deepfreeze, an end table – a lot of junk." Another run scored when pitcher Ray Sadecki threw a wild pitch on an intentional walk.

Thanks to Kanehl's homer and Roger Craig's complete game, the Mets won 10-3, to Mrs. Payson's delight. She was there for next day's doubleheader as well, when they won the first game 5-4 on a Throneberry pinch home run in the bottom of the ninth. The Mets were in a position to win because of a Cardinal mistake which Throneberry must have found familiar. In the eighth, after a double, Dal Maxvill was inserted as a pinch runner. The next batter singled, and Maxvill scored on the play. However, the Mets appealed, and Maxvill was called out at third because he sailed over the base without touching it. This kept the score tied until Curt Flood homered in the ninth to put the Cardinals ahead. The Mets won in the bottom of the frame on Throneberry's two-run homer, giving Ray Daviault his only big league win.

The Cardinals won the nightcap, though, despite another Throneberry homer (Sammy Taylor also homered in both games, two of his three homers on the season). Larry Jackson got two outs on one pickoff play. When Kanehl led too far off second, Jackson nailed him with a great throw, and then Joe Christopher unwisely decided to try to advance from first on the play and was out by a mile. The Mets also dropped the last game of the series by a score of 15-1. They made three throwing errors in one inning and allowed seven unearned runs. Stan Musial, who had homered in his final at-bat the night before, did the same in his first three at-bats. Musial, at 41, thus became the oldest man to hit four consecutive home runs.

With this resounding loss, the Mets limped into the All-Star break with a record of 23-59. At least some of the players were performing. Frank Thomas was hitting with power, Al Jackson had already thrown two shutouts, and Richie Ashburn was hitting well enough to represent the Mets on the All-Star team. There were not many other bright spots, though. Although some observers airily pointed out that the Mets were only six games behind ninth-place Chicago, the team had been dead last for over six weeks and was on a pace to win only 45 games. As it turned out, even this proved to be too optimistic.

CHAPTER EIGHT – THE PLAYERS

> "Players used to sit in the lobbies and talk about baseball. Now they sit in their rooms, watch movies and forget about baseball. A lot of them forget about it on the field, too." – *Casey Stengel, manager of the New York Mets*

As the season wore on, Casey Stengel continually juggled the lineup, trying with increasing frustration to find a working combination. Weiss also kept making deals. Some of their maneuvers were successful, most considerably less so; for every Thomas and Ashburn, there were dozens of Vinegar Bend Mizells and Harry Chitis who contributed little in their often-short stays.

Nowhere were Stengel's exasperating difficulties more apparent than at catcher. The draft-day comments of both Stengel and Weiss indicated the importance they placed on having a quality backstop. In fact, three of the 22 players selected were catchers: Hobie Landrith, Chris Cannizzaro and Choo Choo Coleman. Nonetheless, none of their seven catchers worked out. "The reason for the stockpiling," wrote Ralph Kiner, "was the discovery that Hobie Landrith, who could catch, could not throw; that Chris Cannizzaro, who could throw, could not catch; and that Choo Choo Coleman could catch low pitches but little else." Lindsey Nelson remembered one time where Landrith got too close to the batter and got whacked in the head.

None of the catchers caught more than 56 games, and most appeared in far fewer. Joe Ginsberg made two appearances before being released on May 1. Landrith and Chiti saw action in twenty-three and fifteen games, respectively, before being traded (Landrith for Marv Throneberry, Chiti for himself). Joe Pignatano caught only 25 games in two and a half months after being acquired on July 13.

Only Cannizzaro (56 games), Sammy Taylor (50), and Coleman (44) played the position on anything remotely resembling a regular basis.

Cannizzaro, christened "Canzoneri" by Stengel, was brought up from Syracuse primarily for his defensive skills prior to a series with the Dodgers and Maury Wills. However, his promise was not initially borne out, as Stengel related with frustration: "Wills and those fellows, they start running in circles and they don't stop and it could be embarrassing, which I don't want it to be. Well, we have this Canzoneri at Syracuse, and he catches good and throws real good and he should be able to stop them. So we bring him and he is going to throw out these runners. We come in there and you never seen anything like it in your life. I find I got a defensive catcher who can't catch the ball. The pitcher throws. Wild pitch. Throws again. Passed ball. Throws again. The ball drops out of the glove. And all the time I am dizzy on account of these runners running around in circles on me and so forth. You look up and down the bench and you have to say to yourself, 'Can't *anybody* play this here game?'" [One of Stengel's most well-known Met quotes, this phrase was morphed by Jimmy Breslin into the title of his 1963 book, *Can't Anybody Here Play This Game?*]

Although Cannizzaro spent two years as the regular and was one of the few Original Mets who played into the next decade, his 1962 accomplishments did not endear him to his manager: "He's a remarkable catcher, that Canzoneri. He's the only defensive catcher in baseball who can't catch." Stengel also felt Cannizzaro called for the curve ball too often, stating that "he don't hit it – and he don't think nobody else can."

Nor was Coleman the answer, although he emerged the next season as the starter after Cannizzaro injured his hand. Coleman had originally signed with Washington as a seventeen-year-old in 1955 and had been assigned to the Senators' Class D team at Orlando. Four years later, he was still there. He then rose from Single-A all the way to Triple-A in the Dodgers' system in 1960, and by 1961, he made his major league debut, appearing in 34 games with the Phillies and batting .128. "Choo Choo Coleman was the quintessence of the early New York Mets," asserted Brendan Boyd and Fred Harris. "He was a 5'8", 160-pound catcher who never hit over .250 in the majors, had 9 career home runs, 30 career RBIs, and couldn't handle pitchers. Plus his name was Choo Choo. What more could you ask for?" Walter Pullis remembered that Coleman "was fast, but he wasn't graceful. He was kind of awkward. But he had a couple of big home runs, such as they were on the '62 Mets."

Coleman also proved to be inscrutable. He called everyone "Bub," and he answered most queries with "Yeah, Bub," including those put to him in a now-legendary exchange with Ralph Kiner on "Kiner's Korner." It occurred in spring training, not long after Coleman had hit the first home run in club history, albeit unofficially, in the second exhibition game. Kiner was not looking forward to having Coleman on the show, but finally, he recalled, "after running through virtually the entire roster, I surrendered to the inevitable." Kiner, then an inexperienced interviewer, asked Lindsey Nelson and Bob Murphy how they thought he should deal with Coleman. After some discussion, they agreed that Coleman's nickname was a promising starting point, figuring that there had to be a story there.

The big day arrived, and Kiner imagined himself to be prepared. As precaution, he had also invited Roger Craig. Kiner introduced Coleman as one of the most popular Mets – still true at the time due to his homer – and asked the catcher how he had gotten his nickname. "I had anticipated the answer that as a child he liked to play with trains or that his father worked for the railroad," Kiner wrote in his autobiography. Coleman paused for a second before answering, "I don't know, Bub." Kiner, who had expected a dialogue-provoking response, was stunned. He desperately grasped for the first question that came to him, asking, "Well, what's your wife's name, and what's she like?" Coleman answered, "Mrs. Coleman, Bub . . . and she likes me." That ended the interview.

Kiner recalled that "Roger Craig received more air time that day than both he and I had anticipated." Walter Pullis has fond memories of that show. "You know – 'Mrs. Coleman, Bub,'" he remembers with a chuckle. "My father and I were on the floor laughing at that one." (There is another story, possibly apocryphal, concerning Coleman's nickname, also attributed to Kiner. While in the minors, Coleman allegedly had the habit of stepping on the umpire's shoes while assuming his catcher's crouch. One umpire, tired of having his shoes "chewed" by Coleman's cleats, began calling the catcher "Choo Choo.")

Small wonder that Kiner later described Coleman as his toughest interview. Nor was Choo Choo any easier his teammates. "'Hey, Bub' is about the only thing I've ever heard him say," said Marv Throneberry. "But he says it nice." "He didn't talk very much," said Craig Anderson. "He didn't have much vocabulary at all. Everybody liked him because he was easygoing." Lindsey Nelson said that Coleman "made Gary Cooper sound like a chatterbox," and described his vocabulary as "consisting largely of 'Yup,' 'Nope,' and 'Hi.'" Jerry Mitchell wrote that "The words he uses in a day could be written on one side of half dollar. Explaining victory afterwards, he said, 'We score six. They score six. We score five. They score six. We need two.'"

Kiner also recalled an event during spring training the following year. Charlie Neal had just reported, and he was talking with a bunch of players and reporters behind the batting cage. He spotted Coleman, with whom he had roomed in 1962, and told the others he was going to say hello but doubted that the catcher would remember his name. The group, thinking Neal was kidding but wanting to witness the meeting in case he wasn't, followed him. "Hello, Choo Choo," said Neal. "It's good to see you." Coleman's greeting was the standard "Hi, Bub." "You know my name?" asked Neal. "Yep," said Coleman. "I'll bet you don't," challenged Neal. "I know you, all right." Coleman responded. "You number four."

Coleman's on-the-field performance was similar. When crouched in position, he moved around so much that he presented a difficult target. In fact, when Chuck Churn, Coleman's battery mate with the Phillies the year before, was asked to identify the toughest man to whom he ever pitched, he answered, "Coleman." Roger Craig added that Coleman "was one of the best low-ball catchers I've ever seen. But if it was high stuff, you could forget it." Stengel insisted on keeping him on the roster, saying that Coleman "can handle a low-ball pitcher because he crawls on his belly like a snake." When asked the value of keeping a catcher who would only catch pitches in the dirt, Stengel replied, "Them are the only ones the other teams ain't hitting."

Coleman also had his own brand of logic, as Stengel discovered several weeks after Coleman arrived from Syracuse. When a pitcher failed to cover first base on a play, Stengel reminded him that "you got to yell to the pitcher to cover first." Coleman's wordy response was "I figure they should know what to do up here."

Nor were these the only unique aspects of his performance. Craig recalled that "Choo Choo would give you the sign and then look down to see what it was." After he once called for a pitch that resulted in a monstrous home run, Stengel asked him what pitch it was. "I don't know, Bub," responded Coleman. "Well," said Stengel, "the next time you give a sign out there, take a peek yourself so you'll know what pitch you were calling."

Coleman had so much trouble communicating the signs that there was talk of color-coding his fingers – red for a fastball, blue for a curve, and so on. Craig Anderson and Gene Woodling insisted that something along those lines was actually implemented. "They said his fingers were so black they had to put white tape on them," recalled Anderson. "And they did. He actually put pieces of white strip tape on his fingers so they could see his signs at night." Woodling said that "the sorriest thing I ever saw was Casey trying to teach Choo Choo how to count on his fingers. He had to paint them. I almost busted out."

After Cannizzaro's injury the following year, Coleman became the regular backstop, appearing in 91 games but batting only .178. Stengel, though, remained a firm supporter: "He always runs in to work and anyway he's got some fine points 'cause he don't smoke, don't drink and don't talk like Berra who didn't talk well much when he came up and he made it. I had fifteen pitchers who said they couldn't pitch to him, and it turned out they couldn't pitch to nobody. Maybe he wouldn't be on this club if I wasn't the manager, which might be a mistake. He can throw. He can run. He is very alert. He can dig balls out of the dirt an' he backs up first base in a hurry. If he could hit he'd have five points. I think he'll learn."

Unfortunately, he never did. In yet another of Stengel's memorable quotes, he summed up his dilemma behind the plate: "I got one that can throw but can't catch, and one that can catch but can't throw, and one who can hit but can't do either."

Stengel was equally nonplussed by his rotation, although, unlike the catching-by-committee situation, he mostly relied upon the same starters all year. Roger Craig finished the season 10-24, Al Jackson was 8-20, Jay Hook 8-19, Craig Anderson went 3-17 (with a sixteen-game losing streak after starting 3-1), and Righty Bob Miller chimed in at 1-12, and the leader in earned run average was Jackson at 4.40. The staff surrendered a league record 192 home runs, led by Craig with 35 and Hook with 33. Although their records were indeed awful, the starters were hurt again and again by poor defense and a lack of run support. Although the Mets gave up 948 runs (121 more than the next most allowed), 147 of those – almost one per game – were unearned. Jackson was particularly bedeviled by lousy defensive play. He once pitched fourteen innings of one-run ball only to lose the game in the fifteenth on two Throneberry errors. However, he was clearly not a bad pitcher. Four of his eight 1962 wins were shutouts – the only shutouts thrown by any Mets pitcher that year. Jackson, wrote George Vecsey, "would occasionally pitch a masterful low-run game when he managed to keep his pitches low. When his pitches were high, they took off into outer space."

Moreover, the starters saw a lot of work. Craig and Hook each threw thirteen complete games, with twelve for Jackson, and they each logged more than 200 innings. The entire staff contributed an astounding (by today's standards) total of 43 complete games. Craig had 27 in his two seasons with the Mets, more than most pitchers today complete in their careers. "Back then," notes Jay Hook succinctly, "we were expected to complete games."

In addition, Anderson and Miller saw substantial work as starters and relievers. Craig, the top starter (and former reliever), also pitched in relief nine times, earning three saves. In fact, Stengel often instructed the starters to save their between-starts throwing for late in the game, rather than the more-usual pre-game throwing. On those infrequent occasions when the Mets carried a lead into the late innings, Stengel "wouldn't even have to say anything to me," remembered Craig. "He'd just look at me and I'd get up and go down to the pen and start to throw. A lot of times he'd bring me into the game." Of course, such line-crossing was not always a good thing. "They started me," said Anderson. "I think I knew that I was really a better relief pitcher, but they used me in both capacities in spring. When we broke to go north, they went back to the veteran guys as the starters and they put me back in the bullpen, and that was fine with me, but it didn't take long for them to put me back out as a starter. Some of that going back and forth was not a good thing for me since I really was more inexperienced than some of the other guys."

Of course, one reason why the starters pitched so many innings (and why Craig, Jackson and Hook all made relief appearances in addition to starting over thirty games each) was that the bullpen was terrible. Only one pitcher, Galen Cisco, had an ERA under 4.00, but he wasn't acquired until September and pitched in only four games. The next lowest among the relievers was Bob Moorhead at 4.53. Moorhead was a morose character whose season ended when he broke his hand punching a locker after a bad outing. He appeared in 32 games without winning any (and he pitched another thirteen times in 1965 without winning any of those). Ray Daviault gave up at least one run in ten consecutive appearances between April 13 and July 15. The only pitcher with a winning record was Ken MacKenzie, and he coupled his 5-4 record with a 4.95 ERA. Nine of the thirteen relievers finished with ERAs over 5.00. Anderson led the team with fifty appearances and four saves, while Craig's three saves were good enough for second. The entire staff only managed ten, a league low; of course, with only forty victories, save opportunities were somewhat scarce. As far as statistics went, the only things the Met pitchers had the most of were losses, hits, home runs, runs (earned and unearned), and Bob Millers.

Craig was the Opening Day starter and led the staff in victories with ten. He had spent seven seasons with the Dodgers, compiling a 49-38 record and pitching in the 1956 and 1959 World Series. In 1959, his best year, he finished 11-5 with a 2.01 ERA, leading the team in winning percentage and ERA and tying for the NL lead with four shutouts. He was known primarily as a relief pitcher and was well-regarded throughout the league. He came to the Mets after hurting his shoulder and was presumably washed up at thirty. After two seasons as the Mets' ace, he was mercifully traded to St. Louis, where he made key contributions to the pennant-winning Cardinals in 1964, including winning a World Series game against the Yankees. After his retirement, he enjoyed success as a pitching coach and manager, developing the careers of several ace pitchers and leading the 1989 Giants to the World Series. His Mets career, though, was awful, as he went 15-46 in his two seasons.

Craig was certainly a victim of extreme hard luck. Although he was 5-22 in 1963, with eighteen losses in a row, his ERA was an astonishing 3.78, which would have resulted in a multi-million dollar contract forty years later. Five of his losses came from being on the wrong end of a 1-0 decision. Tracy Stallard, one of Craig's 1963 teammates, commented that if Craig "bought a graveyard, nobody would die."

When the Mets traded Craig after that year, he was at least able to look philosophically at his time in New York: "I lost 24 games my first year with the Mets. You've got to be a pretty good pitcher to lose that many. What manager is going to let you go out there that often? My two seasons with the Mets were a blessing. It taught me how to cope with adversity."

The third starter, Jay Hook, recorded the Mets' first victory with a sparkling five-hit performance. "He was young and seemingly effective," wrote Leonard Shecter. "At the same time he was a failure at crucial moments. He was, then, almost by definition, a Met." "Jay Hook had a great arm, but he threw some of the longest home run balls I've ever seen thrown," Rod Kanehl recalled. "Willie Mays would hit them into the lights in left center at the Polo Grounds on the dead fly." "But the thing you have to realize is where we were playing," said Hook in his own defense. "The second deck really hung over. The upper deck actually seemed like it was closer than the lower deck. I'm not sure it was, but it seemed that way."

Hook was probably the most educated player in the majors that year (or any year), having earned a degree in mechanical engineering from Northwestern University, and he was working towards his masters. Some of Hook's technical knowledge occasionally surfaced in the baseball world as a source of both wonder and amusement. During his studies, he considered the phenomenon of spheroids re-entering the atmosphere, such as the Russian satellite Sputnik. Hook and his colleagues would sit around over coffee and discuss related issues, including why an airplane wing will lift a plane – and why a curve ball curves. All of these actions are governed by Bernoulli's Law. During spring training, columnist Barney Kremenko overheard Hook talking about the application of Bernoulli's Law to baseball. Kremenko went over and said, "Jay, give me a couple lines. I've got this story and I need a couple more lines." Hook was happy to oblige. Early in the season, a home game was rained out. Bob Lipsyte of the *Times*, having thirteen inches to fill, asked Hook for a more detailed explanation of why a curve ball curves. "So I got a piece of paper and a pencil and I drew a baseball," Hook related. "I drew the boundary-layer buildup and the various velocity vectors of the ball going through air, and the angular velocity of the ball spinning. I showed him how the angular velocity would build up on one side of the ball and subtract from the other side of the ball, and as the velocities changed, the forces changed. I drew the force vectors on the ball and wrote out Bernoulli's Law, explained it all to him. Of course, who's going to believe a ballplayer on something like that?" Not Lipsyte, who took what he'd received from Hook and had it reviewed by the head of the physics department at Columbia University, who confirmed that Hook was right. Lipsyte ran the story and was awarded a one hundred dollar cash prize for "Best Article of the Month" in the *Times*. Two weeks later, Hook started a game and was knocked out after a few innings. He showered and dressed and was sitting in front of his locker when the press came into the clubhouse after the game. Lipsyte was talking with Hook when Stengel joined them. "He looks at Lipsyte and he looks at me," related Hook, "and he looks back at Lipsyte, and he says, 'you know, if Hook could only do what he *knows* . . . '"

Stengel's biggest criticism of Hook, though, was his unwillingness to knock hitters down. Once, after he surrendered five homers in a game, Stengel remarked, "There was two outs. How'd I know he couldn't get the third one? I mean, he had good control. He didn't knock anyone down, did he? He looks like he ought to beat anyone. If he pitched like [Sal] Maglie [the notorious

Giant headhunter] nobody would beat him." "I'm sure he was right," said Hook forty years later. "If guys are digging in on you, you brush them back. Nowadays, you can't hardly do that anymore. Everybody wants to fight if they get brushed back. Back when I was playing, a brushback was just part of the game." Hook at least had an excuse. While pitching in a high school game, he had inadvertently hit a batter in the head and fractured his skull. He was thereafter understandably reluctant to throw at batters. On one occasion with the Mets, Hook was ordered to throw at Smokey Burgess, whom Hook had known well when both were with the Reds. Burgess had become one of the league's great pinch hitters, and Stengel wanted to give him something to think about. "Instead of throwing at him up high, I threw down at his legs, because I think he only had one kidney or something," Hook remembered. "I thought, 'Man, I sure don't want to hit him in the back.'"

Stengel also expressed the same frustration with Anderson on learning that he owned a generous annuity plan: "He's got an-noo-i-tees, but he won't knock the batter on his butt."

In fact, none of Stengel's pitchers, it seemed, were willing to throw at opposing batters. Stengel, the quintessential old-school baseball man, knew the value of the brushback and decried what he saw as softness: "All these pitchers we have, I see them with their lovely wives and their lovely children. So they go out there to pitch, and here is the batter. Oh, he digs right in there and he swings that bat and he has a wonderful toehold. And our pitchers, they say they won't throw at him. They say you have to think of the lovely wife and children the batter has. Well, some of these pitchers of mine ought to think about their own children. That batter up there doesn't care about them. He's in there to take the food right off the table from the pitcher's children. These fellows of mine, they better start thinking of their own lovely children and move that batter back off the plate a little."

Stengel's task was no easier with his infield. Initially, he had high hopes for a core of Hodges at first, Charlie Neal at second, Felix Mantilla at shortstop and Don Zimmer at third. However, Hodges was so often injured as to be a non-factor, and Zimmer was gone by May. That left Neal and Mantilla.

Neal was a puzzle to many. In 1959, at the age of 28, he had played second and short, batting .287, driving in 83 runs with 18 homers, 11 triples and 30 doubles, making the All-Star team and helping the Dodgers win the World Series. He was also a Gold Glove fielder who made the hard plays look easy. After that, though, he suffered through abysmal batting slumps, and in the field, he began to make hard plays look hard and then easy plays look hard as well. By the time he came to the Mets, he was 31 and thought to be washed up. However, Neal's former teammate, Maury Wills, believed that Neal's trade to the Mets was a sort of banishment in retaliation for Neal having spoken out against the Dodger establishment. "It shows how the mind affects your ability to play," wrote Wills in his autobiography. "Charlie Neal became ill psychologically and emotionally. Before you knew it, he was through."

Mantilla came in the draft after hitting .215 in spot duty with Milwaukee. Neal and Mantilla both posted respectable batting numbers, but their fielding was another matter. Neal made 28 errors at three positions, including twelve in only 39 games at short. Mantilla was somewhat better, committing twenty errors while spending most of his time at third base following Zimmer's departure. However, Stengel never warmed to him, once benching him after a four-hit performance. Mantilla recalled a pre-game incident in which Solly Hemus hit infield popups to him and Rod Kanehl to determine which of the two would start that day. Kanehl, though, believed it was Weiss who disliked Mantilla and that he and Stengel got along fine. In any event, he produced at the plate; his .275 average was second only to Ashburn.

Over the course of the season, Stengel tried eight different men at first base, six at second, nine at third and five at shortstop. In the middle of it all was Hot Rod Kanehl, who played all four positions (and all three outfield positions). Neal, Elio Chacon and Mantilla, the erstwhile starters at second, short and third, respectively, each saw action at all three positions.

The only consistent factor was the lack of success regardless of who played where, as shown by the 146 errors Mets infielders racked up in 1962. By contrast, the Mets' 2000 infield, featuring John Olerud, Edgardo Alfonso, Rey Ordonez and Robin Ventura, committed only 33. Chacon was the only infielder to play more than 100 games at one position, and he made 22 errors. Throneberry had 17 errors at first, tying Pittsburgh's Dick Stuart (another notoriously bad fielder and, appropriately enough, a future Met) to lead all NL first basemen despite playing in only 97 games there. Ken MacKenzie, speaking in 1969, summed up the infield play as follows: "I still think that was a pretty good team. We were in a very strong league. The big difference was defense. I think guys like Jay Hook and Roger Craig would have done all right for anybody if they had a better defense behind them. Sometimes we'd have to get seven or eight outs an inning." This resulted in 147 earned runs. Craig Anderson, in particular, had an "unearned run average" of 2.06, the highest in baseball in the last 85 years.

At one point, someone realized that Chacon had handled 95 consecutive chances at shortstop without making an error. The team rushed out an announcement to this effect, even though common practice was to wait for a streak at least twice as long. In a masterpiece of timing, Chacon muffed the very next grounder hit to him, allowing two runs to score. Chacon also frustrated traveling secretary Lou Niss by requesting tickets to be left at every ball park in the league for his "cousin," leading Niss to comment that "Elio has the biggest family in the Western Hemisphere." Jerry Mitchell wrote that "Chacon carried a Spanish-English dictionary around with him but the suspicion was that he never opened it." Mitchell also recalled that when the team left Florida and returned to New York, Chacon bought a flashy sports car. Not long after the season opened, Tom Meany saw the car parked outside the Polo Grounds with its headlights and taillights smashed, windshield cracked, fenders dented, and so on. When he asked how all the damage had happened, Chacon answered, "Parking."

Chacon soon became a fan favorite. Like Kanehl, he tried to compensate for his lack of talent by hustling and scrapping. Although he only batted .236, he had almost as many walks (76) as he did hits (87), and his on-base percentage was thus a respectable .368. In fact, he was a big reason that the Mets, surprisingly, ended up leading the league in walks by a wide margin. He also tied Ashburn for the team lead in stolen bases with twelve. Early in the season, Stengel was full of praise for the gritty little Venezuelan shortstop.

However, Chacon only drove in 27 runs despite being among the team leaders in plate appearances, and this was one reason why the 1962 season was his last in the majors. The following spring, when the Mets had acquired Ron Hunt and Al Moran to play second and short, Chacon was consigned to the minors, where he was converted into an outfielder. The experiment was a failure, though, and Stengel asked, "What the hell is the difference where you play him? He's still gonna knock in 27 runs for you." Walter Pullis added, "Chacon was a guy who flabbergasted me. He looked so good sometimes, but his career came to an end that year. He was fast, he looked like a comer, he had a good year before . . . it was just amazing that he played so poorly."

In addition, Chacon and Ashburn contributed a truly memorable bit of Original Met folklore. On occasions when the Met lineup included Ashburn in center and Chacon at shortstop, Chacon was perpetually and recklessly prepared to lay claim to every fly ball hit in the remote vicinity of his position. Ashburn, still an outstanding centerfielder, reasonably felt that balls hit into center were within his purview. Frequently, Ashburn would call out, "I got it!", at which point leftfielder Frank Thomas would stop his pursuit. Chacon, though, spoke insufficient English to understand the complexities of "I got it," and he would continue to chase the ball, sometimes stopping just short of colliding with Ashburn, and sometimes not.

Ashburn eventually got fed up with being run over by Chacon, so he asked bilingual teammate Joe Christopher for the Spanish equivalent of "I got it." "Yo la tengo," responded Christopher. In August, the Mets were clinging to a two-run lead against the Reds with the bases loaded and the dangerous Frank Robinson coming to bat. Robinson, in the midst of a season in which he would finish second in the league with a .342 batting average, hit a fly ball to short left-centerfield. "I see [Chacon] whipping out from shortstop like a little kid on a scooter," recalled Ashburn later. "So I yell, '¡Yo la tengo! ¡Yo la tengo!' And Elio puts on the brakes." Unfortunately, this took care of only half the problem. Just as Ashburn was settling under the ball, he was bowled over by Thomas, who spoke insufficient Spanish to understand the complexities of "¡Yo la tengo!" The ball dropped safely, the runs scored, and the Mets lost. In one version of the story, as Ashburn and Thomas picked themselves up, Thomas asked what a "yellow tango" was.

Thomas, though, disputes this story. "It never happened," he claimed in 2002. "Ashburn told a lot of stories. He told a story about Chacon and I and him – never happened. I'm serious. He fabricated a lot of stories because he was an announcer. I was never that fast to be able to run into him! I always let the centerfielder catch everything."

Still, there was a question as to how much catching was really going on, as the outfield was responsible for another 30 errors. Stengel had an idea on how to solve these difficulties, suggesting that "maybe we should play one of Mrs. Payson's horses out there."

Earlier, during spring training, when informed that astronaut John Glenn had undertaken his second mission to orbit earth, Stengel said, "There's a man who could make this team. He is just what we need – somebody in position to catch a fly ball."

Thomas, the third member of the collision triumvirate, had one of his best years, batting .266 and leading the team in games played, homers, RBIs, doubles, hits, runs, total bases and slugging percentage. Although it has been noted that 25 of his 34 homers came with the bases empty, Thomas still led the team, by a huge margin, with 94 RBIs. He established Mets records for both categories which lasted into the next decade (and setting a still-unequaled mark for a player on a first-year expansion club). Known as the "Big Donkey," he also pursued an unusual habit – working with the stewardesses on the team's flights. As Jimmy Breslin reported, "Once the Mets are airborne, going to or from a game, Thomas jumps out of his seat, strides up the aisle to the kitchenette, and takes over the running of the plane. Trays slide in and out, coffee is poured, and he starts moving rapidly up and down the aisle, serving meals. He is very particular about it, too." Thomas explained his motivation: "I just thought that the players were hungry. I said to the stewardess, 'You get the meals prepared and I'll take 'em up to them. We'll get the meals in and out within half an hour.' And that's what we did. I really enjoyed helping them, and I had a lot of fun with it. As soon as the players said, 'We're ready to eat,' I was up and the girls were ready, and we just fed them very quickly."

Thomas also had another unusual habit. "He used to bet guys that he could catch Aaron and Mays," recalled Craig Anderson. "He'd let them wind up and throw the ball as hard as they could and he'd catch it barehanded. And he would do it, too." Thomas had developed the skill as a boy, when he could not afford a glove. He played shortstop in games of fast-pitch softball, which toughened up his hands. As a farmhand at Waco, he overheard a teammate, Bill Pierro, bragging about how hard he could throw. Thomas interjected that he could catch Pierro's fastball barehanded. Thomas told Pierro to mark out sixty feet six inches and go to the bullpen and warm up. "I don't need to warm up," claimed Pierro. He threw two fastballs, both of which Thomas caught. "I wasn't warmed up," Pierro now said. "I knew you were going to say that," replied Thomas. "Get down there and warm up." Pierro warmed up, only to have Thomas catch five more of his fastballs. "That kind of deflated his ego," observed Thomas.

Thomas kept the stunt in his repertoire and used it to amaze spectators, but also to win bets. His personal favorite incident occurred during 1962. Before a Giant game at the Polo Grounds, Richie Ashburn, ever the ringleader, spied Willie Mays walking nearby. "Hey, Willie," Ashburn called out. "Want to make a quick hundred?" That got Mays' attention. "I'll bet you Thomas catches your fastball barehanded," offered Ashburn. "Like heck he can," responded Mays. They marked off sixty feet six inches, and Thomas dropped his glove and caught Mays' first pitch barehanded. Mays walked back over and said, "Let's make it a ten dollar bet." Thomas caught a couple more, and Mays walked away shaking his head.

In addition to left field and airline stewardess, Thomas also saw action at first and third, although the results were sometimes less than ideal. Thomas also tied two National League records that season. The first was when he hit six home runs in a three-game span. The second, and more archetypical, occurred when he was hit by a pitch twice in a single inning. He also established a club record which survived the decade when he hit safely in 18 consecutive games. As the team's only legitimate power threat, opposing teams sometimes used unusual maneuvers to defense him. For example, the Reds shifted all their infielders to the left and then moved all three outfielders to the left of centerfield.

Rod Kanehl was another Met with an unusual habit. After arriving in New York, he mastered the subway system with such verve that he soon had a nickname: the Mole. He recalled how

Roger Craig would load up his little Corvair with three or four players and head to the Silhouette, a Brooklyn bar at the corner of Utica and Tilden. "So I looked it up on the map," explained Kanehl. "One day I waved goodbye to them, and they waved goodbye. I hopped the subway, got off at Utica and took a cab up to Tilden. And I'm sitting there drinking my second beer when they come in. Here's Ginsberg and Zimmer and Craig and Bell and Ashburn, whoever it was. Can you imagine the double takes? They'd just waved goodbye to me up at the Polo Grounds. They couldn't believe that I was there. It was fun."

Kanehl had an additional ability, one which allowed him to use his natural speed. He became, as he called himself, the "lucky charm pinch runner." He scored the tying or winning runs in a large percentage of the Mets' early wins. "Stengel would put me in as a pinch runner and I'd tie up the game," he recalled, "and we'd go around and I'd get a time at bat and get a base hit. Then I'd score the winning run. That happened more than once." Mostly, though, it was his ability to fill in where needed which made him valuable. "I played over a hundred games as a utility man, which is saying something," he remembered with pride.

Rick Herrscher also played first, third, shortstop and all three outfield positions, all in only 35 games. Ashburn, in addition to centerfield and second base, also played in right field. Jim Marshall played first base and right field in his brief Met career. Joe Christopher saw time in center and left field in addition to platooning with Jim Hickman in right after Gus Bell was dealt. Sammy Drake filled in at second and third. Even Chris Cannizzaro made a single appearance in right field. In fact, only Thomas, Chacon and Hickman played more than 100 games at one position (although Hickman's appearances were often in spot duty or after pinch hitting). Thus, with few exceptions (and with apologies to Kanehl), the Mets were an entire squad of utility players.

The other National League teams seemed to see them that way. Kanehl related how other clubs took the Mets for granted, in this case the pennant-winning Giants in a game in San Francisco. Facing the tough Jack Sanford, on his way to a 24-win season (five against the Mets), with the Mets needing a baserunner, Kanehl attempted to bunt his way on. Sanford took offense for some reason, yelling to Kanehl, "If you want on that bad, I'll put one in your ribs." Still, Kanehl had shaken the Giant ace's concentration, and Sanford walked Kanehl. "So I'm trotting down to first base," Kanehl recalled. "I see [first baseman Orlando] Cepeda looking out into right field, and there's [second baseman] Chuck Hiller looking out into center field, and [shortstop] Jose Pagan looking out into left field. Well, I hit first base and I take off for second. Sanford sees me and he starts to run at me, but he can't catch me. So now he's really mad." On the plane later, Ralph Kiner and Bob Murphy called Kanehl over and said that he had taken them by surprise. They had cut away for a station break as he was trotting down to first, and they used the occasion to take a quick drink of water. They explained, "We come back and you're on second base and we don't know how to explain how you got to second base because nobody saw it." Kanehl later heard from Hiller that Giants manager Alvin Dark fined everyone responsible for Kanehl winding up on second on a base on balls.

Another indicator was the speed with which players disappeared from the team and from the major leagues. Of the 45 players who saw action with the Mets in 1962, only sixteen remained with the team by Opening Day the following year and nineteen never again appeared in a big league game. Even with all the young players the Mets signed, only Al Jackson, Chris Cannizzaro, Jim Hickman, Righty Bob Miller, Galen Cisco and Ed Kranepool (the latter two joining the club in September) were still in the majors five years later, and by the end of the decade, just Cannizzaro, Hickman, Miller and Kranepool remained. However, this was overshadowed by the fact that the Mets won the World

Series in their eighth season – when the Amazin' Mets became truly amazing.

CHAPTER NINE – THE MANAGER

"There's three things you can do in a baseball game. You can win, or you can lose, or it can rain." – *Casey Stengel, manager of the New York Mets*

Long-time observers noted how different Casey Stengel was with the Mets than he had been with the Yankees. He had been grumpy then, given to scathing comments and a low tolerance for fools. With the Mets, though, there emerged a tireless promoter, a patient instructor always willing to take aside a fledgling reporter. "As a loser with the Mets," wrote Leonard Koppett, "he was much more patient, understanding, good-humored, gentle. He had his irascible moments as a Met, too, but usually during periods of better play, not during the frequent losing streaks. He was more tolerant of lack of talent than of talent going to waste." "I heard he could be a real horse's ass with the Yankees," said Rod Kanehl. "But with us, he was loose. He realized there wasn't any reason to be tough on players; there weren't really any prospects. From the first day in the Mets camp, what struck me was his energy and enthusiasm. He seemed an old man with the Yankees, tired, crotchety, aloof from the players. With the Mets he was incredibly energetic, warm, involved, a great teacher." According to Jay Hook, this warmth extended beyond baseball. "In spring training, Casey and his wife Edna had really taken a liking to our two kids, Wesley and Marcie. When we'd go to a press luncheon, he and Edna would come and get the kids, and they'd be sitting up at the head table with Casey and Edna, and Joanne and I would be in the back somewhere."

Roger Craig, himself a successful manager, had this to say: "Casey had something kind to say to everybody, he was good with the media, he was always courteous and would give as much time as he possibly could to 'em. His relationship and communication with the players, even at his age, was just remarkable, and hopefully I've learned something from him." Hook also appreciated what Stengel brought to the team. "Casey really knew who his customer was. It was the fans, and he knew the way you get to the fans was through the sportswriters. So he really did a great job of cultivating the sportswriters. We got front sports page coverage a lot when the Yankees were winning and we were losing."

The press, of course, knew what kind of opportunity they had. "Things were never dull around the Mets and, of course, one of the reasons was Casey Stengel," wrote Leonard Shecter. "Traveling with him was like camping out with mummers. One should have had to pay for the privilege." Stan Isaacs wrote that "I sometimes think that I can make a living on the lecture circuit in my old age by just talking about Casey Stengel and the stories he told and the ones surrounding him." Maury Allen remembered that Stengel "was called the Professor or Old Perfesser because he loved to lecture sportswriters. You'd be out three or four hours before the game and you'd find him on the bench. He'd talk to anyone: groundskeepers, young players."

Stengel, for his part, was well aware of the value he brought to the club. When he came out of retirement, he gave the team instant credibility. Dick Young, who has been credited with popularizing the term "Amazin' Mets," insists it was Stengel who did it. "Casey Stengel, God love him," he recalled in 1986. "He invented the term, 'the amazin' Mets.' They'd get two hits and he'd say it's 'amazin'!' Or if they scored a run, it was 'amazin!' Not that they won a ball game . . . that would be 'amazin' too, when that happened." Craig Anderson confirmed this. "We were 'amazin'.' He used that word a lot."

He used it especially during the early season, when he seemed perpetually upbeat. "If we'd had anyone other than Stengel, they would have run us out of town," stated Kanehl. "I truly believe that. I don't think there was any other manager that could have kept the fan appeal. He was an underdog because the Yankees had fired him." According to Al Jackson, the reason for Stengel's continual good humor was simple. "He knew he had a terrible ball club. I don't think he would have been that jolly if he had been with the Yankees and losing." As Stengel himself said, "if everybody on this team commenced breaking up the furniture every time we did bad, there'd be no place to sit."

As the season wore on, though, his frustration became evident not only in his increasingly cutting remarks but also in his incessant tinkering with the lineup. Stengel had employed his Yankee players as interchangeable parts, for which he was acclaimed as a genius. With his 1952 World Series-winning club, he had used almost a hundred different lineups. With the Mets, though, he didn't have the horses. In fact, it is possible that by switching Neal, Chacon and Mantilla between second, short and third, Stengel contributed to their inconsistent play. He even put Richie Ashburn, one of the greatest defensive centerfielders ever, at second (although some say this was at Ashburn's request). Kanehl played every position other than pitcher and catcher, and he was probably the only utility player ever to make 32 errors in a season. "I look back on that thinking you really don't want to platoon too much when you don't have a strong team," said Anderson. "With the Yankees, it didn't matter who he played. With the Mets, he had some talent, but he only played it half the time."

Hook believed that Stengel overly stressed the finer points rather than the fundamentals. As an example, he described Stengel's actions when there was a runner on first. "He'd watch which way the shortstop or second baseman would break when the ball was pitched. He'd be looking if the weight was on the right or left foot because that would give him a feel if we could have a shot at stealing second. When you're managing the Yankees with outstanding players, that stuff is important. With the Mets, I'm not sure it was that important." Lindsey Nelson held a similar view. Early in the season, Stengel told Nelson that "we got to work on the little finesses: the pickoff of the runner with runners at first and second, and on the first baseman holding a runner in a bunt situation, breaking in and back to take a pickoff throw." Not long after, the Mets lost a game by double digits. Nelson said, "He spotted me and said, 'the little finesses ain't gonna be our problem.'"

Although Stengel's early pronouncements were full of praise, he was not fooled by his own words; he knew the dubious quality of his players. He told Jimmy Breslin, "I got four or five guys who are going to make it up here. The rest of them, we just got to get along with. I'm not goin' to start breakin' furniture because of them. It's the man and I got him and I can't change his life." Craig Anderson stated that "Stengel was probably the only guy who could have gotten through a season like that without killing himself."

From the beginning, he shielded the players from an already-protective press corps. "I think he had an agreement with the newspapermen," theorized Kanehl. "They could write how terrible the Mets were, but they couldn't write about how terrible individual players were." Anderson recalled that the reporters allowed them to say things confidentially without worrying about their remarks winding up in print. The reason, said Anderson, was that "they would go to Stengel and use all of what he had to say." Hook remembered how keenly Stengel understood that the writers had columns to fill. When games were rained out, Stengel would call the writers into his office, get them a drink and tell stories for a few hours. He also made sure the writers knew that they should come to him first, particularly when the team suffered a tough loss. Stengel "worked at helping make their job easier," said Hook. "Maury Allen said that one of the things he remembered was what a great job Casey did in giving the writers material when they needed space filled."

Before long, this process assumed legendary proportions. Lindsey Nelson noted Stengel's facility with doubletalk as a defense against troublesome topics while still giving his interrogators something useful. There were only two words – "no comment" – which he never allowed to cross his lips. Stengel "realized there were three basic objections to 'no comment': it doesn't take up any space in the papers, it is utterly colorless, and it infuriates newspapermen. Instead of 'no comment,' Casey always replied with generous portions of his own brand of 'filler' material. He never answered the question, but he sent everyone away with something."

Many commentators also noted the difference between Stengel's postgame actions depending on how the team did. On those infrequent occasions when the Mets did something remarkable, he would stand aside – sometimes even leaving the clubhouse early – and allow the writers all the time they wanted with the hero of the day. For example, the day the Mets won their first regular season game, which also happened to be a getaway day, he held up the team's plane so as to allow the writers extra time with winning pitcher Jay Hook. When, as was more usually the case, the team's performance was less than amazin', he would take center stage, often remaining for hours while the players scattered.

Still, a few less sympathetic observers began to call attention to the discrepancy between Stengel's buoyant remarks and the team's actual performance. In addition, reports emerged that he fell asleep on the bench during games. Ed Kranepool, a rookie during the 1962 season, commented later: "People said Casey fell asleep on the bench. Sure he did. I did too and I was a hell of a lot younger." Frank Thomas added, "People were saying he was sleeping in the dugout. Well, I never knew that, because I was on the field. Whenever I came in, I always saw him awake." Kanehl, while confirming that Stengel occasionally dozed off, insisted that the manager "knew exactly what was going on. He wouldn't miss anything, but he would doze a bit. When it's 3:00 and you're 72 years old, you need to take a nap. I'd rattle the bats to let him know that something was coming up that he ought to be aware of. If there was a change that needed to be made, I'd make some noise."

Columnist Jack Lang had a similar view, stating that Stengel "might have dozed off between innings, but when anything was going on in the game, he was alert as you could possibly be." Lindsey Nelson was more blunt: "When Casey managed the Mets he was the boss of everything that happened on the field." Stengel's longtime friend Bob Sales had another theory: "The players said he slept in the dugout. He probably couldn't stand watching them play."

The players, almost to a man, staunchly supported their skipper. In addition to his knowledge of the game, in which he was without peer, the ballplayers found that he knew what was going on, on and off the field. For example, Stengel always knew who was staying out late, but no one understood how he knew, since he saw bed checks as demeaning and refused to use them. Rod Kanehl related a recurring conversation he had with Stengel:

Stengel: "What kind of hours you been keeping, Kanehl?"
Kanehl: "Good hours, Case."
Stengel: "Good hours my tit. You better start getting in on time."

Kanehl finally noticed that during the team's many early-morning flights, Stengel would always walk up and down the aisle of the plane. "Anybody that was asleep before the plane left the ground would be called into the office for the talk. 'Good hours my tit.'" Kranepool had another theory, that Stengel would check up on a player by asking him for a match. The player "would pull out a book of matches, [Stengel] would read the name of some bar on the matches and the guy would be out of the lineup."

One self-proclaimed victim of Stengel's craftiness was little-used catcher Joe Ginsberg. Ginsberg and some of the older players did not care much for the two o'clock curfew after night games. On one occasion, several players came back after curfew and entered the hotel elevator, which was an old fashioned lift still run by an operator. The operator pulled a baseball out of his pocket and asked the players to sign it. Ginsberg related what happened next: "The next morning at the ballpark, Casey said, 'Okay, you, you, you and you come into my office.' We all came into his office, and he said, 'You guys didn't make curfew.' We said, 'How do you know that, Case?' He said, 'You see this baseball? I gave it to the elevator operator and told him to get every one of you to sign after two o'clock in the morning.' So that's how he found out we were late." "You couldn't fool Casey," said Yankee star Mickey Mantle, "because he'd pulled every stunt that ever was thought up and he did it fifty years before we even got there."

Stengel, while undeniably clever, still had trouble with names. One memorable event occurred when the Mets acquired veteran catcher Joe Pignatano from the Giants on July 13. It was a homecoming of sorts, as Pignatano had broken in with Brooklyn and had caught the last game at Ebbets Field. Pignatano learned of the trade while the Giants were in Philadelphia. He immediately proceeded to New York and went straight to the Polo Grounds, arriving hours before the game. Eventually the clubhouse man showed up and gave him a locker and a uniform. He got dressed and went and sat in the dugout by himself. After a while, "here come Casey. Casey and I talked for about an hour . . . well, I mean Casey talked for the hour. I just listened. Jack Lang come by, and Jack says, 'Hey, welcome. Glad to see you.' And he turns to Casey, and he says, 'Who's gonna catch today?' He says, 'Well, that Pignatani guy, if he ever gets here.' And I looked at Jack and said, 'This is gonna be a hell of a three months.'"

Not long after, pitching coach Red Ruffing had to leave for a day to take care of some personal business. He made the 33-year-old veteran Pignatano acting pitching coach and stationed him in the bullpen. Stengel's only instruction was, "If the phone rings, pick it up – it's me." In the fifth inning, the phone rang. Pignatano dutifully answered, and Stengel told him to "get up Nelson." "I didn't know what he was talking about," said Pignatano. "We didn't have anybody named Nelson. I told him that but he repeated he wanted 'Nelson' to warm up. So I just took a baseball and put it on the rubber and said to the guys in the bullpen, 'He wants Nelson.' [Righty] Bob Miller got up immediately and grabbed the ball. 'He always calls me Nelson,' Miller said."

While the Mets didn't have a pitcher named Nelson, they did have a broadcaster named Nelson. Just to make things interesting, Stengel referred to him as "Miller." "Casey confused my name with Bob Miller's all season," said the real Nelson. "On the accepted premise that one who is dealing with Casey Stengel must forfeit all right to any identity, both Bob and I were aware of and accepted the switch."

The confusion had arisen when Stengel saw Nelson interview both Bob Millers on the same program. Nelson, though, had another theory: "Maybe he linked our names together because each had six letters." In practical terms, though, there was no distinction. When Stengel told the press that "Nelson" would start the next game, one writer asked whether Stengel meant "Miller" even though he kept saying "Nelson." Stengel responded, "Well, I may say Nelson, but when I say Nelson, Miller knows he's working, and my coaches know he's working, so what difference does it make?"

The same held true for catcher Chris Cannizzaro, whom Stengel referred to as "Canzoneri," presumably after Tony Canzoneri, a boxing champion. As Nelson pointed out, "Whenever Casey said 'Canzoneri' everyone, including Cannizzaro, knew whom he meant. As far as Casey was concerned, that was all that counted."

Others had similar experiences. Kanehl said, "He used to call me 'Canoe.'" Joe Ginsberg, originally from Detroit, was "the left-handed hitter from Detroit." Galen Cisco, who was picked up in September and remained for three more seasons, recalled that

Stengel "always called me 'Ohio State.' I went to school there. For some reason, he associated with that."

Stengel's trouble with names also included outright forgetfulness. Anderson related that Stengel would call Red Ruffing in the bullpen and ask, "Who do you have down there?" Ruffing would then have to go through the whole bench: "MacKenzie, Jones, Anderson . . ." and so on, until he'd named every available pitcher. Stengel would listen while Ruffing recited all the names before saying, "Gimme a righthander" and hanging up. Since Ruffing liked Anderson, this meant that he got a lot of work. Anderson said that "Ruffing told us, 'You know, I have to tell him every player every time he calls down here.'"

Ray Daviault told of one time where Stengel listed Yankee stalwart Moose Skowron batting cleanup and playing first on the lineup card. "The umpire said, 'Hey Casey, you made a mistake. Look who you've got hitting fourth, Skowron.' He said, 'I wish I had him.'"

Ralph Kiner recalled a different type of mishap when Stengel appeared on "Kiner's Korner." Kiner, aware that Stengel would often talk nonstop, was concerned that Stengel would finish at the proper time. As the interview went on, Kiner became increasingly nervous. "But he quit right when he was supposed to," said Kiner. "Then he got up and walked away and tore the whole set down. He was still hooked up to the lavaliere."

As the defeats continued to mount, Stengel's moods swung back between hopeless optimism to bewildered incomprehension to stark gloom. "Everyone thinks this may be a losing ball club," he told Breslin, "but I always try to tell myself after we blow a game, I tell myself like a swami that we'll win the next one." Stengel biographer Robert Creamer noted that "Casey had what I call an existential attitude toward life. When bad things happen, you ride with them. When good things happen, don't take them too seriously. He had no illusions. I admire him tremendously for that."

After a particularly galling loss to the Cardinals, though, Breslin recalled Stengel haranguing a baffled cleaning worker in the early hours of the morning in a St. Louis hotel: "I'm shell-shocked. I'm not used to gettin' any of these shocks at all, and now they come every three innings. This is a disaster. Do you know who my player of the year is? My player of the year is Choo Choo Coleman and I have him for only two days. He runs very good."

Richie Ashburn, though, saw a different side of Stengel: "There was never a game that Casey didn't think we could win. He never gave up, he never lost his enthusiasm."

One characteristic Stengel maintained was his limited willingness to suffer fools lightly or pretend a player was something other than what he was (Dawes Hamilt notwithstanding). Of the team's defense, he once said that "some players lose the ball in the sun. Our guys lose the ball in the moon." Several years later, Stengel compared Kranepool and catcher Greg Goossen, both of whom were then twenty-ish prospects: "Now here's Mr. Kranepool. He can hit left-handed with power and he can field and he can throw. In ten years he has a chance to be a star. Now here's Mr. Goossen. In ten years . . ." He trailed off, trying to think of what Goossen might achieve, before finally concluding, "he's got a chance to be thirty."

Sometimes even the media would feel Stengel's wrath. After the Yankees lost the 1957 World Series to the Braves, one TV interviewer made the mistake of asking whether they had "choked." Stengel first asked the questioner, "Do you choke on your fucking microphone?", thus rendering the audio unusable. Then, as he put it, "when I started scratching my ass I was ruining his video. He ain't gonna ask me a question like that again."

Although it was rare, Stengel occasionally got his dander up with the press after joining the Mets, as the *Times*' Bob Lipsyte discovered during spring training in 1962. It was a thinly veiled secret that the team was staying at the Colonial Inn because that was the only hotel which would allow both white and black players as guests. Lipsyte asked around and learned that none of the Mets, white or black, were allowed to use the swimming pool, ostensibly on the grounds that swimming would use the wrong set of muscles and thus affect baseball performance. "I kind of didn't buy it," explained Lipsyte, "and the rumor was that part of the deal to have the team as an integrated group was that blacks wouldn't mingle with the paying customers, who generally tended to hang around the pool. So I asked Stengel, 'Casey, is it true you are keeping all the ball players out of the pool so that black players wouldn't be there and scandalize . . .' And it was as if for the first time he really recognized who I was. He looked at me very coldly, and he said, 'None of them are allowed to swim, and I've also given them instructions that none of them are allowed to fuck. Now you put that in your *New York Times*.' And that was the end of the discussion."

While with the Mets, Ed Bouchee continually agitated for more playing time and complained when limited to pinch hitting. Bouchee indeed had a frustrating season, batting only 87 times and hitting .161 after expecting to be the everyday first baseman due to Hodges' creaky knees. According to Bouchee, in five early pinch at-bats, he had two home runs, a single and seven RBIs [note: actually five RBIs in a pinch-hit stint and a start the next day]. He started the next four games, went one for eleven, and then started ten games in May and early June before he was demoted, at which time he was batting .153. Recalled in July, he claims to have remained unused for three weeks until he contributed pinch doubles in both games of a Sunday doubleheader in St. Louis [note: There is no record of this occurring. Bouchee had two doubles all year, neither after he was recalled]. "I go into the clubhouse afterward," stated Bouchee, "and Casey says, 'We're sending you back to Syracuse.' I blew up. I told Casey what I thought of him. He didn't say anything. I never played again! [Note: after being recalled, he played in ten games in eleven days, starting two, and had three singles in fifteen at-bats]. So don't give me no bullshit about Stengel being a good manager. It's all politics." On another occasion, Bouchee was even more blunt, calling Stengel "worthless" and asserting that "a manager who falls asleep on the bench every day should not be managing in the majors . . . He was there for no other reason than to attract fans."

It is possible, though, that the Perfesser saw something in Bouchee that the player himself did not, or would not, when he told the media that Hodges "fields better on one leg than anybody else I got on two." Indeed, Bouchee committed four errors in only 19 games at first base, while the 38-year-old Hodges had five in 47 games.

Stengel certainly had ideas on how things should be done. Although the Mets' pitching coach, Red Ruffing, had been a Hall of Fame hurler with the Yankees, Stengel had his own thoughts on the craft. "Casey felt if you couldn't go to the corners, you couldn't win," remembered Solly Hemus. "He believed in getting ahead of the hitter. Get a pitch he doesn't expect over the plate right away – a curve, say, to a fastball hitter." Above all, he believed in never giving a batter a pitch he could hit. "The number one thing he taught me about pitching was to pitch my own game rather than the hitter's," recalled Al Jackson. "That meant having good control, getting ahead of the hitters and staying ahead of them, and using few pitches."

Of course, Stengel's pitchers did not always adhere to this tenet. During a game in St. Louis, Ray Daviault threw a low fastball to Charlie James, a low fastball hitter. James deposited it into the leftfield stands for a game-ending home run. Daviault, who gave up 14 home runs in only 81 innings of work, insisted that he had thrown James a "perfect pitch." "It couldn't have been a perfect pitch," responded Stengel. "Perfect pitches don't travel that far."

Still, Stengel was constantly teaching, sharing his wisdom and experience, especially with his pitchers, with whom he used a number of strategies. Jackson remembered him walking up and down the dugout seemingly talking to no one but somehow getting his message through to the person for whom it was intended. He recalled a situation where there were runners on first and second and the batter coming up to bunt. The batter would almost certainly bunt toward the third base side. Jackson, the only lefthanded pitcher in the dugout, listened as Stengel said, apparently to no one in particular, "If I was a lefthanded pitcher, I'd take a little off a slider and go to the third-base line, and I would throw his ass out at third." Jackson took the advice to heart, and "in eight years I never let a man get bunted to third."

Ron Swoboda, who emerged near the end of Stengel's tenure, also noted the manager's indirect approach. Swoboda learned that within Stengel's lengthy stories were lessons that he wanted a particular person to grasp. "He saw you listening," said Swoboda. "Instead of haranguing you about something over and over again, somehow the story meanders into something that he wants you to listen to. It was a parable."

Although Stengel could be oblique, Jackson appreciated his particular form of directness. "Casey had the guts to tell you what he'd do in a certain situation when it came up," said Jackson. "He didn't wait until after it was over and then second-guess. He'd tell you right now, and he'd tell you what the other team should do. He's the only man I ever saw do that."

Roger Craig recalled how Stengel would use humor to make the players feel at ease. Before a series with San Francisco, the pitchers and coaches were reviewing the Giants' lineup. When they came to Willie McCovey, Craig, who was scheduled to start one of the games, said, "He's a low, outside fastball hitter, so I'm going to play him deep and to pull." "Mr. Craig, let me interrupt," interjected

Stengel. "Where do you want to play your rightfielder: in the upper deck or the lower deck?" On another occasion, after McCovey had already homered twice off of Craig at the Polo Grounds, Stengel went to the mound. He told Craig, "At the end of this year, they're tearin' down this place, and if you keep throwing inside fastballs, they're gonna have a head start in the right field stands."

Another time, Craig was pitching on a cold day and was having difficulties. Stengel came out to find out what the problem was. Craig said that the baseballs were feeling slick, making it difficult to control his pitches. Stengel, as always, had the answer: "Well, Mr. Craig, you've got about four tons of dirt underneath your feet. Why don't you reach down and rub the ball up?" As Craig, the future pitching coach, noted, "The secret in talking to a pitcher in a crucial situation is not so much what you say as how you say it. You want to say something to relax him so that he can be himself and not show pressure. Casey would never say, 'Don't throw a high curve' and put a negative thought in your head. He'd say, 'Oh, Mr. Craig, you know this guy can't hit a low slider. Why don't you throw one and we'll be out of the inning and in the clubhouse.'"

Stengel's advice was realistic, even if it was not well received in the form given. Leonard Shecter recalled the time Daviault was pitching and kept throwing ground ball pitches which his fielders could not handle. After the fourth misplay of the inning, Stengel came out to get Daviault. "I'm doing the job, Casey," he moaned. "What else can I do?" "You can strike them out," replied Stengel. "You know we can't catch grounders."

Stengel also had plenty of ideas about hitting, which did not always coincide with those of his batting coach, Rogers Hornsby. Kanehl asserted that Hornsby was just a figurehead, offering comments about hitting but not actually coaching anyone. Hornsby promoted the idea of hitting up the middle. Stengel, though, believed that the best fielders – the second baseman, shortstop, centerfielder, pitcher and catcher – were up the middle, while the lesser ones – the first and third basemen and right- and leftfielders – were on the lines. Therefore, he wanted his hitters to hit down the lines rather than up the middle. "Casey held a meeting one time," recalled Kanehl. "Hornsby wasn't there. He said, 'Hornsby preaches, "Hit up the middle," but Hornsby could hit up the middle because he could hit home runs hitting straight away. If you guys show me you can do that, you hit up the middle.'"

After twelve years in the American League, Stengel quickly re-adjusted to the Polo Grounds. Even Ashburn, the crafty veteran, benefitted from his insights. Stengel told him to "use both lines and never hit to center," good advice for the Polo Grounds where the porches were short and centerfield was cavernous. Ashburn responded with seven home runs that season, three more than his previous career best. "The other reason Casey said to hit down the foul lines was that double-play balls are usually hit to the shortstop and second baseman. So his advice was good for any park."

This is remarkable coming from a man who had played in the Polo Grounds almost a hundred times. In fact, Ashburn experienced a revival with the Mets. He'd batted only .257 the year before, and his last homer was in 1959. In '62, however, Ashburn hit over .300 to go with his career-high seven home runs.

Nor was Ashburn the only hitter whose numbers went up. "He was always telling us to watch the ball and not overswing," stated Marv Throneberry. "If you overswing, you pull your head out. His main theory was that if you couldn't see the ball, you couldn't hit it." It can hardly be a coincidence that Throneberry had the most productive year of his career. Although he only hit .244, he contributed sixteen homers, good for second on a team badly lacking in power, and he did it in only 116 games.

Once again, though, not everyone got Stengel's message or the means in which it was communicated, as shown when Jim Hickman struck out to end an inning without swinging once. In the clubhouse, Stengel made sure he had Hickman's attention and then launched into a song: "Oh you can't improve your average with the bat on your shoulder, Oh you can't improve your average with the bat on your shoulder, Oh you can't improve your average with the bat on your shoulder, Tra la la la la la la la la." Stengel told Maury Allen that he'd learned the song from Wilbert "Uncle Robby" Robinson, his old manager with the Brooklyn Dodgers, "only I can't teach it to Hickman." Indeed, Hickman was a source of frustration for Stengel, and others. He posted good numbers at times with the Mets, and great numbers for the Cubs in 1970, proving Stengel's sense of Hickman's worth. Walter Pullis remembered that "he looked like he might be a ballplayer, but every time he came to the plate, my dad would say, 'There's Jim Potential.' That was a very sarcastic word in my father's vocabulary – 'potential.' He didn't think Hickman was ever going to make it. But as it turned out, Casey was right about him. The guy had some ability."

In addition, Stengel was not above using the press as a means of addressing his players. Anderson noted that as much as Stengel talked to the press, his coaches and anyone else who would listen, he would not often address the players one to one, or even in groups. "If he wanted to tell you something," the pitcher said, "you'd read about it in the papers the next day. He'd go to the writers and say, 'Anderson screwed up yesterday.' I came in against the Phillies with runners on first and second. He just handed me the ball and he says, 'Here, you know what to do.' And he walks off. So the next day in the paper, he wanted me to throw one high and tight on the guy to see if he was gonna bunt. Well, the guy did bunt, and what happened was I came off the mound and I fielded the ball. I turned to throw to first base and Jim Marshall was standing there right behind me. There was no second baseman there [covering first], so the guy was safe. And we proceeded to lose that game. Well, the next day, you know, Stengel was taking it out on me, because we weren't defensively prepared and 'I wanted Anderson to push him back.' That's the way it was. He never talked to us about what he wanted from us. That was probably the hardest thing. I could never figure Casey out. I'd be warming up in the bullpen and I could never figure out if he was going to bring me in or not."

"There were so many comments made," agreed Jay Hook. "It's part of the game that comments like that are going to get made. You know, when you win a game and he says, 'I'm gonna start Hook every game' . . ."

Not every player appreciated this tactic. Since the writers generally refused to make adverse comments about them, they found it hard to accept that their manager would, and that his comments would end up in print. What they failed to appreciate was that in his own peculiar way, Stengel was protecting them. Better they should read what he had to say than to have the writers apply their own creativity to making them look bad. "The longer he kept us in the office making wisecracks, the less chance we had to go to their lockers and ask them embarrassing questions," pointed out Leonard Koppett. "While he wouldn't show it, he was doing his best to make it as easy as he could for his players. Now remember, Stengel was a man who was born in 1890, so his ideas of employee-employer relationships were very different than what we take for granted now. In many ways, he could be mean and unfeeling, but that was the culture he came from. But in his way, he was trying to do well."

Bob Sales was another who firmly believed that by talking about them, Stengel was deflecting attention from the players. Ashburn was one who understood, but, as Sales points out, "Marv Throneberry was afraid that Casey was destroying his career. Casey *made* his career. He turned him into a folk hero. I was there one day, and Marv was smoking three packs of cigarettes a day and complaining to Richie Ashburn that Casey was turning him into a joke. Ashburn said, 'Relax – don't you understand what he's doing?"

Generally, Stengel did what he could to minimize his team's many weaknesses, and to use what strengths they had to maximum advantage. For example, Felix Mantilla was notorious for being unable to field anything hit to his right. Stengel had him stand a step or two further to his right than he might otherwise have done. "He didn't want to move a player over so far he couldn't get to his weak side," said Hemus. "It was part of Casey's psychology: getting the most out of his players." Ed Kranepool recalled how Stengel "would ask anyone with any credibility to help out. He had Gil Hodges teaching first base and giving us strategic advice. He had us give with the glove on balls to our backhand side. If you lunge at the ball, he said, you'll have stiff hands, but if you give you'll be relaxed."

Some players, like Ashburn, were outspoken in their admiration for Stengel. "He was the best manager I ever saw at handling players," Ashburn recalled. "He got some amazing results from pinch hitters. When he was with the Yankees, of course, he always had that great bench. The Mets didn't have that kind of talent, but we turned in some great pinch-hitting records anyway. When a situation obviously called for a pinch hitter, Casey'd walk up and down the dugout kind of mumbling, talking to himself. But he did it just loud enough for us to hear him. He'd be saying thing like, 'Mr. Hodges. . . no, we'll use him for the long ball. Well, Mr. Ashburn, maybe, but no, I'll save him for later to move a baserunner over.' Then he's stop in front of somebody else and say something about getting on base now. See, what he was doing was making the guy he finally chose feel special about the assignment – to feel that Casey had confidence in only him to get this particular job done. Casey made you feel like you were just the right guy at the right time. Guys would think they were the perfect pinch hitter for some situation or other."

Jesse Gonder, who caught for Stengel between 1963 and 1965, appreciated a well-known piece of Stengel advice: "The most important thing I can remember him saying was that no matter who's talking, when it goes in one ear and comes out the other, if you would let some of it rub off inside your head it might be useful some day. He was right."

Also, his age notwithstanding, he showed himself to be flexible enough to learn how to motivate young ballplayers. Such flexibility was hardly necessary with the Yankees, whose organizational arrogance was such that the pride of being a Yankee was supposed to be enough (it had to be, with George Weiss controlling the purse strings). They were so successful that the players counted on receiving World Series checks every year. A lazy ballplayer would not have lasted long among such a group. With the Mets, though, Stengel had a large collection of sow's ears from which he had to make silk purses, and it was sometimes necessary to invoke the number one motivator – money. Kanehl recalled how, during the second spring training, Stengel approached one of the pitchers, asking his record the year before. Stengel, of course, knew his record, and he also knew that the pitcher did not have a changeup. If he'd had a changeup, Stengel told him, he would have had three more wins and would be making $23,000 instead of $17,000. He used the same logic on Kanehl: "He said to me, 'You run good. You should get ten more hits a year bunting. Instead of hitting .245, you'd be hitting .265. And instead of making your $11,000, you'd be making $15,000."

On another occasion, some players were asked to assist in marketing a phonograph record to supermarkets. The players were to get a flat sum of $1,000 each or a percentage down the road. As they were discussing what they should do, Stengel interjected. "I just want to say one thing," opined the Glendale banker. "A hundred percent of nothing is nothing. Take the thousand dollars now."

Stengel would also use the Mets' lowly status as a motivator, as he showed the first spring training. "Everybody says, 'I want to make the big league,'" he told the media hordes one day. "If you can't make this club, with no regulars, what the hell are you?"In

May, Stengel was asked to speak at a luncheon in Pittsburgh honoring Pirates manager Danny Murtaugh. Stengel used the podium for recruiting purposes. The Pirates, he noted, were only a year removed from being defending World Series champs. How could a rookie play for such a team? "You can't," he concluded, answering his own question. "But you can play for the Mets. If you want rapid advancement, play for the Mets. We've got the bonus money. We'll even buy you a glove. So join us. Take the bonus money. Play a year or two. Then you can go back to school."

For those who performed for him, or at least tried hard, Stengel showed remarkable loyalty. Kanehl was one example, a player over whom Stengel repeatedly clashed with Weiss. Irv Noren had been another, a player who had performed well and then became debilitated by injury. Although Noren was probably not fit to remain on the Yankee roster, Stengel kept him anyway as a gesture of gratitude.

Stengel would sometimes also let a player receive a hard lesson, although it was sometimes difficult to determine what the lesson was. In a March 26 exhibition game in Miami, he let Jay Hook take a pounding at the hands of the Orioles. Hook gave up seventeen hits, and the Mets lost 18-8. "I don't know what I was doing that day, but I didn't have anything," said Hook. "Casey just left me in the game. The writers said to Casey, 'Why'd you leave him in there?' And he said, 'Well, he's gonna be one of my startin' pitchers, and I wanted to get him a lot of work.' Well, he got me a lot of work that day. I gave up a ton of runs. They weren't just bleeders, they were really hit hard."

Stengel was unafraid to impose a bit of humility, if not humiliation, when he thought it necessary to reach an otherwise unreachable player. One example was outfielder Jimmy Piersall, acquired in 1963. Piersall had driven some of his earlier managers to distraction and had himself had a nervous breakdown. He should have been a natural for the Mets. As Ken MacKenzie recalled, though, he made the mistake of upstaging Stengel. The occasion came after Piersall hit the 100th home run of his career. He celebrated by circling the basepaths backwards and sliding head first into home plate. Shortly thereafter, he received a telegram from league president Warren Giles threatening grave consequences should such a performance be repeated. Piersall read the telegram aloud during a clubhouse meeting, and announced that when he hit his 200th home run, "I'm going to slide at every fuckin' base. I guess there's no fuckin' rule against that. HA, HA, HA, HA." Stengel did not usually run such meetings, preferring to let Solly Hemus do the honors, but he happened to be there that day. He got up from where he had been sitting quietly and went and stood in front of Piersall. As MacKenzie remembered, "Casey bent over as though he were going to say something in confidence to him but then for everyone to hear he said, 'And I guess if they throw you a good curve with two strikes there's no rule that says you can't swing, either. HA, HA, HA, HA.' The same cynical laugh that Jimmy had used. It was very clear to everyone that there was room for only one clown and one ringmaster in this circus, and it was going to be Casey." Piersall lasted another month before being released, at which time he was hitting .194.

Stengel's bad side was not somewhere a player wanted to put himself. Swoboda recalled aspring training dinner party Mrs. Payson threw for the players in West Palm Beach. Stengel was addressing the players through a microphone at a podium. After lecturing the players on the wisdom of being careful with their money, he also had some postgame drinking suggestions. He told them not to go out with five or six others after the game, because by the time everybody bought a round they would all be drunk. Go in smaller groups, he advised. Outfielder Duke Carmel, a young hotshot outfielder who was sure he would go north with the team, had had a glass of wine too many. He stood up and announced that he'd seen Stengel out recently with ten others. "That was true, but it wasn't something you should say with Casey up at the microphone," said Swoboda." Suddenly the air conditioner came on – whoooo –

and the place quieted down. 'I seen you too when you didn't see me,' Casey said to Carmel. 'And I'll tell you another thing – you haven't made this club yet.' The next day Duke Carmel's locker was empty. Casey was tough."

Nor was it just the rookies, as veteran Joe Pignatano found out the hard way. Stengel called the bullpen and told Pignatano to "get me Blanchard." One of Stengel's Yankee favorites had been John Blanchard. Although Stengel had referred to first baseman Jim Marshall as "Blanchard," Marshall had been gone for more than two months by the time Pignatano arrived. Stengel insisted that he wanted "Blanchard." "You want me to walk across the river [to Yankee Stadium] or take a cab?" asked Pignatano. "Casey barks, 'I'll make with the jokes.' And I was in Casey's shithouse for a month and never played once and I still have no idea who he wanted to have hit, because no one admitted to being Johnny Blanchard. But Casey didn't forgive me, didn't talk to me and didn't use me."

On balance, though, many more players found Stengel to be a massively positive influence on their careers and their lives, and some were outspoken in their admiration. This included many who'd had their differences with him. A frequently-cited example involved Hank Bauer and Gene Woodling, the two rightfielders Stengel platooned in the early 1950s. Mel Allen recalled one time when Woodling had four hits, only to be pulled in favor of Bauer when the other team brought in a lefthanded pitcher. This went on during Woodling's entire five-year stay with the Yankees (which coincided with Stengel's first five championships). Although Bauer and Woodling were initially passionate Stengel foes, they both later recognized that Stengel helped lengthen their careers. "He used psychology on both of us," said Bauer. "He kept us mad, and when we did get into a game, we'd bust our ass to stay in there. But then at the end of my career – I was 39 – I said, 'Maybe he helped me play two years longer.' Gene played till he was 40. The Old Man knew baseball." Indeed, Stengel brought the 40-year-old Woodling over to the Mets in June of 1962, by which point he, too, was singing a different tune. "I was with him for five championships with the Yankees, and he and I had our differences," Woodling told the press that season. "It's nothing new. Everybody knew that. But I've never seen anybody like him this year. This is a real professional."

Al Jackson recalled a 1962 game in San Francisco which was halted by a thick fog which rolled in off the bay. Lacking anything better to do, the players went back into the clubhouse and sat in front of their lockers. Stengel found a chair and planted it in the middle of the floor. Without singling out any player or group, he just started talking. "Everybody started to look around, and there's that old man sitting in the middle of the room in a chair, talking," remembered Jackson. "It wasn't a matter of a minute or two before all twenty-five players were sitting around him on the floor, just like little kids. He was amazing. He was just talking and talking. I think he told us ten stories. Ten stories! The stories were good, too. But he would start the first story, get halfway, and start another one. There might have been three stories that you were really interested in. But you had to wait until he came back to finish them." This was all part of the method, according to Koppett. "Like all the greatest teachers, Stengel was a superb actor. Every gesture, every facial expression, every tangled word was put to use – first to get attention, then to deliver the message."

Another young player who idolized Stengel was Ed Kranepool. When he came to the team, Kranepool was a first baseman. Because there was a glut at that position, Stengel wanted to play Kranepool in the outfield. This process got underway during spring training in 1963. The 72-year-old Stengel gradually went position by position, working directly with the players individually and in small groups. Finally he got to right field. "First we'd talk about what the job was in each situation," said Kranepool, "then we'd take cutoffs, we took throws, and he'd have a coach hit fly balls. He caught one, reared back to hit the cutoff and threw it . . . right down on his foot. He growled at me, 'That's to teach you to keep the ball low.' He gave me the glove and he was gone, never to teach me outfield again. I loved the old man."

His teaching had several aspects. Although Stengel genuinely enjoyed the instructional process, there was a certain measure of ego gratification involved; after all, when his players performed well, it was a reflection on him. In another respect, the process was a challenge, particularly with the Original Mets. As Koppett pointed out, Stengel stressed five particular virtues – hustle, alertness, practice, study and the correction of weakness. These, of course, are the attributes that can be taught, and the challenge was how to use strengths in these areas to counter weaknesses in the areas – natural ability, speed or strength – which cannot be taught.

However, Stengel also was at his best that season in terms of how he dealt with the older veterans, players who had some talent and knew what to do with it. It is no accident that Richie Ashburn experienced a renaissance under Stengel. Ashburn knew it, too; years after his career, he said, "I learned more baseball and had more fun playing one year under Casey with the Mets than in any other season in my entire career." Roger Craig was even more expansive during his tenure as manager of the Giants: "The bottom line is I'm a better person and a better manager because of the time I spent with Casey Stengel. I only spent two years with him. I wish I could have spent more."

CHAPTER TEN – THE FANS

"I love signing autographs. I'll sign anything but veal cutlets. My ballpoint pen slips on veal cutlets." – Casey Stengel, manager of the New York Mets

From the beginning, Met fans have been a breed apart – a "New Breed," as christened by *Daily News* columnist Dick Young. The enthusiasm they showed was almost unfathomable considering the team's lack of success. The Mets drew over 900,00 fanatics to the Polo Grounds in 1962, paltry by today's standards, but at that time an attendance record for a last place team, and about half again more than the Giants had drawn in their last season at the Polo Grounds in 1957. Although they drew huge crowds when the Dodgers or Giants were in town, a more normal crowd was five thousand or so during the week, particularly for day games, and 20,000 on the weekends. This was during an era in which several teams routinely drew in the low thousands. In a fitting tribute to the faithful, Jimmy Breslin's *Can't Anybody Here Play This Game?* contained this opening dedication: "To the 922,530 brave souls who paid their way into the Polo Grounds in 1962. Never has so much misery loved so much company."

The Mets' early moves were calculated to attract attention, especially the selection of Casey Stengel. He had a track record second to none, and even at his age, he had as sound a baseball mind as anyone in the game. However, there is no mistaking the public relations bonanza George Weiss achieved, nor was Stengel himself blind to his own potential appeal to New Yorkers starved for National League baseball. From the beginning, Stengel went out of his way to connect with the media and the public, as shown by his ebullient performance in the Macy's Thanksgiving Day parade on that freezing afternoon. He resumed his PR campaign during spring training, and he never stopped. However effective Stengel's performance was, though, the fact remains that New York fans were simply ready for the Mets.

One such fan was Jim Fertitta, the former Dodger fan, who was 31 in 1962. Fertitta became a Dodger fan at the age of ten shortly after the Dodgers lost the 1941 World Series – their first appearance – to the Yankees. Brooklyn had the Yanks on the ropes at one point, but catcher Mickey Owen dropped a third strike, allowing New York to win the game and ultimately the Series. Fertitta remembered how the older kids in the neighborhood were upset by the loss. "I didn't know too much about it at that time," he recalled, "but I felt, you know, let me see what this is all about." Fertitta, whose family lived on Franklin Avenue, used to take the trolley right to Ebbets Field. He went to quite a few games over the next fifteen years, even after getting married and starting a family. He was heartbroken when the team departed in 1957. He remembered that it was "very hard to see that a team would just pick up and go. I could never stand the Yankees and I wouldn't go and root for them, so I kind of faded away from baseball until the Mets were born. I had heard almost from the minute that the Dodgers moved out that there would be a new team. The Mayor had always said that they were gonna get another team, and they were gonna form a committee. But it took such a long time that I started to get away from the game. Once in a while I would look at Philadelphia or Cincinnati, but I started to get away from it until the team was born."

Once the Mets arrived, Fertitta became a fan right away. He went to twenty games at the Polo Grounds over the first two seasons, and he attended the Shea Stadium opener in 1964. Before long, he began taking his son, Jim Jr., now one of the most fervent, and best-known, Mets fans in the country. Jim Jr.'s home in Port St. Lucie, Florida, where the Mets have a farm team, is decorated with Mets logos and memorabilia, and he, his home and his wife appeared in a series of commercials for Fox Sports. Jim Sr. moved to in Port St. Lucie as well in 1988.

As ready as the fans may have been, though, the team was still capable of generating controversy. After all, we are talking about New York. One talking point was Weiss' draft strategy, an issue still discussed today. While Houston took unknowns with upside potential, Weiss went for familiar names and was especially attracted to whatever former New York players were available. He was accused of sacrificing the team's long-term prospects in return for immediate gate profits.

Not everyone, though, felt the same way about this strategy. Columnist Jack Lang believed that by drafting familiar players, Weiss was giving the fans what they wanted. "It was obvious," according to Lang, "that he felt that New York at the beginning would welcome them back, and they did." Jim Fertitta was one of these fans. "I think that the organization felt that maybe the people wouldn't go to see the games," he stated, "so they were gonna grab these old players. I said to myself, 'They're getting a lot of good ballplayers, they're gonna be a hell of a team.' I don't think Weiss knew at the time whether people would come out, but they did."

The opposing view is typified by Walter Pullis, who believes Weiss' strategy was a mistake. Houston, having no legacy to contend with, could draft anybody they wanted. They did not have to compete with the Yankees – or anyone else – for attention. As a result, they could take unknowns like Roman Mejias, Bob Lillis and Bob Aspromonte, all of whom were able to contribute right away. "But I understand the premise," said Pullis with four decades of perspective. "You see this today with the Rangers or the Knicks. They never want to develop anything. They always feel you have to have a name team there or nobody will go see it. But the Mets? I'm going to answer that as a fan. The fact that Gil Hodges was on the team . . . that didn't mean anything to me. I think if they could have had Lillis at short, Aspromonte at third . . . if you would have put that team in New York, they probably would have drawn the same attendance and they would have gone 64-96."

Leonard Shecter, writing in the wake of the Mets' 1969 World Series victory, was also critical of Weiss' belief that "he needed big-name players in order to induce the foolish multitudes to pay their way into the ancient and decrepit Polo Grounds . . . He was wrong."

He was wrong because the fans were happy enough just to have the return of National League baseball to New York, with or without familiar faces. From the beginning, they proved to be supportive. As Shecter noted, National League fans differed from their American League counterparts, especially in New York. The crowds at Yankee Stadium tended to be better dressed, better behaved and less informed, a far cry from the "noisy, tough and knowledgeable" masses who populated Ebbets Field and the Polo Grounds prior to 1957, often becoming part of the ceremony. This latter group made the easy transition to Met fandom in 1962, according to Ed Wolff, who attended games both at Yankee Stadium and the Polo Grounds in 1962. Based on his observations, "the Yankee fans were a little more quiet, more reserved, and the Mets fans were more boisterous." Another was Jimmy Breslin, who, in a widely-reported quote in a 1962 *Sports Illustrated* piece, stated that Met fans, like the old Dodger rooters before them, never would have tolerated Joe DiMaggio on their team, as he was too perfect.

The Mets' broadcasters believed the fans were worthy inheritors of the legacy. Bob Murphy, speaking during the Mets' 25th anniversary season, stated that "the fans were just about as much a part of that ball game, a part of the entertainment, as the game was itself . . . they were having a good time at the ball game." In his autobiography, Lindsey Nelson referred to them as "part of the spectacle. They go out as much to watch other people as to watch the ball game. They laugh and wave flags and signs and sing songs and write poetry and enjoy themselves, much as they did at

Ebbets Field when the Dodgers were there. The Mets had something to offer the serious fan, too – the chance to see National League baseball, a chance that had been denied him for four years."

Casey Stengel went one better during the season. "Ebbets Field was never like this," said the Perfesser. "Some of these people are maybe a little nutsy, but you gotta like the tremendous support they give you. They sure jazz you up."

As the season wore on and the losses mounted, their enthusiasm never wavered. Even when they were scarce in number (when Houston or Milwaukee came to town), they cheered from wire to wire. Leading the way, as in many ballparks, were the denizens of the bleachers, which were divided in half by two loud and antagonistic (towards the opponents as well as each other) old Giant fans, Looie Kleppel, a hulking former piano mover in his sixties, and a large African-American woman who called herself Mother of the Mets.

Lindsey Nelson discovered that Met fans would pop up in unlikely places. On his way to the ballpark one night, he was pulled over for speeding on the Cross-Bronx Expressway. The officer took his license and registration and retreated to the patrol car. After a few minutes, the officer returned and asked Nelson to identify himself. When Nelson said he was a broadcaster for the New York Mets, the patrolman handed back his documents and said, "Hell, buddy, you got enough troubles." On another occasion, during a visit to a movie set at the Twentieth Century-Fox studios in Hollywood, Nelson was continually surrounded by stage hands, all Met fans, who came over to chat whenever they had a moment. One particularly memorable situation occurred when the Dodgers returned to New York for the first time. During a rain delay, Nelson, doing the television call, found himself increasingly desperate to keep from losing the huge viewing audience. He was unexpectedly joined in the booth by superstar entertainer Danny Kaye, then being wooed by all three major networks to do a TV special. Kaye almost pre-empted himself, giving an impromptu performance in the booth and sticking around for an hour. On a more mundane level, Nelson received daily greetings, cheers and probing questions from people he met on the street – police and firemen, cabbies, shoeshine boys, and other complete strangers who knew who he was.

The Mets themselves, while clearly grateful for this outpouring, seemed unsure about how to deal with such unstinting loyalty, especially those who had not previously played in New York. "Some of them had been jeered in other cities for being merely mediocre, but now they were being applauded in supposedly the most critical city in the country for being collectively and colossally abysmal," wrote George Vecsey. The competitive Richie Ashburn, though grateful, felt that the fans shouldn't settle for "losing good;" still, he acknowledged that, as an alternative, "they could make it real miserable for us." Roger Craig recalled how a cabbie would disregard a thirty-dollar fare, or attempting to settle his restaurant check only to find that some unknown person had already paid it. "It got to the point where we were enjoyable losers," said Craig Anderson. "They came to be entertained by figuring out how we were going to lose the next game. It was like, 'okay, they're a bunch of losers, so let's just go watch them and have fun.'" Jay Hook added, "The thing that made it good was the fans. The fans in New York were terrific. They really cheered and were very positive toward the Mets." These sentiments were confirmed by Frank Thomas: "No team got more enthusiastic support. The fans were just fantastic. No matter what you did, they cheered you on. They never booed you. New York treats me better than my hometown of Pittsburgh. And they still do. I can't say enough about them."

Longtime fan Ed Wolff attributes this support to several factors. First and most obviously, the Mets filled a void in the lives of their fans just by existing. Second, he believes the overwhelming majority of fans had low expectations, since they were aware of how the players had been assembled. "They wanted a team," he says.

"They would take it any way they could get it." He draws a contrast between fans of the Original Mets and those of the present-day New York Knicks. When the Knicks – a big-budget team with high expectations and glory years now well in the past – have a bad season, the fans abandon them and wait until the next season. With the Original Mets, though, "it was different, because they knew what they had. Nobody was pulling the wool over their eyes. New Yorkers wanted a team so much that they were willing to stick with the Mets through thick and thin. And they were lovable and accessible in many ways that the Yankees weren't. One might consider them the people's team. Having been in sales and talking to a lot of people, a cross-section of New York City, a lot of people were rooting for the Mets. I guess they just liked the spirit of it. 'They're not the best, but they try, and if they screw up, they screw up. It's okay. I can relate to that.' People went out to be entertained. If they won, that was great. If they didn't win – okay, they saw the Mets. It really didn't matter. If they won, that was a bonus."

Lindsey Nelson drew similar conclusions in his autobiography, noting than fans came to the Polo Grounds "clad in T-shirts and slacks, dungarees and sneakers, business suits, silk dresses, cashmere sweaters, and mink stoles." They were likely to cheer any honest effort or actual accomplishment they witnessed, and when they laughed at the team's many mistakes, "the laugh is one of fondness, not ridicule."

Of course, opponents found the terrain significantly less hospitable. One of these was Reds pitcher Jim O'Toole, who hated the dimensions of the Polo Grounds. "Everything looked on top of you because the fences were so close down the lines," he remembered after his career. He particularly disliked the Met fans: "When you walked up the runway in center field, they would spit and throw things at you."

The organization was certainly grateful for the fan support, especially in light of the woeful performance on the field. This gratitude was reflected in an extraordinary advertisement in the *New York Times* on June 6, 1962, at the tail end of a seventeen-game losing streak:

HOW COLD IS NEW YORK?

Never in sports history has there been such a heart-warming demonstration of loyalty and affection as we have received from the Met fans, the New Breed. They are the new Miracle of Coogan's Bluff. Once and for all the myth has been shattered that New York is a cynical sports city, settling only for a winner. Our Met fans have proved that New York is the warmest, the most sympathetic, the most tolerant city in the nation and we are grateful. The Met fans have shown that they appreciate the battling of Casey Stengel and his team against tremendous odds. The Met fans have shown an understanding of unstinting efforts, regardless of expense, to bring National League baseball back to New York under the best conditions possible. We thank all of those who came to the Polo Grounds to see us play. We thank the press and the other media of communication, but above all, we thank the Met fans. Our fans, you see, have shown that they love us and we love them.

THE BOARD OF DIRECTORS

Mrs. Charles S. Payson
G. Herbert Walker, Jr.
Frederick H. Trask
James M. Carlisle
George M. Weiss, PRESIDENT

M. Donald Grant, Chairman

Of course, not all Mets observers were completely sympathetic. Some supported the team but expected better results and were not reluctant to say so, such as Joseph Landsman, the self-appointed poet laureate of the Mets. Landsman would post frequent letters to the club's Fifth Avenue offices and also many of the city's leading sportswriters, explaining himself in long, detailed handwritten communiqués. Of course, criticism was often disseminated on a more grassroots level too. Jay Hook recalled going into a barbershop and being asked why he hung a curve ball to so-and-so. He compared it to working for a car company. "Everybody knows about their car," he points out. "If they have a problem with their car, and if you happen to be working for the company that makes that car, they got a lot to say to you. And the same thing was true in baseball."

Another method of fan expression was the display of banners. The earliest of these celebrated Rod Kanehl, the Mets' unlikely first hero. Soon the banners were common, incurring the wrath of George Weiss and Don Grant. Grant's ire was understandable – one of the early banners said "Welcome To Grant's Tomb." He had it confiscated. Weiss also ordered the banners to be confiscated, ostensibly on the grounds that they obstructed the view of the non-banner-displaying public. However, Dick Young reported the confiscations, and the fans brought even more banners. Eventually, Weiss quietly relented, and banners soon became an integral part of Met games. The following year, Weiss even allowed a "Banner Day" at the Polo Grounds, and before the game that day, the fans paraded on the field displaying their creations. Banner Day was such a success that it became an annual event.

One of the first and most inventive of the banneristas was Karl Ehrhardt, a commercial artist from Queens. He was the author of the "Grant's Tomb" banner, which was confiscated by a Met employee named Matt Burns, who had been with the franchise since the Continental League days. Undaunted, Ehrhardt soon returned with another banner, this one saying "WE SCRIBBLE WHILE MATT BURNS." With that, Ehrhardt was off to the races, and he was soon bringing with him a variety of messages, often dozens at a time, which he would display whenever he deemed it appropriate to what was happening on the field. However, columnist Stan Isaacs, writing in 1969, believed that Ehrhardt never topped the simple, straightforward genius of "WE SCRIBBLE WHILE MATT BURNS."

At first, the banners were simple affairs, containing straightforward sentiments such as "LET'S GO METS," and, on one memorable occasion, "PRAY!" As the season (and the losing) went on, though, the fans became more creative. Soon, there were "TO ERR IS HUMAN, TO FORGIVE IS A METS FAN," "THE METS AIN'T FIRST, 'TIS SAD BUT TRUE, BUT DEAR OLD METS, WE LOVE YOU" and "WE DON'T WANT TO SET THE WORLD ON FIRE – WE JUST WANT TO FINISH NINTH." There was even a high-brow parody of the standard cheer, "LET US PROCEED, METROPOLITANS" (along with the Latin version, "EAMUS METROPOLI"). The phenomenon went national when the Mets visited the West Coast and were greeted by a group of UCLA students holding a banner stating "FLASH – KENNEDY DISCUSSES THE RAILROAD STRIKE WITH CHOO CHOO COLEMAN." Even Homer the beagle got into the act, displaying a mini "LET'S GO METS" banner in his teeth. Of course, the fans saved their best efforts for when the Dodgers came to town. In addition to the window shades spelling out "OMALLEY GO HOME," another banner announced that "DA BUMS ARE CRUMS."

Even if Weiss never liked the banners, others in the organization recognized their value. One of these was publicity director Tom Meany, who must have understood that the fans were doing his job for him. Meany was enthused by the more literate banners; among his favorites were "CHASTISE THOSE CINCINNATIANS" and "PRESS ON METROPOLITANS." Lindsey Nelson was a big fan, and the broadcasters included banner shots in their telecasts whenever they could. He also related the story, perhaps apocryphal, that when President Kennedy visited Berlin in 1963, among the hundreds of banners displayed in a huge crowd greeting him was one reading, "LET'S GO METS." Ed Wolff believes the banners were a stroke of genius, but one which took the club completely by surprise. In fact, he recalls hearing an interview to the effect that "management was totally shocked by the number of people that came out with banners. It was part of that euphoria." When reminded of Weiss' early opposition, Wolff responded, "Well, he wasn't always right."

Another tradition which originated that year was the "Let's Go Mets" chant. Although it began tentatively, it quickly caught on, and it has continues as an unofficial slogan today. Rod Kanehl recalled how the fans could rock the stadium at times.

Another observer taking note of the sheer noise the fans could generate was Roger Angell of *The New Yorker*, who was in attendance the first time the Dodgers returned to the Polo Grounds. The visitors staked themselves to a ten-run lead in the first four innings on a number of long home runs. When the Dodgers were finally retired in the top of the fourth, the crowd responded with a derisive and sarcastic cheer. However, the cheers became genuine when Gil Hodges led off the home half of the fourth with a Polo Grounds pop-fly homer off Sandy Koufax, cutting the lead to 10-1. The crowd exploded with fervent cries of "Let's go, Mets! Let's go, Mets!" Jim Hickman doubled, Felix Mantilla singled and then was driven home by Joe Christopher, and the noise grew louder. As Angell put it, the fans "screeched, yawped, pounded their palms, leaped up and down, and raised such a din that players in both dugouts ducked forward and peered nervously back over the dugout roofs at the vast assemblage that had suddenly gone daft behind them." The Dodgers got the runs back the next time they came to bat and went to the bottom of the ninth leading 13-4. The fans erupted again as the Mets scratched out four singles and two runs before Koufax, looking slightly dazed, managed to put them away.

No one there seemed to take any notice that it was the Dodgers' ninth win in a row and the Mets' ninth consecutive loss. "Sandy Koufax and I had learned the same odd lesson," concluded Angell. "It is safe to assume that the Mets are going to lose, but dangerous to assume that they won't startle you in the process."

In his 1970 history, *The New York Mets – the Whole Story*, Leonard Koppett examined the makeup of the early Met audience, breaking it up into several subcategories. The first was the subgroup of young fans, the "New Breed," the ones unlikely to be touched by the wave of nostalgia Weiss expected when he made his draft selections. Many had no personal memories of Gil Hodges or Don Zimmer wearing Brooklyn uniforms. More to the point, the Dodgers and Giants belonged to their fathers or even older brothers, while the youngsters could claim the new Mets for themselves. Moreover, there was no rich decades-long tradition they had to go back and learn. Since they were supporters of a team in its infancy, they were aware of – and involved in – the club's entire history as it developed.

John MacMaster, an example of this subgroup, grew up in New Milford, New Jersey, as a Yankee fan, joining the ranks when New York played the Pirates in the 1960 World Series. At that time, of course, the Yankees were the only team in New York (and thus the only team to which he had access), and he was drawn to them by their tremendous success. However, he never got to see a game, because his father was a Giants fan and Yankee hater.

MacMaster experienced a sudden conversion after attending his first Mets game in 1962 at the age of eight. His father had instantly taken to the Mets simply because they were in the National League and played at the Polo Grounds. MacMaster's father and grandfather soon took him to a game. He still remembers the awe he felt leaving New Jersey, driving over the George Washington Bridge and suddenly being in Manhattan. "It was culturally like a million miles away from New Jersey," he recalls. "Driving to the Polo

Grounds and seeing this thing you'd seen on television was incredible. It kind of linked you to what you saw on television actually existing in your life. People who know the geography of Manhattan know that if you go down Harlem River Drive, the Polo Grounds were on one side of the East River and Yankee Stadium is on the other. So you can literally see one when you're in the other. It was the first time I ever saw anything live that I'd seen on television." That was all it took for MacMaster, who was a Mets supporter from that point on. "All the guys I knew were superstars were guys in the National League, and they would come in and play the Mets every once in a while. The Mets were sort of an amusement, but they were also the link to the National League, and I got to see a lot of guys I had read about but had never been able to see. My father was a National League fan and always talked about Stan the Man, Willie Mays and Willie McCovey. Gil Hodges was someone else to admire. Every team had at least one or two guys to admire, players you wanted to see. And everything was fresh and new, and I got a kick out of watching them as part of the National League in general."

Walter Pullis was another youthful booster who rallied to the new team. He was born in 1947 in Jersey City and grew up in Union City, across the river from New York. His parents were both Giants fans, and he attended the last Giants game at the Polo Grounds with his mother at the age of ten. Pullis was fifteen when the Mets began play, and they instantly became his team. Although he had no illusions as to the quality of play, he followed them game by game, even in August and September after the Mets had been eliminated. He attended eighteen games that year and saw six or seven wins, including two come-from-behind walkoff home runs in the bottom of the ninth. "My memories of that year and of all the games I went to are crystal clear," he stated in 2002, "even though it was 40 years ago. I went to about nine doubleheaders that season. My mom and dad would give me five dollars to go with a friend. For five dollars, I'd get a ticket, a hot dog, a soda, and pay my bus fare and subway fare. I'd go with my friends, and we'd sit through a doubleheader. We'd be there for eight hours."

Another young fan was Rick Williams, who came by his fandom via an unusual route. He was born in 1949 in Hartford, Connecticut, the youngest of three children. His father graduated from Hillier College in 1956 after nine years of study, and the family moved to West Hartford. Williams' first baseball memory was of the 1957 World Series between the Yankees and the Milwaukee Braves. "Arriving home from school one fall afternoon," he remembers, "I found my mother in the front room sitting on the edge of the couch ignoring her ironing board and laundry, agonizing over each pitch Lew Burdette was making as the Braves were upsetting the Yankees. I sat down beside her and started to learn the importance of each pitch." Once he became interested in baseball, he followed the Red Sox, whose games were broadcast (and televised, but only on Sunday afternoons) in the Hartford area. He and his brother memorized all the players by position and their batting averages.

Williams still recalls, with crystal clarity, the moment everything changed for him in April 1962, several months before his thirteenth birthday. His mother had taken a job working afternoons as sales clerk, so he was accustomed to having the house to himself after school. He turned on the TV and surfed through the three channels he had at his disposal. The third was showing something called "The Rheingold Rest," featuring an odd-looking man named Leon Janney. Janney was dressed as a bartender and was wearing an apron, and he stood behind a bar which had signs for Rheingold Beer and the New York Mets. Williams had been dimly aware, from reading *Sports Illustrated*, that the Mets were the new team in New York and that they were managed by Casey Stengel, but he wasn't interested. After all, that was the National League, and he was a Red Sox fan. As he watched, he realized that Janney was doing a spot for Rheingold Beer. This itself was something of a revelation; Williams had not realized there was any beer other than

Narragansett, which sponsored the Red Sox. The commercial ended, and the scene then switched to the Polo Grounds, where a game was in progress. "It looked old and dark," Williams described, "as if the game was being played in a place where there was no sun." He listened with growing interest as Bob Murphy told how the Mets were going to pinch-hit Jim Marshall, whom Murphy described as the "sweet swinging, powerful left handed hitting first baseman who could take advantage of that short porch in right." Williams quickly grew excited, thinking he had tuned in at a crucial point in the game, with the Mets looking for one big hit to win. He discovered his error when Marshall popped out to end the inning, and he realized the Mets were getting hammered. "It didn't matter, though," he explained. "It was baseball on TV. My TV in my house. It wasn't Sunday afternoon with the Red Sox. It was the middle of the week and they would be on again tomorrow after school. It didn't matter to me that Frank Malzone wasn't at third or Carl Yastrzemski wasn't in left field. It didn't matter that I didn't know any of these players. It was baseball."

Fascinated, Williams watched the last two innings. When the game ended, the scene returned to the Rheingold Rest, and Leon Janney returned to explain that "someone named Ralph Kiner was going to do something called 'Kiner's Korner.'" Williams watched "Kiner's Korner" with a sense of disbelief. "Watching him stumble through his live postgame show, I couldn't believe how many mistakes he was making. He kept correcting himself by saying 'or I should say.' He was worse than the local Hartford weatherman. He seemed very nervous and there wasn't a lot of positive things to talk about." Still, Williams enthuses, "I was hooked. I called my best friend Billy Regan to see if had been watching all of this and he told me I was a jerk. When my father got home that night, I asked him question after question about the National League, the Polo Grounds and the Met players. He told me about Gil Hodges, Richie Ashburn and the ones he knew about."

The effect on Williams was immediate and dramatic and went well beyond simply becoming a fan of the new team. Every day, he would come home to his empty house and watch the Mets, "Rheingold Rest" and "Kiner's Korner." "It's odd," he states. "The last thing a twelve-year-old wants to be is different. You want to be like everyone else. You had to wear the same clothes, say the same things, hang out with the popular kids and stay away from the unpopular kids. But this was nothing like any of that. It was okay for me to be different." He was a committed Mets fan living in the land of diehard Red Sox rooters, but he didn't care. He soon had all of the Mets players committed to memory, as well as what teams they had come from. Nor did he care that they weren't winning; they were his team. More than that, he made himself personally responsible for their success. "If I didn't do what I was supposed to do," he states, "I was convinced bad things would happen to the Mets. That wild pitch was because I didn't finish mowing the backyard. That bases-loaded strikeout by Frank Thomas was because I didn't vacuum the cellar stairs. My Little League games took on a new significance. My hits were Met hits. Our wins were against the Reds or Dodgers, not against Civitan or Herb's Sporting Goods. When summer came we could play baseball all day and that meant games against Billy Regan, who was still rooting for the Red Sox. I was always Al Jackson and he was always Don Schwall. Jackson had become my favorite pitcher. Bob Murphy would gleefully refer to him as 'the battling little lefthander from Waco, Texas.' He was just like me. He would pitch his heart out and it was never his fault if he lost. That was the catch with the Mets for me. It was never their fault. It was always shoulda, coulda, woulda."

Williams' big day – a visit to the Polo Grounds to see the Mets play the Reds – came near the end of 1962, and the joy and wonder he felt were still evident four decades later. The occasion was his thirteenth birthday on September 15. As his father drove down the Major Deegan Expressway, Williams was able to see the Polo Grounds for the first time as it loomed across the river from

Yankee Stadium. Williams likened it to a "stepchild" next to Yankee Stadium, which looked huge, clean and bright in comparison. The park looked like a giant horseshoe, old and gray despite the brilliant green grass and the colorful team flags fluttering along the line of the roof. Jay Hook, the former Red, was on the mound for the Mets, facing Bob Purkey, on his way to a 23-5 season. Williams was sure of a win based on his sense that Hook would have the advantage over his former mates. He even recalls the starting lineup that day: Throneberry, Sammy Drake, Elio Chacon and Charlie Neal from first to third, an outfield of Thomas, Jim Hickman and Joe Christopher from left to right, and Choo Choo Coleman behind the plate. Despite Williams' confidence, the Reds won 9-6 behind Frank Robinson and Vada Pinson, managing to overcome home runs by Throneberry and Christopher.

Williams and his father availed themselves of one of the more unique aspects of the Polo Grounds experience when, during the seventh inning stretch, they visited the rest room, which he described as "the foulest smelling place I had ever been in. There was water dripping everywhere and long troughs on the floor. There was no privacy; you were standing next to strangers peeing down into floor troughs. 'I don't think I gotta go, Dad.' And I walked over to wash my hands at the sink which had water pouring out of the faucet. The handles were long since gone, so there was no way to stop the water." It wasn't a wasted trip, though; on their way back to their seats, his father gave him fifty cents and suggested that he buy a Mets yearbook. "I couldn't put it down the entire trip home," he recalls. "I still have it to this day and it remains one of my most prized possessions. As I got older and entered high school and college, the Mets slipped away, as did baseball. My horizons were expanding and when I did return to baseball I went back to my first love, the Boston Red Sox. As to why the Mets lost their charm, I don't know. I turned from them in the early seventies and never came back. But my memories of the early years, especially 1962 and 1963 at the Polo Grounds, will never fade. I have probably gone to well over fifty big league games during my life, but no gameday is as memorable as my thirteenth birthday in 1962. It has become a standing family joke, when I take my son and nephew to Yankee Stadium, when we pass Coogan's Bluff, that I say, 'Richard and Daniel, look over there, do you realize that's where the Polo Grounds used to be?'"

In fact, the Polo Grounds, then in what was supposed to have been its last year of use, was integral part of what the early Mets were about. "It was a dump by that time," remembers Walter Pullis. "It was just such an old-fashioned park. It had terrible sightlines – unless you had great seats, it was awful. And they didn't always clean it up after every game. I couldn't wait till they went to Shea Stadium." John MacMaster recalls it as a "weird-looking field . . . centerfield was such a long way off and left and right field were so short. A very oddly-designed baseball stadium." Jim Fertitta states that "almost anybody could hit a home run there, although centerfield was a very great distance. The ballpark needed a lot of repairs. I remember it was a long train ride from Brooklyn."

One of the few improvements the club had managed, and one which the youthful fans were unlikely to visit, was the Met Lounge. This was reserved for season ticket holders, and it bore a Draconian sign stating that "gentlemen must wear coats, ladies, inclusive of girls twelve years of age and over, will not be permitted to wear slacks of any type or abbreviated clothing." There, columnist Murray Kempton wrote, the visitor "was first inspected for dress and credentials by a pretty girl in a pin stripe jacket and with eyes like a house detective. This ordeal entitles the elite to a fifty-cent hot dog."

Koppett's second subcategory was comprised of "intellectuals," people who ordinarily would not partake in such a foolish and immature activity as rooting for a baseball team. For these people, batting averages, home run titles and even wins and losses didn't matter. However, the Mets gave even such supposedly hardheaded fans something else to appreciate – the simple escapism, and even comedy, afforded by cheering on a team which not only had no hope of winning but which actually made losing enjoyable (to watch, anyway; the players would surely not have shared this view). Koppett reasoned that since the Mets were true underdogs in every sense of the term, and since support of an underdog "was an acceptable stance for any intellectual, the Mets clearly qualified on that ground alone."

Shortly before his death, Koppett elaborated on his 30-year-old analysis, pointing out that it wasn't just the fans who succumbed to this sentiment. It even extended to the Mets press corps. "Remember, this is the first half of the sixties, before the social revolution gets rolling. There was a feeling that we're too sophisticated to be dedicated baseball fans. The Dodgers, the liberal darlings, are gone. The Giants are gone. You can't root for the Yankees because they win all the time. But although we don't like to admit it, we like to root for teams. And the Mets give us an excuse. We can laugh it off that they lose all the time and still engage in the passions of rooting."

Ed Wolff grew up in Brooklyn, but he was a Yankee fan as a child. He saw games at Ebbets Field and Yankee Stadium, but prior to the arrival of the Mets, he had never been to the Polo Grounds. He was 23 in 1962 and working for his father as a salesman. The company bought a box at the Polo Grounds, and Wolff began to go see the Mets. The company also gave tickets to clients, and demand was high. Wolff remembers people being "very friendly and enthusiastic. It was still in that earlier stage of the way they respected the game and the teams. They felt close to them, so they would dress appropriately and root hard for their team. I don't recall any violence in the stands or people getting angry at each other. I'm sure it happened, but I don't recall any of that. It was very social, a joyous type of event, and people looked forward to it. There were a couple of games the box wasn't attended, but most of the time, it was a sought-after ticket. Everybody had their own reasons for wanting to go to a particular game. Sometimes the league leader was in town. Sometimes they just had a favorite other team they wanted to see. But people were enthusiastic about going. They always wanted to go."

He believes that the personal appeal of the players helped generate early fan loyalty and identification. Now in his sixties, it has been years since he has attended a Mets game. Of course, as he points out, baseball is a different game as compared with when the Mets first appeared. "It's always been a business. We know that. From the time that Ruth was traded from Boston to the Yankees, everything was done for economic reasons. It's so much so now that there are no loyalties. It's about 'I don't care who I play for this year as long as I make my money.' Those types of things didn't happen then. We were more naive about it. We could just root on a very personal level, and everybody could take away from the game what they wanted to take away from it. Today, because it's so intrinsically tied to business, it's lost that personal appeal."

More than one Met became the subject of the personal identification to which Wolff refers. Not surprisingly, Marv Throneberry received considerable attention from the fans. Although they booed him at first, they quickly came to appreciate his misadventures, and his actual accomplishments were rewarded with genuine affection. One September game featured five young men dressed in white t-shirts, the first four of which had M-A-R-V written on them in huge letters, and the fifth, an explanation point. At one point they danced on top of the Mets' dugout, proudly displaying their t-shirts. For that feat, they were ejected from the ballpark. Once outside, they turned their shirts inside out, bought new tickets and re-entered the park, where they were later seen in the bleachers, their shirts now spelling V-R-A-M-!

Nor was Throneberry the only subject of cultish adulation. Another was Rod Kanehl, the first real Met hero, an immensely popular player during his years in New York. Just as Throneberry became emblematic of the Mets, Kanehl also came to symbolize what the team was about. Walter Pullis was one fan who particularly enjoyed Kanehl. "You could tell this guy didn't belong in the major leagues," he relates, "and yet at the same time, he was a hustler, you could play him anywhere, and he never embarrassed you. I got a kick out of journeymen, and, of course, you got a lot of opportunity to watch them on the Mets."

This leads nicely into an examination of Koppett's third subcategory, those who really were underdogs, or who viewed themselves that way – the poor, the disadvantaged, the unsuccessful. Koppett noted that for anyone who felt alienated, the Mets "were, instinctively, partners in misery." From this viewpoint, each rare Met victory was that much more special.

Koppett's belief regarding this subgroup were reinforced by Roger Angell, who reached a similar conclusion during the first home stand with the Dodgers. The Mets' lousy play led Angell to direct his attention elsewhere, and he chose to examine the wildly enthusiastic Polo Grounds faithful. Angell experienced an epiphany during that home series, becoming the first to understand, and the first to report, how the losing Mets quickly came to rival the winning Yankees for the affection of New York fans. "Suddenly the Mets fans made sense to me," he wrote in *The New Yorker*. "What we were witnessing was precisely the opposite of the kind of rooting that goes on across the river. This was the losing cheer, the gallant yell for a good try – antimatter to the sounds of Yankee Stadium. This was a new recognition that perfection is admirable but a trifle inhuman, and that a stumbling kind of semi-success can be much more warming. Most of all, perhaps, these exultant yells for the Mets were also yells for ourselves, and came from a wry, half-understood recognition that there is more Met than Yankee in every one of us. I knew for whom that foghorn blew; it blew for me."

This worldview, of course, highlights the contrasts between supporters of the Mets and Yankees. The latter group expected something approaching perfection. It was not enough to just win pennants, let alone mere ballgames. Bringing home a World Series triumph was the only acceptable result. It is mind-boggling to consider a 103-win season a disappointment, but this was precisely how many Yankee fans viewed the 1954 campaign in which the team turned in its best showing under Stengel but still finished a distant second to the Indians. The same was said about the 1955, 1957 and 1960 seasons, which saw the Yankees win pennants but lose the Series to the Dodgers, Braves and Pirates, respectively.

Eventually, the Yankees, and their fans, began to suffer from the burden of their own expectations, which had been elevated to such sublime heights by the team's unprecedented success under Stengel. Since the Yankees could not win the Series every year, disappointment became inevitable. By contrast, the Mets and their fans had no such expectation, and thus, no such burden. The Yankees had to win, failing which their fans would become disgruntled, while for Mets fans, any rare win was a cause for celebration.

There is no better proof of this than the speed with which the Mets began to outdraw the Yankees even when the Yanks were winning and the Mets could not escape the cellar. To the Mets' devoted followers, such things simply were not as important as, in the words of Met chronicler Stanley Cohen, "extending the promise of unexpected triumph. For the underdog, every victory has a spiritual message; it speaks of the conquest of forces larger than itself. Winners, and those who back them, carry with them always the relentless burden of their own success." Fundamentally, wrote Robert Lipsyte in 1963, the Met fan is a dreamer. Radio host Charles Collingwood took it a step further, stating that the Mets were beneficiaries of the Underdog Factor, which he defined as "something deep in the human psychology which draws us to the underdog, the competitor who doesn't figure to win, whose skills are not commensurate with his goals but which, far from giving up the struggle, fights even harder." Thus, Collingwood posited, Mets fans were better positioned to enjoy the team's rare wins, and even the more usual losses afforded "at least the satisfaction of having done valiant battle."

It is hard to imagine the fans of any other team in any era adopting such a sentiment. Of course, no one summed up the results of such fan support better than Stengel. "I wanna say that the Mets fans has been marvelous," he gushed after the season. "And they come out and done better than we have on the field and I'm glad we got 'em. If we could do as well as them it'd be better and we're tryin' 'cause in supportin' us the attendance has got trimmed. I'm glad to see that we got so many of the ladies turnin' out to see our team 'cause it proves that we got effeminate appeal which is the result of my charm school which I run as chief instructor in effeminate appeal and we got 'em turnin' out with their dates, the young 'uns and the old 'uns, and I wish we could do it better on the field."

CHAPTER ELEVEN – THE MEDIA

"[When looking at the Mets' batting averages in the newspaper] I make out they're a misprint and turn to the financial section." – *Casey Stengel, manager of the New York Mets*

One of the more overlooked contributions to the legend of the Original Mets is that of the media. Although Stengel's attributes and the fans' support were crucial, the writers covering the team were just as important. Without them, Stengel would have lacked an audience, and the fans would have been slower to realize that something special was going on at the Polo Grounds.

Larry Merchant of the *New York Post* identified six men as being "largely responsible for the Mets as a phenomenon." The first two were Casey Stengel, who saw the Mets for what they were, and Richie Ashburn, the first to celebrate Hot Rod Kanehl and Marvelous Marv Throneberry. And, said Merchant, "four writers saw the Mets in perspective and wrote the poetry that made them as big as life anyway: Len Shecter of the *Post*, Leonard Koppett of the *Times*, Stan Isaacs of *Newsday* and Dick Young of the *News*." Koppett, when told of Merchant's assessment, said that he "would include Jack Lang and Barney Kremenko in that."

Dick Young was the most esteemed baseball writer in New York, and possibly the country. Until 1957, he covered the Dodgers, developing a huge following. Longtime fans Jim Fertitta and John MacMaster thought Young was the best. Walter Pullis believed, as did others, that Young went through several phases and should be viewed differently in each phase. Prior to the return of National League ball to New York, he seemed rootless, almost angry, particularly with Walter O'Malley. Later, in the 1970s and 1980s, Pullis remembers him as being very bitter, a pro-team man. With the birth of the Mets, though, Young too seemed reborn, at the wise old age of 45. Pullis found him to be "just great . . . the column sparkled. He was probably the best sportswriter in New York at the time." Young was so influential that when he reported the Mets' efforts to stamp out the Polo Grounds banners, the team was sufficiently embarrassed to back off.

Another important writer was Leonard Koppett, who, while not quite of Young's stature, was still one of the more experienced writers covering the early Mets. As a child, Koppett lived up the block from Yankee Stadium. By the age of ten, he had his ideal career in mind. "I decided that when it was time to earn a living," he recalled shortly before his death, "writing is a good idea because it involves no heavy lifting. But even at that age, I understood that whatever you do, you have to get paid every week, and the only way I could think of that combined writing and getting paid every week was to work for a newspaper." Koppett wrote for the school papers in high school and at Columbia. He also got sports exposure by working for a radio station that was just starting at Columbia. During his junior year of college, he entered the Army, serving three years during World War II. By the time he returned to finish his schooling, he had developed a number of journalism contacts and was able to do stringing jobs for several newspapers and wire associations. In the summer of 1948, he joined the *Herald Tribune* on the sports desk with the understanding that he would soon be out writing. At that time, with three teams in New York, the practice among the nine New York dailies (not counting the suburban papers) was to have four full-time baseball writers, the fourth being known as the swing man, who would fill in on the traveling writers' days off. By the following year, Koppett was writing full-time, and by 1951, he was well-known as a baseball writer.

In 1954, Koppett moved over to the *Post*. He had begun to cover the fledgling National Basketball Association, and the *Post* encouraged him to cover basketball and football as well as baseball. "I had a ball over there," he later remembered. "It was a great place in those days." However, by the fall of 1962, he had topped out his earning capacity at the *Post*, in addition to which the paper suffered through a strike lasting 114 days. During the strike, a vacancy opened up at the *Times*, and since Koppett had contacts there and could make more money, he jumped at the chance.

In the spring of 1962, though, Koppett was still with the *Post* and was eager to devote more attention to baseball. "When the Giants and Dodgers left New York, Leonard Shecter and I were the two ranking baseball writers on the *Post*, so we had to share one team. The way we did it was he would take the Yankees half the year and I would take them the other half. When the Mets came into existence, we had two teams, so we could both be full-time baseball writers again. However, I was never free to go to spring training because the basketball playoffs were still on. I would pick up when the team came north and baseball season started." Shecter went to spring training with the Mets in 1962, and Koppett went with the Yankees. Three weeks into the season, they switched, and they continued to switch from time to time during the season. "So," he said, "my firsthand exposure to the Mets was sometime in early or middle May. I fell in love with them right away."

Others making significant print contributions were Robert Lipsyte, also of the *Times*, Dan Parker of the *Mirror*, Harold Rosenthal of the *Tribune*, Barney Kremenko of the *Journal American*, and Jack Lang of the *Long Island Press*. Koppett referred to those assigned to the Mets as "the cream of the crop, the most experienced baseball writers around – Dick Young, Jack Lang, Barney Kremenko, me by that time. The next generation – Stan Isaacs, George Vecsey, Maury Allen – they may have had some of their generation's feeling about the Mets. The coverage that created the Mets was led by Young and Lang primarily." Vecsey himself echoed this sentiment, writing that if Young was the leader of the press corps, Lang was "the quartermaster – perhaps a Sancho Panza to Young's Don Quixote." Lang also handled all the press charter trips, whether by plane, train or bus.

Lang was also one of the first to posit that the Mets could represent a new benchmark in baseball futility, which he demonstrated by negative statistics. He believed that the Mets' establishment – up to, including and especially George Weiss – failed to understand or appreciate the way the press covered the team's foibles. "Realizing the potential of being in on the club's birth," he wrote decades afterward, "I began collecting statistics and anecdotes during that first year. Unfortunately, most of them were on the negative side." He soon found himself labeled as a "negative reporter" by the team, but this did not stop him from gleefully sharing his "neggies" with other reporters – often in the crowded press box during games, with Met officials in attendance. However, the club brass did not make it easy on him. He recalled one incident when, as the team was approaching another negative milestone, he attempted to borrow the press box copy of *The Little Red Book of Baseball*, the official record book. Publicity director Tom Meany and promotions director Julius Adler refused to give it to him. Lang, undaunted, called Seymour Siwoff, owner of the book's publisher, the Elias Sports Bureau, who gave Lang the information he needed.

Koppett later recalled that "neggies were easy to come by." A personal favorite of his was the number of times the Mets managed to get the tying run up to bat in the ninth inning before losing, no matter how far behind they had been earlier in the game. He put the figure at something like two-thirds of their games in 1962.

A couple of the younger writers deserve special mention. One of these was Stan Isaacs, who wrote a column entitled "Out Of Left Field" for Long Island's *Newsday*. Isaac's approach was different from most of his colleagues. Rather than focusing on the team's on-the-field play, he instead sought to appreciate the behavioral and sociological aspects of what was going on at the Polo Grounds. Indeed, he was one of the first to draw attention to the cult which developed around Marv Throneberry.

Another was Robert Lipsyte, a recent Columbia graduate who began his career at the *Times* doing night rewrites. Eventually, his superiors noted his abilities and sent him into the field. Before long, he wound up with the Mets at the first spring training. George Vecsey, himself a fine reporter for the *Times*, wrote that Lipsyte "was not familiar with baseball. For all he knew, all ball clubs were funny like the Mets: tired old players ate soup in the clubhouse; eccentric geniuses like Casey Stengel told anecdotes until four in the morning." However, Lipsyte's comparative inexperience gave his work a unique flavor, one which hit home with readers. The John Pappas spring training saga, which Lipsyte and Isaacs uncovered, was but one example. Lipsyte himself recalled his first spring training experience warmly. Although he was, as he described himself, "a young reporter who really didn't know what he was doing," he quickly found himself under the wing of veterans like Young, Lang and Shecter. He singled out Young as being especially warm and collegial, although he apparently never wrote anything Young agreed with. This was a heady experience for a neophyte writer. Lipsyte suffered a sour moment, though, when he flew home and was met by the recently-arrived Louie Effrat, a veteran *Times* writer, on the way to catch his flight. Effrat told him, "Everybody is talking about you in New York, kid. You can really write, but you don't know shit about baseball." When he returned to New York, though, he found that he had a regular readership which appreciated his humorous writing. This was crucial to the team's early publicity successes. According to Vecsey, "if the Mets had been described in standard runs-hits-and-errors form in the *Times*, it would have taken much longer for many fans to catch on. But this excellent young writer helped give the Mets their official *New York Times* stamp of approval."

Clearly, the press corps would draw attention to the new team by any means possible; if that meant writing about negative benchmarks and skinny kids from Queens showing up for unsolicited tryouts, then that was what they wrote about. Of course, the Mets themselves helped in that regard, keeping the pot boiling by being bad in an unprecedented fashion. As Jay Hook put it, "if we were just mediocre, nobody would've ever paid attention."

Therein lies the crucial point. Spring euphoria notwithstanding, no one expected the Mets to be any good. Therefore, the media collectively decided that it would be pointless to report something everyone already knew. It was the Mets' good fortune – and that of their fans – that the press corps consisted of writers with imagination, creativity and foresight. Dick Young led the way here as well, pointing out that "you don't spank a child until it reaches the age of reason. Usually, a child reaches the age of reason when it's seven." Longstanding fan Ed Wolff recalled, too, the unorthodox approach taken by the writers: "There was a lot of parody, a lot of satire, a lot of second-guessing. The media stayed with them because they were entertaining. They could never predict what Throneberry would do. They were following personalities then. When you have people you can relate to, it's still newsworthy. The media just stayed with them through thick and thin."

Indeed, the relationship between the team and the beat writers would astonish today's observers. From the first moment of the Mets' existence, the reporters often acted as though they had a vested interest in seeing the team succeed and thus devoted themselves to giving their readers stories which were optimistic and fun, rather than critical and muckraking. This "we're-all-in-this-together" mentality, unfathomable now, reflected itself in interesting ways. For example, the youthfully idealistic Bob Lipsyte unabashedly recalled taking his glove with him to the first spring training. After all, he reasoned, maybe this brand new team might need a backup infielder. His fantasy abruptly ended when he took batting practice against Met coach Solly Hemus: "He threw a couple of pitches, and I realized I had no business having a bat in my hand. I had never seen anything so fast. I took a couple of pitches, and I walked away. I bailed out. It was just too fast."

Even comparatively grizzled veterans like Koppett were not immune. He had been a rookie baseball writer in 1949, which had also been Stengel's first year managing the Yankees. He had enjoyed the benefits of Stengel's well-known partiality to younger writers and his career flourished as a result. He even referred to Stengel having been "very much my baseball guru" during the 1950s. When Stengel returned to New York to manage the Mets and Koppett became part of the press corps covering the team, he referred to it as "a great reunion for me."

In 2002, the venerable Koppett elaborated on the writers' collective awareness that their journalistic challenge was different than anything they'd faced previously. Their approach was simply to have fun with the job, and their enjoyment was translated to the public through their writing. Since there were no daily cable outlets with professional spinmeisters rendering wry comments on highlights and lowlights, and since many fans were not even watching the games on television, the majority of fans depended on the papers for their information – and their entertainment. Luckily, the reporters were up to the task, as Koppett was happy to confirm: "We had a game in Cincinnati the second year, and the pitching staff got beaten up something terrible. It happened that all five of the pitchers were college guys – Hook, Cisco, MacKenzie, and the rest of them. So we're all toying with the lead with the same thought – all that education and being smart doesn't do you any good if you can't pitch. But Dick Young got to the heart of it with one of the best lead sentences I've ever seen. He wrote, 'The Mets got their Brains' – capital B – 'beaten out tonight.' And that tells it all. Well, somebody was writing things like that every day, and it was terrific. I can't think of any situation where the writers had as much fun as they did those first three or four years with the Mets."

Their importance to the Original Mets' fortunes cannot be overestimated. In disseminating information, the Mets had to overcome an unexpected liability: Tom Meany, the publicity director. Meany had been a highly regarded baseball writer for years, and he was a witty and entertaining after-dinner speaker as well. Unfortunately, he hated newspapermen, which was something of a drawback in a publicity director. He saw no reason to make their lives any easier by giving them the information it was his job to provide. Had the reporters returned his animosity, the team would have been in trouble.

Instead, they simply ignored the hostile Meany (and the secretive Weiss) and turned their attention a rung down the ladder toward the ever-obliging Casey Stengel. Unlike the rest of management, to whom every bit of information, no matter how minute, was proprietary, Stengel would freely discuss anything and everything – including trade rumors and players' shortcomings – after every game, and often well into the night at various watering holes. Using what he bestowed on them, as well as what they observed with their own eyes and ears, the reporters gave the Mets exposure and publicity well beyond anything the team could have purchased or begged. As a result, Vecsey pointed out, "the people were conditioned to expect a bad, funny ball club, whose merit was in merely existing – never mind winning."

"We had that effect," confirmed Koppett. "It fit perfectly the goals of our newspapers and ourselves and Stengel, and it was the rest of the Met family which benefitted from becoming the successful darlings that they did become, selling tickets when there was nothing to sell tickets to." There were several factors leading to this result. First and foremost, of course, was Stengel himself. He made sure there was something to write about every day, even if there was no game. Indeed, Jay Hook recalled how, on days when a game was rained out, Stengel would bring the writers into his office and tell stories for a few hours.

In addition, though, there was the newness inherent in every aspect of the Mets. After all, the Mets were just the third expansion team ever, and the first two were only in their second season. Therefore, everything that happened was a milestone of some kind.

Not just Jack Lang but also Koppett enjoyed the fact that "everything that happened, we could make fun of as setting a record of some sort or another . . . so we jumped all over that."

Then there was the simple fact that everyone knew the Mets would be bad. "We knew that the team couldn't be competitive because we knew the circumstances under which those players had been selected," Koppett stated. Again, it was as if the team's lack of ability was the last thing anyone wanted to write about – or at least write critically about. There were plenty of people around the club who understood that and gave the reporters something else to print. Stengel was the major contributor, of course, but some of the veterans got into the act as well – Roger Craig, Gil Hodges and especially Richie Ashburn. "It was just a wonderful opportunity," summarized Koppett, "to treat the Mets and baseball itself – in our basic view – that it was fun and games and not life and death." Stan Isaacs viewed things in much the same way. "We weren't there to promote the Mets," he told the author, "but we did recognize that baseball was fun and games, and the Mets in their futility brought out a certain lovability in people. I, like Len Shecter and Dick Young, among others, seized on such instances where we could be humorous and show that baseball was more than who won and who lost when you had a team with players who weren't competitive with the other teams."

Another important factor in the nurturing of fan support was the Mets' broadcasting triumvirate of Lindsey Nelson, Ralph Kiner and Bob Murphy. The three were popular with fans immediately, and Kiner and Murphy, who were still with the team four decades later, remain much-loved figures.

They understood right away that it was incumbent on them to sell the new team to New York, and they were not above resorting to gimmicks. Nelson visited a clothing store at 49th and Broadway and told a salesman to "show me all the jackets you got you can't sell." The man brought seven terrible jackets from the back of the store.

Nelson bought them all and started wearing a different one every night. The jackets quickly became Nelson's calling card. Early in the season, he got into a cab in Manhattan and was asked by the driver, "Hey, Mack, you're the guy with all those jackets, aren't you?" He began to use road trips as jacket hunts, and Murphy and Kiner soon joined in. Even the Nelson family got involved. Nelson's daughter Nancy bought him a particularly hideous jacket while vacationing in Ireland. When she brought it back to the U.S., she told by a customs official that nobody would ever wear a jacket like that. "My daddy will," replied Nancy.

By the time he retired in 1979, Nelson had accumulated over 300 jackets. When he was inducted into the Baseball Hall of Fame in 1988, he was asked to wear one of his classics to the ceremony. Just before he took the podium, a representative asked him if they could keep the jacket. It now resides in the broadcasters' wing of the Hall of Fame. Murphy joined Nelson in the Hall in 1994. Kiner had previously been inducted as a player in 1975, based on his 369 career homers and seven home run titles.

One of the early issues facing the three was the extent to which they would be "homers," or outright rooters. Such an approach, common today, was much less so then, and they debated the issue amongst themselves. "We decided to play it straight," Nelson reported. "We agreed simply to report events as they happened in the manner of their happening." Of course, this straightforwardness itself became a source of humor. They just had to report a Throneberry miscue or a ball going through Kanehl's legs and the fans would laugh. "Those three guys were on the same wavelength we were," said Koppett. "They weren't pretending anything great was happening. They were enjoying whatever went on."

From the beginning, the broadcast trio managed to create a desire in the new Mets fans, especially the younger ones, to see what it was all about. John MacMaster, one of the early young fans, remembered "listening to Mets games on the radio right from the go-get, and watching them on Channel 9." He was particularly enamored of Nelson's charisma and enthusiasm: "you could listen to the guy announcing you going to the mailbox and getting your mail, and you'd get excited about it." He also found Kiner's analysis valuable, since he had a wealth of experience as a star player to draw on. He also enjoyed staying up after the game to watch "Kiner's Korner." "Ralph Kiner would do an interview with the star," MacMaster remembered, "usually someone from the other team." Although MacMaster liked Bob Murphy, he felt Murphy was "clearly the number three guy in the booth." He also enjoyed the way the broadcasters alternated between television and radio during the games – two would do the television broadcast and one would be on the radio, and they would switch every three innings.

Another young fan was Greg Ortiz, who was nine in 1962. Ortiz had a special reason to appreciate the broadcasters – he was blind. He enjoyed all three, but Murphy was his favorite, the one who always made him feel as if he were there. When Ortiz finally made it to the Polo Grounds for a game against the Reds, he made sure to bring his radio.

Walter Pullis recalled that the announcers would say something positive whenever possible. His personal favorite occurred on June 30, 1962, when Sandy Koufax no-hit the Mets in Los Angeles the night after the Mets had taken the series opener. Nelson's first comment after Koufax had recorded the last out was, "Well, the series is tied up. The rubber game will be played tomorrow." "Even I thought that was a little strange in my fifteen-year-old mind," said Pullis. "You know, come on." As Rick Williams, yet another young fan, put it, "Bob Murphy could have put a positive spin on the Titanic."

The broadcasters were also instrumental in drawing attention to the banner craze, no doubt influencing untold numbers of other would-be banneristas. A good tight shot of a clever handmade sign would provoke discussion amongst the broadcasters and audience, and it would serve as a tacit challenge to other artisans to do better. Baseball being the somewhat leisurely game that it is, there were plenty of opportunities for those seeking attention by means of a well-placed and creative banner. The broadcast team and cameramen seemed to recognize this, as early Met telecasts featured plenty of crowd shots. After all, as Stengel pointed out, the banners were often more interesting to watch than the players.

It wasn't long before incidents involving the broadcasters began to become an integral part of the Mets folklore quilt. Even today, fans still recall Kiner's abortive interview of Choo Choo Coleman and Nelson's attempt to get a starting lineup out of Stengel. In addition, the three did what they could to support the organization's own efforts to make a trip to the ballpark an entertaining and enjoyable experience, despite the club's poor record and the decrepitude of the Polo Grounds.

One of the team's important early attractions, whose fame was spread through the efforts of Kiner and Nelson and the television crew, wasn't even a player or manager. This, of course, was Homer, the Mets' first mascot. Homer was a beagle who carried his plump body on four stubby legs and, as Kiner pointed out, he always seemed to wear a mournful expression which suited his surroundings. Homer was dreamed up by Phil Liebmann, the owner of Liebmann Breweries, the Mets' chief sponsor. Liebmann originally wanted to name the animal "Mr. Met," but the team had already given that name to a cartoon character, and later, an actual mascot with a large baseball for a head.

Homer was ensconced in the Waldorf Towers and lived a life of canine luxury. He was instructed by Rudd Weatherwax, who also trained television's Lassie. The original plan of stationing Homer in the Met dugout was scuttled by Stengel, who reportedly hated the dog. Therefore, Homer was instead given a stage set up on top of four box seats behind home plate, a location which received a substantial camera attention during telecasts. The broadcasters referred to him at every opportunity, realizing that here, at least, they were onto a winner. Homer often wore a little Met cap and was trained by Weatherwax to perform a number of stunts. These included holding a "Let's Go Mets" banner in his mouth and waving it back and forth, doing flips and barking on cue. The cost of his lodgings, upkeep and training, as well as the four box seats supporting his platform, was estimated to exceed $20,000 annually. "Oh, what a wonderful time that was to be young and single and a beagle living in Gotham," wrote Steve Rushin in a Mets tribute piece in *Sports Illustrated*. "And if you happened to be a big league mascot on top of that, then the world was indeed your Gaines-Burger."

Homer became a celebrity and received as much fan mail as anyone else associated with the team. This avalanche of mail was forwarded to the broadcasters, who claimed to have answered every letter, always thanking the correspondent and signing Homer's name.

Homer's downfall, though, came the following year, when the brewery sponsored Miss Rheingold Day at the Polo Grounds. Aside from the charming young lady performing in the title role, the star attraction was to be Homer, who would run around the basepaths. This was to have been Homer's signature stunt, and Weatherwax had been training him for months under a veil of secrecy.

On the big day, Weatherwax and Homer arrived early at the ballpark, and the trainer ran the dog around the bases again and again until he was sure nothing would go wrong. During the festivities, Lindsey Nelson introduced Homer from home plate, and the beagle was led out from his staging area to tremendous applause. At Weatherwax's beckoning, Homer started at the plate and scooted down to first. As the crowd cheered, Homer made an expert turn at first and headed for second. The applause grew louder as the dog touched second. Without missing a step, though, Homer then turned abruptly, cut across the pitcher's mound and crossed the plate, never even casting a glance in the direction of third base. It took six people, including Weatherwax and three Met players, to corral him. Of course, the crowd loved it, and the inevitable comparisons with Marv Throneberry ensued in the press. Homer was, as Ralph Kiner posited, a true Met.

After the 1963 season, Homer was retired. He was taken by Al Moore, a Rheingold vice president, to his Long Island home. This led to another discovery – despite his extensive training and life of luxury, Homer was not housebroken.

CHAPTER TWELVE – THE SEASON CONTINUES

> "The only thing worse than a Mets game is a Mets doubleheader." – *Casey Stengel*, manager of the New York Mets

After the All-Star break, the Mets picked up where they left off. Jimmy Breslin, writing the following year, summed it up as follows: "The second half of the season consisted of the months of July, August and September, although some of the more responsible players on the team insisted it never really happened." Craig Anderson stated that "we sure did some crazy things to lose games." Frank Thomas remembered that the players would even go to the ballpark wondering how they would lose that day. "That was in the back of your mind, because every conceivable way that you can lose a ball game, we lost it. It was a player making a bad throw over the cutoff man's head, an error, a dribbler off the end of the bat to score a run to beat us. Every which way you could lose a game, we did it." Lindsey Nelson recalled the season more historically. "The Mets in action looked like the Light Brigade at Balaclava," he wrote. "They bravely took the field each day and were systematically destroyed."

At least the All-Star game in Washington was fun. Stengel was there, having been named a first base coach by Reds manager Fred Hutchinson. Lindsey Nelson was also there as part of the broadcast team, and he learned that Stengel's conversation-dominating style was not limited to players, coaches and writers. President John F. Kennedy was in attendance in a box by the first base dugout. Stengel was serving his mostly honorary functions when he received word that the President would like a word with him. As it was between innings, Stengel walked over and, as always, dominated the brief conversation. However, as the game was about to resume, Stengel said, "Mr. President, I'd love to stay here and talk to you, and if I was running this here team I'd do that, but I'm working for this here other fellow today, and Mr. Hutchinson, I am sure, would like for me to get back on my job at the first base, and I enjoyed visiting with you but I gotta go." Nelson recalled that as Stengel trotted back to his coaching box, President Kennedy was doubled over with laughter.

The Nationals lost the game by failing to hit in crucial situations, leading Stengel to observe that "here I was coachin' these wonderful All-Stars, an' what happens? They don't get enough hits either. It was just like another game with the Mets."

Stengel was not the only one to have a good time during the All-Star break. Jay Hook, the Mets' player rep, was contacted by Grossingers, the popular Catskills resort, and told that any of the players and families that wanted to could come up as guests of Grossingers. The resort made the same offer to the Yankees. Hook was the only Met to accept, and he took his wife and two children. Several Yankees attended, including Whitey Ford, Moose Skowron and Joe Pepitone. The only consideration asked of Hook was that he participate in a joint interview with Whitey Ford by the resident comedian. "The comedian interviewed Whitey, and talked about the Yankees and their great year," says Hook. "Then he asked me, 'Now, tell me, Jay – what's it like? You know, you're out there, you throw your best pitch. You see the guy swinging. He's hit the ball. It's goin', it's goin', it's gone, over the left field fence for a home run. What's it feel like out on the mound?' And I don't know why I said this, because I'm not this quick-witted, but I said, 'Abe, tell me – what's it like when you tell your best joke and nobody laughs?' I don't know how that came to me so quickly. You know how these bar comedians are – they've got to come back to everybody, because they're dealing with drunks all the time. And he didn't have a thing to say."

After the break, the Mets got things under way by dropping three straight to the Dodgers at home. After losses to Sandy Koufax and Don Drysdale, the Sunday game was preceded by, of all things, an Old Timers' Day. Since it was ludicrous for a team in its fourth month of play to host such an event ("Who were they going to bring back?" a journalist wrote later. "Harry Chiti?"), Weiss used the occasion to recall former New York heroes, many of whom, including Gil Hodges, played in an Old Timers' Game. "It worked, too," wrote Leonard Koppett. "A crowd of 37,253 turned out, properly indifferent to the fact that July 14 was also Bastille Day." Ralph Branca, who had surrendered Bobby Thomson's legendary home run, was even persuaded to participate, and he actually faced Thomson, getting him to pop out this time.

The actual game did nothing to add dignity to the proceedings. Starter Craig Anderson only gave up a Willie Davis solo homer in the first, but the wheels fell off in the second, when he was charged with four runs without getting an out. All three batters facing the next pitcher, Ray Daviault, also scored. Daviault gave up a bases-loaded walk to force in a run. The Dodgers sent up eight men and scored six times before the Mets managed to record the first out of the inning. Dodger catcher John Roseboro hit a high popup down the right field line. Throneberry called for it, and twisted and turned under the ball. Charlie Neal, backing up the play, slipped and fell, but he nonetheless made the catch while lying flat on his back. Ken MacKenzie followed, giving up eight runs in four and two-thirds innings, and Bob Moorhead allowed another run through the rest of the sixth and seventh. Finally, Vinegar Bend Mizell stopped the bleeding with two innings of no-hit ball. In all, the five Met pitchers gave up sixteen hits and nine walks. After the Dodgers ran the score to 17-0 by the sixth inning, the Mets finally managed some runs of their own, two scoring on Richie Ashburn's sixth homer of the season. Dodger star Maury Wills, who had no home runs against the rest of the league to that point, hit his fourth against the Mets. He also stole three bases on the way to breaking Ty Cobb's single-season record. Dodger pitcher Stan Williams also homered, as did Duke Snider, who reached the second deck in right field. Frank Howard hit a pitch 450 feet to straightaway center which bounced into the bleachers on a single hop, likely one of the longest ground-rule doubles ever. John Drebinger, writing for the *Times*, wrote that "Casey Stengel might have done infinitely better had he loaned his Met uniforms to such legendary figures as Rube Marquard, Carl Hubbell, Bill Terry and Thomson, and had them battle the Dodgers." Paul Zimmerman summed up the day's proceedings, noting that "exactly 173 years after the storming of the French prison [the Bastille], the Los Angeles Dodgers stormed another monument, the Polo Grounds, with similarly devastating results. While Walt Alston, the Dodgers manager, sat and watched – he might as well have been knitting – his hitters beheaded the Met pitching staff." Eventually, Stengel sent in Gil Hodges as a defensive replacement for Throneberry, leading Zimmerman to conclude: "Los Angeles won the game, of course, but Hodges' flawless fielding helped the Mets limit the Dodgers to seventeen runs."

It was Hodges' last hurrah, such as it was, for a while. Shortly after the game, he had to have a kidney stone removed and was hospitalized until August 3. The Old Timers' Day defeat was the Mets' fifth in a row. They broke this losing string with a rare triumph over the Giants the next day, with Jay Hook getting the win in front of 35,000 fans in the first of a twin-bill. The win raised Hook's record to a respectable 7-9, but unfortunately, he was to go 1-10 the rest of the way. The reporter covering the doubleheader for the *Times* compared the Giants' performance to that more typically associated with the Mets, especially after the Giants botched a rundown in the second game.

However, after the opening victory on Sunday, the Mets didn't win again until July 26, dropping eleven games in a row and sixteen of seventeen going back before the All-Star break. They started the streak by losing two to the Giants by a run apiece, the first featuring a six-run late-inning rally that fell short, the other occurring when Righty Bob Miller threw his second wild pitch of the day to allow the winning run in the ninth. The Mets wasted a gem from Roger Craig, who held San Francisco to two runs, one unearned, through seven innings. Part of the reason was the Mets' half of the seventh, when they loaded the bases but could not score, due to another Throneberry baserunning problem. Throneberry led off with his second hit of the game. Stengel signaled a hit and run, and Neal singled sharply between first and second. In trying to make sure he didn't get hit by Neal's drive, Throneberry got his feet tangled and fell on the way to second. He got there safely, but he should have made third easily, in which case he would have scored instead of being stranded at third.

The series featured the debut of twenty-year-old Giant pitcher Bob Garibaldi. In the first game of the Sunday doubleheader, he pitched a hitless eighth inning, while in the finale, he got the final out, earning a save. He had previously been scouted by Mets pitching coach Red Ruffing, who sent back a glowing report. On July 3, while the Mets were losing 10-1 to the Giants in San Francisco, Stengel and Weiss ducked out early for a stealth trip to the Garibaldi household in Stockton, 60 miles away, to convince the young man to join Stengel's "youth of America." Although the Giants had offered Garibaldi a mind-boggling $135,000, Weiss told him the Mets would top this sum. Garibaldi declined and signed with the Giants the next day. Within two weeks, he had already victimized the Mets twice. For once, though, the Mets had the last laugh, as Garibaldi was destined to appear in only fifteen big-league games between 1962 and 1969, never recording a victory.

Another two of the consecutive losses occurred against Pittsburgh on July 19. In the second game, Hook lost 7-6 despite striking out ten Pirates in ten innings. The next day, Roger Craig dropped his fourteenth decision despite going the distance against the Reds in an uncharacteristically error-free game. The day after, Throneberry and Thomas homered early to pull the Mets into a tie with the Reds. After New York took the lead in the top of the fifth, the usual problems occurred. Anderson retired the first two hitters in the bottom of the inning, but Throneberry booted a Don

Blasingame grounder. This allowed Vada Pinson to bat, and he made the Mets pay with a homer. Anderson thus became the third consecutive starter to pitch a complete game and lose.

Two more defeats came in Cincinnati the following day, July 22. In the opener, the Reds pounded Jackson, MacKenzie and Righty Bob Miller, overcoming an early 4-1 Mets lead to win 11-4. Earlier in the day, Craig, the former reliever, went to Stengel and volunteered to pitch in relief if needed (although the bullpen should have been well-rested with three consecutive complete games preceding the doubleheader). In the second game, Stengel sent Craig in with the score tied 3-3 in the ninth. Marty Keogh hit Craig's second pitch for a long homer, giving Cincinnati a 4-3 win. In the two losses that day, the Mets also had four runners thrown out at the plate. "What made it frightening was the ease with which the Mets brought it off," Breslin wrote in *Sports Illustrated*. "You got the idea that they could get four runners thrown out at the plate any day they wanted to."

On July 17, during the losing streak, the Mets called up Lefty Bob Miller from Syracuse. The player sent down to clear a spot was Cliff Cook, the infielder who came with Miller in return for Don Zimmer. Miller had agreed with Wid Matthews' suggestion that he try to stick around long enough to accumulate the eighteen days of service time he needed to qualify for the major league pension. He had done well at Syracuse, posting a 4-1 record, and now he was on the big club, where he proceeded to sit unused for a week. On July 24, in Milwaukee, with Stengel in Kansas City for his brother's funeral, interim manager Cookie Lavagetto brought Miller in to face Del Crandall, the Braves' catcher, with the score tied at four in the twelfth inning. Crandall promptly hit Miller's first Met pitch over the left field wall. One pitch, one hit, one run, one loss. [Note: Ralph Kiner reported that Miller's second pitch as a Met also left the yard, leading Kiner to conclude that "Miller had grasped the true spirit of the team sooner than anyone had a right to expect." However, this is not accurate. Miller only gave up one more home run, and it was not until his eighth appearance.]. Miller managed to earn his eighteen days' service time, finishing 2-2 with a 7.08 ERA. Only one other pitcher, Ken MacKenzie, finished with a better winning percentage.

The next day, the Braves hammered the Mets 11-5, handing Roger Craig his sixteenth loss. Milwaukee broke the game open in the eighth, when Vinegar Bend Mizell, in his last appearance, walked the bases loaded and then gave up a grand slam to Joe Adcock, his second homer of the game. In two-and-a-third innings, Mizell allowed five walks, three hits and six runs. Third baseman Eddie Mathews also homered twice. The Mets staged another too-little too-late rally, scoring four in the ninth. Things got no better in the finale, when Warren Spahn made quick work of the Mets in a 6-1 triumph, homering in his own cause (the 31st of his career, a National League record for a pitcher) and aided by three Met errors, two by Chacon and Mantilla, both of whom had also erred the day before. The loss was their eleventh in a row, and their 73rd of the season, against only 24 wins.

The game which finally broke the losing streak was a near thing as well. In the first of a doubleheader against St. Louis, Al Jackson was locked in a dogfight with Cardinal ace Bob Gibson, taking a 1-0 lead into the ninth inning. The Mets had scored the only run of the game on a bunt single, a sacrifice and an error in the third inning, and they had kept Jackson in the game by turning three double plays in the field. Leading off the ninth, third baseman Ken Boyer hit a ball to his counterpart, Mantilla, who broke the wrong way, allowing the ball to go into left field. Leftfielder Joe Christopher, in the game as a defensive replacement for Frank Thomas, had trouble picking up the ball, and Boyer reached second, representing the tying run. Jackson got the next two batters out and then induced Red Schoendienst to hit what should have been a game-ending popup to Throneberry, who dropped it. Jackson walked Schoendienst. The next batter, Fred Whitfield, hit a shot back to Jackson. Although it was a tricky play, Jackson was disinclined to trust his infielders any more. He dove on the ball himself and threw to Throneberry, who held on for the final out. It was Jackson's third shutout of the year.

Although they lost the second game despite triples by Throneberry and Choo Choo Coleman, they beat the Cardinals again the next day, 9-8. Ken MacKenzie pitched well enough to keep the Mets in the game until Gene Woodling contributed a pinch-hit two-run homer, and Craig Anderson saved it for MacKenzie, who helped himself with an RBI single. After the game, there was a party at the Chase Hotel (the scene of the season-opening elevator incident) to honor Stengel's 72nd birthday two days early. In another legendary performance, he not only outlasted all the guests but was also the first to turn up when the dining room opened for breakfast the next morning.

After another win, Mets followed with five consecutive defeats. On the last Sunday of July, they dropped another doubleheader to St. Louis. In the eighth inning of the first game, the Mets had Ken Boyer caught in a rundown between Throneberry at first and Neal at second. Throneberry threw caution to the wind and chased Boyer almost all the way to second, finally flipping the ball to Neal, who made the tag. However, in his dogged pursuit of Boyer, Throneberry forgot all about Stan Musial, who scored standing up from third. "When Throneberry finally gave up the pursuit and tossed the ball to shortstop Charlie Neal for the tag," Jerry Mitchell reported later, "Musial was at the water fountain getting a swallow."

Musial's run put the Cardinals up by three. The Mets got two runs in the ninth to pull within one but could get no closer, so Musial's tally turned out to be the game-winner. The Mets' five errors (along with one by Throneberry, Neal and Chris Cannizzaro had two each) didn't help. It was the Mets' 75th loss of the season, against only 26 wins. The Cardinals showed themselves to be good hosts after a fashion, honoring Stengel with a birthday cake between the games. In the second game, Roger Craig was cruising along through six innings. In the seventh, though, he ran into trouble so quickly that Stengel didn't have time to get a reliever ready. The Mets lost that game as well. "I keep tellin' myself I'm dreamin' these terrible things that happen," Stengel said after the game. "But I ain't."

In yet another roster shuffling, the Mets sent Ed Bouchee to Syracuse and purchased Rick Herrscher, a utility player. The day after brought the second All-Star game (1962 was the last year baseball held two All-Star games). Richie Ashburn, who hadn't played in the first contest, entered the game in the seventh inning, singled against Hank Aguirre of Detroit and scored a run.

By now, there were rumblings even in the sympathetic press that this team just might be the worst of all time. In an August piece for *Sports Illustrated* entitled "The Worst Baseball Team Ever," Jimmy Breslin recounted some of the events he would chronicle the following year in *Can't Anybody Here Play This Game?* He quoted George Weiss and Don Grant concerning the progress, or lack thereof, of the team: "I've been in baseball since 1919, and this is only the second time I have had a second-division team. My first year in baseball I had the New Haven club and we finished seventh. This year is, I must say, a bit of an experience. No, it is certainly not a funny thing to me. But you could say I am not doing things halfway. When I finally get in the second division, I really get there." Grant said, "It is annoying to lose by one run [the Mets had already lost more than 20 one-run games], but Mrs. Payson and I are pleased with the team's progress. She is perfectly understanding about it. After all, you do not breed a thoroughbred horse overnight."

The debate was not limited to the press, however. Bill Veeck, who had owned the Indians, Browns and White Sox, and whose father had owned the Cubs, knew something about bad baseball, and he spoke wistfully as summer wore on: "They are without a doubt the worst team in the history of baseball. I speak with authority. I had the St. Louis Browns. I also speak with longing. I'd love to spend the rest of the summer around the team. If you couldn't have any fun with the Mets, you couldn't have any fun any place."

August, though, was when things really got interesting. At the beginning of the month, the team released Vinegar Bend Mizell, who retired, and recalled infielder Sammy Drake from Syracuse. Frank Thomas then tied a league record by homering six times in three consecutive games (from August 1st to the 3rd), all Met losses. One of these homers, on August 1st, was the team's second and final grand slam of the season. "It was a twilight game," Thomas recalled. "I put on these yellow glasses that made it look like daylight. I hit the first home run, then the second, and I come into the dugout. Casey says, 'Where'd you get those glasses?' And I said, 'The trainer gave 'em to me.' He said, 'Tell him to order a gross for the other players also.'" However, it came during an 11-9 loss to Philadelphia, in which Mets pitchers (including, as usual, Al Jackson) were victimized by four errors. The next day, Art Mahaffey held the Mets to five hits, four of which were solo homers by Thomas and Throneberry, and helped his own cause with a grand slam as the Phillies won 9-4. The day after, Thomas concluded his home run tear as the team lost to the Reds by the score of 10-8. They made it interesting with another abortive late-inning rally. Down by six in the bottom of the seventh, Thomas, Throneberry and Coleman homered, putting up four runs, but it was not enough.

Then they broke their losing streak by winning three in a row, all home games against the Reds. These included a doubleheader sweep on August 4, the only one they managed all season besides the two against the Braves in May. The Mets won the first game 9-1, scoring six times in the first inning. In addition to Coleman's second homer in two days, Throneberry hit his fourth in three games and Neal added one. Craig went the distance to pull his record to 6-17. In between the games, the crowd was entertained by hundreds of balloons and a parade of young women vying to be "Miss Rheingold of 1963."

The loss upset Reds manager Fred Hutchinson, whose trauma was only beginning. Don Zimmer, now playing for the Reds, recalled the nightcap: "Now you have to remember, the Reds were the defending National League champions in 1962, and to lose to the Mets was unacceptable – especially to Hutch. So Hutch was already hot when we started the second game." Hot Rod Kanehl led off the third with an outstanding bunt up the third base line. Zimmer fielded the ball cleanly, but his throw could not beat the speedy Kanehl. "From the dugout I heard this crash," Zimmer wrote, "and when I looked over, I saw that Hutch had kicked an ammonia bucket clear into the back wall. Guys were scattering all over the place and I knew I didn't want to get anywhere close to Hutch when I came in after the inning was over."

As usual, the Mets fell behind early, but they tied it in the eighth, when Neal tripled and Thomas scored him with a sacrifice fly. Although the Reds loaded the bases in the ninth, they were unable to push any runs across the plate off Ken MacKenzie. Nor were they able to score over the next five innings, despite putting the leadoff man on base three times. The Mets finally won on a Thomas homer (his seventh of the month) off Moe Drabowsky in the fourteenth, eight hours after the start of the first game. Hutchinson was so upset by his team's doubleheader loss that he stayed by himself in the visitors' dugout for half an hour afterward, refusing to leave until all of his players had already boarded the bus. Reds pitcher Jim O'Toole remembered that "Hutch just about went nuts when we lost a doubleheader to them. He told us to be out of the clubhouse in fifteen minutes because if anyone was still there by the time he walked in, they were in deep shit. So everyone ran up those stairs, got dressed without showering, and – boom! – was gone. I'd never seen him so mad. He was totally right. We played like a bunch of women." Hutchinson's mood did not go unnoticed by the Mets. "We were kind of celebrating," said Anderson, "and people brought it to our attention. 'Take a look there in the dugout.' And there he was. He was not going to leave that dugout until every single Cincinnati player had left the clubhouse. I think he had told the trainer or one of the coaches to call him in the dugout when everyone else was gone. He was not going to face those players. Well, we got a kick out of that." Kanehl recalled that Hutchinson "called the locker room and told everybody to get out. Then he demolished it. He broke about every chair in the place." As Zimmer explained to *Sports Illustrated* thirty years later: "If you were playing the Mets you had to win four. Winning three of four wasn't good enough."

The Mets took the Reds again the following day in the first of another doubleheader, as Al Jackson pitched a complete game, aided by Rick Herrscher's only major league homer. However, the team followed up the three-game win streak by losing three in a row. In the second of these losses, on August 6, Jay Hook pitched a gem against the Dodgers, giving up no walks and only five hits. Once again, though, the defense failed the Mets. In the sixth, with the score tied at one, Maury Wills beat out a bunt and then attempted to steal second. A good throw would have caught him, but Chris Cannizzaro threw the ball so high that centerfielder Jim Hickman caught it on the fly. Wills then scored what proved to be the winning run on a Willie Davis grounder, and the Mets lost 2-1. The following day, as Don Drysdale won his eleventh in a row (and Craig Anderson dropped his twelfth), Davis provided another memorable moment. With a runner on first, Davis swung hard at a pitch and his bat took off on a mission of its own. The bat sailed over the Mets' dugout and hit Mrs. Stengel on the arm. "Human nature says that you'd watch the bat go over there," asserted Anderson. "I know I would be watching it go over there. Well, Choo Choo Coleman was going to pick that guy off of first base, and he fires the ball to first. But Throneberry's watching the bat go over there. Ashburn, in right field, is watching the bat. The coach and the runner are watching this bat. The ball rolls out into right field.

The ball's laying out in right field. One of the infielders went and got the ball, and the runner took off and went to second."

This loss was the 82nd of the season, against only 29 victories. In thus clinching a losing season, the Mets, as *SI* noted, were also mathematically eliminated from the pennant race, not that this had been much of a concern to anybody. Rod Kanehl recalled that Stengel called a meeting and said, "You guys can relax now. We're mathematically eliminated from the pennant. You can loosen up now." "So we loosened up," said Kanehl. "We won just eleven more games in the last two months."

There was a limit, though, to how much the team "loosened up." Being pros, they still went out every day to win. Hook remembered being "terribly competitive" the first half of the season, which led him to be extremely upset after losses. He realized, though, that he could not go on like that without becoming a basket case. "That probably hurt me more than helped me, because, you know, you want to be competitive," he recalled. "But every day was a new day. Every day we had the opportunity to go out there and win. I think that's a great life lesson." "Absolutely," confirmed Kanehl on learning of Hook's remarks. "We went out there every day to win the ballgame, with the attitude that we could win the ballgame. It was such a great attitude all year long. Ashburn, you know, he played every inning, every ball, every pitch. Everybody else was the same way." Thomas agreed too, noting that "you play football on a Sunday, and you've got all week to drool about it. With baseball, if you lose today, everything is forgotten because you can play right again tomorrow. You can go out and forget what you did the day before. That's why baseball's such a great game."

In any event, they celebrated by recording their only win of the year in San Francisco, with Craig earning his second complete game victory in a row. Thomas hit his eighth homer of the month, and Mantilla added another. The Mets' infield defense helped, as Mantilla, Neal, Kanehl and Throneberry turned five double plays behind Craig, blunting potential Giant rallies in the sixth, seventh and eighth. Giant bonus baby Bob Garibaldi, though, continued his dominance of the Mets (perhaps the only team he pitched well against), retiring nine hitters in a row. The next day, things returned to normal, as Jack Sanford went to 5-0 over the Mets, with Thomas making an error and getting picked off.

On August 10, the Mets visited Crosley Field in Cincinnati, where they were destined to be winless all year. In the third, Al Jackson gave up a double to Frank Robinson, retired the next batter, with Robinson moving to third, and then walked Don Pavletich. With one out and runners at the corners, the infield moved in, anticipating an inning-ending double play ground ball. Jackson induced Hank Foiles to hit a grounder directly to Throneberry, who had time to do one of two things. He could either step on first and throw to second for the double play, or he could throw to second and then take the relay at first for the double play, either of which would have ended the inning. Instead, he threw home in an effort to get Robinson at the plate. His throw arrived too late, and the Reds now had runners on first and second and a run in, still with only one out. Jackson walked the next batter on four pitches, loading the bases. Bearing down, he got Don Blasingame to hit another double play ground ball, which Kanehl booted, allowing a run to score. Now the bases were still loaded, two runs were in and there was still only one out. Jim Maloney, the Reds' pitcher, hit another ground ball to Kanehl, who fielded it cleanly this time and attempted to force Blasingame at second. Unfortunately, Blasingame was running with the pitch and he arrived just ahead of Kanehl's toss. In the meantime, the third run had scored, the bases were *still* loaded and there was *still* only one out. Leo Cardenas hit yet another double-play ball, this time to shortstop Neal, who for some reason chose to bypass the double play and throw directly to first. He got the second out, but another run scored on the play, and there were now men on second and third. Jackson steeled himself and got the next man out to end the inning. He had given up four runs, despite the fact that he had caused four batters to hit into what should have been inning-ending double plays and had given up only one hit – Robinson's leadoff double – which got out of the infield. Not even Throneberry's three-run homer and yet another by Thomas could prevent an 8-4 defeat.

The following day, Throneberry defended his decision to try for Robinson at the plate, telling the *New York Times*: "[The fans] will probably call me stupid for that, but baseball fans may not understand as much as they think. If Robinson slides the way he's supposed to slide, the throw gets him. But he comes in head-first and all he gives the catcher to touch is fingers. So I'm a bum 'cause he slides wrong." Richie Ashburn, who had watched it all from centerfield, had his own thoughts on the matter, stating, "I don't know what's going on, but I know I've never seen it before."

Nor did Jackson's travails end with that inning. Stengel, in order to spare him any further trauma, lifted him and directed Ray Daviault to pitch the fourth. However, he failed to tell Jackson, who went to the mound and prepared to make his first warmup pitch as the public address announcer said, "Now pitching for New York, number 35, Ray Daviault."

Jay Hook then lost a heartbreaker the next day. For eight innings, he held the Reds to one run on three hits and five walks. In the ninth, though, they pushed a two-out run across the plate. The Mets, who scored their only run on a 400-foot homer by Throneberry, left nine men on base against Reds ace Bob Purkey, who went to 17-4 with the win. The Reds closed out the series by pounding Craig 8-4, thus winning all nine games at Crosley Field that season.

On August 14, four days after throwing four unsuccessful double play balls in one inning, Al Jackson was victimized again. For fourteen innings, he turned in one of the true gems of which he was capable, holding Philadelphia to just one run. The Mets failed to cash in several times, such as when they loaded the bases with no outs in extra innings but failed to score when Joe Pignatano grounded into an inning-ending double play. In the top of the fifteenth, the Phillies scored two runs off Jackson when Throneberry misplayed a bad hop ground ball for his third error of the game. Throneberry then blew a chance to make up for his miscue when he struck out with runners on first and third, and the Mets lost 3-1. Jackson, who had thrown 215 pitches in his fifteen innings of work, showed remarkable equanimity, telling the *Times*, "The guys have played real good behind me. Why say something when they boot one?" Stengel, though, was less than happy, stating that Throneberry "ended up swinging on balls they was gonna walk him on." Another unhappy party was Craig Anderson, whom Stengel warmed up six different times during the game but didn't use.

The loss was the fifth in what was to become a thirteen-game losing streak, the second longest of the season. During the streak, which began after the Mets beat the Giants on August 8, they lost three times each to the Reds, Phillies, Dodgers and Pirates and did not win again until August 21, when they took the second game of a doubleheader with the Pirates.

The first game of that doubleheader, the thirteenth loss, featured another late-inning blown lead. With the Mets leading 6-4 in the ninth, Anderson (who hadn't won a game in over three months and wouldn't ever win another) retired the first batter but then gave up a hit and a walk. Stengel pulled Anderson and called in Craig to get the last two outs. Craig got off to a bad start, though, walking Roberto Clemente to fill the bases. This brought former Met Jim Marshall to the plate with the bases full and only one out. Craig induced Marshall to hit an easy grounder to Mantilla at third. Faced with the choice of throwing to second and starting a game-ending double play or firing to the catcher to nail the lead runner at home, Mantilla instead went to first base. His wild throw wound up in right field, and three runs crossed the plate, Clemente scoring all the way from first. After facing just two batters, Craig was tagged with his twentieth loss. "I had my mind made up to go home with the ball," said Mantilla after the game. "Then I got it and threw it away. I don't know why. I wanted to go find a hole in the ground and hide."

However, the second game allowed Marv Throneberry to be the hero for once. In the fifth inning, third base coach Solly Hemus was ejected by umpire Frank Walsh for arguing. "Hemus was the coach who would fight the umpires when he felt they were wrong, which was often," reported George Vecsey. "He and Ashburn had developed a theory that the umpires 'screw us because we're horseshit.' This theory got him excused early from several games." With Hemus' departure, Stengel moved first base coach Cookie Lavagetto to third and summoned the veteran Gene Woodling to coach at first. Then Stengel sent Woodling up to pinch hit and needed another first base coach. Ashburn suggested Throneberry, who was cheered when he made his way to the coach's box. In the bottom of the ninth, the Mets were down 4-1, with the Pirates' star reliever, Elroy Face (who had already saved the first game), on the mound. Ashburn led off with a single, and after two outs, Joe Christopher and Jim Hickman followed with hits as Ashburn scored. Now it was 4-2, and the fans began chanting "We want Throneberry!" Stengel obligingly called in Throneberry from the box and gave him an encouraging pat on the rump. As Throneberry approached the plate, Stengel himself went out to the coach's box to replace him. Throneberry then hit a three-run homer into the right field seats, and the Mets won 5-4. Many fans remained after the game to celebrate, and some of the other players gleefully ejected Throneberry from the clubhouse in his torn underwear and told him to go meet his public.

Three days later, the Mets won their only game against the Dodgers at the Polo Grounds, one of only two wins against Los Angeles that season. Jay Hook's 6-3 triumph (his last win of the year) over Don Drysdale, who would win the Cy Young Award that year. The score was tied at three in the eighth, the Met runs coming on solo homers by Throneberry, Kanehl and Coleman. After the

Mets loaded the bases against Drysdale with no outs, Kanehl singled home the lead run, but Throneberry was thrown out at the plate. Pinch-hitter Gene Woodling singled, scoring a run, and Hook beat out a drag bunt, scoring another. Hook then pitched a perfect ninth, helped out by fine fielding from Throneberry, of all people. After two infield assists, Throneberry made a diving grab of a line drive off the bat of Willie Davis to end the contest. The game was preceded by a tribute to Gil Hodges, who had been out of the lineup for weeks due to his kidney stone. "Richie Ashburn rode onto the field to present Gil Hodges a golf cart," Herman Weiskopf reported in *Sports Illustrated*. "As he put-putted past the dugout, Ashburn yelled, 'how do you stop this thing?'"

Although Hodges was an obvious fan favorite, even though he wasn't playing, the gritty Ashburn was also a hero, especially in the second half. The fans could certainly see the effort he gave on the field, but there was more to him than his hitting and fielding. Jay Hook recalled that after his July 15 win over the Giants, catcher Chris Cannizzaro asked him what he thought of the way the pitches were called. "I said, 'I thought you called a good game,'" Hook related. "'We were throwing more fastballs than we normally have.' He said, 'Well, I didn't call the game. Richie Ashburn called the game.' I said, 'What do you mean?' He said, 'Before the game, Richie came to me, and he said, "Chris, I want to call all the pitches today."' I don't know what [signals] he used, whether he raised his hand or stepped, or whatever. But he would signal every pitch to Cannizzaro, and Chris would give me the signal. Richie came up later and said, 'What did you think of the game I called?' I said, 'Gee, I wish you'd call every game.'"

The home win against the Dodgers was the first of a three-game set. The Mets followed their moment of triumph by getting buried 8-2 and 16-5. In the second game, the Dodgers pounded Craig and MacKenzie, with Junior Gilliam, Willie Davis, Tommie Davis and Ron Fairly all homering. In the finale, the Dodgers pounded everybody. Twelve of the Dodgers' sixteen runs were unearned; Craig Anderson, who took the loss, was charged with eleven runs, but only three were earned. However, the Dodgers also provided the home crowd with some badly-needed comic relief when, taking a page from the Mets' book, a Dodger baserunner was caught off second base after a flyout to the outfield; he'd wandered off, thinking the flyout was the end of the inning. In fact, there were only two outs, although the more alert Mets took care of that by tagging the errant runner to retire the side.

During this time, people began to notice that the number of one-run losses was piling up. They ultimately finished with 39 one-run defeats, six of which occurred in the nightmarish seventeen-game losing streak back in May and June. Ashburn explained that "Casey used his bench well enough to keep the games close until the late innings. There just wasn't enough talent available to win them." Hook remembered that "I lost thirteen games by one run. The motto I coined that year was, 'Don't give up a run 'cause you'll lose a chance for a tie.'"

Of course, as Breslin pointed out early in the month when the team was 28-79, one-run losses were hardly the only problem: "[Some people] say the Mets have a poor record because they lose so many one-run games. They point out that the Mets have lost 28 games by one run so far. However, this figure also means the Mets lost 51 other games by more than one run. Whether the Mets lose by a run or by 14 runs (and they have done this, too), it doesn't matter. They still lose. They lose at night and in the daytime and they lose so much that the only charge you can't make against them is that their pitchers throw spitters. 'Spitters?' Stengel says. 'I can't get them to throw regular pitches good.'"

The hundredth loss of the season, on August 29, was another one-run decision, as Hook went ten innings in losing 3-2 to the Phillies. At one point, Charlie Neal fielded a ground ball and threw wildly to Throneberry at first. Throneberry had to come off the bag into foul territory to make the catch, which he did just as the batter went by him. Throneberry attempted to tag the runner as he went by but slipped as he did so, missing the tag and falling on his face.

The following day, the Mets lost again to the Phillies, 8-7, a game in which Frank Thomas' season-best eighteen-game hitting streak came to a conclusion. During the streak, Thomas batted .378 with four doubles, two triples, five homers, sixteen runs batted in, eleven runs scored, and a slugging percentage of .689. Unfortunately, the Mets won only four of the eighteen games.

On September 1, major league rosters expanded as teams were allowed to call up minor leaguers and add other players. Weiss purchased two more pitchers, Larry Foss from the Pirates and Galen Cisco from the Red Sox. Stengel threw them in at the deep end, calling on each to start games. Cisco, who went 1-1 in four September appearances, wound up as one of only three Mets pitchers without a losing record (another of whom was Lefty Bob Miller, who, like Cisco, was with the team only briefly), though he took care of that by posting 7-15 and 6-19 records in 1963 and 1964. He was also the only pitcher with an ERA under 4.00. The Mets also brought up Ed Kranepool at the end of the season, giving the fans a glimpse of the future. Kranepool was still only seventeen when he came up, 23 years younger than Gene Woodling, and he appeared in three games, managing one hit in six at-bats.

On September 2, the Mets celebrated Throneberry's birthday by beating the Cardinals 4-3, breaking a five-game losing streak. The celebration continued into the clubhouse after the game and culminated in another folkloric Met moment when the team produced a cake in Throneberry's honor. Throneberry complained that he had not been given a piece of the cake, to which Stengel responded, "We was gonna give you a piece, Marv, but we was afraid you'd drop it." Of course, in other versions, there was no cake, and Stengel delivered his immortal punch line when Throneberry complained because Stengel had received a cake for his birthday in July and Throneberry did not. Naturally, Throneberry remembered the event differently, allowing him to again vent his spleen on New York sportswriters: "Casey got credit for a line I made up. It was Casey's birthday, July 30, and we got him a cake and I said to him, 'They were gonna get me a cake too, but they were afraid I'd drop it.' It was reported that Casey said it to me, but the writers got that one wrong, too." Of course, Throneberry's version is highly unlikely, since his birthday would have had to have come before Stengel's, when in fact it was six weeks afterward. Lindsey Nelson also recalled a distinct scenario, writing that "Stengel's birthday was in late July, and there was a big celebration, complete with cake. About six weeks later, Marv also had a birthday, but it was ignored. He grumbled to Casey that nobody had thought to give him a cake. Casey scratched his chin, looked at him a moment, and said, 'Well, we was going to get you one, but we figured you'd drop it.'"

Six days later, on September 8, Craig Anderson lost his seventeenth decision, his sixteenth in a row since his two wins in the long-ago doubleheader on May 12. Hook had started the game and shut Houston down through six innings. With the Mets up 2-0, Ray Daviault came in to pitch the seventh, and Houston scored on two infield errors and a base hit. Hal Smith homered off Daviault to tie the game in the eighth, but the Mets got the lead back in the top of the ninth when Joe Christopher tripled and scored on Kanehl's single. Daviault gave way to Willard Hunter, who surrendered up singles to Bob Lillis and Johnny Temple to start the bottom of the ninth. Stengel lifted Hunter and inserted Anderson, who got Joey Amalfitano to hit into a double play but then walked the next man he faced, Norm Larker. "[Stengel] made me walk him," says Anderson. "Stengel came out and says, 'I want you to put him on. He's the winning run but I don't care. Put him on.'" Now there were runners at the corners with two outs. The next hitter, Bob Aspromonte, hit a short fly ball to left, which Frank Thomas dove for unsuccessfully. Lillis, the lead runner, scored as Larker headed for third. Thomas might have thrown in time to catch Larker, but instead he decided to try to nail Aspromonte at second. However,

Aspromonte had not gone for second and was, in fact, standing a few feet off first. Because there was no play to be made at second, neither shortstop Kanehl or second baseman Neal was covering the bag. Thomas' throw whizzed by the unattended base as Larker rounded third and broke for home. Thomas' throw was the Mets' fifth error of the game. "I don't know what the hell he was doing out there, but he didn't catch the ball," recalls Anderson. "He picks it up and throws it into the Mets dugout." Throneberry, backing up the play, had a chance to beat Larker with a good throw but instead held the ball just long enough for Larker to slide across the plate with the winning run. "Larker came in from third when Marv took what was practically a time-out to throw," wrote Jerry Mitchell. "And I got the loss because [Stengel] made me put Larker on," asserted Anderson. "And I had come in there with nobody out and got two outs. All I had to do was pitch to the next batter. Let me pitch to *him*, you know."

The loss was the first game of a doubleheader, and the Mets dropped the nightcap, 6-5, as Roger Craig and Dick Farrell gave up a combined 25 hits and eight walks. The teams finished nine innings tied at five, and the Mets went out in order in the tenth. In the bottom, though, Craig gave up a leadoff single to Bob Lillis, who moved to second on a sacrifice by Al Spangler and to third on a Roman Mejias groundout. Craig then uncorked a wild pitch, and Lillis scored the winning run. It was the 23rd loss of the season for Craig, who gave up six runs on twelve hits, six walks and the wild pitch. The next day, the two teams played a curfew-shortened 7-7 draw, which, mercifully, was never completed. Sherman "Roadblock" Jones, recently recalled from the minors, pitched an inning, giving up two runs. It was his first big league action in more than four months, and his last.

Finally, the last home stand was at hand, ten games which were to close out the Polo Grounds' existence. The Mets got the ball rolling with a 5-2 loss to Milwaukee, their seventh in a row (not counting the tie). They then took two of three from the defending champion Reds, scoring 24 runs in the three games. Craig got the win in game one when he came on in relief, then he pitched a complete game for the win in the series closer. After the Reds left, the Mets dropped four in a row to the Colt 45s in two doubleheader sweeps, during which they set a season record for losses at home. The Cubs came in for the last three-game home series and split the first two.

The final home game of the season was the rubber match on September 23. To pay tribute to the fans before the game, someone in the organization came up with the idea of giving the players lettered placards, so that when the team held up the placards, the letters would read "WE LOVE YOU METS FANS TOO." "Can you imagine anybody doing that today?" asked Anderson in wonderment in 2002. "At the beginning of the series, they said, 'We would like for all the players to hold up a letter and run out on the field, "We love you Met fans too."' We had this clubhouse meeting prior to this. The players really didn't want to do it. I didn't care one way or the other, but some of the veteran players were a little more uptight about being made fun of by holding placards out there." As always, though, it was Stengel to the rescue. "Stengel came in and made a 15-minute speech that began, 'You guys don't have to do this,'" remembers Anderson. "Fifteen minutes later we *ran* out there with our placards. I don't know what the hell Casey said, but we did it." After the players lined up in formation and held up their placards, Stengel ran to the end of the line and held up his own card, on which was printed an exclamation point.

The game was also to have marked another momentous occasion, the last game played in the Polo Grounds, as the team was scheduled to open Shea Stadium the following spring. The fans watched Ed Kranepool get his only hit of the season, a double down the leftfield line. After the business with the placards and the game itself (a 2-1 Mets victory, with Craig earning his third straight win when he came on in relief of Righty Bob Miller in the ninth), the public address system played "Till We Meet Again" as the paid attendance of ten thousand fans stood and cheered. Stengel was awarded home plate and made a few remarks. He recalled playing for and against John McGraw there, as well as facing pitchers like Christy Mathewson. "They may tear it down, if they ever get around to it, which you never know, but they'll always talk about it. Years from now the newspaper fellas will come up to that young fella Kranepool, an' say, 'Did you ever play in the Polo Grounds, Mr. Kranepool?' 'Indeed I did,' he'll say. 'Why, I made my first major league hit at the Polo Grounds!'"

Before taking his leave, Stengel thanked the broadcast crew for having done such a fine job announcing the team's games on behalf of the club's sponsor, Ballantine Beer. The only trouble was that Ballantine was the Yankees' benefactor; the Mets, of course, were sponsored by Rheingold. As Stengel then turned and walked 600 feet to the Mets' clubhouse behind the centerfield fence, the PA system played "Auld Lang Syne," as many of the fans wept openly in the stands. "And we all stood outside the clubhouse and we cried," Kanehl recalled. "I sat up in [Stengel's] office and cried like a baby. Most everybody cried. If you play 'Auld Lang Syne,' I'll cry every time."

However, as with virtually everything else that season, there was a problem. It was soon discovered that the Polo Grounds farewell was premature. Shea Stadium was sinking into the ground, and there was absolutely no way it would be ready for the 1963 season. This meant that the Polo Grounds, intended to be the Mets' home only for 1962, had to be used for their 81 home dates in 1963 as well. At the end of the 1963 season, they held the exact same farewell ceremony – Stengel was presented with home plate, the PA played "Auld Lang Syne" as Stengel walked to the centerfield clubhouse, and Kanehl cried again.

CHAPTER THIRTEEN – JOURNEY'S END

"We've got to learn to stay out of triple plays." – *Casey Stengel, manager of the New York Mets*

As their manager had predicted, the Mets finished not seventh, not eighth, not even ninth, but in Chicago. After posting their 117th defeat to Warren Spahn in Milwaukee, followed by Roger Craig's twenty-fourth loss the next day, in which the team broke the season loss record set by the 1916 Philadelphia Athletics, the Mets played out the string with three games at Wrigley Field. They dropped the series opener, their 119th loss, before winning the next day, only their fortieth victory. Righty Bob Miller narrowly avoided a record for pitching futility. His record to that point was 0-12. No other National League pitcher had ever gone 0-13 in a season, and only one American Leaguer had done it. Miller's trip to immortality was not to be, though, as he beat the Cubs for his only win. However, it didn't look that way for a while. When Miller loaded the bases, Stengel came out for a conference. Miller chased him off, telling the manager to "let me lose it by myself." Stengel did, and Miller pitched out of the jam. Finally he got some support. With Frank Thomas on second and the score tied in the seventh, Jim Hickman singled, but Thomas fell down rounding third with the potential lead run and was tagged out. However, Throneberry came to the rescue with a two-out double, scoring Hickman. Miller managed to hold the lead and the Mets won 2-1. Only 595 diehard Cubs fans showed up to witness the event.

Not only was the stadium empty, but so was the victors' clubhouse. The day before the game, the writers covering the Mets were pulled off the team to cover the thrilling pennant race between the Giants and Dodgers, which ultimately had to be settled by a playoff. "I waited for the reporters in front of my locker, and nobody came," Miller said later. "When I lost they were always there. Now that I won I was all alone. It could only happen with the Mets." Maury Allen wrote that "Miller had saved his finest hour for an empty theater without a critic in sight." Paul Zimmerman postulated that "In the Mets' first season, every bit as much as Marvelous Marv Throneberry symbolized the team's fielding skill, Bob L. Miller symbolized the team's pitching skill. By Met standards, he was absolute perfection – twelve consecutive defeats unmarred by victory – until the next-to-last day of the season. Then Miller committed his first, and last, victory of the season."

Finally, things concluded on September 30, a chilly day in Chicago. It was just like a typical Mets game, only more so. They went into the eighth inning trailing 5-1, having done little against Cubs starter Bob Buhl. However, they showed signs of life when the little-used Sammy Drake led off with a single (only his tenth hit of the year, all singles) and Ashburn followed with another, moving Drake to second. Catcher Joe Pignatano came up with no outs, two on and the tying run on deck. He hit a short fly ball toward right field. Drake and Ashburn, thinking it would fall safely, took off. However, second baseman Ken Hubbs caught the ball to retire Pignatano and threw to first baseman Ernie Banks, doubling up Ashburn, who had almost reached second. Banks then threw to shortstop Andre Rogers, nailing Drake, who had already rounded third, completing the triple play. The Mets went quietly in the ninth, ending the game and the season with their 120th loss. There could not have been a more appropriate conclusion. Neither Ashburn, Drake nor Pignatano ever appeared in another major league game, the triple play thus also marking the denouement to three big league careers.

Pignatano, the unintentional instigator, said that "I had a lousy career, so it was fitting that I was on a lousy team to finish it up. It was a long, long two-and-a-half months with the Mets, but it was fun, and so was my career, so it was fitting that I ended it in a losing game, our 120th loss of the year – worst in this century – and on the last at-bat of my career, I hit into a triple play. Perfect."

The end of the season brought another of the year's historical curiosities. The Dodgers and the Giants finished in a dead heat for first. Therefore, as they had in 1951 when both were still in New York, they met in a three-game playoff to determine who would face the Yankees in the World Series. Once again, the Giants won, although this time they did it 3,000 miles from the Polo Grounds. Although the playoff took place after the season had ended, the results counted in the standings. This meant that the Mets fell behind by a further game and a half even after the season was over. The Giants wound up 103-62. The Mets, at the other end of the spectrum, finished at 40-120, an unbelievable 60½ games behind San Francisco. Houston, the other expansion team, had a record of 64-96, which was good enough for eighth place, 24 games ahead of New York. The Cubs, who were involved in so many memorable moments of the Mets' debut season, were in ninth at 59-103, tied for the worst record in franchise history, but still 18 games ahead of the Mets.

The Perfesser, subdued for once, addressed his troops after the loss, telling them, "This was a group effort. No one player could've done all this." Lou Effrat of the *Times* asked Stengel whether, despite all the losing, the season had been fun. Stengel responded, "I would have to say no to that one." He later elaborated, stating, "I have to say that it wasn't any fun. It had to be bad. I had to get used to losing all over again. It was worse than in those seasons in Brooklyn an' Boston. It was shocking because we didn't win at least 50 games. There were at least 10 easy lost that should have been won. Imagine 40 games I won with this club – 40. That's what I used to lose with the Yankees!"

Sports Illustrated's Herman Weiskopf offered this year-end summary: "When Casey Stengel is back home in Glendale, Calif., this winter, he will be able to recall many highlights from this season. Just recently, for example, he suffered through his 2,500th loss as a manager. And he will certainly recall the high point of the year. That was when the Mets were about to land in New York after a fairly successful road trip. 'O.K., men,' Casey said, 'straighten your ties; you're in ninth place now.' Unfortunately it was a command Casey never got to repeat." Maury Allen was more succinct: "It could have been worse. They might never have gotten out of the elevator."

Joe Pignatano agreed with his manager's dour sentiments, as the triple play was his career finale. Richie Ashburn also made his feelings known. Ashburn jumped up after being called out and ran to the dugout, grabbed his glove and kept going. He stopped long enough to tell Kanehl, "That's a fine fucking finish to this year. I'll see ya next year." "And he went right on up the ramp to the clubhouse," said Kanehl. "And by the time the game was over, he was packed and gone. We thought we'd see him the next spring, but we never saw him again. [The triple play] was his last play in the big leagues."

Despite hitting .306 and being offered a reported $10,000 raise to return in 1963, Ashburn chose instead to take a broadcasting job with his beloved Phillies for far less money. Don Zimmer, Ashburn's teammate with the Cubs in 1961 and briefly with the Mets in 1962, saw him in spring training the following year. He asked how Ashburn could have quit after hitting .300. Ashburn responded that the Mets were sure to lose 100 games again in 1963 and he couldn't bear to be a part of that. Jimmy Breslin put it another way, reporting that Ashburn "meant he was taking a big cut in pay for the privilege of not having to go through another year with the Mets." Ashburn also rejected the idea of being a part-time player, a realistic possibility considering the club's hopes for Jim Hickman and Joe Christopher. "If I have to be a bench warmer for the Mets," he told a reporter, "I'll commit suicide."

Ashburn was selected by the writers as the club's Most Valuable Player, for which he was awarded a 24-foot Owens powerboat. Ashburn accepted both the award and the events which followed with typical humor. "Most Valuable Player on the worst team ever?" he asked. "Just how do they mean that?" The boat presented another conundrum, since Ashburn lived in Nebraska. He also still had a home in Philadelphia, so he moored the boat across the Delaware River in Ocean City, New Jersey. Unfortunately, a short time after, the boat sank. "But it didn't just sink," he recalled later. "The sucker took five or six days to go down." Apparently the drainage plug had never been installed. "So they dragged it up, and I sold it," Ashburn explained to *Sports Illustrated*. "Oh, and the guy I sold it to – his check bounced." Don Zimmer, who also recalled the story in his memoirs, said, "That pretty much typified what the 1962 Mets were all about."

Ashburn's boat was not the only nautical craft to figure into Mets lore than season. Early in the year, the Howard Clothing store (which also provided the boat Ashburn won) erected a sign in left field just by the foul pole. As part of its promotion, the company decreed that Met batters hitting the sign and the adjacent circles on the wall would receive points, and the player with the most points at year's end would also win a boat. Stengel complained mightily about this, stating: "We get to the season, and I might need a couple of games to finish higher and what am I going to get? Everybody will be standing up there and going, whoom! Just trying to win themselves a nice boat, while I'm sittin' there hopin' they'll butcher boy the ball onto the ground and get me a run or two. I don't like it at all." In an unsuccessful attempt to mollify the manager, the Howard company erected a similar sign in right field.

Ashburn remembered that ball boys were stationed down both the first- and third-base lines for the purpose of monitoring whether any hit ball landed in one of the circles. "Well, I hit one ball that I know was in the circle, but the ball boy didn't see it," Ashburn said thirty years later. "And there was no appeals process. That ball would have given me enough points to win the boat. So I should have won two boats that season. But what the hell, I didn't even know what to do with one. I lived in Nebraska." Another keen competitor for the boat was Frank Thomas. On one occasion, after watching Thomas jerk foul ball after foul ball down the leftfield line toward the sign, Stengel came out to the box and told him, "If you want to be a sailor, join the Navy!" "When he said that, I had to get out of the batter's box and try to get my composure," recalled Thomas with a laugh.

In any event, neither Ashburn nor Thomas won the second boat. That honor went to none other than Marv Throneberry, who had hit the sign in right four times and put two other balls inside the circle. He was presented with his boat, a Chris Craft cabin cruiser valued at over $6,000, between games of a September doubleheader with Houston. Fewer than 1,500 fans were there to watch the presentation. Walter Pullis pointed out that "they had to make up some games, and they played two doubleheaders with Houston in September, and the one on September 18, they had 1,800 people there. The one on September 20, which was an afternoon doubleheader – I came home from school and watched the Mets lose both games – was like fifteen hundred. And that was the day Throneberry got the boat in between games. There was no one in the stands to watch it. That must have been really weird."

Throneberry, who still lived in Collierville, Tennessee, miles away from any navigable water, was in fine humor, telling the tiny crowd that he and the similarly-landlocked Ashburn would "both sail our boats all over the bathtub." Ashburn said, "We're going to arm these boats and invade Cuba."

Throneberry's good spirits abruptly vanished a few days later during a conversation with Robert Cannon, legal advisor to the Major League Baseball Players Association. Cannon said that unlike Ashburn, whose boat was a gift bestowed upon him by the writers, Throneberry had earned his by winning it in a competition of skill. Since the boat represented earnings, he would have to declare its full value ("To who?" asked Throneberry, "the Coast Guard?") and pay taxes on it. Throneberry bemoaned his fate to

Jimmy Breslin: "In my whole life I never believed they'd be as rough a year as there was my last season. And here I am, I'm still not out of it. I got a boat in a warehouse someplace and the man tells me I got to pay taxes on it and all we got around here is a filled-up bathtub and maybe a crick or two. I think maybe I'll be able to sell it off someplace. I think you could say prospects is all right. But I still don't know what to do about that tax thing."

Speaking long afterward, Ashburn put the year into a positive perspective. When the team reported to spring training, he thought things would be tough, but the team would score some runs. He pointed out that although the pitching and defense were bad, the hitting was not terrible, and in fact, the '62 Mets' home run total was not bested by another Met team until the 1986 World Series champions. "I'll tell you, it was a bunch of good guys," he added. "Usually on a losing team you have dissension. We didn't have any of that. We were miserable sometimes, but we didn't take it out on anybody, and we didn't blame each other. I give Casey a lot of credit for that. Stengel was a guy who deflected all the criticism you would have with that kind of team. Any losing team I've ever been on had several things going on. One, the players gave up. Or they hated the manager. Or the fans turned into wolves. But there was none of this with the Mets. Nobody stopped trying. The manager was absolutely great, nobody grumbled about being with the club, and the fans we had, well, there haven't been fans like this in baseball history. So we lose 120 games and there isn't a gripe on the club. It was remarkable."

Ken MacKenzie, speaking right after the season, had a similar view. "You hear about clubs that win pennants. What happens is one guy picks up if another lets down. We've worked in reverse. We found a different way to lose every day. I don't think we were quite as bad as we looked. Our pitching had a pattern. Error, base hit, error, base hit. When you're pitching good ball and there's an error behind you, you bend your back and make the pitches. This is exactly what we didn't do. We probably set a record for unearned runs. [Note: They did not. However, the team's 147 unearned runs were the most in baseball since the World War II-era Philadelphia Athletics, who gave up 168 in 1945. Since 1962, no other team has come within twenty unearned runs of the Original Mets; the 1974 Chicago Cubs were the closest, with 126.] That's no alibi for a pitcher, not when he's giving up the runs after the error."

Frank Thomas, though, "had fun on the Mets. I happened to have a good year. I played 156 games and hit 34 homers and drove in 94 runs batting cleanup. In one three-game period, I hit six homers, hitting two homers in each game. I just missed hitting another and setting the major league record. That was exciting. Because of my star status, I hoped I'd make a lot of money in New York through endorsements. I made about $2,000."

Not everyone viewed the season with such equanimity, though. One outspoken critic was Ed Bouchee, whose bitterness continued long after the season ended. "I resented the portrayal of the 1962 Mets as a comedy act," he said. "But it was a circus. I don't really think there were good things about being on that Mets team. I'm not even sure the Mets fans were as great as they were cracked up to be. I just remember that they liked to boo. But I didn't hate the players. We got along well. There was no division between old and young players and no infighting between those who played and those who didn't. We were all in the boat [presumably no pun intended] together."

Nor was Throneberry prepared to look at the bright side. When it was suggested to him that the team should be better in 1963 since the players had had a year together, he responded, "You know, they's teams been playing together forty years and they's still finishin' down in last place or something. Just because you have a team, that don't mean it got to finish on top."

The Mets certainly knew what Throneberry was talking about. The first year expansion schedule called for the teams to play each other 18 times, for a total of 162 games. In setting a modern record for losses in a season, the Mets had posted a respectable record against only one other National League team, the Cubs, winning nine times against nine losses. Their next-best showing was versus the Braves, against whom they were 6-12 (five of those wins coming in May, with the sixth on June 19, after which the Braves took the final eight games), followed by the Reds and Cardinals at 5-13, the Giants and Phillies at 4-14, and the Colt 45s, the other expansion team, against whom they went only 3-13, with two postponements. Against the Dodgers and Pirates, they were a woeful 2-16. Four of the losses to the Dodgers were by scores of 17-8, 13-6, 17-3 and 16-5.

The Mets' futility, particularly against good teams, was remarked upon by players on those teams. "Playing the Mets was kind of funny," said Pirates infielder Dick Schofield. "Casey Stengel would be in the other dugout sleeping, and since they had drafted a lot of old guys, we thought we should beat them every game. When we didn't, it was frustrating." Reds pitcher Jim Brosnan was blunter: "Pitching against the Mets was one of my pleasures in the 1962 season. I didn't have to pay attention to what I was doing to strike them out."

Of their 80 home games, the Mets lost 58, setting another mark for futility. In fact, they had a winning home record against only one team, a 5-4 showing against the Reds. They also dropped 62 of their 80 road games (another record), again finishing ahead against only one team, edging the Cubs 5-4 at Wrigley Field. They failed to win a single road game against the same Cincinnati team they'd bested at home, and they only had one road win each against Los Angeles, Pittsburgh and lowly Houston. Aided by the peculiar Polo Grounds dimensions, the Mets hit twice as many home runs (93) at home as they did on the road (46), where they managed not much more than a third of the total of their opponents (120), who also connected for 72 homers in New York. The 192 total home runs given up by Mets pitching (49 more than the ninth-place Cubs) established another NL record.

They also wound up on the losing end of seventeen doubleheader sweeps, while sweeping only three themselves (two against Milwaukee in the halcyon days of mid-May and the third against the Reds in August, resulting in Fred Hutchinson's tantrum). They were 18-39 in games decided by one run and 4-13 in extra-inning matches. Their longest winning streak was three games, which they did twice, while compiling separate losing strings of seventeen, thirteen, eleven, nine, seven (twice), five (three times) and four (four times) games.

In addition, certain players were able to elevate their personal statistics at the Mets' expense. The Giants' Willie Mays and Willie McCovey feasted on New York pitching all season. Mays, who batted .298 against the rest of the league, torched Met pitchers for a .346 clip (27 hits in 78 at-bats), eight of his league-leading 49 homers, and 23 runs batted in. McCovey, who hit .283 against the other eight teams, batted .357 against New York, with four of his 20 homers and 11 of his 54 RBIs. Braves star Henry Aaron was even better. He hit safely in 16 of 18 games against the Mets, batting .400 (28 hits in 70 at-bats) with nine homers, 28 RBIs, five doubles and ten walks (which raised his on-base percentage versus the Mets to .475). His homers and RBIs against the Mets accounted for a fifth of his total homers (45) and almost a quarter of his RBIs (128). Ernie Banks and Don Demeter went deep seven times against the Mets (out of total counts of 37 and 29), respectively, while Eddie Mathews and Frank Howard connected five times each (four of Mathews' homers were against Roger Craig). Giant pitcher and Cy Young runner-up Jack Sanford beat the Mets five times without a loss; in those five wins, three of which were complete games, he surrendered a total of three earned runs in 40 innings (an ERA of 0.675) and twice struck out nine batters. Dodger shortstop Maury Wills, the NL Most Valuable Player, hit six home runs all year, four in the Polo Grounds, while three of Curt Flood's twelve came from Met pitching. Perhaps no one benefitted more than Cardinal great Stan Musial. Reportedly, Musial, who turned 42 during the season, considered retiring in 1961 but decided to return when he realized he would be playing 36 games against two expansion teams. Musial hit .468 against the Mets (and .313 against the rest of the league), with 22 hits in 47 at-bats, four home runs (in consecutive at-bats, and out of a season total of nineteen) and fifteen RBIs (out of 82). This performance helped Musial to a batting average of .330 (his highest average since 1958, and 42 points better than in 1961), good enough for third in the league.

Of course, the Mets had some statistical gems of their own. In addition to Ashburn's and Thomas' team-leading contributions in average and power, there were Jackson's four shutouts, including a one-hitter against Houston. The Mets' 617 runs and 40 triples (of which Charlie Neal had nine, a club record until 1984) were not equaled until 1969, and the team's 139 home runs would not be bested for 24 years. The Mets came up with nine pinch-hit home runs, a club record until 1983, led by Throneberry, Ed Bouchee and Choo Choo Coleman with two each (with Coleman and Hickman hitting pinch homers in the same game, tying a league record), and Throneberry and Coleman each won games with pinch homers. Thomas also hit safely in eighteen straight games, and Felix Mantilla and Ashburn added streaks of fourteen and thirteen games, respectively.

After the season ended, the experts – real and self-proclaimed – continued to weigh in on whether the '62 Mets had been the worst baseball team of all time. Since the Cleveland Spiders had finished the NL 1899 season with a record of 20-134, 80 games out of first, the consensus was that the Mets were the worst team of the twentieth century. In particular, Bill Veeck continued to offer his views. When Veeck owned the Browns (whom he once described as "a charitable organization formed to provide work for the otherwise unemployable"), he resorted to gimmicks to bring people into the ballpark, such as sending Eddie Gaedel, a midget, into a game to pinch hit. Some of Veeck's Browns teams were considered to be the worst ever, with justification. Veeck now reacted with mock umbrage to any comparison between the Mets and his Browns: "I was always secure in the knowledge that when I owned the St. Louis Browns, I had the worst. Now it's different. You can say anything you want, but don't you dare say my Brownies were this bad. There are still a few Browns in the major leagues and this is nine years later. How many Mets do you think are going to be around even two years from now? I'm being soft here. [The Mets] achieved total incompetence in a single year, while the Browns worked industriously for almost a decade to gain equal proficiency." Veeck's exceptions are well-taken – to a point. More than half of the 45 players who saw time with the '62 Mets were indeed gone from the majors within two years, and only four were still around nine years later. However, one can imagine Veeck's jealousy at seeing the Mets' attendance figures, a record for a last-place team, and almost four times what the Browns drew in their last year in St. Louis.

On October 22, 1962, three weeks after the end of the season, President Kennedy declared an embargo on Cuba, triggering the Cuban missile crisis. As the world held its breath, fearing an imminent nuclear war, Lee Allen, the Hall of Fame's official historian, received a letter from a Mets fan, who wanted to know the team's record in games played on Thursday. "My first impulse was to toss it into the waste basket," Allen told Jerry Mitchell. "But it occurred to me that the writer must have had a purpose in asking the question, as unusual a one as I ever received. I checked the records and found that the work of the Mets on Thursdays showed no victories and 15 defeats." Allen notified the fan of the answer to his question. He also sent a copy of the letter and response to the team, stating, "With the world on the verge of ruin, I thought you might be interested in what the Mets' fans are worried about."

The Mets organizational leaders had their own worries. Mrs. Payson put the year in perspective in her own way: "Nothing went right, did it? Well, let's hope it is better. It has to be. I simply cannot stand 120 losses this year. If we can't get anything, we are going to cut those losses down. At least to 119."

The players also predicted improvement in the coming year, although for differing reasons. Charlie Neal, coming off his second bad season in a row, said simply, "I'd better be better." Kanehl opined that "I think we have a faster ball club with a much better defense. The fact that many of the guys have been playing together for a year should be worth ten ball games right there. I'd say we ought to win twenty more than last year." Roger Craig was more straightforward: "Sure we'll be better. How in hell could we be any worse?"

Meanwhile, George Weiss began the re-shaping as soon as the season ended. On October 11, he purchased catcher Norm Sherry and first baseman-outfielder Dick Smith from Los Angeles. On December 1, he sent Righty Bob Miller to Los Angeles in return for infielders Tim Harkness (continually referred to by Stengel as "Harshman") and Larry Burright. In discussing the trade, Paul Zimmerman later described Harkness and Burright as "two young major-leaguers who later, when they realized their full potential, became minor-leaguers."

Ten days later, Felix Mantilla went to Boston for third baseman Elijah "Pumpsie" Green, shortstop Al Moran and pitcher Tracy Stallard. Green was a character – another made-to-be-a-Met ballplayer. He had been the first African-American player for the Red Sox, the last team to integrate (in 1959, twelve years after Jackie Robinson's debut). Green, who was less than impressive over parts of four seasons with the Sox, achieved a level of notoriety during the summer of 1962. After a 13-3 loss to the Yankees in New York, Green and pitcher Gene Conley (who had started the game, lasted two and two-thirds innings and walked in two runs), got off the team bus in the middle of a Bronx traffic jam, ostensibly to use the bathroom, and disappeared. The rest of the team continued to the airport and on to Washington for a series with the Senators. Green and Conley repaired to a local hotel and considered their next move. After a couple of days, they were still debating what to do in the comforts of a local watering hole. Conley suggested that the two of them go to Israel. Green initially agreed, but then he happened to glance at the sports section of the newspaper being read by another customer, which described how he and Conley had deserted the Red Sox and that their careers were in jeopardy. He decided that perhaps he should go to Washington after all. Conley, disgusted, left Green there and took a taxi to Idlewild Airport, where, in the words of one observer, he attempted to board a plane for Israel "with no luggage, no passport, and in what in all candor must be described as a markedly inebriated condition." Green made it to Washington, where he was confronted by reporters asking why he had not gone to Israel after all. "I'm not Jewish," Green replied. He was hit with a heavy fine and demoted to Boston's Louisville farm team soon thereafter. Conley, who ended up tied for the team lead in wins with 15, lasted through the end of 1963 before being released.

Green had one additional claim to fame, which was, of course, his name. One theory was that it was a childhood nickname; another was that he used to be a gas station attendant. Green himself was always coy on the subject. "Almost the first thing people do is ask me how I got my nickname," he said upon coming to the Mets. "I figure eight million people have asked me so far, almost half of them sportswriters. When I get out of baseball, I'm gonna write a book entitled How I Got the Name of Pumpsie and sell it for one dollar. And if everybody who has ever asked me that question buys the book, I will be a millionaire."

In 1963, Green was one of an astounding eleven third basemen the Mets tried, only four of whom had been on the team in

1962. The sixteen players at third in two years would grow to 79 by 1986, and 122 by 1999.

Tracy Stallard, also acquired in the Mantilla trade, had his own moment of immortality, one more permanent than Green's. He threw the pitch that Roger Maris hit for his sixty-first home run in 1961. In 1962, he appeared in a grand total of one game with the Red Sox, retiring all three batters he faced. Stallard stayed with the Mets for two years, compiling a record of 16-37, before being traded after becoming the Mets' third twenty-game loser in 1964. However, compared with the other players Weiss acquired in the fall of 1962, Stallard was a find. Al Moran became the regular shortstop in 1963 but batted only .193 and was gone early in 1964. Pumpsie Green's Met stint lasted seventeen games (the last of his career) as a September call-up. Harkness stepped in at first base, batted .211, and like Moran, disappeared during 1964. Burright played in 44 games, went to the plate 107 times and hit .206 before he too was sent off. Norm Sherry went .136 in 63 games before being released. Dick Smith saw spot duty for two seasons; however, he managed to tie for the team lead in stolen bases in 1964 with a total of six, despite having only 95 plate appearances.

Naturally, the primary beneficiaries of the Mantilla trade were the Red Sox and Mantilla. Although his defense in his only season with the Mets had been shaky at best, his .275 batting average was second only to Ashburn's .306. He also added eleven homers, tied for fourth, and his 59 runs batted in were second (albeit distantly) to Frank Thomas' 94. In 1963, he batted .315 with the Red Sox, but he only appeared in 66 games. In 1964, though, he suddenly exploded, hitting 30 home runs in only 133 games, and the following year he added 18 round-trippers and drove in 92 runs. In 1965, though, he began to fade, and he was done the following year.

Weiss also entered into an agreement with Triple-A Buffalo, which became the Mets' affiliate in place of Syracuse. Many of the 1962 Mets wound up in Buffalo the next year, including Craig

Anderson, Elio Chacon, Ed Bouchee, Bob Moorhead and even Marv Throneberry.

In retrospect, Weiss seems to have been following the path he laid out to *Sports Illustrated* several months after the draft: "It's obvious we can't sit back and wait for younger players to develop. For two or three years we might have to go with one-year men, players good enough for that length of time. By then, we hope, our scouts and farm system will be showing results." Although the Mets had already signed Ed Kranepool and Cleon Jones, with Bud Harrelson and Ron Swoboda soon to follow, it took several years for these players to reach the majors and contribute. In the meantime, Weiss had no choice but to bring in a series of "one-year" (or one-month) men like Norm Sherry and Pumpsie Green.

In January, the Mets did add three young pitchers from the minors in anticipation of spring training. These were Larry Bearnarth, who had posted a 2-13 mark at Syracuse after signing in June (and to whom Stengel referred as "Big Ben"); Tom Belcher, who was 1-12 at Syracuse in 1962; and Grover Powell, who went a combined 4-12 in stints with Auburn and Syracuse. Bearnarth, a fan favorite, lasted four seasons, going 13-21 with a 3.52 ERA and eight saves. Powell briefly aroused hopes by pitching a complete game shutout in his first Met start, but it would be his only big league win. Belcher never appeared in a game with the team.

With all the changes, at least one thing would stay the same. Although Stengel had originally signed only a one-year contract and Cookie Lavagetto and Solly Hemus had each been promised a chance to manage the team after what was expected to be Stengel's only year, the Perfesser agreed to another one-year contract to return in 1963. Jimmy Breslin noted that "even if the players don't belong, Stengel does. He'll be back next year. God help him." *The Sporting News* also approved the move: "He won in [Yankee] Stadium with gusto, and he lost at the Polo Grounds with spirit, sportsmanship and realism. He never entered excuses when no excuses were permissible. He took his trouncings like a man, and it was not easy to follow up his bright years with the Bombers with his dour season with perhaps the worst peacetime club in the last 40 years."

For his part, Stengel expressed optimism for the coming year: "I wish the season opened tomorrow because we're going to surprise a lot of people. Everybody tells me I look wonderful and maybe I do – on the outside. But I don't look so good on the inside. Those 120 losses we had last season do something to you. But our organization hasn't been sleeping this winter and I'll guarantee we'll be better next year." When asked by reporters how long he intended to stay on, Stengel reminded them of his earlier non-promise when he originally joined the team: "A lot of people my age are dead at the present time and I didn't say I would stay five years or fifty."

His coaching staff, though, would be very different. Red Kress and Rogers Hornsby died within five weeks of each other at year's end, and Red Ruffing resigned to become the Mets' roving minor-league instructor. Clyde McCullough and Ernie White joined Hemus and Lavagetto to make up Stengel's coaching roster for 1963. White, the pitching coach, found himself being called "Mr. Weiss" by Stengel. McCullough handled the catchers.

Another constant was the fan support which had sustained the team all year. In January, more than 400 fans attended an event called "Nassau County Welcomes the Mets" at a hotel in Garden City, Long Island. Stengel was the principal speaker, praising the fans for their loyalty and their "tree-mendous spirit." During a question-and-answer session, a fan asked Stengel what Mets fans would have to look forward. Stengel responded that the team would have a "big new scoreboard that is going to be just magnificent. Oh, it's huge. Grand. Nothing ever like it before. But it's not going to be so useful to us if you don't get the man to home plate."

Also in attendance that night was Throneberry, who in spite (or perhaps because) of his struggles was now a sought-after banquet speaker. A young fan got Throneberry's attention and requested an autograph on a ball. Throneberry nodded and held out his hands as the boy tossed him the ball. He dropped it.

CHAPTER FOURTEEN – THE AFTERMATH

"The public that has survived one full season of this team got to be congratulated." – *Casey Stengel, manager of the New York Mets*

When the Mets began play in 1963, there were quite a few new faces. Of the 45 men who had donned the orange and blue at one time or another the season before, only sixteen were still around, with another nineteen gone from the major leagues for good. Of the position players who had opened the previous year, only Frank Thomas and Charlie Neal were left, and Neal, the Opening Day second baseman in 1962, was now at third. In addition to the many players traded or released during the '62 season, Richie Ashburn, Elio Chacon, Felix Mantilla, Ray Daviault and both Bob Millers, among others, were no longer there. Also gone was Gene Woodling, by then a forty-year-old player-coach, after an absurd attempt to involve himself in Marv Throneberry's salary negotiations.

Throneberry himself had spent the off-season appearing at banquets, including the one hosted by the New York Baseball Writers Association, who gave Throneberry their annual Ben Epstein Good Guy Award, given to the player who had been the most good-natured and cooperative. When Throneberry accepted the plaque at the banquet in January, he showed how well he understood his own image, telling the crowd, "I was a little afraid to come up and get this for fear I might drop it."

Soon after, though, he seemed to lose his perspective. In March, George Weiss offered Throneberry a pay cut, rather than the raise he thought he deserved. Leonard Shecter recorded this snippet of dialogue between Throneberry and Weiss' assistant, Johnny Murphy:

Throneberry: "People came to the park to holler at me, just like Mantle and Maris. I drew people to games."
Murphy: "You drove some away, too."
Throneberry: "I took a lot of abuse."
Murphy: "You brought most of it on yourself."
Throneberry: "I played in the most games of my career, 116."
Murphy: "But you didn't play well in any of them."

Weiss reacted badly to Throneberry's inflated sense of worth, telling reporters that "Marv got the Good Guy Award mixed up with the Most Valuable Player Award."

Along came Woodling, asserting that Throneberry was entitled to a raise, which led Weiss to unceremoniously dump him. It was the end of his seventeen-year career. "We were at spring training," said Craig Anderson, "and all of a sudden Gene Woodling decided that they were screwing Marv Throneberry. Unbelievable. He got quoted in the press and he became the in-between guy between Johnny Murphy and Throneberry. Well, to make a long story short, he got released in spring training. You're not supposed to speak up, you know."

However, Woodling, who (other evidence to the contrary) was nobody's fool, had prepared himself well for his life after baseball. He had already entered the business world, understanding earlier than most that his career could end at any time, even though his end came later than most. He was very successful in business and as the owner of farm property.

Most of the players Weiss picked up in the off-season contributed nothing. However, Tracy Stallard, acquired in the Mantilla trade, wound up in the starting rotation. He was joined by

Carlton Willey, who came from the Braves that spring and became one of the team's most effective pitchers.

Weiss also continued the nostalgia parade, purchasing Dodger centerfielder Duke Snider just before the start of the season. "Being sold was humiliating enough," Snider wrote in his autobiography, "but being sold to the Mets seemed like the ultimate humiliation." Unlike his former teammate Gil Hodges, though, Snider wasn't completely done; he contributed fourteen homers, good enough for third on the team. In fact, his first Met hit was a home run off Braves ace (and future Met) Warren Spahn. The Duke, for his part, was stunned by the reception he received, and he dealt well with the prospect of playing in former enemy territory, telling the press, "I look up into the stands and it looks like Ebbets Field." Towards the end of the year, the team sponsored a Duke Snider Night at the Polo Grounds (the very concept of a Duke Snider Night at the Polo Grounds being unthinkable six years earlier), at which Snider was awarded a golf cart, as Hodges had been the year before. "Without Casey there, I would have gone nuts," Snider said, summing up his one year with the Mets. "He used to call me 'kid,' which at my age, thirty-seven, was nice of him. I learned Stengelese that summer and listened to him talk about the '49, '52, '53 World Series, but never about the '55 Series, when we Dodgers won over the Yanks."

The reshaping of the bullpen and the addition of Willey and Stallard to a rotation already including Roger Craig, Al Jackson and Jay Hook spelled doom for Craig Anderson. Although Anderson had led the team in appearances and saves the year before, he found himself the odd man out. After the 1962 season, he went to St. Petersburg for Instructional League ball. After six weeks there, he was asked to go to Puerto Rico to finish the fall season. He came to spring training in 1963 in excellent shape but was suddenly and unexpectedly cut. "That was probably one of my toughest days in baseball, because I did not expect to get cut," he explained. "I felt I had contributed as much as anybody else the year before. They were just buying players and bringing them in. So I got caught up in that."

While the faces were different in '63, the results were not. Once again the Mets staggered out of the gate, losing their first eight. The opener, a 7-0 shellacking by the Cardinals in which the Mets managed two hits, led Stengel to comment that "we're still a fraud – the audience got trimmed." Charlie Neal fielded a grounder hit by the first batter and threw the ball away, thus setting the tone for the rest of the year. They spent the entire season lodged squarely in tenth place and finished with a final record of 51-111, miles out of contention.

Although the '62 team sometimes had trouble putting runs on the board, the '63 Mets made them look like an offensive machine, batting an anemic .219 (down from .240 in 1962), averaging three runs a game and getting shut out 30 times. Frank Thomas' homer production fell from 34 to 15, second to Jim Hickman's 17, but his 60 RBIs (down from 94) were still enough to lead the team. Roger Craig was the primary victim of the team's lack of scoring. He finished 5-22 but sported a respectable 3.78 ERA, indicative of a chronic lack of run support. He also experienced a nightmarish eighteen-game losing streak, tying the league record for consecutive defeats set by Boston's Cliff Curtis back in 1910. During the streak, he lost five 1-0 games, and the Mets were shut out in three of his other losses. As the trading deadline approached in June, Craig made no secret of his wish to be moved, but it didn't happen. The Mets finally showed mercy after the season, dealing him to St. Louis, with whom he was to pitch in the 1964 World Series. "No prisoner ever felt better when he was pardoned," Craig stated. "My two seasons with the Mets taught me to cope with adversity."

Although Craig was the only twenty-game loser this time, five other pitchers lost at least fourteen games – Al Jackson (13-17), Tracy Stallard (6-17), Galen Cisco (7-15), Carlton Willey (9-14) and

Jay Hook (4-14) – although Craig, Jackson and Willey all had ERAs under 4.00. As he was in '62, Ken MacKenzie, at 3-1, was the only pitcher with a winning record, but he was traded to the Cardinals on August 5. Nor did the team's fielding help, as they equaled their 1962 total of 210 errors, a mark unequaled by any team in either league in almost fifty years since. Although the Mets were pitching better than the year before, their defense was as bad and their hitting was considerably worse. This meant that instead of losing games by eight runs, they were losing by one or two instead. But they were still losing.

More positively constant, though, was the attendance – almost 1.1 million fans despite the team's poor performance, drawing only slightly less than their crosstown rivals, who went to their fourth straight World Series. The Mets also beat the Yankees in the Mayor's Trophy exhibition game at Yankee Stadium on June 20. Mets fans made up many of the 50,000 who attended, and although their banners were confiscated at the gate, they made a lot of noise. As he had against the Yankees in the first spring training, Stengel started his regulars and his best pitchers, even using starter Willey in relief, and the Mets came away with a 6-2 victory.

At the end of the year, Craig Anderson made a brief return appearance, losing two more decisions to run his string to eighteen straight defeats. He did achieve one milestone, though, starting the last game ever played in the Polo Grounds – a loss. Fewer than two thousand fans showed up to witness the stadium's third farewell in seven seasons. This one, though, turned out to be final.

1963 also brought Throneberry's farewell. He was in Weiss' doghouse after his misguided holdout, and he rode the bench during spring training and the early season. In May, Stengel sent him to the outfield, where he had rarely played. His performance in right field was about what it had been at first base the year before. When the first fly ball was hit to him during a game, he said to himself, "Oh God, what do I do now?" It bounced in front of him, and as he tried to pick it up on the run, he fell flat on his rear and slid for several feet. After the game, Throneberry said that if Ashburn had still been in center, he would have yelled, "Safe!" Centerfielder Duke Snider came over to cover on the play. He was laughing so hard he barely had enough breath to tell Throneberry to throw to second.

It was the beginning of the end for Marvelous Marv, and the end came quickly. On May 12, he was demoted to Buffalo. At the time of his demotion, he was hitting .143, with no homers and one RBI in only fourteen at-bats, and he hadn't played in the week since his outfield debacle. Stengel told him to go to Buffalo and hit 50 home runs and they would bring him back. Shortly after, a reporter mentioned to Stengel that Throneberry had homered twice in a game for Buffalo. Stengel replied, "Well, he's got only 48 more to go before he gets back."

His departure provided one last Marvelous Marv sequence, beginning with when he was summoned to Stengel's office to get the news. He kept turning the doorknob the wrong way, requiring Gil Hodges to come help him. After the meeting, he took his time saying his goodbyes, and when he was alone in the clubhouse, he took off his uniform, showered, packed his stuff and tried to leave. Unfortunately, the door to the clubhouse had been locked from the outside. Throneberry spent a half hour yelling for help before anyone heard him and let him out. Despite his brave announcement that "I ain't gave up yet," Throneberry never appeared in another major league game. He retired from baseball the following season, at the age of thirty, and returned to Tennessee to become a beer salesman.

Unlike 1962, though, there was a positive sign. Before the 'season, Weiss acquired yet another player from Milwaukee, an unknown minor-league infielder named Ron Hunt. He was the sort of gritty dirty-uniform player that Stengel treasured, and against expectations, he made the club. After riding the bench for the first eight losses, he confronted Stengel and demanded to be put in the lineup. Stengel, no doubt admiring the kid's nerve, played him at second base the next day and was rewarded when Hunt went three for five with a double and a triple and drove in the winning run in the ninth inning, giving the team its first victory of the year. Hunt was a fixture the rest of the way and led the club in hits, runs, doubles and total bases, along with his team-best .272 average. He finished second to Cincinnati's Pete Rose in the balloting for Rookie of the Year. Like Rose, his hustle and ability also made him a fan favorite. Hunt was important because he was the first Met star whose best years lay in the future.

In 1964, the Mets were finally able to open Shea Stadium. The opening had been delayed for a year due to labor and weather problems, and even after the '63 season, there was some doubt as to whether it would be ready by the following Opening Day. Work continued all through the spring while the Mets were in Florida, and even as the stadium opened, workers were still making last-minute adjustments. Located adjacent to the World's Fair, which also debuted that spring, the park was easily accessible by the several train lines which fed directly into the area (although the first game, before the fans learned to use public transportation, featured an enormous traffic jam on the surrounding expressways). Everything about the park was new and shiny, especially compared to the Polo Grounds. When asked for his thoughts, Stengel responded, "Lovely, just lovely. The place is lovelier than my team."

On April 10, a week before the Mets made their Shea Stadium debut, the long-delayed demolition of the Polo Grounds finally got under way. The wrecking ball used to knock it down was the same one used to demolish Ebbets Field four years earlier.

The Mets drew 1.7 million fans to their new stadium, compared with 1.3 million for the Yankees, who won their fifth straight pennant. In fact, the Yankees would not outdraw the Mets until 1976. Shea also hosted the All-Star game that year, and the Mets' first homegrown star, Ron Hunt, started at second base on his way to a team-best .303 average. Another memorable day was a 23-inning marathon with the Giants on June 29 which took more than seven hours to complete. Since it was the second game of a doubleheader, they played ten hours of baseball that day. The game was full of strange moments, such as when Stengel lifted Rod Kanehl for a pinch-hitter in the second inning, or when the Mets pulled off a triple play in the fourteenth. Kanehl was supposed to have dinner with disc jockey Jim Lowe after the game. Lowe asked what time the doubleheader would be over; Kanehl guessed six or seven, eight at the latest. Having been lifted, Kanehl ended up delivering hot soup to the bench late in the game, and when it ended at midnight, he called Lowe. Lowe told him, "I turned it off in the ninth inning, and you guys were getting beat." In short, the events of the day were more memorable than the results, which were two more defeats.

On Father's Day, Jim Bunning of the Phillies pitched a perfect game at Shea, while his wife and daughter visited the World's Fair next door. It was only the eighth perfect game in baseball history and the first in a National League regular season game in over eighty years. One of the road highlights occurred in Chicago on May 26, when the Mets racked up 23 hits and pounded the Cubs 19-1. That night, a fan called a local newspaper to see how the Mets had done. When informed that they had scored 19 runs, he asked, "But did they win?" Also, on May 4, a game in Milwaukee featured a bench-clearing brawl. One of the fiercest combatants was the seventy-three-year-old Casey Stengel, who leapt into the fray with determination. Tracy Stallard said, "I laughed so hard when I saw Casey that I couldn't hit anybody."

On the season's final weekend, the Mets went to St. Louis with a chance to play the spoiler. The Cardinals were in a three-way dogfight with the Reds and the Phillies. If the Mets could somehow sweep the three-game series, admittedly an improbable event, they would eliminate the Cardinals. Stengel held his ace, Al Jackson, out of the preceding series to pitch him against Bob Gibson in the first game. Jackson outdueled Gibson for a 1-0 victory, with Ed Kranepool driving in the only run. The next day, Kranepool and four other Mets homered, and they pounded the Cards 15-5, chasing twenty-game winner Ray Sadecki in the first inning. In the third game, though, both teams reverted to form, and the Cardinals won the pennant (with Gibson pitching in relief on one day's rest), going on to defeat the Yankees in the Series. However, the Cardinals appeared to have been so shaken by the first two losses that they didn't seem to believe they'd won until the game actually ended. With two outs in the ninth and Barney Schultz on the hill, Stengel sent Kanehl in to pinch hit. On reaching the batter's box, Kanehl congratulated Cardinal catcher (and future Met broadcaster) Tim McCarver. McCarver told him, "We haven't won yet." Kanehl singled, driving in two runs. On reaching first, he congratulated first baseman Bill White, who responded, "We haven't got the last out yet." Then Kranepool popped to McCarver, and the game was over. For a brief moment, the Mets enjoyed being at least a factor in a pennant race. However, it was Kanehl's last hurrah.

As for the team which was less lovely than the ballpark, Stengel predicted before the season that they would finish in "thirtieth," presumably meaning a third straight year in tenth place. He was right. The Mets had a final record of 53-109, only two games better than the year before. For his part, Stengel came up with an innovative way to improve his club: "This here team won't go anywhere unless we spread enough of our players around the league and make the other teams horseshit too."

By the time the season was over, only Kanehl, Jackson, Chris Cannizzaro, Jim Hickman and Joe Christopher remained from the Original Mets. Although Craig Anderson resurfaced long enough to lose one game, his nineteenth in a row, he was finished with the Mets. So was Kanehl. Of the others, only Hickman lasted into the 1966 season with the big club.

Anderson had spent most of 1963 at Buffalo, going 9-12 before being called up in September. In 1964, he was having a fine spring and was sure he would make the team. "Then I got hit by a pitch and broke my hand," he remembers ruefully, "and the next day – the next day – they sent me to Buffalo. I mean, what the hell is going on?" He reported to Buffalo, spent a frustrating month on the disabled list and then got hot, saving three games in a ten-day period. Called back up, he pitched well in a relief appearance in Los Angeles, started a game in Houston and then made his first visit to Shea Stadium. "I got into the 23-inning game with the Giants, and I didn't do very well," he related. "The only guy I got out was Mays, who hit a hard grounder to third. There were a couple guys on, and they scored a run off of me. So they brought in another relief pitcher, and I ended up getting charged with four runs. So now I got to stay in that stadium for . . . it must have been eight hours, plus we'd already played a nine-inning game in the first game. That was my last game in the big leagues. I was there one more night and then they sent me back to Buffalo. That was disappointing. I really wanted to get out of the Met organization at that point. I really didn't want to deal with them anymore. Well, I went down to Buffalo and I had the best year in my career. I was 13-7, and we won the playoffs. I had the best record, I think, in the Mets system. And you know, they didn't even invite me to spring training the next year. So I knew that was the end of it. I couldn't do anything. I didn't have a good year in '65, but I had a good year in '66, and then I said I'm packing it in. They weren't doing anything with me, they were cutting my salary every year, and it wasn't worth it. So I moved on."

Kanehl's situation was even sadder. He returned home after the 1964 season, expecting to return in 1965. For each of his three seasons with the Mets, he had been sent a minor league contract and an invitation to spring training, whereupon he would go down to Florida and make the team. In the winter of 1964, though, the club sent him a Buffalo contract but did not invite him to spring training. At this point, Kanehl was thirty years old with four kids in school, and he had no intention of going back to the minors after spending eight pre-Mets years there. Unfortunately, the Mets still retained his rights, and despite being a Stengel favorite who always gave more than his ability would allow, he was done in the majors. He announced he would not report and waited to see what happened next.

The Yankees, hearing of Kanehl's plight, offered him a managerial position in their farm system. Kanehl was very interested, believing that Stengel had been grooming him for a career in managing. The Yankees' Johnny Johnson called to ask if he wanted the job, and Kanehl said of course. Johnson said he would call back. "Well, I was thinking maybe I'll hear from him and maybe I won't," Kanehl said. "He called back within an hour and said, 'They want two ballplayers for you.'" George Weiss demanded this exorbitant compensation in return for releasing the Mets' rights to a player he had never wanted in the first place. He didn't even think enough of Kanehl to offer him a similar position within the Mets system. Since the Yankees were not about to give up two players for a minor-league manager, Kanehl's baseball days were over, although the Mets did not release his rights until five years later, in 1969. He didn't even have enough service time to qualify for the pension. Therefore, he had to get on with the rest of his life. After all, it was Kanehl, in an oft-quoted line, who noted that "baseball is a lot like life . . . the line drives are caught, and the squibblers go for base hits. It's an unfair game."

Kanehl had worked as a cement contractor in Springfield, Missouri, during the off-season. After his career ended, he worked building houses in 1965 and 1966, also playing semi-pro ball. In 1965, he played with former Met teammate Charlie Neal on a team known, appropriately enough, as the Dreamliners, and they won the league championship. In 1967, he moved from Springfield to Los Angeles and went into the insurance business. "That didn't pan out too well," he recalled. He soon changed careers again, becoming the caddy master at Bel Air Country Club before going into restaurant management in 1978. After fifteen years in the restaurant business, he went back to Bel Air Country Club as a caddy, where he worked his remaining years. He died of a heart attack on December 14, 2004, at the age of seventy.

After leaving the game, Kanehl soon found that his notoriety, such as it was, had not gone away. During a Met game against the Cardinals, he was playing centerfield with the bases loaded. Tim McCarver hit a fly ball to center, but Kanehl slipped while playing it and the ball went to the wall. McCarver and all three runners scored on the play. "Three years later I'm out of baseball, sitting at home listening to a ballgame with my kids around," laughed Kanehl. "McCarver hits a grand slam home run. Harry Caray says, 'That's [McCarver's] second grand slam home run. The first one was when Rod Kanehl fell on his face in centerfield.' I saw Harry a couple times in Palm Springs. He came down here in the offseason. When he'd come into a club I was managing, I'd get the band to play 'Take Me Out to the Ballgame.'"

Jay Hook also left during the 1964 season, having been swapped on May 8 for shortstop Roy McMillan (who later managed the Mets) in yet another trade with the Braves. The Braves wanted to farm him out to Denver. Hook needed about ten days of big league service time to vest in the pension plan, and he agreed to go to Denver if the Braves would bring him up at the end of the season so he could get his time. Shortly after pitching ten innings of no-hit ball only to lose the game in the eleventh, Hook tore up his knee on the basepaths trying to break up a double play. Although it effectively ended his year, the Braves kept their word and called him up for the last month of the season, though he didn't get into a single game.

His pension rights thus vested, Hook found himself at a crossroads. When he first entered baseball, he set an objective for himself to try and stay in the majors for five years and then decide what he wanted to do with his life. The Braves sent him a contract for the 1965 season, but Hook sent it back unsigned and took a job with Chrysler. "I had five years and about eight days in the major leagues," he explained. "I couldn't achieve the consistency that I felt it took to really have a lasting career. You know, we didn't make that much money at that time, and the first seven years we were married, we moved 22 times. It was great, and if I had the opportunity to do it again I would, but it's tough to realize that you're just an average player." Hook finished with a career record of 29-62, with an ERA of 5.23.

Hook, though, made up for his lack of baseball success many times over, showing that he was anything but average. He spent four years at Chrysler, beginning in product planning before moving to marketing and then to the Dodge sales division. He was then recruited to Rockwell International, where he remained for nine years. He started running the product planning department and went on to market research, and he soon ran Research and Development. Before long, he went into general management and headed three divisions. He was recruited again, this time to Masco, a plumbing manufacturer, where he was given six companies to run. At that time, Masco generated about $600 million in sales. By the time Hook left the company in the early nineties as Group President, the Masco umbrella spread over twenty companies with sales of six billion dollars. He retired in 1991 but remained with the company in a consulting role. At that point, Hook began his third career. The Dean of Northwestern University's engineering program was a friend, and Hook become involved in starting a masters program in manufacturing management at his alma mater, the teaching of which was divided between the engineering school and the Kellogg business school. Hook became a full professor, committing to travel to Northwestern from his home in Michigan for a week every month. "That was a fun thing," Hook enthused two years after retiring from Northwestern in 2000. "We had changed the engineering curriculum, and I was involved in that. I was kind of an ombudsman. I would do things that nobody else wanted to do. But I got along with people, because I didn't want anybody's job. I also went on the Board of Trustees of the Garrett Evangelical Seminary, which is a Methodist seminary on the Northwestern campus." As of this writing, Hook owns a 170-acre farm in northern Michigan while continuing to volunteer his time with local foundations.

Another Original Met departing during 1964 was Frank Thomas, who was traded to Philadelphia on August 7. The deal gave Thomas the chance to finally make the postseason, something he had never done in fourteen seasons, as the Phillies were going for the pennant. After 39 games with his new team, in which he batted .294 and hit seven home runs, Thomas broke his thumb, and the Phillies faded. He began 1965 with the Phillies but was traded after an altercation with the team's rising star, Richie Allen. After leaving Philadelphia, Thomas played 23 games with Houston and 15 with the Braves. When the season ended, Thomas, who was 36 by then, still hoped to play with the Braves the coming year. He had a discussion with his old nemesis, general manager John McHale, upon receiving his 1966 contract. He told McHale that if he wasn't going to be given a chance to play, he would prefer to just get on with his life. McHale assured Thomas that he would get a chance. "So I go to spring training and I don't play a ballgame," he stated. "Not one." Released shortly after, he attempted to pursue opportunities with the Red Sox and Cubs, but neither panned out. His 1966 season consisted of five hitless at-bats with the Cubs, after which his career was over. In his sixteen seasons, he amassed 286 home runs and 962 runs batted in along with a .266 batting average.

The end of Thomas' career left him somewhat rootless at first. "I walked the streets for quite a long time because no one wants to hire you if you only have a high school education," he told the author in 2002. Then he had a chance meeting with Pittsburgh Steelers announcer Joe Tucker, who told him, "Don't sell yourself short. You weren't just a good ballplayer. You were a great ballplayer, and let those people know it." Thomas took the advice to heart. "A friend of mine who owned a computer school asked me if I'd come down. I knew nothing about computers. I still don't, though I'm learning – my kids are trying to teach me. So I worked for them for eighteen years." He spent his time going to high schools to encourage kids to pursue their education. After all, he stated, $100,000 might seem like a lot of money, but it doesn't go very far when you're 23, you've hurt your arm and your career is over. He retired in 1984. "It had started to bother my throat because I was making 35 presentations a week – five days, seven presentations each day in each school. I said, 'It's time for some young kid to get up at four in the morning and make a two hundred-mile trip to speak for seven periods. I was 55 when I retired, which I'd set as a goal for myself. I play in a lot of charity golf tournaments, and my wife and I, we travel. We have eight kids, twelve grandkids, three step-grandkids and two step-great-grandkids." In 2005, Thomas published his autobiography, *Kiss it Goodbye: The Frank Thomas Story*.

When the Mets began the 1965 season, Casey Stengel was 74 years old. The team, however, was getting younger, as the farm system was delivering players like outfielders Cleon Jones and Ron Swoboda and pitcher Tug McGraw. Ed Kranepool, signed during 1962, was already in his third full season. At the same time, Weiss picked up Yogi Berra and Warren Spahn, two more players at the end of their Hall of Fame careers. Spahn was brought in as a pitcher and pitching coach, which proved to be a bad idea. The proud and stubborn Spahn refused to acknowledge that the end was at hand, and he kept pitching while the younger hurlers suffered. Berra had not even played the year before. The Yankees relieved manager Ralph Houk of his duties after the 1963 season, despite the fact that Houk had won pennants in each of his three years at the helm. Noting the Mets' PR success with Stengel, the Yankees elevated Berra, their own version of a folksy character, for 1964. All Berra did that year was lead the Yankees to another pennant, their fifth in a row (going back to Stengel's final year), although they lost to the World Series to St. Louis in seven games. However, Berra was moody and elusive, hardly the lovable figure he had been previously thought to be (in fact, it was well-known among insiders that Berra's public image as a humorous gnome had been manufactured by Stengel and Yankee coach Frank Crosetti). The Yankees rewarded Berra for his success – one year, one pennant – by firing him after the Series, whereupon he joined the Mets. Neither Berra nor Spahn contributed anything on the field, and both were released during the season. Spahn, possibly the greatest lefthanded pitcher of all time, had a 4-12 record when the Mets let him go. He was picked up by the Giants, for whom he went 3-4 before retiring at the end of the season. Berra, though, returned as a coach and ultimately became the Mets' manager in 1972, leading the team to a pennant in 1973.

On July 24, Stengel was holding court at Toots Shor's nightclub. The Mets had planned to honor his seventy-fifth birthday between games of the next day's doubleheader. During the evening, though, he suffered a fall in the men's room and was rushed to the hospital in terrible pain. The doctor diagnosed a broken hip, and Stengel underwent surgery to replace the hip with an artificial joint. Stengel spent several weeks in the hospital and designated one of his coaches, Wes Westrum, as interim manager. On August 30, though, Stengel bowed to the inevitable and resigned, and Westrum took over officially. "I couldn't strut out to the mound to take out a pitcher," Stengel told the press. "It was time to step down."

On September 2, walking on a crooked cane, Stengel was honored at Shea for his inestimable contributions, and his uniform was retired and put on display in a glass case in the stadium's Diamond Club. Stengel had mixed feelings about receiving such an honor. "I'd like to see them give that number 37 to some young player so it can go on and do some good for the Mets," he announced. "I hope they don't put a mummy in the glass case."

There weren't many other memorable moments that season. The team's 50-112 record was the worst since year one. None of the veterans Weiss brought in had produced, and after good years in 1964, Chris Cannizzaro and Joe Christopher slumped badly. After the season, the club showed mercy on Al Jackson, trading him to the Cardinals.

During the offseason, the Baseball Writers Association petitioned the Baseball Hall of Fame to waive the mandatory five-year waiting period required for Stengel's induction. The Hall unanimously granted the petition. On July 25, 1966, a year and a day after Stengel broke his hip, he was inducted into Cooperstown. Despite his many years managing the Dodgers and Braves, not to mention his spectacular success with the Yankees, Stengel made it clear during his induction speech where his loyalties were: "I want to thank the tree-mendous fans. We appreciate every boys group, girls group, poem and song. And keep going to see the Mets play."

Four other momentous events occurred in 1966. First, the Mets finally escaped the cellar, coming in ahead of the Cubs to finish ninth. Also, with a 66-95 record, they lost fewer than 100 games for the first time. Third, and most incredibly, they even managed to wind up ahead of the Yankees. Since losing the World Series in 1964, and firing Berra thereafter, the Yankees had been in free-fall, finishing sixth in 1965 and, unbelievably, dead last in 1966. The Yankees were in last place and the Mets were not – such a thing would have been unthinkable just two years earlier.

The most significant event, though, was the signing of a California pitcher named George Thomas Seaver on April 3, 1966. In true Mets fashion, they won him in a raffle. Seaver signed with the Braves for $50,000 while still in college, but the contract was voided by baseball's commissioner, William Eckert, because the Braves had signed Seaver after his college season had started. In addition, by signing the now-void contract, Seaver lost his college eligibility and was thus in limbo. After Seaver's father threatened a lawsuit, Eckert decreed that any club other than the Braves could have Seaver for the same $50,000 the Braves had paid. After three teams, including the Mets, staked a claim, Eckert chose the winner by pulling a name from a hat, and for once the Mets won something of value.

1966 also saw the departure of the last of the Original Mets. On November 29, Jim Hickman, the last expansion draftee on the big league roster, was sent to the Dodgers with Ron Hunt for outfielder Tommy Davis. "We used to sit around in those days [in 1962] and talk about who might be the last player to stay with the team," Hickman later reminisced. "They started trading and farming out guys pretty quickly and we used to wonder about the last of us. Frank Thomas always thought it would be him. Some people thought it might be Jackson. Nobody ever thought it would be me, not even me."

Eight days later, the Mets sold Chris Cannizzaro to the Yankees. Cannizzaro had a good year in 1964 and had been the regular catcher in 1965, appearing in 112 games but hitting only .183. He'd spent the entire 1966 season in the minors. Now he was gone.

Hickman and Cannizzaro were preceded out the door by George Weiss, who retired as president on November 14, and was replaced by former Cardinal general manager Vaughan "Bing" Devine. "This culminates a lifetime of the happiest work I could ever indulge in," said Weiss in his farewell announcement. "This time I go out with the right kind of taste in my mouth. I would have to say that the thing I am most proud of was hiring Casey Stengel twice."

That left Craig Anderson, by now a forgotten man, having spent all of 1965 and 1966 in the minors. He retired at the end of the 1966 season with a 7-23 career record and 5.10 ERA and moved on with his life while still staying involved with the game. He decided to use the job placement service offered by Lehigh University, from which he had graduated in 1960 with a business degree. "I got quite a few letters and interviews and things,"

Anderson stated. "Then Lehigh called and said would I be interested in working for the University, and they hired me. Never did I believe I'd be there 34 years later. I was a fundraiser for two years, and then an athletic administrator for one or two years, and I was the pitching coach of the baseball team for 34 years. I enjoyed that immensely, and that helped to bridge the gap when I came out of baseball. I retired from there in 2000. I coached one guy who went to the big leagues, Paul Hartzell. He was a pitcher in the Angels' system and played in the big leagues for about five years. I was real proud of that. And my son got to play. He got drafted by the Texas Rangers. I coached him for years. He was a nice player, and he signed as a pitcher. The year of the strike [1981], he got released, but he played three years, and that was a good experience for him. And me. I still love baseball." After retiring, Anderson and his wife Judy toured the country in an RV before settling in Dunnellon, Florida, where Anderson served as part-time pitching coach at the local high school. Anderson is in the Lehigh Sports Hall of Fame.

Anderson was not the only Met pitcher to maintain his ties to the game. Roger Craig and Al Jackson enjoyed long coaching careers, and Jay Hook was involved on a more informal level. He would always volunteer to help with school or Little League pitchers. "We live on a farm now in northern Michigan," he explained, "and I go to all the high school football, basketball and baseball games and I help the baseball team. It's just a fun thing to do. In fact, one of the things I did when I went down to spring training [in 2002] was, I wanted to know more about a split-finger fastball. That was something Roger Craig really developed, more after he was active. I wanted to make sure that what I was telling these kids was still consistent with what is being taught. I used that time to update myself so I could pass that along to these young kids. It's what we used to call 'benchmarking' in business."

Although no one could have known it then, 1967 was the year the worm began to turn. From its ninth place finish in 1966, the team slid back into last with a record of 61-101. With eleven games left in the season, Wes Westrum decided he couldn't take it anymore and resigned. He was replaced by Salty Parker, one of his coaches. However, 1967 saw the arrival of the first franchise player in the club's brief history. Once Tom Seaver hit the big leagues after just one season in the minors, he was there to stay. He finished 16 13 as a rookie on a last-place team, accounting for more than a quarter of the team's victories, and he was the Mets' first Rookie of the Year. He went on to win more than 300 games in his career (198 with the Mets), and he became the first player inducted into the Hall of Fame for what he accomplished in a Met uniform.

After the 1967 season, Bing Devine resigned as general manager. He was replaced by Weiss' favorite, Johnny Murphy, whose star had risen in the organization since he first joined as a scout in 1961. Murphy had broken in with the Yankees in 1932, and he pitched twelve seasons in New York and one in Boston, primarily in relief, although his playing days were interrupted by World War II. On retiring in 1947, he had a 93-53 career record. He then joined the Red Sox' front office and ultimately ran the farm system, remaining there until Weiss hired him in 1961, and he quickly became Weiss' most valued assistant. His appointment as the Mets' general manager was the culmination of almost forty years in baseball.

1968 also marked the return of Gil Hodges to New York. Hodges' tenure as a Met player had been beset by injuries and ailments, and the team had released him early in 1963 so he could become manager of the Washington Senators. There, he had taken another lousy expansion team and improved them incrementally each year. The Mets sent $100,000 and pitcher Bill Denehy to Washington in return for the rights to Hodges, who signed a three-year deal to manage the Mets. Even with his yearly progress while managing the Senators, no one could have foreseen what he would accomplish now that he was back in New York.

In his first season, the Mets finished 73-89, still good enough only for ninth place but by far the team's best record yet. Lefty starter Jerry Koosman emerged from the minors to join Seaver in the rotation, winning 19 games to set a team record and giving the Mets a killer one-two punch. In addition, players developed from within, such as Tug McGraw and Cleon Jones, continued to blossom, and outfielder Tommy Agee was acquired from the White Sox for Tommy Davis.

1969, though, was when everything came together, the year the lovable losers became the Miracle Mets. The National League had expanded again, and the twelve clubs were divided into two divisions, with the division winners to meet in a playoff for the pennant. The team stumbled early, losing their opening game to the expansion Montreal Expos and leading many to conclude that nothing had changed. In late spring, though, the Mets went on an eleven-game tear which put them in the thick of the division race. The Cubs, also perennial doormats for most of the decade, had a powerful veteran team, and they led the new Eastern Division for most of the way. Beginning in June, though, the Mets stayed just close enough to keep things interesting, as pennant fever swept New York. In August, the club faltered, and by the 19th, they trailed the Cubs by 9 ½ games. At that point, they rallied, winning 26 of their next 33 decisions, including a ten-game winning streak, and they moved into first place for the first time in franchise history on September 10. From then on, they buried the Cubs (many of whose old-time fans, the Bleacher Bums, have never fully recovered), ultimately converting a 9 ½ game deficit into an 8 ½ game lead in six weeks. The team which had lost 101 games only two years before and finished ninth in 1968 wound up with a record of 100-62. Seaver and Koosman won their last fifteen starts, and Seaver's 25-7 record earned him the Cy Young Award. The Mets swept the heavily-favored Atlanta Braves in the division playoff and faced the even more heavily-favored Baltimore Orioles in the World Series. The skeptics nodded knowingly at one another when the Orioles took the first game. However, the Mets made believers out of millions when they won the next four and the championship. The Miracle of '69 was complete. The Amazin' Mets had finally, truly and without a doubt, become amazing.

In the forty years since 1969, the Mets have known triumph and tragedy, victory and defeat. After third-place finishes in 1970 and 1971, Gil Hodges died of a massive heart attack just before the 1972 season, and Yogi Berra took over as the Mets finished third again. They got off slowly in 1973, suffering a number of early injuries and spending the spring mired in last place. As they had four years earlier, though, the Mets came to life over the summer, and they ended up winning the pennant but losing the World Series to the Oakland Athletics. They did not repeat their success, though, and Berra was fired during the 1975 season. In September, Casey Stengel and Joan Whitney Payson died within a few days of each other. It was the end of an era in more ways than one. The club fell into disarray, with management and players squabbling amongst themselves and with each other. An acrimonious dispute between Tom Seaver and Don Grant resulted in the most popular Met ever being traded to Cincinnati on June 15, 1977, a date which will forever live in infamy among Met fans (Dave Kingman, who two years earlier had broken Frank Thomas' Met single season home run record, was traded to San Diego that same evening, leading New York fans to refer to the night's events as the Midnight Massacre). The team spent the rest of the decade in the cellar, and for the only time in franchise history, the fans stayed away. In 1970, the Mets had drawn just under 2.7 million fans to Shea; nine years later, less than 800,000 showed up to see what had become a listless, hopeless team.

At the end of the decade, Mrs. Payson's daughter sold the Mets to a group headed by Nelson Doubleday, president of the Doubleday publishing empire, and Fred Wilpon of Sterling Equities. The Doubleday-Wilpon group paid over $21 million for the club – roughly seven times what Mrs. Payson had paid to get the franchise going less than twenty years earlier. Doubleday and Wilpon rebuilt the team with Frank Cashen as general manager and a cast of homegrown and imported players such as Keith Hernandez, Darryl Strawberry, Dwight Gooden and Gary Carter. The Mets, led by manager Davey Johnson, celebrated the franchise's twenty-fifth campaign with a 108-win season and a thrilling seven-game World Series victory over the Boston Red Sox in 1986.

Johnson led the Mets to a division title in 1988 but was fired in the early 1990s, another dry period. "We're just as bad as the old Mets," said general manager Dallas Green in 1993, "but this time nobody's laughing." Once again, though, they revived themselves by the end of the decade under manager Bobby Valentine, winning the wild card in 1999 and the pennant in 2000. Although they lost the World Series to the Yankees, they at least gave New York fans the thrill of the first subway series since the Yankees and Brooklyn Dodgers squared off in 1956. The fans came back, too – the Mets drew over 2.5 million in 1999, 2000 and 2001. Once again, though, the team fell into disarray. The Doubleday-Wilpon partnership ended badly, and little of the high-priced talent the team imported prior to the 2002 season produced anything, leading to Valentine being fired. The Mets went an entire month without winning a single home game – something even the 1962 team couldn't manage. 2003 and 2004 were little better, as the Mets lost 95 and 91 games, respectively. This time, though, the fans did not desert them. Although attendance slumped from 2002, over 2.3 million fans paid their way into Shea Stadium to see a fourth place team. By 2005, the Mets had improved to 83-79, their first winning mark in four years, and had drawn over 2.8 million fans. For the remainder of the decade, with a number of high-profile players, the Mets remained in contention although they fell short at season's end.

At any rate, the forty-eighth anniversary of that first season seems as good a time as any to re-visit the Original Mets (other than Anderson, Hook, Kanehl and Thomas, already discussed herein) and examine what has happened with them since 1962:

After Richie Ashburn retired following the 1962 season, he broadcast Phillies games for 35 years. From 1974 to 1991, he was also a columnist for the *Philadelphia Bulletin* and *Daily News*, and he found time to compile *The Phillies Trivia Book* and write the introduction for a 1981 pictorial history of the team. A lifetime .308 hitter, he was elected to the Baseball Hall of Fame by the Veterans Committee in 1995. The crowd attending his induction ceremony was estimated at 30,000, one of the largest ever. During his speech, he paraphrased Casey Stengel's summation of the 1962 season, acknowledging that his success had been a team effort. After calling a Phillies game against the Mets in New York, Ashburn died suddenly of a heart attack on September 9, 1997, in his room at the Grand Hyatt Hotel. He was seventy years old. An estimated 40,000 attended his viewing, and the centerfield entertainment area of the Phillies' ballpark is now named "Ashburn Alley." He is remembered as one of the greatest defensive centerfielders ever, and his career total of 2,754 hits ranks him ahead of such high-profile Hall of Famers as Joe DiMaggio, Hank Greenberg, Joe Cronin and Mickey Mantle.

Gus Bell wound up his fifteen-year career with Milwaukee in 1964, although he played just three games in 1963 and three more in 1964. He was a career .281 hitter with 206 home runs. His son, Buddy, was an All-Star player and also managed several teams, and Buddy's son David played twelve big league seasons, batting .291 with the Phillies in 2004. Another grandson, Mike, also played briefly in the majors. Bell, who was with the Reds for nine of his fifteen seasons, returned to the Cincinnati area after he retired. He suffered a heart attack on May 1, 1995, and died six days later in Montgomery, Ohio, at the age of 66. Four days after Bell's death, David made his major-league debut. The Bells remain one of only three three-generation major league families, the others being Ray, Bob and Aaron Boone and Sam, Jerry and Jerry Hairston Jr.

Ed Bouchee's demotion in July 1962 marked the end of his major league career, which totaled seven seasons and a batting average of .265 with 61 homers. He remained in the minors until the end of 1963, when he retired at the age of thirty. After a long tenure in management with AC Delco in Des Plaines, Illinois, he retired to Gilbert, Arizona, where he now resides.

Chris Cannizzaro remained with the Mets until 1965. He was sold to the Yankees after spending the 1966 season in the minors. He batted .236 in his Met career, with no home runs in 581 at bats and one stolen base in nine attempts. In 1969, he found himself with the new San Diego Padres, thus becoming the second player to experience two initial expansion seasons (former Met teammate Gene Woodling, drafted by the Senators in 1960, was the first). He became the Padres' starting catcher for two seasons and made the All-Star team in 1969. He retired after the 1974 season, one of only three Met draftees to remain in the major leagues until then. His career batting average in thirteen seasons was .235. After coaching and managing in the minor leagues, he served as a high school and college coach and is now the director of baseball operations at the University of San Diego.

Elio Chacon never appeared in a major league game after 1962, and after two years in the minors, the Mets traded him to St. Louis in 1964. Chacon then spent the next five seasons with the Cardinals' Triple-A Tulsa team without ever being called up. His last season, 1970, was spent with the Milwaukee Brewers' Triple-A franchise in Portland. In his three major league years, he appeared in 228 games, batting .232 but with an on-base percentage of .351. He died on April 24, 1992, in Caracas, Venezuela, at the age of 55.

Harry Chiti did not play a single game for the Indians after the Mets returned him to Cleveland as the player to be named later in the Chiti-for-Chiti trade. He never appeared in another major league game after leaving the Mets. Although Chiti was in his tenth big league season at the time his career ended, he was only 29 years old. He had a career average of .238 with 41 homers in 502 games over ten seasons. After his career ended, he and his family moved to

Tennessee, where he worked as a district manager for Columbia Pictures and then as a bailiff. His son Dom was drafted by the Atlanta Braves as a pitcher in 1976. Although Dom never made it to the majors, he has had a lengthy career as a scout and a coach and now works for the Texas Rangers. Chiti died on January 31, 2002, in Haines City, Florida, at the age of 69.

Joe Christopher had the distinction of being the first major leaguer born in the Virgin Islands. One of the last of the expansion draftees to leave the team, he remained with the Mets until 1965. He was a platoon player until 1964, when he suddenly exploded, batting .300 with 16 home runs and 76 runs batted in while appearing in 154 games. The following year, though, his production fell to .249, five homers and forty RBIs. Traded to Boston after the season, he appeared in only twelve games with the Red Sox in 1966 and was traded to the Tigers in June. He bounced around the minors in the Tigers, Cardinals, Pirates and Phillies systems before retiring in 1968. After retiring, he operated a baseball school in the Virgin Islands before returning to the US and becoming a freelance artist. Christopher currently lives in Baltimore.

A late-season acquisition after being waived by the Red Sox, Galen Cisco appeared in four September games in which he went 1-1 with a complete game and a 3.26 ERA. He started 59 games for the Mets between 1963 and 1965, going 7-15, 6-19 and 4-8. He next appeared in eleven games with the 1967 Red Sox and fifteen with the expansion Kansas City Royals in 1969, following which his major league career ended at the age of 33. In seven seasons, he won twenty-five games and lost fifty-six, with an ERA of 4.56. After two years in the minors, he became a Royals coach in 1971, beginning a thirty-year coaching career which included stops in Montreal, San Diego, Toronto and Philadelphia. He was Toronto's pitching coach from 1990 to 1995, a tenure which included the Blue Jays' World Series championships in 1992 and 1993. Cisco's sons, Jeff and Galen Jr., also played in the minors, and his grandson Mike was selected in the 2008 draft. Cisco, born in St. Mary's, Ohio and educated at Ohio State, now resides in Celina, Ohio.

Clarence "Choo Choo" Coleman began 1963 as the regular catcher, but he batted only .178 in 247 at-bats and had 15 errors and 11 passed balls. He also managed the singular feat of hitting 41 singles and three home runs but no doubles or triples. After 1963, he did not return to the majors until he played six games with the 1966 Mets. He was then out of baseball until 1969, when he appeared in 94 games with the Mets' Triple-A team in Tidewater. He batted .197 in 201 games over four major league seasons with nine homers and thirty runs batted in. After retiring, he returned to Philadelphia where he had begun his career and became a butcher.

Cliff Cook appeared in 40 games with the Mets after coming over in the Don Zimmer trade, and 50 games the following year, his last in the big leagues. In five seasons, he batted less than 400 times and compiled an average of .201. After spending all of 1964 with Buffalo, he retired at the age of 27 and ran a sporting goods store in Ft. Worth, Texas.

Roger Craig was traded to St. Louis after the 1963 season. In 1964, he helped the Cardinals win their first pennant since 1946, and he won his second World Series game that fall (the first was with the Dodgers in 1956). He pitched for the Reds in 1965 and the Phillies in 1966. He finished with a record of 74-98 in twelve seasons but had an ERA of only 3.83. Without his 15-46 Mets record, he was a career winning pitcher. Following his retirement, he enjoyed considerable success as both a pitching coach and manager. He managed the San Diego Padres to their first-ever winning season in 1978. As pitching coach for Detroit in 1984, he supervised one of the best staffs in baseball, as the Tigers won the World Series. Craig is credited with teaching the split-finger fastball to two of the decade's premium pitchers, Detroit's Jack Morris and Mike Scott of the Astros (a former Met who came to prominence after leaving the team). He also managed the San

Francisco Giants to a Western Division title in 1987 and the National League pennant in 1989. In his eleven seasons as a manager (nine with the Giants), he compiled a record of 738-737.

As a 28-year-old rookie in 1962, Ray Daviault spent most of the season – his only big league campaign – with the Mets, going 1-5 with a 6.22 ERA in 36 games. He gave up runs in 30 of his 36 appearances, surrendering 64 runs in 81 innings. Returning to the minors for his eleventh season in 1963, he retired at the end of the year. He then coached amateur baseball following his playing days. Daviault, born in Montreal, is one of two Canadian-born members of the 1962 Mets, the other being Ken MacKenzie.

John DeMerit's fourteen games with the Mets in 1962 – in which he had sixteen at-bats with a .188 average – turned out to be the last of his career. He retired at the age of 26 after he was sent down in May, choosing to go back to school instead. He played in 93 games spread over five seasons, with 132 at-bats and a .174 average. DeMerit, a Wisconsin native who had originally signed with Milwaukee for a $100,000 bonus, earned a masters degree at the University of Wisconsin and went to work for an insurance company. After seven years in insurance, he became Director of the Parks and Recreation Department in Port Washington, Wisconsin. He retired after 26 years with the Department and still lives in Port Washington.

An expansion draftee, Sammy Drake appeared in 25 games with the 1962 Mets, batting 52 times with an average of .192 and seven runs batted in. These were all career highs. It was the last of his three big league seasons. For his career, he appeared in 53 games with only 72 at-bats, eleven hits and a .153 batting average. He remained in the Mets farm system for three more years, retiring after the 1965 season at the age of 31. Drake's older brother Solly was a little-used catcher, but the Drake brothers have the distinction of being the first African-American brothers to play in the major leagues since integration in 1947. Drake retired to southern

California, where he became an investigator with the U.S. Department of Housing and Urban Development. He was also a Sunday school teacher at the Greater Ebenezer Missionary Baptist Church, where Solly remains the pastor. He died of cancer in Los Angeles on January 27, 2010, at the age of 75.

Larry Foss spent the last month of the 1962 season with the Mets after being acquired on September 6. He got into five games with one start and finished 0-1 with an ERA of 4.63. Foss never appeared in another major league game. He reported to spring training in 1963 but was traded to Milwaukee before camp broke and spent the entire season with the Braves' farm club at Denver. He retired that fall at the age of 27, having appeared in eight big league games, going 1-2 with a 5.33 ERA. After spending time in the oil and gas industry and then as a business owner in Colorado, Foss is now retired and lives in Kansas.

Joe Ginsberg retired after being released by the Mets on May 1, 1962. He batted .241 in thirteen seasons with seven teams. After a business career which included sixteen years with the Jack Daniels distillery, he retired to Florida in 1986. He has made frequent appearances at Detroit Tigers fantasy camps, and he has often been quoted in articles about the Original Mets, for whom he played two games, batting five times without a hit. He is the only player to play on teams posting over 110 wins – the 1954 Cleveland Indians, with whom Ginsberg appeared in three games – and over 110 losses the Original Mets.

M. Donald Grant remained as chairman of the Metropolitan Baseball Club of New York until 1978. After the passing of owner Joan Payson in 1975, he assumed a larger role, presiding over one of the most tumultuous periods in the club's history. It was his decision to trade Tom Seaver on June 15, 1977, for which Grant was never forgiven by the fans. He was forced out as chairman on November 8, 1978, after the Mets had finished last for the second year in a row, and was succeeded by Payson's daughter, Lorinda de

Roulet. After Grant's removal, he remarked that his demise was due to the press making a martyr out of Seaver. He remained on the board until de Roulet sold the team in January 1980. He died on November 27, 1998, at the age of 94. Controversial even today, he remains the only one of the Mets' principal founding figures who has not been inducted into the team's Hall of Fame.

Solly Hemus remained a Mets coach until the end of the 1963 season. He then coached for the Cleveland Indians in 1964 and 1965 and managed the Mets' farm team at Jacksonville in 1966. He then left baseball and went into the oil business in Houston. He eventually formed his own company, Hemus Inc., focusing on drilling wells and buying royalty rights.

Rick Herrscher spent the last two months of the 1962 season with the Mets, appearing in 35 games at six positions but batting only 50 times, with a .220 average, one home run and six RBIs. This was his only big league action. He spent the next two seasons in the minors before retiring in 1964 at the age of 27. He then went to Baylor University's dental school, graduating in 1968, and he became an orthodontist in 1972. He is still in practice in Athens, Texas.

Jim Hickman, the last of the Original Mets to leave the major league roster, stayed with the team through the 1966 campaign before moving on to the Dodgers, Cubs and Cardinals. He was the first Met to hit for the cycle and the first to post a three-homer game. In 1970 he hit .315 for the Cubs, with 32 homers and 115 RBIs, making the NL All-Star team (and driving in the winning run in the game) and finishing eighth in the voting for the league's Most Valuable Player award. He was also awarded the "Comeback Player of the Year" by *The Sporting News*. It was the only year of his career, which lasted until 1974, in which he hit over .272, homered more than 21 times or drove in more than 64 runs. He batted .252 with 159 home runs over his thirteen seasons. After retiring, Hickman returned to his birthplace of Henning, Tennessee, where he spent the next decade farming tobacco and soybeans. In 1985, the Reds made Hickman their minor league hitting instructor, a position he still holds as of this writing.

Dave Hillman's thirteen games with the 1962 Mets, in which he had no record and a 6.32 ERA, marked the end of a thirteen-year pro career. In his eight major league seasons, he appeared in 188 games with a 21-37 record with a 3.87 earned run average. His best year, and only winning season, came in 1961 when, at the age of 33, he went 3-2 with a 2.77 ERA for the Boston Red Sox. After retiring from baseball, he became the owner of a clothing store in Kingsport, Tennessee.

Gil Hodges remained with the Mets until early in 1963, although his tenure was beset by injuries. After the Washington Senators expressed interest in having the 39-year-old Hodges become their manager, the Mets traded his rights to allow him to begin his second career. Under Hodges, the Senators improved every year. In 1968, he returned as the Mets' skipper and led New York to its unbelievable World Series title in 1969, as the result of which Hodges was named the NL manager of the year. He died of a massive heart attack on April 2, 1972, in West Palm Beach, Florida, two days before his 48th birthday. He was inducted into the Mets Hall of Fame in 1982. A lifetime .273 hitter with 370 career home runs, eight All-Star appearances, two forty-home-run seasons and three Gold Gloves while playing in seven World Series, Hodges remains one of the best players not yet admitted into baseball's Hall of Fame. His record as the Mets' manager was 339-309. He became the first Met skipper to compile a career winning record and he remains one of only five of the Mets' nineteen managers to do so, the others being Bud Harrelson, Davey Johnson, Willie Randolph and Bobby Valentine. Although Hodges managed the Mets for just four seasons, only Johnson and Valentine have more wins. Hodges is one of only three Mets (the other two being Casey Stengel and Tom Seaver) whose numbers have been retired by the team, and he remains a beloved figure in the hearts and minds of New York. "Gil was the best human being I ever met," said Joe Pignatano, Hodges' teammate in 1962 and a coach under Hodges as well. "He was a super guy."

Rogers Hornsby remains one of the most controversial personalities in baseball history. No one can doubt his accomplishments as a player. In his lengthy career, which spanned from 1915 to 1937 and included stays with six teams, he batted .380 or better seven times, setting a record (which still stands) in 1924 by hitting .424. He finished with an incredible .358 lifetime average, second only to Ty Cobb, with 301 home runs, and was an early entry into the Hall of Fame. He also managed six teams, winning two pennants and a World Series, with a career record of 701-812. Hornsby drove his teams hard and was hated by many of his players, and he was also a devoted horseplayer, traits which did not endear him to baseball's establishment. By the time he joined the Mets as a scout, his last managerial job had been nine years earlier. He also served as the team's batting coach in 1962, as well as an instructor throughout the minor-league system. After his only season with the Mets, his health failed. Upon entering a Chicago hospital on December 10 for cataract surgery, he developed cardiac fibrillation and suffered a stroke. His condition worsened and he remained hospitalized until he died from heart failure on January 5, 1963, at the age of 66.

Willard Hunter spent the entire 1963 season in the minors and re-appeared with the Mets in 1964. He pitched much more effectively than in 1962, going 3-3 with five saves. As with Craig Anderson two years earlier, two of those three wins came when he won both ends of a doubleheader against the Cubs; as also with Anderson, though, those two wins were his last. 1964 saw the end of his big league career with a 4-9 record, and after spending the 1965 season in the minors, he quit baseball and entered the nascent computer industry. Now retired, he lives in Nebraska and reportedly refuses to discuss the Mets or the 1962 season.

Al Jackson's big league career lasted until 1969. A Stengel favorite, he was traded to St. Louis following the 1965 season, after Stengel retired, having compiled a 40-73 record with the Mets and leading the team in victories three years in a row. His hard luck did not end in New York, though; in 1966, with the Cardinals, he was only 13-15 but had an ERA of 2.51, fifth in the league. The following year, he went 9-4 with a 3.96 ERA. After the Cardinals returned him to New York in 1968, he opened the season with the '69 Mets before being sold to Cincinnati in June, thus missing out on the miracle. A pitcher who clearly deserved better, he finished his career with a record of 67-99 (24-19 when not with the Mets), coupled with a respectable earned run average of 3.98. After his retirement, Jackson went into the restaurant business and then rejoined the Mets as a minor league pitching instructor in 1971, becoming a full-time minor league pitching coach in 1976. In 1977, ex-teammate Don Zimmer became manager of the Red Sox, and Jackson became his pitching coach. After being fired in 1979, he returned to the Mets as minor league manager before joining the Orioles as pitching coach in 1989. He wound up his career as the Mets' bullpen and assistant pitching coach in 1999 and 2000, serving as interim pitching coach when GM Steve Philips purged manager Bobby Valentine's coaching staff. He retired after the 2000 season but continued to serve as a roving pitching instructor for the team, and he lives in Port St. Lucie, Florida, where the Mets now conduct spring training and have a minor league affiliate. His son, Reggie, spent four years in the Mets' minor league system before he too went into coaching. He is presently a pitching coach in the Kansas City organization.

Sherman "Roadblock" Jones was demoted to Syracuse in April 1962 after beginning the season in the starting rotation. Recalled in September, he pitched once more. As with so many other Original Mets, he never appeared in another major league game after 1962. After treatment and rehabilitation for gout in his throwing shoulder, he spent a couple of years in the minors, even making the International League all-star team, before retiring in

1964. The following year, he began a 23-year career as a police officer in Kansas City, Kansas, and he also coached semi-pro ball. In 1988, he was elected to the Kansas House of Representatives, and in 1992, to the Kansas Senate, in which he served two terms before retiring to Kansas City in 2000. He died on February 25, 2007, in Lawrence, Kansas, at the age of 72.

Ed Kranepool went back and forth between the Mets and the minors before sticking in 1965. For years, he was viewed as a player who never realized his potential, although he made valuable contributions to the Miracle Mets' pennant-winning teams of 1969 and 1973, and he eventually became a reliable first baseman and pinch-hitter. In 1974, he batted .486 in 35 pinch at-bats. Kranepool retired in 1979, having spent his entire career with the team, and he was inducted into the Mets Hall of Fame in 1990. After making an unsuccessful bid to buy the Mets, he resumed his employment as a stockbroker, a job he had held throughout his playing career. He also owned a restaurant with former teammate Ron Swoboda and continues to own businesses in the New York area. Kranepool still holds the franchise career records for games played, at-bats, hits, doubles, total bases and pinch hits, and he ranks among the top ten for virtually every offensive statistical category. In August 2002, he also was named to the "All Amazin' Team" – as a pinch hitter – as part of the Mets' fortieth anniversary celebrations.

Ralph "Red" Kress returned to his home in Los Angeles after the 1962 season. He had a heart attack and died on November 29, 1962, at the age of 55. His coaching career was preceded by fourteen major league seasons in which he batted .286 with 89 home runs.

Clem Labine retired after being released by the Mets in 1962. He finished with a record of 77-56 with 96 saves and an ERA of 3.63 in thirteen seasons and is recognized as one of the premier relief pitchers of the 1950s. He devoted himself full-time to Sports Apparel Company, a business he had started while still a player.

Upon the demise of the business in 1979, Labine joined a banking company, serving as a loan officer and business development representative. He died on March 2, 2007, in Vero Beach, Florida, at the age of eighty.

After being traded in May 1962, Hobie Landrith played with the Orioles and Senators before retiring in 1963. After a short stint as a Senators coach, he returned to the San Francisco area and went into the car business, ultimately becoming the director of sales for numerous Volkswagen dealerships in northern California, where he still resides. His major league career spanned fourteen seasons, and his lifetime batting average was .233.

Harry "Cookie" Lavagetto remained a Mets coach until after the 1963 season, when he was diagnosed – incorrectly, as it turned out – with lung cancer. He took a coaching position with the San Francisco Giants so he could be near his family home in Oakland. He remained with the Giants until 1967, when he retired. He then focused on assisting his wife with her business selling therapy equipment. He died of a heart attack in his sleep on August 10, 1990, 27 years after being mistakenly diagnosed, at the ripe old age of 77.

Ken MacKenzie was traded to the St. Louis Cardinals during the 1963 season. In 1964, he pitched for San Francisco, and in 1965, with the Astros, before retiring at the age of 31. Unlike every other pitcher with the Mets in 1962 and 1963, most notably Roger Craig, his winning records with the Mets those two years were the only winning seasons of his career. His lifetime record was 8-10 with a 4.80 earned run average and five saves. After retiring, he returned to Yale University as the baseball coach. In the late sixties, the Major League Baseball Players Association lowered the threshold for pension eligibility from five years of service time to four. MacKenzie found himself 27 days short of the required time, so in 1969, at the age of 35, he wrote to his former employers seeking a comeback. John McHale, general manager of the expansion

Montreal Expos, and also MacKenzie's GM at Milwaukee, brought him to Montreal when the big leagues expanded their rosters in September so MacKenzie could earn his service time. He pitched batting practice but did not appear in a game with the Expos. MacKenzie now lives in Connecticut and is involved with Yale hockey. He is also reportedly working on a book about the Original Mets.

Felix Mantilla played three seasons with the Red Sox after being traded following the 1962 season. In 1964, he hit 30 home runs (19 above his previous career best), and the following year, he made the American League All-Star team. He was dealt to the Astros in 1966, and he retired that season at the age of 31. He finished with a career average of .261 in eleven seasons. After a stint managing a minor league team in Canada, Mantilla returned to Milwaukee, where he had begun his career. He worked for a chapter of the Boys and Girls Clubs of Milwaukee until his retirement.

Jim Marshall was traded to the Pirates on May 6, 1962, at which point he was batting .344, having appeared in 17 games. He spent the rest of the year with the Pirates, hitting .220 in spot duty. He never appeared in another game, finishing at the age of 31 with a career average of .242, having never batted more than 300 times in a season. He then played in Japan from 1963 to 1965. After retiring, he became a coach and eventually managed the Cubs from 1974-76 and the Oakland Athletics in 1979. His teams never finished higher than fourth or with a winning record, and his managerial career ended after Oakland went 54-108. His major league managerial record was 229-326. Thereafter, Marshall served in a number of capacities before signing on with the expansion Arizona Diamondbacks in 1998. He has been with the Diamondbacks ever since and is currently the team's director of scouting for the Pacific Rim.

"Lefty" Bob G. Miller was acquired in the Don Zimmer trade after pitching in six games for the Reds, his first big league action since 1956. He appeared in seventeen games for the Mets after being called up from Syracuse, posting a 2-2 record with a 7.08 ERA. He retired after the season at the age of 26, with a career record of 6-8.

"Righty" Bob L. Miller was traded to Los Angeles after the 1962 season. The following year was his best, in which he went 10-8 with a 2.79 ERA for the Dodgers, although one of his losses was to his former team. Like Cannizzaro and Hickman, he remained in the majors until 1974, pitching for ten teams after leaving the Mets, with whom he also ended his seventeen-season career. During his tenure, he played for five pennant winners and four clubs which lost 100 games, and he also appeared in three World Series. He finished with a 69-81 record but had a career ERA of 3.37, and he also had 51 saves. He gave the following brutally honest reason when he finally hung it up: "I got tired of ducking line drives and backing up home plate." After his retirement, he stayed in baseball, serving as the first pitching coach for the expansion Toronto Blue Jays, ultimately becoming an advance scout for the Giants, for whom he had previously served as pitching coach as well. He was killed in a car accident on August 6, 1993, in Rancho Bernardo, California, at the age of 53. He lived just long enough to see the record he tied in 1962 for consecutive losses to start a season be broken by another Met, Anthony Young.

Wilmer "Vinegar Bend" Mizell's nine year major league career ended with his release by the Mets in August of 1962. After briefly attempting to come back with the Pirates who had traded him to the Mets earlier in the year, he retired with a record of 90-88 and an ERA of 3.85. He settled in North Carolina and began a sales and marketing career for Pepsi Cola before being elected county commissioner in Davidson County. He was elected to the U.S. House of Representatives as a Republican in 1968, serving three terms before being defeated in 1974. After losing his third re-election bid, he served in a number of capacities under Presidents

Ford, Reagan and Bush. He died in Kerrville, Texas, on February 21, 1999, at the age of 68.

Herb Moford was sent down to Syracuse in May 1962 after appearing in seven games with the Mets, his last big league action. He remained in the minors before retiring the following year at age 34 after seventeen pro seasons. His totals in a major league career that spanned parts of four seasons over an eight-year period were 5-13 with an earned run average of 5.03. He returned to his native Kentucky and became a tobacco farmer, an occupation he pursued until his death from emphysema on December 3, 2005, at the age of 77.

Bob Moorhead's 1962 season ended when he broke his pitching hand punching a wall. He appeared in 38 games that season, starting seven, without recording a win. He did not return to the big leagues until 1965, appearing in another nine games without winning any of those either. He retired after spending the 1966 season in the minors. His two years with the Mets were his only big-league campaigns, and he finished 0-3 and an ERA of 4.51. He became employed with a trucking company in Lemoyne, Pennsylvania, and left the company shortly before his death on December 3, 1986, at the age of 48.

Johnny Murphy served as George Weiss' number-one assistant until Weiss retired after the 1966 season. Murphy ultimately succeeded Weiss' successor, Bing Devine, becoming general manager before the 1968 season and remained in that position until suffering a fatal heart attack. He died on January 14, 1970, at the age of 61. He was inducted into the Mets Hall of Fame in 1983.

Charlie Neal was traded to Cincinnati on July 1, 1963. He retired after that season and played semi-pro baseball for several years, during which time Rod Kanehl was his teammate on a team named the Dreamliners, which won the league championship. He died of heart failure on November 18, 1996, in Dallas, Texas, at the age of 65. In eight seasons, he batted .259.

Lindsey Nelson retired from the broadcast team in 1979 after seventeen years. That same year he was elected to the National Sportswriters and Sportscasters Hall of Fame. He was so much a part of the team that he was awarded a World Series ring after the 1969 victory. After resigning, he announced for the Giants until 1981. In 1988, he was awarded the Ford C. Frick Award, gaining him admission to the Baseball Hall of Fame. Bob Murphy joined Nelson in the Hall of Fame in 1994 by being awarded the Frick Award (Ralph Kiner, of course, has already been inducted as player). Nelson, Murphy and Kiner were collectively inducted into the Mets Hall of Fame in 1984. Nelson died of Parkinson's disease on June 10, 1995, in Atlanta, Georgia, at the age of 76. Murphy remained at his post until retiring at the end of the 2003 season. He died after a brief battle with lung cancer on August 3, 2004, six weeks before his eightieth birthday. Kiner remains part of the Mets broadcast team to this day, and in 2002, the television booth at Shea Stadium was renamed in his honor. The booth at the Mets' new stadium, Citi Field, is also named for Kiner.

Joan Whitney Payson continued to own and love the Mets until her death on October 4, 1975, at the age of 72, within five days of Casey Stengel's passing. Ownership of the team passed to her daughter, Lorinda de Roulet, and the Mets went into a nosedive which did not end until de Roulet sold the team in January 1980. The following year, Mrs. Payson and Casey Stengel became the first two inductees to the Mets Hall of Fame.

Joe Pignatano retired after hitting into the infamous triple play at the conclusion of the 1962 season. He hit .234 in 307 games over six big-league seasons. He entered the coaching ranks and rejoined the Mets as part of Gil Hodges' staff in 1968. He enjoyed the heights of 1969 and 1973 and endured the lean years of the late 1970s, serving several managers before leaving in 1981. He finished his coaching career with the Braves in 1986. Most closely associated with the Dodgers, he still lives in Brooklyn.

Charles "Red" Ruffing resigned as pitching coach after the 1962 season and became a roving minor-league instructor for the team. Based on his lifetime record of 273 wins and 225 losses, he was elected to the Baseball Hall of Fame in 1967. He is still considered to be one of the best-hitting pitchers in history, with a career batting average of .269, and he hit at least .300 eight times with thirty-six home runs. In 1973, Ruffing suffered a stroke and remained in poor health until his death thirteen years later, on February 17, 1986, at the age of 81.

Although Bill Shea did more than anyone else to achieve the return of National League baseball to New York, he had no formal relationship with the team after his group was granted the charter. He had no ownership interest and never served in any capacity. Following his return to practice, his reputation as a politically-connected behind-the-scenes law giant grew, as did his firm, which was hired by many large and influential clients, including the Mets and Yankees. Shea practiced law for almost fifty years, winning many civic awards and serving on numerous boards. He also remained active in the sporting world, helping the city retain the New York Jets in the 1960s and attract two more expansion teams, the NBA's New York (now New Jersey) Nets and the NHL's New York Islanders. He was inducted into the Mets Hall of Fame in 1983. He died in New York at the age of 84 on October 2, 1991, as the result of complications from a stroke he had suffered two years earlier. When the Mets' stadium, which he'd worked so hard to bring about, opened in 1964, Shea was asked how long he thought the team would continue to name it after him. "Oh, until about five minutes after I'm dead," he responded. In fact, Shea Stadium remained the team's home for the next 45 seasons under its original name, despite the fact that most other teams had long since sold the naming rights to their ballparks. On April 8, 2008, during the Mets' final season at Shea, the team held a night honoring Shea and announced that his last name would be treated as a retired number by the club. The outfield bridge at Citi Field was also been named in Shea's honor.

Bobby Gene Smith's eight-game Met career ended two weeks into the 1962 season when he was traded to the Cubs for Sammy Taylor. Five weeks later, the Cubs traded him to the Cardinals. After 1962, he did not return to the majors until 1965, when he appeared in 23 games for the California Angels. He batted .246 in 476 games over seven seasons. After two more years in the minors, he went to work as a maintenance technician for Pierce County in Tacoma, Washington. He is now retired and lives in Surprise, Arizona.

Casey Stengel continued his affiliation with his amazin' Mets long after he retired as the team's manager (and the team, in turn, retired his number, an honor that the Yankees did not bestow upon him until five years later). In fact, he was the only baseball personality who wore the uniforms of the Brooklyn Dodgers, New York Giants, New York Yankees and New York Mets. Even with his atrocious winning percentage with the Mets. Dodgers and Braves, he still finished with a record of 1,905 wins and 1,842 losses. Although he and Edna returned home to Glendale, California, after his retirement, he was named Vice President of the team's West Coast operations, and he frequently visited the Mets' Florida spring training camp thereafter. He remained on the Mets payroll for the remaining nine years of his life. "The Mets have been paying me for the past ten years and people ask me what I do for them," he explained in 1974. "I don't bother them, that's what." In addition, he resumed his former duties as a vice president at the Valley National Bank and attended many games in California, never relinquishing his status as baseball's Perfesser Emeritus. Stengel, Ashburn, George Weiss, Hornsby, Ruffing and the three broadcasters remain the only figures associated with the 1962 Mets to be enshrined in Cooperstown. After suffering a stroke, he died on September 25, 1975, in Glendale, at the age of 85. When Stengel's death was announced, columnist Jim Murray of the *Los Angeles Times* printed the following eulogy: "Well, God is getting an earful today. I hope He understands the infield fly rule, the hit and run, how to pitch to Hornsby with men on, when to platoon, when it would do you some good to bunt, and what really happened in the 1913 World Series. He will get an illustrated lecture on the hook slide, the best place to play Babe Ruth, when to order the infield in, and how to steal on left-handers. At the end of all this, the narrator will doff his cap and a sparrow will fly out [Stengel had pulled this famous stunt as a player]. They finally slipped a called third strike past Casey Stengel. He can't argue the call. The game is over. Dusk is settling on the bleachers, the lights are turned on in the press box where 'my writers' are putting '30' to the final bits of Stengelese they will ever type." He was buried with his 1962 Mets home uniform, his 1960 Yankees road uniform, a set of cleats and a picture of Edna. Stengel, inducted as a charter member of the Mets Hall of Fame in 1981, remains dead at the present time.

Acquired during the 1962 season, Sammy Taylor remained with the Mets until July 1, 1963, when he and Charlie Neal were traded to the Reds for Jesse Gonder. After a month with the Reds, in which he appeared in three games, he was traded to the Indians, for whom he appeared in four games, his last in the majors. He appeared in 245 games over six seasons, batting .245. As of this writing, he lives in Boiling Springs in his native South Carolina.

After playing eight games with Buffalo in 1964, Marv Throneberry retired with a career average of .237 and 53 home runs. He returned to Collierville, Tennessee, and became a beer season. He returned to public life in the 1980s, when the Miller Beer Company featured him in a series of television and radio commercials. In 1983, he was inducted into the Tennessee Sports Hall of Fame. He died of cancer on June 23, 1994, in Fisherville, Tennessee, at the age of 60. He is remembered still as the personification of lovable baseball incompetence.

George Weiss retired as president of the Mets in November 1966. In the 29 seasons between 1936 and 1964, the Yankee teams that he built won 22 pennants and sixteen World Series. He was inducted into the Baseball Hall of Fame in 1971, one of only four general managers to have been so honored, and the Mets Hall of Fame in 1982. He died on August 13, 1972, in Greenwich, Connecticut, at the age of 77.

Gene Woodling, the oldest player on the 1962 Mets, retired after being released just prior to the following year at the age of 40. He had 1585 career hits with a lifetime average of .284, and he batted .318 in five World Series. After coaching and scouting, he became a successful businessman, most notably with the Eaton Corporation, and the value of some farmland he owned in Ohio skyrocketed after oil was discovered. He suffered a stroke in 1997 which left him largely crippled, and he died on June 2, 2001, at the age of 78.

After being traded in May 1962, Don Zimmer played with the Reds and Senators before retiring after the 1965 season. After playing briefly in Japan, he then managed teams in the Reds and Padres systems before becoming a Padres coach. He managed the Padres (1972-73), Red Sox (1976-80), Rangers (1980-82) and Cubs (1987-91), winning a division title with Chicago in 1989 and being named NL Manager of the Year. He experienced expansion baseball a second time, signing on with the new Colorado Rockies as a coach in 1993. In 1996, he joined the Yankees, serving manager Joe Torre as bench coach, a position from which he retired in 2003. Zimmer was with the Yankees for their six World Series appearances during that period. In 2001, he published his autobiography, *Zim: A Baseball Life*, thus joining Frank Thomas as the only Original Met players to do so – so far, anyway. Approaching his sixtieth year in baseball, he now serves as a special advisor for the Tampa Bay Rays.

CHAPTER FIFTEEN – THE LEGEND

"This was a group effort. No one player could've done all this." – *Casey Stengel, manager of the New York Mets*

Nearly fifty years after their initial season, the Original Mets are still a beloved team. Legions of true baseball fans have heard about Throneberry's fielding misadventures and his failure to step on first base, the fate of Ashburn's boat, Roger Craig's 24 losses, the two Bob Millers, "yo la tengo," and the triple play in the last game. Casey Stengel remains a revered figure, renowned as much for his time with the Mets as for his unequaled success with the Yankees. The '62 Mets remain the yardstick against which true incompetence on the diamond is measured. Any exceptionally bad team (most recently, the 2003 Detroit Tigers, who lost 119 games) is inevitably compared to the Original Mets, and the names of Marvelous Marv, Hot Rod Kanehl and Choo Choo Coleman are fondly recalled all over again. The same thing occurred when baseball expanded in 1969, 1977, 1993 and 1997. Mets devotees still contribute their memories and thoughts about the team to various fan websites, where other Mets devotees read them and offer their own memories and thoughts, or in the alternative, explanations why the author of the first memories and thoughts is full of shit. Autographed baseballs, copies of the Mets souvenir yearbook and other memorabilia command substantial sums at auctions. Clearly, a lot of people still care about the Original Mets.

But why? What makes a horrible ball club worthy of such reverence after five decades? Why should Rod Kanehl and Elio Chacon still be remembered after hundreds, if not thousands, of better ballplayers have been forgotten?

There are several reasons. Not the least of these is that the Original Mets represented the return of National League baseball to New York after four long empty seasons. There is a phenomenon which occurs in cities with teams in different leagues, which is that fans of one club can't be fans of the other. Ask any Chicago White Sox fan what he thinks of the Cubs, and vice versa. The same was just as true for New York baseball fans prior to 1957, due in no small part to the fact that the Dodgers and Giants so regularly competed for the pennant, especially in the golden age following World War II, with the winner almost invariably facing the Yankees in the World Series.

"In Brooklyn, we would sit on the stoop and argue about baseball," recalls Ed Wolff. We'd argue for the personalities, more than the team. Mays, Mantle, Snider . . . the arguments would never get resolved. And people would choose the beer they'd drink not for the way it tasted, but for which team the beer company sponsored. Ballantine for the Yankees. Knickerbocker for the Giants. Schaefer was the Dodgers' beer. I remember when they poured beer when the guys came around [at the ballpark], it was all head and very little beer. And the announcers . . . if you were a Brooklyn fan, you thought Red Barber was such a fantastic broadcaster. If you were a Yankee fan, he was no damn good. You would like Mel Allen better. Whether it was the beer, or the announcer, or the field they were playing on . . . that was the best, according to who you were a fan of."

Jim Fertitta's memories are similar. "We were always arguing with each other. We always compared our centerfielders. I loved Duke Snider. But there were guys who liked Willie Mays, there were guys who liked Joe DiMaggio and then Mickey Mantle. We always compared Mantle and Snider and Mays, and of course, all the kids who were Dodger fans thought Snider was the best. When the Dodgers and Giants played each other, there were plenty guys arguing with each other. The kids on my block and across from me were mostly Dodger fans, but the ones down on Franklin

Avenue near DeKalb were mostly Giant fans. We would just go at it. We argued a lot."

In fact, the only thing Dodger and Giant fans could agree on was their disaffection, if not outright hatred, for the Yankees. It has been well documented that the Yankees' attendance did not substantially increase once they had the city to themselves. This was because most hardcore Dodger and Giant fans would rather insult their own mothers than attend a game at Yankee Stadium. There is no better proof of this fact than the speed with which the Mets began to outdraw the Yankees, even as the Yankees were winning pennants and the Mets were in the cellar. In 1962, the Mets' attendance was less than their competitors but still respectable. In 1963, the figures were almost even. In 1964, when Shea Stadium opened, the Mets drew 400,000 more fans. The common denominators in each of those three years were that the Yankees won the pennant and the Mets finished last. Clearly, a large segment of New York fans felt disenfranchised after the exodus, and as a result they were ready to embrace any new National League team in the city. As Joseph Durso explained: "Where the Yankees were successful as ball players, the Mets became monumentally unsuccessful. Where the Yankees were cool cats, the Mets grew up as warm ugly ducklings. Where the Yankees were institutional, the Mets lunged into the public domain. The Yankees, on top, had everything to lose; the Mets, on bottom, had everything to gain. And they set out to gain it with those Yankees renegades, Weiss and Stengel, who discovered now that the same public that had criticized them in the later Yankee years was clamoring to adopt them in their new roles, to idolize them – to support them at the box office. Weiss gave full credit for this support to two things: 'The latent interest in the National League after the Dodgers and Giants left, and the energies and personalities of people like Casey Stengel and Mrs. Joan Payson."

In a 2002 email to the author, Stan Isaacs stated that "I find it hard to say why people have such a feeling for the Mets to this day.

I think the Mets meant a lot to people because they brought National League baseball back to New York after the Giants and Dodgers deserted New York. Casey Stengel made them lovable at the beginning, as did Richie Ashburn. I think the fans knew that they had to make their own fun by bringing an attitude over and above seeing their team win – because it was obvious the pioneer Mets couldn't win very often. The sign man, Karl Ehrhardt, is not to be overlooked because he captured the essence of the fans' feeling about actions on the field in the early days." Leonard Koppett added that "[t]he secret of their success was this: with the Yankees winning a hundred games every year, the Yankee fan had sixty disappointments, and the Met fan, when they won fifty games, had fifty thrills. The losses didn't count for the Met fans, and only the losses counted for the Yankee fans."

Along this same theme, Roger Angell, writing after the Mets' first exhibition victory over the Yankees, offered this analysis, which still rings true almost fifty years later: "What cheered me as I tramped through the peanut shells and discarded programs and out into the hot late sunlight was not just the score and not just Casey's triumph but a freshly renewed appreciation of the marvelous complexity and balance of baseball. Offhand, I can think of no other sport in which the world's champions, one of the great teams of the era, would not instantly demolish inferior opposition and reduce a game such as the one we had just seen to cruel ludicrousness. Baseball is harder than that; it requires a full season, hundreds and hundreds of separate games, before quality can emerge, and in that summer span every home-town fan, every doomed admirer of underdogs will have his afternoon of revenge and joy."

The Mets' continuing popularity is another factor contributing to the longstanding interest in the 1962 team. With the exception of some down seasons in the late seventies, the Mets have been the number one team in New York almost since their creation. Because of their popularity, there has always been considerable interest in the team's roots, as Craig Anderson explained in 2002:

"The term that came up was 'Original Mets.' Whoever did that put a label on us that has stuck for forty years. I was an Original Met. New York fans are unbelievable baseball people for remembering things. They are historians of baseball. They keep the stats and they're just more up on things. When they did that expansion draft, it was like . . . these are the Original Mets. This was the first New York Metropolitan team. You never hear the term 'Original Colt 45s.' That's a minor trivia question. But you start talking about Original Mets, you start bringing all these names back up again. I don't think they were trying . . . I think it just fell into place, that we were the Original Mets. And that stuck with us for forty years. I get letters, you know, people writing me with bubble gum cards, and it's amazing – you see, I use that word too – that they're still using that term in these requests for autographs; they're collecting autographs and they want to get the Original Mets."

Writing in 1970, shortly after the Miracle Mets' triumph, George Vecsey wrote that "someday when the Mets are hailed as the greatest dynasty in sports, the fusing process of history will make millions of fans assume that New York baseball sprang full-grown out of Shea Stadium sometime in the middle 1960s. The truth is that New Yorkers had been conditioned to love the Mets even before there was a Mets. The seeds of mad devotion and ironic appreciation had been planted for generations and needed only the bright sunshine of the new Mets in 1962 to make them flourish."

Jay Hook offered this to the author in 2002: "Maury Allen said that, with all the famous Yankee teams, his belief is that there's still more interest in the '62 Mets than there is in any of those great Yankee teams. I was quizzing him a little about that. I guess my perspective on it was that the writers were so involved with the Met players that they created a great mystique about that team. Secondly, it seemed to me at the time that we had more fans who were cab drivers and bartenders . . . we had maybe the more blue collar kind of fan, and the Yankees had more of the white collar fan. Maybe we related better with the average person."

Long-time fan John MacMaster told the author that "most of these guys, at some point, must have been really, really good. I mean, they were professional baseball players in a sixteen-team sport. Because they were still considered respectable, it was interesting to see whether these guys could really do anything, and it was kind of a disappointment to me that they were that bad. I really thought, 'These guys are pretty good. I don't really know a lot about them, but I've heard of them,' and the fact that they failed so miserably was almost hard to believe. There must have been something else going on besides bad luck – it was some kind of negative charisma that they had. You could probably pick twenty-five other guys and they would have at least won fifty or sixty games the way Houston did. It was like this sort of death wish that they had which made it like there was something greater going on than just the fact that they were lousy. And again, growing up in the New York metropolitan area, they got a lot of press. I read the sports section and didn't really care about anything else, so I was immersed in, every day, 'what's going on with these guys, they're just a comedy of errors.' I kind of felt sorry for them. I really wanted to see them break out. When they won a game, like the game I went to, it was almost hard to believe. They'd lose ten games in a row and then suddenly out of nowhere they'd play great and win a game, and you'd be thinking, 'Why can't they do that every game?' And I'd get caught up in that."

Another fan, Walter Pullis, offered this analysis: "Let's take it from a psychological point of view. You can't get away from the fact that we didn't have National League ball for four years. So people were willing to wait to bring back almost anybody. Second, Casey. That had a lot to do with it. If you had [Houston manager] Harry Craft, you would have won more games, but probably the team wouldn't have been as memorable. So you've got no National League ball, you've got Casey, and you've got the fact that they not only lost but they lost in a colorful manner. You take the Mets in '93, when they lost a heck of a lot of games – that's not colorful, that's just lousy ball. This is a team that was obviously outmanned, and everybody above a very casual fan knew that. When they did the expansion draft, people knew that they got lousy players and you couldn't expect much of them. So winning a game a week was kind of fun. And even when they didn't win, they lost with a certain aplomb. They were colorful, in a nutshell. And people accepted it. Now Breslin's book the following year . . . I read that at the time it came out. He was talking about how people could relate to losing or something. I don't know whether that was true. Leonard Koppett wrote an article about it being an interesting point in time. This, of course, was the Kennedy era. I can remember the inauguration, the whole bit, and it was a very hopeful time. It was before Vietnam and after the fifties . . . I think people were happy, and the so-called average person was maybe a little more happy and not as ironic or cynical as people are today. And I think the Mets just hit it at that time, and you remembered the players. There was just something very memorable about the team. Forty years later, I have almost total memory of it. And of course I wasn't an adult then, I was only a kid. I was fifteen years old. I had nothing on my mind but the next Met game. I had my little transistor radio wherever I went – listening to the day game, or through my pillow at night if it was after my bedtime like with the California games. So it made more of an impression. That was my life that summer, following the Mets. I've always stayed a Mets fan, but as I got older, I lost some interest. I'm not one who's followed the team for forty years and remembers all forty years. I don't remember things from the last ten or fifteen years. I only remember games from when I was a teenager. I remember those vividly."

Mets chronicler Stanley Cohen elaborates as follows: "The 1962 Mets, who forever will remain the prototype of the losing cause, could not have come upon the scene at a better time. The early sixties was a fairly blissful period in America's history. The serene but monotonous years of the fifties had given way to breezier days. Camelot had opened its gates to a new generation. A sense of subtlety, of irony and wit, was more the fashion than the ponderous sincerity, the unwinking commitment to purpose that had given the Silent Generation its name. In New York, sports championships had become as routine as the turning of the season. In 1962, the Yankees were on their way to their third straight pennant, and two more would follow. The football Giants were winning division titles with almost equal regularity. So when the Mets came to town, it meant more than the return of National League baseball. Here, at last, was a team one could root for and remain free of the anxiety of defeat. If fans drew sustenance from a winner, there were nonetheless few who could easily identify with one. The Yankees and Giants might reflect our fondest hopes and aspirations, but the Mets – ah, the Mets! – embodied the harsh reality of our workaday lives."

Writing in 1970, Leonard Koppett summarized that "a few years earlier, the New Breed might have felt too intimidated to come out of the woodwork; a few years later, it might have aroused only hostility. The Kennedy Years were not only the right period for the New Breed to take root but also the right time for its character to be met with acceptance and amusement at its kookiness."

Thirty-two years thereafter, and not long before his death, Koppett offered another take on what made the Original Mets special: "There hadn't been anything like that. The first expansion team was the Angels. They're on the other end of the country. Who's paying attention? Completely overshadowed by the Dodgers and Hollywood. The second expansion team is the Washington Senators Two. The Washington Senators One hadn't been getting any attention for the last ten years. Why should the Washington Senators Two? Here's this thing starting from scratch, in New York, in the famous Polo Grounds, controversial on every level, Stengel clowning it up and being Stengel, and Stengel and Weiss as a combination who had taken the Yankees to the highest possible levels now dealing with this. It was a story circumstance that was unique."

Journalist Brian Heyman, who wrote a fine article in the *White Plains Journal News* about the Original Mets in 2002, added this perspective in an email to the author: "The 1962 Mets earned their place in baseball history with that worst record ever, a record that may never be broken. But even if it is, the profound failures of that team keep the memory alive. It's more than that, though. Those Mets were the first Mets, the foundation for a franchise and the foundation for National League baseball's return to the city. The indelible images of the way they lost also make that team endure, the grounders through legs, the catchable flies falling in, the bad pitching, the blown leads, the almost-comical mistakes in the field and on the bases by Marv Throneberry, a fitting symbol of the lovable losers. And there are those clips shown from time to time of Casey Stengel clowning in his unique double-speak way. Perhaps his act and all the losing wouldn't have been tolerated in New York in this day and age with the intense multi-media coverage and the 24-hour sports call-in shows. That was a different time, though. But it's interesting when you talk with many of the surviving players from that team, and the Mets went through 45 players that year. They're not generally ashamed of their association with it. Some like being known for something. Some simply enjoyed the experience and have countless funny stories to tell. Many were just grateful for the chance to play in the big leagues or to keep playing in the big leagues."

Although the public's fondness for the Original Mets has never gone away, there have been chronological and literary triggers which have led to increased attention being focused on the '62 team. For example, in the franchise's second season, there appeared *Can't Anybody Here Play This Game?* written by a then-little-known New York writer named Jimmy Breslin (the title was based on the mangling of a well-known Stengel quote – see Chapter 8). It was a short book and was based largely on material which had already appeared in *Sports Illustrated*, *Reader's Digest* and elsewhere. Although Marvelous Marv Throneberry was on his way out of New York and out of baseball by the time the book appeared, the public got to enjoy him one more time through Breslin's work, which focused on some memorable Throneberryisms. As Throneberry himself put it thirty years later, "Jimmy Breslin went on the TV once and said that I made him famous. I think it was on Johnny Carson. He admitted it."

The hysteria following the Mets' improbable World Series victory in 1969 inevitably led to a revival of interest in the Original Mets. It was an instance where the literary and the chronological factors converged, as five books about the Mets, all written by New York sportswriters, emerged in 1970: *Once Upon The Polo Grounds: The Mets That Were*, by Leonard Shecter of the *Post*, *The Amazing Mets*, by Jerry Mitchell, also of the *Post*, *The New York Mets – the Whole Story*, by Leonard Koppett of the *Times*, *Joy In Mudville*, by George Vecsey, also of the *Times*, and Maury Allen's *The Incredible Mets*. Another similarly celebratory book, *The Year the Mets Lost Last Place*, by Paul D. Zimmerman and Dick Schaap, appeared while the 1969 season was still going on. Although these books are well-written (and observant readers of this text will notice frequent quotations therefrom), their focus was not the Original Mets, but rather, the development of the team from lovable losers into lovable winners. That these books were all published in the wake of the Series could hardly be a coincidence. Of course, folded into the euphoria was the sense that everything which had happened before had led to the triumph. For example, on the day the Mets clinched the pennant, the ever-present Leonard Shecter recorded this exchange: "The most moving thing said about the Mets had been said the day the clinched the pennant. George Weiss, the elderly retired president of the Mets, stuck his head into Gil Hodges' crowded office, smiled his tight little smile and said, '1962.' Hodges smiled a big-toothed grin. His eyes shone with amused understanding. '1962,' he said. That was the year the Mets started paying their dues."

One of those who paid dues along the way was Tug McGraw, who pitched for the Mets from 1965 through 1974. After the World Series win, he stated that "when the Mets were born, management did a tremendous job of public relations in making the team popular. The theme was: 'To err is human, but to forgive is to be a Mets' fan.' From the fans' standpoint, the idea was to take this little baby of a team, and they were going to feed it and bathe it and stroke it and change its diapers and forgive it when it messed up. They were going to give it love and affection, and some day this little baby was going to grow up, and when those Dodger bullies and those Giant bullies came to town it was gonna kick their ass so high they'd have to shit through their ribs. Finally, in 1969, that little Met baby had grown up. He was young and innocent and naive, but he was also strong and powerful. Nobody knew yet what he was capable of, but when we beat the Dodgers and the Giants [by consecutive sweeps, signaling the team's rise to power] it was like saying, 'Okay, folks, no more kicking sand in our faces.'"

The ballclub's 25th season in 1986 also led many to pay homage anew to the Original Mets. Before the season began, the club, in conjunction with Major League Baseball Productions, released an anniversary video called *An Amazin' Era – The New York Mets*, which featured invaluable (and otherwise unavailable) footage of Bill Shea, Mayor Wagner, the ticker-tape parade and Stengel at the first spring training, as well as interviews with Roger Craig, Al Jackson, Jay Hook and Frank Thomas. Again, though, coverage of the Original Mets was limited, as the producers had 25 years to get through in the video's 71 minutes. Another sportswriter-produced book, *The New York Mets – Twenty-Five Years of Baseball Magic*, written by Jack Lang with Peter Simon, also appeared during this time.

The eighties also provided an unlikely source of celebrity for one Original Met. The Miller Brewing Company had been using retired athletes in its Miller Lite television commercials for several years. Some of these commercials featured Marv Throneberry, usually uttering his standard introductory line: "I don't know why they asked me to do this commercial." "I heard a great story about him and the Miller beer ad he did," recalled Rod Kanehl. "They called him up and said, 'We want you to come to New York and make this commercial.' Marv laughed and hung up the phone. He thought this was a prank. They had to call him three times before they could convince him they weren't kidding." Longtime author and editor Dick Schaap added that *"Can't Anybody* . . .will always be remembered for one of Breslin's most delightful images, his suggestion that having Marv Throneberry play first base for your baseball team is like having [convicted robber] Willie Sutton work in your bank. Nobody could have guessed when Breslin wrote that line that almost twenty years later, in the early 1980s, he and Throneberry would both be on television, doing beer commercials. Willie Sutton only did time." For his part, Throneberry was quoted as saying that if he did for Miller what he did for baseball, he would hurt their sales.

Throneberry went on to make about a dozen TV and radio commercials for Miller Lite, all of which featured his folksy, good-natured and self-deprecating delivery, and in most of them, he professed ignorance as to what he was doing there anyway. His appearance, noted George Vecsey, was "rubbery-shaped and sad-eyed as a basset hound, musing, 'I still don't know why I'm in this commercial.'" Of course, there is the possibility that some of his ignorance was genuine; during his interview with Steve Rushin in 1992, it seemed he still didn't quite understand what all the fuss was about. "People always ask me to tell them some of the funny stuff that happened that year," Throneberry said. "Really, I don't remember that much funny stuff happening."

Occasionally, though, Throneberry's remarks went from ignorance, feigned or not, to outright revisionism. He told author Mike Blake that "though we lost 120 games, we were not a bad team. We had good players, but we had poor pitching and relief help and lost 35 one-run games [actually 39]. When I was with the Yankees in 1958 and we came back from a 3-1 deficit to beat Milwaukee in the World Series, it was a big team effort . . . the

Yankee way. On the Mets, we had Frank Thomas, Charlie Neal, Jim Hickman and Richie Ashburn – good ballplayers. But they were taught the Dodger way, the Yankee way, the Kansas City way, the Phillies way; they were 25 players all taught different ways to play. They didn't mesh and made mistakes. But I always looked at it this way: There were eight teams in each league and only 400 players in the majors out of millions of athletes in the country who wanted to be. We were all pretty damn good players, among the top 400 out of millions, but the press talked us down so much, they talked us into losing. One final dig at the writers and official scorers. I wasn't a great fielder, of course, but I wasn't as bad as the writers made out. I got errors in the Polo Grounds in the cab on the way to the ballpark. I got errors on throws by infielders that went over my head and into the stands. True. I got errors as part of my reputation."

The Mets' thirtieth and fortieth anniversaries also renewed interest in the debut Mets. In 1992, Steve Rushin's outstanding commemorative article, entitled "Bad Beyond Belief," appeared in *Sports Illustrated*. In 2002, three more comprehensive works, *The Mets Encyclopedia* by Peter Bjarkman, Peter Golenbock's *Amazin'* and *Amazin' Met Memories* by Howard Blatt, all histories of the Mets' first forty years, were published. As with the video, though, these books are limited in their coverage of the Original Mets based on the scope of the projects as a whole.

Oddly enough, the one entity that has been reluctant to acknowledge the Original Mets in recent years has been the Met organization itself. The team was invited back in 1986 on the occasion of the franchise's twenty-fifth season. However, the club's thirtieth and fortieth anniversaries went by without similar festivities, and another gathering at a card show in December 2002 also occurred without team sanction. Craig Anderson noted that "back in 1990, a group of baseball card collectors organized a reunion of the '62 Mets and brought the guys all back to New York for a big show. And twenty-eight guys came back. And you know what? That's the last time we've been together. The New York

Mets have not invited any of us back since 1986. That was the last time they brought us back as a team. Now you would think since this is the fortieth anniversary [in 2002] that they would bring us back and give us a chance to reunite with New York fans."

As it happened, the Original Mets did feature briefly in a video montage prepared by the team, but this was done more to celebrate the franchise's history rather than to commemorate those who came first. Even then, participation by members of the Original Mets has been spotty. As Rod Kanehl noted, "I get one or two cards to sign every month. You know, kids sending cards. One year I didn't get invited back to an Old Timers Game for some reason, and someone said, 'We didn't know how to get hold of you.' I said, 'Well, a couple hundred kids a year know how to get hold of me.'"

As of this writing, Richie Ashburn, Marv Throneberry, Rod Kanehl, Gus Bell, Charley Neal, Elio Chacon, Gil Hodges, Righty Bob Miller, Gene Woodling, Harry Chiti, Sherman Jones, Herb Moford, Bob Moorhead, Clem Labine, Sammy Drake and Vinegar Bend Mizell have died, and of the coaches, only Solly Hemus is still alive. Those players still around are in their sixties and seventies. Therefore, one hopes the Mets will arrange something while the opportunity to do so still exists.

In the face of such official indifference, it has been private individuals who have been responsible for sustaining interest in the Original Mets. The fans are the ones who still tell the tales, who continue to debate Stengel's managerial strategies and the effectiveness of Weiss' approach in building the team, and who continue to write letters to the players and request autographs or information from them. As Marv Throneberry told Steve Rushin in 1992, "I get three to five letters every day. I throw 'em all in a box. When it rains, I answer 'em."

Taken at face value, this statement is astounding. The notion that Throneberry would still be receiving so much correspondence (even allowing for exaggeration) thirty years later speaks volumes about the undying fan interest in the Original Mets. Similarly, Hall of Famer Richie Ashburn was a beloved figure in Philadelphia, where he played most of his fifteen-year career (and was one of the pennant-winning Whiz Kids of 1950) and returned to serve as the Phillies' broadcaster for thirty-five years after his career ended. Yet he told Rushin in 1992 that he got more mail concerning his 1962 adventures than he did for his fourteen preceding years. Indeed, the players' membership on the worst baseball team of the twentieth century certainly provided them with both the memories of a once-in-a-lifetime thrill and the ability to turn adversity into valuable experience.

Jay Hook, perhaps the Original Met who most transcended his experience as a player, told the author in 2002: "I've retired three times now. People say, 'Do you look at yourself as a success or a failure?' I look at baseball. I wanted to win twenty games. I wanted to win a World Series. I didn't do it. But I got to the major leagues and spent five years there. In industry, I wanted to be president of a corporation. Well, I wasn't president of a corporation. I was a group president, which is right next to the top, and I made a lot of money doing that. Well, am I a success or failure because of that? I guess the thing I achieved most was a professorship at Northwestern, and becoming chairman of the board of this seminary. I've been chairman for seven years. About a year ago, they awarded me an honorary doctorate degree. I have a sister that's a professor at the University of Wisconsin. She went and got a Ph.D. and then worked her way up to full professor and went through the tenure process. I called her up after this guy made me a full professor and said, 'Joy, how tough is this? All these years, you've been telling me how hard it was to get there.' I've been chairman of the board for seven years and I've done a lot of things for the seminary, and they awarded me a doctorate for this. Those are real successes. Seeing your four kids doing something, and your thirteen grandchildren, those are successes. When you measure your life's cycle, if you will, there's losses, there's wins . . . but there's always tomorrow."

Similarly, Frank Thomas told the author that "a person wrote to me not too long ago, and he said, 'Do you realize that you're in the top one percent of your business as far as hitting home runs is concerned?' How many people in industry can say they're in the top one percent of their business? I had a great year for Casey. I would always go out and give a hundred and ten percent. If I made five errors in a ballgame, I didn't care what the fans said, as long as I could go into the clubhouse, take off my uniform and say I gave a hundred percent of the God-given talent given to me, I didn't care what anybody said. I love the game of baseball. You know, when you get between those lines, I don't care how old you are, you're like a little kid. I've always been that way. Even in fantasy camps, when I go to those places . . . I played 21 innings this past January 21 [2002] with the Pirates in a fantasy camp. I just love the game."

Craig Anderson explained, too, that "a lot of the players on that Met team became coaches and stayed in baseball for years. I count myself, even though I was on the collegiate level. Roger Craig, and Jackson, there were a lot of guys that stayed in it, and I thought that was good. Maybe going through the hard knocks makes you a better coach. Builds character, yes. It built a lot of characters."

Certainly, the intervening forty-plus years have given the Original Mets a good deal of perspective about what went on that first year and how it affected the rest of their lives. When asked to sum up their experiences in one word, they provided the following answers and explanations:

ROD KANEHL: "Thrilled. It was a thrill to play in the Polo Grounds and play against such players as my idol, Stan Musial. I grew up when there were only sixteen teams in both leagues. I played with guys like Hodges and Zimmer. I saw [then-Yankee manager Joe] Torre this winter, and he said Zimmer [then a Yankee coach] talks about me all the time. It was a thrill. I wasn't intimidated by New York City, and that's one thing that New Yorkers appreciate. They don't mean to be intimidating, because they're just as thrilled to be associated with you as you are with them. I found New York a very friendly town, and my kids learned a lot. My wife took them everywhere, took them to all the museums, Fire Island and all the beaches. It was a great learning process for the whole family."

CRAIG ANDERSON: "Topsy-turvy. Even were things were going bad, there were a lot of positive things around us which kept us going."

FRANK THOMAS: "Fantastic. I had a great year, and I did everything that they thought I would do as far as power is concerned and driving in runs. I played almost all the ballgames, and I did everything that was asked of me. So I'd say that it was fantastic as far as I was concerned. I'm looking at it in that light, but if I'm looking at the overall picture, you know, I'd have to use probably another word . . . it was an experience."

JAY HOOK: "My word was going to be 'terrific.' But, you know, there were terrific times, and there were bad times. There were some wonderful times in New York. Some of our best friends today . . . that was one of the terrific things that came out of that experience. The people that we met, the experiences we had . . . we had some really fun times. It was a wonderful time in our life. Did we have some heartache? Sure. But there was always tomorrow."

As with any oral history, the final word should be left to the participants.

ANDERSON: "I'm glad that season was part of my career. I got to play with Gil Hodges. I got to meet Stan Musial. I got to play for Casey Stengel. I still get letters. How many people can say they were in a ticker-tape parade through New York City?"

GENE WOODLING: "Casey said that we were all going into the Hall of Fame, not as individuals but as a team." Boy, were the Mets bad. I still can't believe the way we played. Yet they weren't an embarrassment for me. I was still in the big leagues. That's a pretty good deal for a forty-year-old, even if my favorite memory of 1962 was my getting ready to go home."

THOMAS: "I really enjoyed playing in New York for the Mets, even though things didn't work out the way you'd want to them to work out."

JOE GINSBERG: "Being a part of that original Mets team, you can't believe what that has done for me in later years. The fans just seemed to take the Mets to heart."

AL JACKSON: "I really enjoyed playing for that team. Casey made us feel as if we could win every game. When we did actually win one it was like New Year's Eve. The guys really celebrated our few victories. Even though I had a losing record with a bad ball club I convinced everybody I could pitch in the big leagues. I wondered, sometimes, how well I would have done with a good club like the Pirates. I had no regrets about being with the Mets. Casey pitched me. The Pirates didn't."

ROGER CRAIG (1991): "[People say] 'Roger Craig, you're the guy who lost forty-six games with the Mets!' I still hear that. But as I look back, it's magnified now. I know that I pitched well, and I also know that I learned by the way we lost games. And frankly, that experience has helped me as a manager. Now when my teams go into a slump and they lose three or four games in a row, I can bring up some things and relate to them because I went through all that. Yes, we lost a lot with the Mets but baseball has always been a lot of fun to me. I also took it as a job. I just said to myself, I know we're not going to win much and we're going to lose a lot of games but I'm going to start. I'm going to go out every time thinking that I'm going to win and I'm going to do the best job I can. I took it more as a job because we weren't going to win anything. It was the best possible thing I could do. And of course Casey was fun to play for."

KEN MACKENZIE (1969): "I'm proud of having been an original Met. If people want to think that I was a clown, that's all right. But I always remember what the old man said after I was traded. As we shook hands, he said, 'You always tried your best.' We all tried our best. I've always thought of the Mets as my team."

RICHIE ASHBURN (1992): "That last season was a year I didn't want to go through twice. But I am glad I went through it once. I made great friends – I still talk to Marv a couple of times a year. I got to spend a year with Casey."

THRONEBERRY: "I still wouldn't trade one moment of my career for anything else in the world. I got to do what only 400 other guys did each year, and I did it for seven years, playing at the same time as my brother [Faye Throneberry, who played eight seasons with the Red Sox, Senators and Angels], so both of us, from one family, were luckier than millions of families out there who could only dream. We lived the dream."

HOOK: "People have asked me, 'Would you do it again?' Boy, I'd do it tomorrow. And I'd hope I was more effective than I was the first time."

ASHBURN: "Play for the Mets? I wouldn't have missed it for anything."

AFTERWORD

"There comes a time in every man's life at least once, and I've had plenty of them." – Casey Stengel, manager of the New York Mets

June 17, 2010, Indianapolis, Indiana: This is a special day, an anniversary of sorts. It was forty-eight years ago today that two signal events occurred in the history of the Original Mets. The first was Lou Brock's homer off Al Jackson into the centerfield seats of the Polo Grounds – only the second time anyone had reached the centerfield bleachers in the long history of the ballpark (with the third time happening the very next day). The other,of course, was the Throneberry Triple Event, possibly the single most immortal event in an entire year full of them. It is fair to say that June 17 was the apotheosis of the Mets' first season.

If anyone were to take on the task of spending years writing a book about the inaugural edition of the New York Mets, I don't think thatI would be the obvious first choice. In fact – and this is going to sound unusual coming from someone who has just spent more than eight years writing such a book – I was never really a Mets fan (although being so Mets-intensive for the last eight years has certainly rubbed off on me to the point where I have a new appreciation for the team; if you spend any time talking with Jim Fertitta Jr., I think such a result is inevitable). Since the tender age of six, I've been a consistent and devoted follower of the Chicago White Sox (heaven help me). Before I started this project, I never actually even rooted for the Mets. Ever. Well, that's not entirely true. There was that two-week period in the fall of 1984 where I rooted passionately and fervently for Doc Gooden, Gary Carter and Mookie Wilson, but that's only because the Mets represented the last (and ultimately unsuccessful) hope of keeping the Cubs out of the playoffs. And, of course, there was the 1986 World Series, in which I actively cheered against the Mets, but I realize now that I did so only because of a particularly obnoxious classmate of mine from New York. He made an interesting Series bet with a classmate from Boston. After the Mets took the Series in seven games, the Bostonian had to stand up in front of about a hundred thirty other students wearing a plastic Mets batting helmet and extolling the virtue of both the Mets and the winning classmate. It was pretty amusing, really – but it did nothing to endear the team to me. Or the winning classmate.

In fact, now that I think about it, I had a pretty compelling reason to begrudge the Mets, which is this: until 2005, my beloved White Sox had last made it to the World Series in 1959, three seasons before the Mets existed, at a time when they were nothing more than a gleam in Bill Shea's calculating eye. In the intervening 46 years between 1959 and 2005, the Mets appeared in four World Series, winning two. If you're a White Sox fan, how annoying is that? In any case, I certainly didn't write this book out of any personal longstanding Mets fandom.

Nor do I possess any sort of Mets fan gene in my lineage. My father grew up in Detroit as, of course, a Tigers fan. He still remembers seeing Hank Greenberg play. Since transplanting himself to Chicago, he's managed to become an aficionado of both the White Sox and Cubs. Of course, this is a trick that only a transplantee can pull off – can you imagine a native New Yorker pulling for both the Mets and Yankees? Or the Dodgers and the Giants before the cataclysm of 1957? Such a mindset would be completely unthinkable. My maternal grandfather, may he rest in peace, lived for decades in Brooklyn. Of course, his sympathies lay with the Dodgers, and once they bolted for the West Coast, he ignored baseball, choosing to focus his considerable sports energies on college basketball and boxing. Nope – no Mets fans in my immediate or moderately extended family.

So why, then, did I want to write this book? I think the answer is really pretty simple. The catalyst was Steve Rushin's excellent article in *Sports Illustrated* celebrating the team's thirty-year anniversary in 1992. Rushin's article showed me then, and has continued to show me every time I re-read it, that there is something inherently compelling about a team which loses seventy-five percent of its games but has more personality than the last four Yankees Series-winning teams put together. Such a sense is reinforced in my mind when, after spending years tracking down and reading virtually every word ever written about the Original Mets, I get to talk with guys like Craig Anderson, Jay Hook, Rod Kanehl and Frank Thomas, and have them tell me stories which have never appeared in print until now (and which would never have seen the light of day had not somebody simply asked them the question; I'm glad it was me). It is one thing to re-live these experiences through the words of gifted writers such as Leonard Shecter, Leonard Koppett or George Vecsey. It is quite another to have them told by the players who actually lived through them, to hear these tales from a perspective that virtually none of us can share, and to appreciate the players' understanding of their own unique place in baseball history. After all, this was a ball club consisting entirely of spare parts, of castoffs no other teams wanted, but which was, at the same time, the result of such a monumental effort to bring the franchise into existence in the first place. Of course, the more jaded and cynical among those who know me may suggest that a sustained diet of White Sox and Cubs baseball during my lifetime (not to mention plenty of astoundingly bad Bears and Bulls teams) has bred in me a natural sympathy with losers, and maybe they're right. But as Jimmy Breslin so aptly pointed out, can any red-blooded American honestly say he doesn't love a team that loses 120 games in a single season? Certainly, there were hundreds of thousands, if not millions, of New Yorkers that year who would have agreed.

But it isn't just the fact that they were bad. Met fans largely abandoned the team in the late 1970s. The large-budget disasters the franchise fielded in the 1990s did not make anyone happy.

Similarly, when the Tigers lost 119 games in 2003, it seemed that there were many, many more Tiger fans angered by what they saw as the players' supreme underachievement than there were those who were amused by the team's collective incompetence. The fact that the Tigers appeared in the World Series just three years later suggests that maybe the fans had a point. The difference is that these were not bad teams with character, or characters, about whom not much could be expected given the circumstances. They were just bad teams.

Maybe that's what makes today such a significant anniversary. You can hardly open a sports section without reading that on such and such day, Joe DiMaggio hit safely in his fifty-sixth consecutive game, or Henry Aaron broke Babe Ruth's career home run record, or Warren Spahn won the last of his record tally for victories by a lefthander, or some other hero achieved some other unassailable height of unimaginable proportion. Who among us can identify with such feats? Now, Al Jackson surrendering a mammoth home run, or Marv Throneberry damaging his team's chances with mistakes in the field and at the plate – these are things to which most of us ordinary people can relate. As *The New Yorker*'s Roger Angell so aptly noted, it was as if the fans of the Original Mets recognized that perfection (as embodied by the Yankees) was admirable but almost inhuman, and the bumbling Mets personified something more readily familiar.

I started out the prologue of this book by comparing the '62 Mets to American legends such as Casey Jones and Davy Crockett in that the precise nature of their deeds and misdeeds have tended to become obscured by the mists of time. However, there is another reason, a far simpler one, why the Original Mets deserve consideration as a genuine American legend, and it is this: they are still being talked about with affection and reverence, even passion and emotion, almost five decades later. If I accomplish anything with this book (beyond personal fame and glory, riches, et cetera), I hope that it will be the continuation of these tales so that they can be enjoyed anew by those who knew about them already and discovered and appreciated by those who didn't. After all, as with any legend, it is the story itself which is paramount, not the person who tells it. And the story of the Original Mets is one which deserves to live on. It was, without a doubt, a year in Mudville – but what a year it turned out to be.

BIBLIOGRAPHY

BOOKS:

Alexander, Charles C. *Rogers Hornsby: A Biography*. New York: Henry Holt and Company, 1995.

Allen, Maury. *The Incredible Mets*. New York: Paperback Library, 1969.

Allen, Maury. *You Could Look It Up: The Life of Casey Stengel*. New York: Times Books, 1979.

Allen, Maury. *Baseball: The Lives Behind the Seams*. New York: MacMillan Publishing Company, 1990.

Amoruso, Marino. *Gil Hodges: The Quiet Man*. Middlebury, Vermont: Paul S. Eriksson, 1991.

Anderson, Dave, ed. *The Red Smith Reader*. New York: Vintage Books, 1982.

Angell, Roger. *The Summer Game*. New York: The Viking Press, 1972.

Angell, Roger. *Once More Around The Park – A Baseball Reader*. New York: Ballantine Books, 1991.

Bak, Richard. *Casey Stengel – A Splendid Baseball Life*. Dallas: Taylor Publishing Company, 1997.

Benson, Michael. *Ballparks of North America*. Jefferson, North Carolina: MacFarland & Company, 1989.

Berkow, Ira, and Jim Kaplan. *The Gospel According to Casey*. New York: St. Martin's Press, 1992.

Bjarkman, Peter C. *The New York Mets Encyclopedia*. Champaign, Illinois: Sports Publishing, 2001.

Blake, Mike. *Baseball Chronicles – An Oral History of Baseball Through the Decades*. Cincinnati: Betterway Books, 1994.

Blatt, Howard. *Amazin' Met Memories – Four Decades Of Unforgettable Moments*. Tampa: Albion Press, 2002.

Bloss, Bob. *Baseball Managers: Stats, Stories & Strategies*. Philadelphia: Temple University Press, 1999.

Bock, Duncan, and John Jordan. *The Complete Year-By-Year N.Y. Mets Fan's Almanac*. New York: Crown Publishing, Inc., 1992.

Bouton, Jim, and Neil Offen. *I Managed Good, But Boy Did They Play Bad*. Chicago: Playboy Press, 1973.

Boyd, Brendan C., and Fred C. Harris. *The Great American Baseball Card Flipping, Trading and Bubble Gum Book*. New York: Ticknor & Fields, 1973.

Breslin, Jimmy. *Can't Anybody Here Play This Game?* New York: Penguin Sports Library, 1963.

Buege, Bob. *The Milwaukee Braves – A Baseball Eulogy*. New York: Douglas American Sports Publications, 1988.

Cairns, Bob. *Pen Men*. New York: St. Martin's Press, 1992.

Cataneo, David. *Hornsby Hit One Over My Head: A Fans' Oral History Of Baseball*. San Diego: Harcourt Brace &

Company, 1997.

Cataneo, David. *Casey Stengel: Baseball's "Old Professor."* Nashville: Cumberland House, 2003.

Cohen, Stanley. *A Magic Summer.* San Diego: Harcourt Brace Jovanovich, 1988.

Creamer, Robert W. *Stengel: His Life and Times.* New York: Simon and Schuster, 1984.

D'Amore, Jonathan. *Rogers Hornsby: A Biography.* Westport, CT: Greenwood Press, 2004.

D'Antonio, Michael. *Forever Blue: The True Story of Walter O'Malley, Baseball's Most Controversial Owner, and the Dodgers of Brooklyn and Los Angeles.* New York: Riverhead Books, 2009.

Dawidoff, Nicholas, ed. *Baseball: A Literary Anthology.* New York: The Library of America, 2002.

Dickson, Paul. *Baseball's Greatest Quotations.* New York: Edward Burlingame Books, 1994.

Durso, Joseph. *Casey – The Life and Legend of Charles Dillon Stengel.* Englewood Cliffs, New Jersey: Prentice-Hall, Inc, 1967.

Durso, Joseph. *Amazing: The Miracle of the Mets.* Boston: Houghton Mifflin Company, 1970.

Durso, Joseph. *Casey & Mr. McGraw.* St. Louis: *The Sporting News*, 1989.

Editors of the *New York Daily News. Amazing Mets: The Miracle of*

1969. Champaign, Illinois: Sports Publishing, 1999.

Fehler, Gene. *Tales From Baseball's Golden Age*. Champaign, Illinois: Sports Publishing, 2000.

Fitzgerald, Ed, ed. *The National League*. New York: Grosset & Dunlap, 1963.

Golenbock, Peter. *Amazin': The Miraculous History of New York's Most Beloved Team*. New York: St. Martin's Press, 2002.

Golenbock, Peter. *Bums: An Oral History of the Brooklyn Dodgers*. Chicago: Contemporary Books, 1984.

Golenbock, Peter. *Dynasty: The New York Yankees, 1949-1964*. Chicago: Contemporary Books, 1975.

Goodwin, Doris Kearns. *Wait Till Next Year – A Memoir*. New York: Simon & Schuster, 1997.

Halberstam, David. *Summer of '49*. New York: Avon Books, 1989.

Heiman, Lee, Dave Weiner and Bill Gutman. *When The Cheering Stops*. New York: MacMillan Publishing Company, 1990.

Helyar, John. *Lords of the Realm –The Real History of Baseball*. New York: Villard Books, 1994.

Holtzman, Jerome. *The Commissioners: Baseball's Midlife Crisis*. New York: Total Sports, 1998.

Honig, Donald. *The New York Mets: The First Quarter Century*. New York: Crown Publishing, Inc., 1986.

Kahn, Roger. *The Era*. New York: Ticknor & Fields, 1993.

Kalinsky, George. *The New York Mets: A Photographic History*. New York: MacMillan, 1995.

Kiersh, Edward. *Where Have You Gone, Vince DiMaggio?* New York: Bantam Books, 1983.

Kiner, Ralph, and Joe Gergen. *Kiner's Korner*. New York: Arbor House, 1987.

Koppett, Leonard. *The Man in the Dugout: Baseball's Top Managers and How They Got That Way*. Philadelphia: Temple University Press, 2000.

Koppett, Leonard. *The New York Mets – the Whole Story*. London: MacMillan Company, 1970.

Koppett, Leonard.*The New Thinking Fan's Guide to Baseball*. New York: Simon & Schuster/Fireside, 1991.

Koppett, Leonard. *The Thinking Fan's Guide to Baseball*. New York: *Sports Illustrated*, 2001.

Lang, Jack, and Peter Simon. *The New York Mets – Twenty-Five Years of Baseball Magic*. New York: Henry Holt and Company, 1986.

Liebman, Glenn. *Baseball Shorts – 1,000 of the Game's Funniest One-Liners*. Chicago: Contemporary Books, 1991.

MacLean, Norman. *Casey Stengel – A Biography*. New York: Drake Publishers, Inc., 1976.

Mitchell, Jerry. *The Amazing Mets*. New York: Tempo Books, 1970.

Nathan, David, ed. *Baseball Quotations*. New York: Ballantine

Books, 1991.

Nelson, Lindsey, and Al Hirshberg. *Backstage at the Mets.* New York: The Viking Press, 1966.

Nelson, Lindsey. *Hello Everybody, I'm Lindsey Nelson.* New York: Beech Tree Books, 1985.

Parrott, Harold. *The Lords of Baseball.* Atlanta: Longstreet Press, 2001.

Peary, Danny, ed. *Cult Baseball Players: The Greats, the Flakes, the Weird and the Wonderful.* New York: Fireside Books, 1990.

Peary, Danny, ed. *We Played The Game.* New York: Hyperion, 1994.

Polner, Murray. *Branch Rickey – A Biography.* New York: Antheneum, 1982.

Reichler, Joseph L., ed. *The Baseball Encyclopedia.* New York: MacMillan, 1978.

Ritter, Lawrence S. *Lost Ballparks: A Celebration of Baseball's Legendary Fields.* New York: Penguin Books, 1992.

Schaap, Dick, and Mort Gerberg, eds. *Joy In Mudville: The Big Book Of Baseball Humor.* New York: Broadway Books, 1992.

Seaver, Tom, and Marty Appel. *Great Moments in Baseball.* New York: Birch Lane Press, 1992.

Shannon, Mike. *Tales From The Dugout – The Greatest True Baseball Stories Ever Told.* New York: Contemporary

Books, 1997.

Shapiro, Michael. *Bottom of the Ninth – Branch Rickey, Casey Stengel, and the Daring Scheme to Save Baseball from Itself.* New York: Times Books, 2009.

Shecter, Leonard. *Once Upon the Polo Grounds.* New York: The Dial Press, 1970.

Shecter, Leonard. *The Jocks.* New York: Paperback Library, 1969.

Sheed, Wilfrid. *My Life as a Fan.* New York: Simon & Shuster, 1993.

Smith, Curt. *The Storytellers.* New York: Macmillan USA, 1995.

Smith, Red, ed. *Press Box: Red Smith's Favorite Sports Stories.* New York: W.W. Norton & Company, 1976.

Smith, Red. *Red Smith on Baseball.* Chicago: Ivan R. Dee, 2000.

Snider, Duke. *The Duke of Flatbush.* New York: Zebra Books, 1988.

Stengel, Casey. *Casey at the Bat – The Story of My Life in Baseball.* New York: Random House, 1962.

Stewart, Wayne, ed. *The Gigantic Book of Baseball Quotations.* New York: Skyhorse, 2007.

Sullivan, Neil J. *The Dodgers Move West.* New York: Oxford University Press, 1987.

Thorn, John, ed. *The Armchair Book of Baseball II.* New York: Charles Scribner's Sons, 1987.

Tygiel, Jules. *Past Time – Baseball as History*. London: Oxford University Press, 2000.

Vecsey, George. *Joy In Mudville*. New York: The McCall Publishing Company, 1970.

Veeck, Bill, with Ed Linn. *Veeck – As In Wreck*. 2nd ed. Chicago: University of Chicago Press, 2001.

Wilber, Cynthia J. *For the Love of the Game*. New York: William Morrow and Company, Inc., 1992.

Williams, Peter, ed. *The Joe Williams Baseball Reader*. Chapel Hill: Algonquin Books, 1989.

Wills, Maury, and Mike Celizic. *On the Run – The Never Dull and Often Shocking Life of Maury Wills*. New York: Carroll & Graf Publishers, Inc., 1991.

Wisnia, Saul, with Dan Schlossberg. *Wit & Wisdom of Baseball*. Lincolnwood, Illinois: Publications International, Ltd., 1998.

Zimmer, Don, and Bill Madden. *Zim: A Baseball Life*. New York: Contemporary Books, 2001.

Zimmerman, Paul D., and Dick Schaap. *The Year the Mets Lost Last Place*. New York: The World Publishing Company, 1969.

ARTICLES:

Acocella, Nick. "Casey's Corner." ESPNClassic.com. http://espn.go.com/classic/s/add_stengel_casey.html

Acocella, Nick. "Wisecracking Stengel Made Baseball Fun."

ESPNClassic.com.
http://espn.go.com/classic/biography/s/Stengel_Casey.html

Allen, Maury. "Memories Of Mets Gone By."
TheColumnists.Com, 2002.
http://www.thecolumnists.com/allen/allen21.html

Allen, Maury. "That Mets Book: Avoid This Disappointing New Book On The Mets."
TheColumnists.Com, 2002.
http://www.thecolumnists.com/allen/allen21.html

Batten, Sammy. "'Bad News' Cubs Aren't Worst Team."
Fayetteville Observer-Times, April 21, 1997.

Blau, Clifford. "New York Metropolitans Of The American Association."
http://users.erols.com/brak/mets1.htm

Blau, Jon. "Where Are They Now? Jay Hook." mlb.com, August 22, 2008.
http://mlb.mlb.com/news/article.jsp?ymd=20080820&content_id=3338765&vkey=news_mlb&fext=.jsp&c_id=mlb

Breslin, Jimmy. "Worst Baseball Team Ever." *Sports Illustrated*, August 13, 1962.

Buck, Ray. "Devil Rays, Diamondbacks In It To Win It NOW!"
CBS Sportsline, November 13, 1997.
http://cbs.sportsline.com/b/page/pressbox/archive/nov97/buckr111397.htm

Crino, Larry. "The Old Man Really Taught Me To Love The Game." BallparkGuys.Com, 2001.
http://www.ballparkguys.com/columnist/articles/crino/casey.html

Czerwinski, Kevin T. "The Mandt Of The House: Mets Legend Has Literally Seen It All With Amazin's." Mets.com. http://www.mets.com/nym_news_story

Daley, Arthur. "Sports of The Times." *The New York Times*, April 24, 1962.

Deford, Frank. "Baseball's Week." *Sports Illustrated*, July 23, 1962.

Dierker, Larry. "Larry Dierker's Baseball Library, No. 23." The Herring Design Quarterlies, 2001 http://www.herringdesign.com/hd/hdq/dierker/baseball2.html

Diunte, Nicholas. "Sammy Drake member of the original 1962 Mets dies at 75." *NY Baseball Examiner*, February 19, 2010. http://www.examiner.com/x-33368-NY-Baseball-History-Examiner~y2010m2d19-Sammy-Drake-member-of-the-original-1962-Mets-dies-at-age-75

Drebinger, John. "16-Hit Attack Beats Mets." *TheNew York Times*, July 15, 2002.

Frommer, Harvey. "The Mets Have Always Been Amazing." Travel-watch.com. http://www.travel-watch.com/amazingmets.htm

Hamill, Pete. "Hamill On Series," October 21, 2000. http://www.petehamill.com/stengle1st.html

Heyman, Brian. "Finding Their Way." *The Journal News*, March 31, 2002.

Holland, Gerald. "Casey In The Stretch." *Sports Illustrated*, October 1, 1956.

Isaacs, Stan. "Hit This Sign & Win A New Suit!" TheColumnists.Com, November 10, 2000. http://www.thecolumnists.com/isaacs/isaacs8.html

Isaacs, Stan. "Chapter 1: The Amazing Mets." http://www.izix.com/stan

Isaacs, Stan. "September 12: Guess Who Came To The Great Mets Party." Originally printed September 12, 1969. http://www.izix.com/stan

Isaacs, Stan. "September 24: A Sentimental Journey To Nostalgia." Originally printed September 24, 1969. http://www.izix.com/stan

Isaacs, Stan. "September 26: Mets Finally Hook The Prodigal Fan." Originally printed September 26, 1969. http://www.izix.com/stan

Isaacs, Stan. "October 8: Youth Of America Answered Casey's Call." Originally printed October 8, 1969. http://www.izix.com/stan

Isaacs, Stan. "October 14: The Crazy Bunch Of Kids Own 1969." Originally printed October 14, 1969. http://www.izix.com/stan

Isaacs, Stan. "October 21: The Little Old Signmaker Takes A Bow." Originally printed October 21, 1969. http://www.izix.com/stan

Kaplan, Ron. "Ya Gotta Believe! The Mets Are Forty." Mets Online, March 21, 2002. http://www.metsonline.net/news/kaplan-golenbock.shtml

Lipsyte, Robert. "Homer and Misplays Top Mets, 8-7, 4-3, At Polo Grounds." *TheNew York Times*, June 18, 1962.

Maloney, C.J. "'Marvelous' Marv Throneberry." Mets Online, March 4, 2002.
http://www.metsonline.net/news/throneberry.shtml

Maloney, C.J. "Once Upon the Polo Grounds." Mets Online, February 28, 2002.
http://www.metsonline.net/news/pologrounds.shtml

Maloney, C.J. "'Steady' Eddie Kranepool: Casey Stengel's First Youth Of America." MetsOnline, March 4, 2002.
http://www.metsonline.net/news/kranepool.shtml

Margolick, David. "William A. Shea, 84, Dies; Lawyer Behind the Mets." *TheNew YorkTimes*, October 4, 1991.

McCarron, Anthony. "Nationals on Same Pace as 1962 Mets as They Stumble into Series with Yanks." *New York Daily News*, June 15, 2009.

Mitchell, Maryann Hudson Houston. "Expansion Drafts Past." November 18, 1992.americast.latimes.sports

Newville, Todd. "The Original! Frank Thomas Was a Versatile Slugger Who Made His Own Niche in Baseball."
http://www.baseballtoddsdugout.com/frankthomas.html

Newville, Todd. "A Rare Bird! Former Cardinal Solly Hemus was one of the Last Player-Managers in the Major Leagues." www.baseballtoddsdugout.com/sollyhemus.html

Phillips, McCandlish. "40,000 Hail Mets, A Broadway Hit." *The New York Times*, April 13,   1962.

Robinson, James. "Break Up The Mets!" CBS Sportsline, April 23, 2002. http://cbs.sportsline.com/u/ce/feature/0,1518,953389_52,00.html

Rushin, Steve. "Bad Beyond Belief." *Sports Illustrated*, May 25, 1992.

Sargent, Jim. "Gene Woodling – A Champion Outfielder In Baseball's Glory Years." BaseballLibrary.com, June 15, 2001. http://www.pubdim.net/baseballlibrary/submit/Sargent_Jim3.stm

Shaplen, Robert. "How to Build a Ball Club." *Sports Illustrated*, March 5, 1962.

Shelton, Gary. "Laughter Is The Best Medicine." *St. Petersburg Times*, June 10, 2001.

Thomas, Robert McG. "Cookie Lavagetto Is Dead At 77; Hit In '47 Series Ruined No-Hitter." *The New York Times*, August 12, 1990. Reprinted at http://thedeadballera.crosswinds.net/Obits/LavagettoCookiesObit.html

Thursby, Keith. "Samuel Drake dies at 75; infielder for the Cubs, Mets." *Los Angeles Times*, March 7, 2010. Reprinted at http://articles.latimes.com/2010/mar/07/local/la-me-sammy-drake7-2010mar07

Treder, Steve. "Not Just Any Bob Miller." *The Hardball Times*, September 6, 2005. http://www.hardballtimes.com/main/article/not-just-any-bob-miller/

Tuckner, Howard M. "Mets Bow as Rally Fails; Get Woodling of Senators." *TheNew York Times*, June 17, 1962.

Tuckner, Howard M. "Giants Beat Mets." *TheNew York Times*, July 17, 1962.

Unknown. "Features – Forty Years Ago." TheBaseballPage.com. http://www.thebaseballpage.com/features/mets_debut.htm

Unknown. "Johnny Murphy Is Dead At 61; General Manager Of The Mets." *TheNew York Times*, January 15, 1970. Reprinted at http://thedeadballera.crosswinds.net/Obits/MurphyJohnnysObit.html

Unknown. "The Language of Casey Stengel." ESPNClassic.com, February 23, 2001. http://espn.go.com/classic/s/Stengelese.html

Unknown. "M. Donald Grant Dies At 94." *Associated Press*, November 28, 1998. Reprinted at http://thedeadballera.crosswinds.net/Obits/GrantMDonaldsObit.html

Unknown. "Meet Our (Circa 1880) Mets." Staten Island Advance, December 26, 1999. Reprinted at http://www.silive.com/si2000/games/1226y2kmets.html

Unknown. "Red Kress, Coach For Mets, Dead." *TheNew York Times*, November 30, 1962. Reprinted at http://thedeadballera.crosswinds.net/Obits/KressRedsObit.html

Unknown. "Red Ruffing, 81, Star Pitcher on 7 Yankee Pennant Teams." *TheNew York Times*, February 20, 1986. Reprinted at http://thedeadballera.crosswinds.net/Obits/RuffingRedsObit.html

Unknown. "Stengel Steals Space For Mets, Giving Admen Soft-Sell Lesson," *TheNew YorkTimes*, May 4, 1962.

Unknown. "With 'Marvelous,' Pay's The Thing." *TheNew York Times*, August 11, 1962.

Ventrella, Tony. "The Worst Team Ever." *The Seattle Insider*, March 29, 2002. Reprinted at http://www.seattleinsider.com/partners/kirotv/sports/0329tonyv.html

Weiskopf, Herman. "Baseball's Week." *Sports Illustrated*, April 30, 1962.

Weiskopf, Herman. "Baseball's Week." *Sports Illustrated*, May 21, 1962.

Weiskopf, Herman. "Baseball's Week." *Sports Illustrated*, June 11, 1962.

Weiskopf, Herman. "Baseball's Week." *Sports Illustrated*, July 2, 1962.

Weiskopf, Herman. "Baseball's Week." *Sports Illustrated*, July 9, 1962.

Weiskopf, Herman. "Baseball's Week." *Sports Illustrated*, July 16, 1962.

Weiskopf, Herman. "Baseball's Week." *Sports Illustrated*, August 20, 1962.

Weiskopf, Herman. "Baseball's Week." *Sports Illustrated*, August

27, 1962.

Weiskopf, Herman. "Baseball's Week." *Sports Illustrated*, September 3, 1962.

Weiskopf, Herman. "Baseball's Week." *Sports Illustrated*, September 10, 1962.

Weiskopf, Herman. "Baseball's Week." *Sports Illustrated*, October 1, 1962.

White, Jr., Gordon S. "Braves Win, 5-4, With a Home Run." *The New York Times*. July 25, 1962.

White, Jr., Gordon S. "Mets Drop Two For Good Old Casey." *The New York Times*. July 30, 1962.

Wright, Alfred. "Happy Blend of Sport and Cash." *Sports Illustrated*, May 14, 1962.

INTERVIEWS:

Craig Anderson, March 10, 2002, with author.

Jim Fertitta, Jr., June 12, 2002, with author.

Jim Fertitta, Sr., July 24, 2002, with author.

Jay Hook, April 13, 2002, with author.

Rod Kanehl, April 25, 2002, and May 6, 2002, with author.

Leonard Koppett, August 26, 2002, with author.

Hobie Landrith, April 12, 2002, with Marty Lurie,

www.loveofthegameproductions.com.

John MacMaster, July 15, 2002, with author.

Joe Pignatano, May 22, 2002, with Marty Lurie, www.loveofthegameproductions.com.

Walter Pullis, July 15, 2002, with author.

Frank Thomas, July 3, 2002, with author.

Ed Wolff, April 14, 2002, with author.

VIDEO:

An Amazin' Era: The New York Mets, 1962-86, Major League Baseball Productions, 71 minutes, 1986. Videocassette.

OTHER SOURCES:

Brian Heyman, e-mail to author, August 14, 2002.

Stan Isaacs, e-mail to author, August 7, 2002.

Rick Williams, e-mail to author, July 21, 2002.

NOTES ON QUOTATIONS

PROLOGUE

Casey Stengel: Richard Bak, *Casey Stengel – A Splendid Baseball Life*, p. 165.

CHAPTER 1 -- THE VOID AND THE IDEA

Casey Stengel: Bak, p. 184.

Red Smith: Red Smith, Dave Anderson, ed., *The Red Smith Reader*, p. 147.

Leonard Koppett: Leonard Koppett, *The New York Mets – the Whole Story*, p. 17.

"Slicker…": John Helyar, *Lords Of The Realm – The Real History Of Baseball*, p. 59.

Press release: Neil Sullivan, *The Dodgers Move West*, p. 136.

Koppett: Koppett, *New York Mets*, p. 19.

Veeck: Jules Tygiel, *Past Time – Baseball as History*, p. 186.

"Dancing bear…" Peter Golenbock, *Bums – An Oral History of the Brooklyn Dodgers*, p. 75.

Shea and Rickey's statement: Murray Polner, *Branch Rickey – A Biography*, p. 260.

George Vecsey: George Vecsey, *Joy in Mudville*, p. 24.

Press release: quoted by Koppett, *New York Mets*, p. 25.

Craig Cullinan: Michael Shapiro, *Bottom of the Ninth*, p. 267.

CHAPTER 2 -- THE ORGANIZATION

Casey Stengel: Allen, *The Incredible Mets*, p. 31; Paul Dickson, *Baseball's Greatest Quotations*, p. 419.

Joan Whitney Payson: Alfred Wright, "Happy Blend Of Sport And Cash," *Sports Illustrated*, May 14, 1962, p. 84.

Grant: Robert Shaplen, "How To Build A Ball Club," *Sports Illustrated*, March 5, 1962, p. 37.

Hazel Weiss: B Jimmy Breslin, *Can't Anybody Here Play This Game?*, p. 59; Ed Fitzgerald, ed., *The National League*, p. 286.

Murray Kempton: Murray Kempton, "Back at the Polo Grounds," reprinted in *Baseball: A Literary Anthology*.

Weiss: Shaplen, pp. 38-39.

Weiss: Koppett, *New York Mets*, p. 30.

Branch Rickey: Polner, p. 262.

Mayor Wagner: Margolick, David. "William A. Shea, 84, Dies; Lawyer Behind the Mets," *TheNew York Times*, October 4, 1991.

Jim Fertitta, Sr.: interview with author, June 24, 2002.

Steve Rushin: "Bad Beyond Belief," *Sports Illustrated*.

"Two for...": Lindsey Nelson and Al Hirshberg, *Backstage at the Mets*, p. 29.

CHAPTER 3 -- CASEY AT THE HELM

Casey Stengel: Maury Allen, *You Could Look It Up: The Life Of Casey Stengel*, p. 219.

Leonard Shecter: Leonard Shecter, *The Jocks*, p. 171.

Leonard Koppett: Leonard Koppett, *The Thinking Fan's Guide to Baseball*, p. 343-44.

Robert Lipsyte: Golenbock, *Amazin':The Miraculous History of New York's Most Beloved Team*, p. 110.

Maury Allen: Ira Berkow and Jim Kaplan, *The Gospel According To Casey*, p. 8.

Jimmy Dudley: Curt Smith, *The Storytellers*, p. 138.

Jim Murray: David H. Nathan, ed., *Baseball Quotations*, p. 158.

Jay Hook: transcribed from *An Amazin' Era: The New York Mets, 1962-86*, Major League Baseball Productions.

Stengel: "My Own Story," *Saturday Evening Post*,

"Casey is a clown...": Gerald Holland, "Casey in the Stretch," *Sports Illustrated*, October 1, 1956.

David Cataneo: David Cataneo, Casey Stengel: *Baseball's "Old Professor"*, p. 82.

Jack Lang: *ibid.*, p. 86.

Red Smith: Berkow, p. 13.

Mel Allen: Curt Smith, p. 139.

George Gobel: Glenn Liebman, *Baseball Shorts – 1,000 Of the Game's Funniest One-Liners*, p. 36.

Richard Nixon: Curt Smith, p. 135.

Hobie Landrith: interview with Marty Lurie, www.loveofthegameproductions.com, April 12, 2002.

Richie Ashburn: Cataneo, p. 82.

Stengel: Halberstam, p. 312; Jerry Mitchell, *The Amazing Mets*, pp. 38-39.

Jack Lawson: Maury Allen, *You Could Look It Up: The Life of Casey Stengel*, p. 211.

Edna Stengel: Joseph Durso, *Casey – The Life and Legend of Charles Dillon Stengel*, p. 159.

Stengel: Casey Stengel, *Casey atthe Bat – The Story of My Life in Baseball*, pp. 249-50.

Stengel: Durso, Casey, pp. 159-60.

Jimmy Cannon: Shapiro, p. 262.

Cannon: Shecter, *Polo Grounds*, pp. 19-20.

Stengel: Stengel, p. 250.

George Weiss: Durso, *Casey*, p. 160.

Weiss: Shaplen, p. 42.

Stengel: Stengel, pp. 250-51.

Stengel: Vecsey, pp. 36-37.

Shecter: Shecter, *Polo Grounds*, p. 21.

Stengel: Jordan A. Deutsch, et al., *The Scrapbook History of Baseball*, p. 238.

Stengel: Stengel, pp. 251-52.

Stengel: Allen, *You Could Look It Up*, p. 214.

Stengel: Vecsey, p. 46.

Edna Stengel: Berkow and Kaplan, p. 7.

Edna Stengel: Wright, p. 91.

Jack Lawson: Allen, *You Could Look It Up*, p. 214.

Edna Stengel: Mitchell, p. 62.

Koppett: interview with author, August 26, 2002.

Nelson: Nelson and Hirshberg, pp. 110-11.

Shecter: Shecter, *Polo Grounds*, pp. 25-26.

CHAPTER 4 -- ASSEMBLING THE TEAM

Casey Stengel: Breslin, *Can't Anybody*, p. 62.

Paul Richards: Helyar, p. 465.

Jimmy Breslin: Jimmy Breslin, "Worst Baseball Team Ever," *Sports Illustrated*, August 13, 1962, p. 23.

Stengel: *ibid.*

Rogers Hornsby: Breslin, *Can't Anybody*, pp. 24-25.

Lindsey Nelson: Nelson and Hirshberg, p. 166.

Weiss: Paul D. Zimmerman and Dick Schaap, *The Year The Mets Lost Last Place*, p. 111.

Stengel: Nelson and Hirshberg, p. 116.

Joan Whitney Payson: Wright, p. 91.

Stengel: Nelson and Hirshberg, p. 64.

Craig Anderson: interview with author, March 10, 2002.

Anderson: *ibid.*

Anderson: *ibid.*

Anderson: *ibid.*

Jay Hook: interview with author, April 13, 2002.

Hook: *ibid.*

Hook: *ibid.*

Hook: *ibid.*

Hook: *ibid.*

Hook: *ibid.*

Hook: *ibid.*

Al Jackson: Allen, *Baseball: The Lives Behind The Seams*, pp. 183-84.

Jackson: *ibid.*, pp. 184-85.

Jackson: Mitchell, p. 88.

Jackson: Allen, *Baseball*, pp, 186-87.

Stengel: Shecter, *Polo Grounds*, p. 25.

Weiss: *ibid.*, p. 24.

Frank Thomas: interview with author, July 3, 2002.

Thomas: *ibid.*

Thomas: *ibid.*

Thomas: *ibid.*

Thomas: *ibid.*

Roger Craig: Mitchell, p. 93.

Rod Kanehl: interview with author, April 25, 2002.

Kanehl: *ibid.*

Kanehl: *ibid.*

Kanehl: *ibid.*

Kanehl: *ibid.*

Kanehl: Golenbock, *Amazin'*, p. 123; interview with author, April 25, 2002.

Stengel: Allen, *The Incredible Mets*, p. 37.

Kanehl: interview with author, April 25, 2002.

Kanehl: *ibid.*

Kanehl: *ibid.*

Stengel: Mitchell, p. 69.

Lindsey Nelson: Nelson and Hirshberg, pp. 64-65.

Weiss: Shaplen, p. 44.

CHAPTER 5 -- SPRING TRAINING

Casey Stengel: Bak, p. 159.

Don Zimmer: Don Zimmer and Bill Madden, *Zim: A Baseball Life*, p. 54.

Craig Anderson: interview with author, March 10, 2002.

Anderson: *ibid.*

Anderson: *ibid.*

Jay Hook: interview with author, April 13, 2002.

Frank Thomas: interview with author, July 3, 2002.

Hook: interview with author, April 13, 2002.

Thomas: interview with author, July 3, 2002.

Robert Lipsyte: Golenbock, *Amazin'*, pp. 112-13.

Nelson: *Hello Everybody, I'm Lindsey Nelson*, p. 273.

Billy Loes: Breslin, *Can't Anybody*, p. 15.

Anderson: interview with author, March 10, 2002.

Casey Stengel: Allen, *The Incredible Mets*, pp. 37-38.

Hobie Landrith: interview with Marty Lurie, www.loveofthegameproductions.com, April 12, 2002.

Anderson: interview with author, March 10, 2002.

Joe Ginsberg: Bryan Heyman, "Finding Their Way," *The Journal News*, March 31, 2002.

Leonard Shecter: Shecter, *The Jocks*, p. 164.

Allen: Allen, *The Incredible Mets*, p. 37.

Bob Sales: Cataneo, *Casey Stengel*, p. 51.

Rod Kanehl: Cataneo, *Casey Stengel*, p. 52.

Stengel: Vecsey, p. 59.

Kanehl: Allen, *You Could Look It Up*, p. 221.

Kanehl: Golenbock, *Amazin'*, pp. 129-30.

Kanehl: *ibid.*, p. 130; interview with author, April 25, 2002.

Kanehl: Allen, *You Could Look It Up*, p. 221.

Ashburn: Berkow and Kaplan, p. 153.

Kanehl: Golenbock, *Amazin'*, p. 130; interview with author, April 25, 2002.

Bob Murphy: Curt Smith, pp. 139-40.

Anderson: interview with author, March 10, 2002.

Zimmer: Zimmer and Madden, p. 54.

Anderson: interview with author, March 10, 2002.

Stengel: Shaplen, p. 44.

George Weiss: *ibid.*

Bill Veeck: Veeck, p. 264.

Shecter: Shecter, *Polo Grounds*, p. 55.

Shecter: Shecter, *The Jocks*, p. 175.

Hook: interview with author, April 13, 2002.

Stengel: Vecsey, p. 54.

Lipsyte: Golenbock, *Amazin'*, p. 112.

John Pappas: Vecsey, p. 51.

Ernie Harwell: Curt Smith, p. 137.

Anderson: interview with author, March 10, 2002.

Nelson: Nelson and Hirshberg, pp. 92-93.

Bromo Seltzer commercial: Allen, *The Incredible Mets*, p. 39; Shecter, *Polo Grounds*, p. 39.

Lou Niss: Shecter, *Polo Grounds*, p. 33.

Chacon interview: *ibid.*

Dick Young: Vecsey, p. 49.

Rogers Hornsby: Breslin, *Can't Anybody*, p. 29.

Weiss: Shaplen, p. 45.

Ginsberg: Shecter, *Polo Grounds*, p. 39.

Kanehl: Allen, *The Incredible Mets*, pp. 96-97; Golenbock, *Amazin'*, p. 136.

Kanehl: Shecter, *The Jocks*, pp. 165-66.

Stengel: Shecter, *Polo Grounds*, p. 45.

Joe Christopher: Heyman.

Anderson: interview with author, March 10, 2002.

Kanehl: interview with author, April 25, 2002.

Anderson: interview with author, March 10, 2002.

Kanehl: Golenbock, *Amazin'*, p. 131; interview with author, April 25, 2002.

Craig Anderson: interview with author, March 10, 2002.

Hook: interview with author, April 13, 2002.

Team prediction:*Sports Illustrated*, April 7, 1962.

Robert Shaplen: Shaplen, p. 44.

Angell: Roger Angell, *The Summer Game*, pp. 14-15.

Ashburn: Bak, p. 161.

Zimmer: Zimmer and Madden, p. 55.

Thomas: interview with author, July 3, 2002.

Anderson: interview with author, March 10, 2002.

Kanehl: interview with author, April 25, 2002.

Stengel: Mitchell, p. 57.

Stengel: Shecter, *Polo Grounds*, p. 46.

CHAPTER 6 – THE FIRST MONTH

Casey Stengel: Bak, p. 156.

Lindsey Nelson: Nelson and Hirshberg, p. 70.

Roger Craig: Shecter, *Polo Grounds*, p. 58.

Jay Hook: interview with author, April 13, 2002.

Stengel: Nelson and Hirshberg, pp. 66-67; Rushin, p. 46.

Stengel: Paul Dickson, *Baseball's Greatest Quotations*, p. 419.

Richie Ashburn: Allen, *You Could Look It Up*, p. 225.

Stengel: Shecter, *Polo Grounds*, p. 59.

Ashburn: Stan Isaacs, "September 24: A Sentimental Journey to Nostalgia." http:\www.izix.com\stan

McCandlish Phillips: McCandlish Phillips, "40,000 Hail Mets, A Broadway Hit," *TheNew York Times*, April 13, 1962.

Rod Kanehl: interview with author, April 25, 2002.

Stengel: Robert W. Creamer, *Stengel: His Life And Times*, p. 298.

Ashburn: Rushin, p. 45.

Anderson: interview with author, March 10, 2002.

Joe Ginsburg: Heyman.

Shecter: Shecter, *Polo Grounds*, p. 62.

Ralph Kiner: Ralph Kiner and Joe Gergen, *Kiner's Korner*, p. 38.

Jim Marshall: *ibid*.

Anderson: interview with author, March 10, 2002.

Walter Pullis: interview with author, July 15, 2002.

Anderson: interview with author, March 10, 2002.

Pullis: interview with author, July 15, 2002.

Stengel: Shecter, *Polo Grounds*, p. 73; Breslin, *Can't Anybody*, p. 70.

Stengel: Breslin, *Can't Anybody*, pp. 70-71.

Kanehl: Golenbock, *Amazin'*, p. 132.

Anderson: interview with author, March 10, 2002.

Stengel: Allen, *You Could Look It Up*, p. 225.

Elio Chacon: *ibid.*

Hook: interview with author, April 13, 2002.

"Violation…": Mitchell, p 62.

Stengel: "Stengel Steals Space For Mets, Giving Admen Soft-Sell Lesson," *TheNew York Times*, May 4, 1962.

Brendan Boyd and Fred Harris: Brendan C. Boyd and Fred C. Harris, *The Great American Baseball Card Flipping, Trading and Bubble Gum Book*, p. 134.

Steve Rushin: Rushin, p. 46.

Clem Labine: Heiman, et al., pp. 109-10.

Joe Ginsberg: Shecter, *Polo Grounds*, p. 81.

Stengel: Bak, p. 164.

Zimmer: Zimmer and Madden, pp. 56-57.

Lou Niss: Vecsey, p. 82.

Stengel: Kiner and Gergen, p. 39.

Nelson: Nelson and Hirshberg, p. 168.

CHAPTER 7 – BEING EMBALMED

Casey Stengel: Allen, *You Could Look It Up*, p. 224.

Walter Pullis: interview with author, July 15, 2002.

Jimmy Breslin: Breslin, *Can't Anybody*, p. 72.

Craig Anderson: interview with author, March 10, 2002.

Hobie Landrith: Vecsey, p. 82.

Stengel: Allen, *You Could Look It Up*, p. 225.

Anderson: interview with author, March 10, 2002.

Lindsey Nelson: Nelson and Hirshberg, pp. 126-27.

Jay Hook: transcribed from *An Amazing Era*.

Marv Throneberry: Mike Blake, *Baseball Chronicles – An Oral History of Baseball throughthe Decades*, p. 198.

Rod Kanehl: interview with author, April 25, 2002.

Anderson: interview with author, March 10, 2002.

Hook: interview with author, April 13, 2002.

Throneberry: Allen, *The Incredible Mets*, pp. 44-45.

Leonard Shecter: Shecter, *Polo Grounds*, pp. 85-86.

Allen, *The Incredible Mets*, pp. 44-45.

Nelson: Nelson and Hirshberg, p. 127.

Shecter: Shecter, *Polo Grounds*, pp. 85-86.

Pullis: interview with author, July 15, 2002.

Ken MacKenzie: Isaacs, September 12.

Anderson: interview with author, March 10, 2002.

John Lardner: Wayne Stewart, ed., *The Gigantic Book of Baseball Quotations*, p. 164.

Stengel: Bak, p. 157.

Stengel: Cataneo, *Casey Stengel*, p. 175.

Roger Angell: Angell, *Once More aroundthe Park – A Baseball Reader*, pp. 6-7.

Kanehl: interview with author, April 25, 2002.

Stengel: Berkow and Kaplan, p. 17.

Pullis: interview with author, July 15, 2002.

Hook: interview with author, April 13, 2002.

Anderson: interview with author, March 10, 2002.

Gene Woodling, George Weiss: Howard M. Tuckner, "Mets Bow as Rally Fails; Get Woodling of Senators," *TheNew York Times*, June 17, 1962.

Stengel: Golenbock, *Dynasty*, pp. 119-20.

Gene Woodling: Danny Peary, ed., *We Played the Game*, p. 543.

Pullis: interview with author, July 15, 2002.

Nelson: Larry Dierker, *The Herring Design Quarterlies*, No. 23.

Kanehl: interview with author, April 25, 2002.

Richie Ashburn: Rushin, p. 45.

Stengel: Dickson, p. 418.

Pullis: interview with author, July 15, 2002.

Throneberry: Kiner and Gergen, p. 43.

Jack Lang: David Nathan, ed., *Baseball Quotations*, p. 34.

Leonard Koppett: interview with author, August 26, 2002.

Hook: interview with author, April 13, 2002.

Stan Isaacs: Vecsey, p. 77.

Maury Allen: Allen, *The Incredible Mets*, p. 45.

Ralph Houk: Breslin, *Can't Anybody*, p. 97.

Throneberry: *ibid.*

Breslin: Red Smith, ed., *Press Box: Red Smith's Favorite Sports Stories*, p. 32.

Kanehl: interview with author, April 25, 2002.

Ashburn: Shecter, *Polo Grounds*, p. 94.

Throneberry: Vecsey, p. 77.

Stengel: Shecter, *Polo Grounds*, p. 90.

Stengel: Breslin, *Can't Anybody*, p. 97.

Stengel: Duncan Bock and John Jordan, *The Complete Year-By-Year N.Y. Mets Fan's Almanac*, p. 16.

Stengel: Dickson, p. 428.

Throneberry: Vecsey, p. 76.

Dick Young: Breslin, *Can't Anybody*, p. 65.

Ed Kranepool: Durso, *Amazing: The Miracle Of The Mets*, pp. 2-3.

Kranepool: Stanley Cohen, *A Magic Summer*, p. 108.

Joan Payson: Breslin, *Can't Anybody*, p. 52.

Stengel: *ibid.*

Kanehl: Rushin, p. 45.

CHAPTER 8 – THE PLAYERS

Casey Stengel: Bak, p. 168.

Ralph Kiner: Kiner and Gergen, p. 39.

Stengel: Breslin, *Can't Anybody*, p. 30.

Stengel: Berkow and Kaplan, p. 72.

Stengel: Dickson, p. 415.

Boyd and Harris: Boyd and Harris, p. 37.

Walter Pullis: interview with author, July 15, 2002.

Kiner: Kiner and Gergen, p. 49.

Kiner: *ibid.*

Pullis: interview with author, July 15, 2002.

Marv Throneberry: Kiner and Gergen, p. 49.

Craig Anderson: interview with author, March 10, 2002.

Nelson: Nelson and Hirshberg, p. 120.

Jerry Mitchell: Mitchell, p. 113.

Kiner: Kiner and Gergen, p. 50.

Roger Craig: Rushin, p. 47.

Stengel: Bak, p. 168.

Kiner: Kiner and Gergen, p. 39.

Craig: Rushin, p. 47.

Stengel: Kiner and Gergen, p. 49.

Stengel: Gordon S. White, Jr., "Mets Drop Two For Good Old Casey," *TheNew York Times*, July 30, 1962; Mitchell, p. 113.

Stengel: Dickson, p. 417.

Anderson: interview with author, March 10, 2002.

Gene Woodling: Peary, p. 543.

George Vecsey: Vecsey, p. 80.

Jay Hook: interview with author, April 13, 2002.

Craig: Bob Cairns, *Pen Men*, p. 180.

Anderson: interview with author, March 10, 2002.

Tracy Stallard: Mitchell, p. 132.

Craig: Weaver, p. 241; Mitchell, p. 135.

Leonard Shecter: Shecter, *Polo Grounds*, p. 77.

Kanehl: Golenbock, *Amazin'*, p. 135.

Hook: interview with author, April 13, 2002.

Hook: *ibid.*

Stengel: Shecter, *Polo Grounds*, p. 77.

Hook: interview with author, April 13, 2002.

Stengel: Breslin, *Can't Anybody*, p. 102.

Hook: interview with author, April 13, 2002.

Stengel: Vecsey, p. 80.

Maury Wills: Maury Wills and Mike Celizic, *On the Run – The Never Dull and Often Shocking Life of Maury Wills*, p. 156.

Ken MacKenzie: Isaacs, September 12.

Lou Niss: Vecsey, p. 84.

Mitchell: Mitchell, pp. 85-86.

Stengel: Golenbock, p. 145.

Pullis: interview with author, July 15, 2002.

Richie Ashburn: Rushin, p. 46.

Frank Thomas: interview with author, July 3, 2002.

Stengel: Bock and Jordan, p. 9.

Jimmy Breslin: Breslin, *Can't Anybody*, pp. 98-99.

Thomas: interview with author, July 3, 2002.

Anderson: interview with author, March 10, 2002.

Thomas: interview with author, July 3, 2002.

Kanehl: interview with author, April 25, 2002.

Kanehl: *ibid.*

Kanehl: Golenbock, *Amazin'*, p. 141.

Kanehl: interview with author, April 25, 2002.

CHAPTER 9 – THE MANAGER

Casey Stengel: Berkow and Kaplan, p. 22.

Leonard Koppett: Koppett, *Thinking Fan's Guide*, p. 346.

Rod Kanehl: Cataneo, *Casey Stengel*, p. 45.

Jay Hook: interview with author, April 13, 2002.

Roger Craig: transcribed from *An Amazin' Era*.

Hook: interview with author, April 13, 2002.

Leonard Shecter: Shecter, *Polo Grounds*, p. 82.

Maury Allen: Berkow and Kaplan, p. 8.

Dick Young: Transcribed from *An Amazing Era*.

Anderson: interview with author, March 10, 2002.

Kanehl: interview with author, April 25, 2002.

Al Jackson: Cataneo, *Casey Stengel*, p. 45.

Stengel: Wayne Stewart, ed., *The Gigantic Book of Baseball Quotations*, p. 60.

Anderson: interview with author, March 10, 2002.

Hook: interview with author, April 13, 2002.

Lindsey Nelson: Curt Smith, p. 164.

Stengel: Breslin, "Worst Team Ever," p. 53, *Sports Illustrated*, August 13, 1962.

Anderson: interview with author, March 10, 2002.

Kanehl: interview with author, April 25, 2002.

Anderson: interview with author, March 10, 2002.

Hook: interview with author, April 13, 2002.

Nelson: Nelson and Hirshberg, p. 118.

Ed Kranepool: Allen, *You Could Look It Up*, pp. 228-29.

Frank Thomas: interview with author, July 3, 2002.

Kanehl: Cataneo, Casey Stengel, p. 158.

Jack Lang: *ibid.*, p. 161.

Nelson: Nelson and Hirshberg, p. 146.

Bob Sales: Cataneo, *Casey Stengel*, p. 158.

Kanehl: Shecter, *The Jocks*, p. 176.

Kranepool: Allen, p. 229.

Joe Ginsberg: Gene Fehler, *Tales from Baseball's Golden Age*, pp. 82-83.

Mickey Mantle: Wayne Stewart, ed., *The Gigantic Book of Baseball Quotations*, p. 420.

Pignatano: interview with Marty Lurie, www.loveofthegameproductions.com, May 22, 2002.

Pignatano: Jack Lang and Peter Simon, *The New York Mets – Twenty-Five Years of Baseball Magic*, p. 30; Blake, p. 199-200.

Nelson: Curt Smith, p. 142; Nelson, p. 281.

Nelson: Nelson and Hirshberg, pp. 114-15.

Nelson: *ibid.*, p. 115.

Kanehl: Cataneo, *Casey Stengel*, p. 91.

Ginsberg: Cairns, p. 96.

Galen Cisco: *ibid.*

Anderson: interview with author, March 10, 2002.

Ray Daviault: Heyman.

Ralph Kiner: Bak, p. 165.

Stengel: Shaplen, p. 42.

Robert W. Creamer: Berkow and Kaplan, p. 15.

Stengel: Breslin, Cataneo, *Casey Stengel*, p. 91.

Breslin: Breslin, "Worst Team Ever," p. 52.

Richie Ashburn: *Casey Stengel*, p. 92.

Stengel: Cataneo, *Casey Stengel*, p. 50.

Stengel: Allen, *You Could Look It Up*, p. 229.

Stengel: Berkow and Kaplan, p. 11.

Robert Lipsyte: Golenbock, *Amazin'*, pp. 110-11.

Ed Bouchee: Bak, p. 167; Perry, p. 542.

Stengel: Breslin, *Worst Team Ever*, p. 52.

Solly Hemus: Berkow and Kaplan, p. 63.

Jackson: *ibid.*, p. 65.

Jimmy Breslin: Breslin, *Can't Anybody*, p. 23.

Jackson: Berkow and Kaplan, p. 71.

Ron Swoboda: *ibid.*

Jackson: transcribed from *An Amazin' Era*.

Craig: *ibid.*, pp. 43-44.

Stengel: Nelson, p. 276.

Craig: Berkow and Kaplan, pp. 54-55.

Shecter: Shecter, *Polo Grounds*, pp. 91-92.

Kanehl: Golenbock, *Amazin'*, p. 129.

Ashburn: Berkow and Kaplan, p. 98.

Marv Throneberry: *ibid.*, p. 94.

Stengel: *ibid.*, pp. 96-97.

Walter Pullis: interview with author, July 15, 2002.

Anderson: interview with author, March 10, 2002.

Hook: interview with author, April 13, 2002.

Koppett: interview with author, August 26, 2002.

Bob Sales: Cataneo, *Casey Stengel*, p. 68.

Hemus: Berkow and Kaplan, p. 77.

Kranepool: Allen, *You Could Look It Up*, p. 229; Berkow and Kaplan, p. 76.

Ashburn: Berkow and Kaplan, p. 123; Bob Bloss, *Baseball Managers: Stats, Stories & Strategies*, pp. 240-41.

Jesse Gonder: Berkow and Kaplan, p. 18.

Kanehl: Cataneo, Casey Stengel, pp. 28-29.

Stengel: Shecter, *Polo Grounds*, p. 82.

Hook: interview with author, April 13, 2002.

Ken MacKenzie: Berkow and Kaplan, p. 130.

Ron Swoboda: Berkow and Kaplan, pp. 131-32.

Pignatano: Blake, p. 200.

Hank Bauer: Golenbock, *Dynasty*, p. 144.

Gene Woodling: Breslin, "Worst Team Ever," pp. 52-53.

Jackson: Cataneo, *Casey Stengel*, pp. 25-26.

Koppett: Koppett, *Thinking Fan's Guide*, p. 345.

Kranepool: Blake, p. 201.

Ashburn: Berkow and Kaplan, p. 48.

Craig: *ibid.*, p. 44.

CHAPTER 10 – THE FANS

Casey Stengel: Bak, p. 164.

Jimmy Breslin: Breslin, *Can't Anybody*, p. 7.

Jim Fertitta, Sr.: interview with author, June 24, 2002.

Jack Lang: transcribed from *An Amazin' Era*.

Jim Fertitta, Sr.: interview with author, June 24, 2002.

Walter Pullis: interview with author, July 15, 2002.

Leonard Shecter: Shecter, *Polo Grounds*, p. 92.

Shecter: *ibid.*, p. 93.

Ed Wolff: interview with author, April 14, 2002.

Bob Murphy: transcribed from *An Amazin' Era*.

Nelson: Nelson and Hirshberg, pp. 77-78.

Stengel: Mitchell, p. 2.

Nelson: Curt Smith, p. 118.

Vecsey: Vecsey, p. 68.

Richie Ashburn: *ibid.*

Jay Hook: *ibid.*, p. 69.

Roger Craig: Cynthia J. Wilber, *For the Love of the Game*, p. 80.

Craig Anderson: interview with author, March 10, 2002.

Hook: interview with author, April 13, 2002.

Frank Thomas: Peary, p. 541; interview with author, July 3, 2002.

Ed Wolff: interview with author, April 14, 2002.

Nelson: Nelson and Hirshberg, p. 82.

Jim O'Toole: Peary, p. 546.

Newspaper advertisement: Vecsey, p. 70.

Hook: interview with author, April 13, 2002.

Wolff: interview with author, April 14, 2002.

Roger Angell: Angell, *Once More around the Park*, p. 7.

Leonard Koppett: Koppett, *New York Mets*, p. 58.

John MacMaster: interview with author, July 15, 2002.

Pullis: interview with author, July 15, 2002.

Rick Williams: e-mail to author, July 21, 2002.

Williams: *ibid.*

Williams: *ibid.*

Williams: *ibid.*

Pullis: interview with author, July 15, 2002.

MacMaster: interview with author, July 15, 2002.

Fertitta, Sr.: interview with author, June 24, 2002.

Murray Kempton: Kempton.

Koppett: Koppett, *New York Mets*, pp. 58-59.

Koppett: interview with author, August 26, 2002.

Wolff: interview with author, April 14, 2002.

Wolff: *ibid.*

Pullis: interview with author, July 15, 2002.

Koppett: Koppett, *New York Mets*, p. 59.

Angell: Angell, *Once More aroundthe Park*, pp. 8-9.

Angell: *ibid.*, p. 9.

Robert Lipsyte: Cohen, p. 98.

Stanley Cohen: *ibid.*, p. 97.

Charles Collingwood: Mitchell, p. 5.

Stengel: Nelson and Hirshberg, pp. 132-33.

CHAPTER 11 – THE MEDIA

Casey Stengel: Dickson, p. 418.

Larry Merchant: Stan Isaacs, October 14

Leonard Koppett: interview with author, August 26, 2002.

Walter Pullis: interview with author, July 15, 2002.

Koppett: interview with author, August 26, 2002.

Koppett: *ibid.*

Koppett: *ibid.*

Koppett: Koppett, *New York Mets*, pp. 61-62.

Vecsey: Vecsey, p. 48.

Koppett: interview with author, August 26, 2002.

Jack Lang: Lang and Simon, p. 28.

Robert Lipsyte: Golenbock, *Amazin'*, p. 113.

Vecsey: Vecsey, pp. 48-49.

Hook: Heyman.

Dick Young: *ibid.*, p. 48.

Ed Wolff: interview with author, April 14, 2002.

Koppett: interview with author, August 26, 2002.

Lipsyte: Golenbock, *Amazin'*, p. 109.

Koppett: interview with author, August 26, 2002.

Koppett: *ibid.*

Koppett: *ibid.*

Stan Isaacs: e-mail to author, August 7, 2002.

Lindsey Nelson: Curt Smith, p. 118.

Nelson: *ibid.*, p. 119.

Koppett: Koppett, *New York Mets*, pp. 60-61.

Nelson: Nelson and Hirshberg, p. 89.

MacMaster: interview with author, July 15, 2002.

Pullis: interview with author, July 15, 2002.

Rick Williams: e-mail to author, July 21, 2002.

Steve Rushin: Rushin, p. 48.

CHAPTER 12 – THE SEASON CONTINUES

Casey Stengel: Berkow and Kaplan, p. 19.

Jimmy Breslin: Breslin, *Can't Anybody*, p. 85.

Craig Anderson: interview with author, March 10, 2002.

Frank Thomas: interview with author, July 3, 2002.

Stengel: Mitchell, p. 78.

Stengel: *ibid.*

Jay Hook: interview with author, April 13, 2002.

John Drebinger: John Drebinger, "16-Hit Attack Beats Mets," *TheNew York Times*, July 15, 2002.

Paul D. Zimmerman: Zimmerman, p. 158.

Breslin: Breslin, "Worst Team Ever," p. 23.

Ralph Kiner: Kiner and Gergen, p. 40.

Jerry Mitchell: Mitchell, p. 72.

Stengel: *ibid.*, p. 73.

George Weiss: Breslin, "Worst Team Ever," p. 24.

M. Donald Grant: *ibid.*

Bill Veeck: *ibid.*

Thomas: interview with author, July 3, 2002.

Don Zimmer: Zimmer and Madden, p. 58.

Jim O'Toole: Peary, p. 546.

Anderson: interview with author, March 10, 2002.

Kanehl: interview with author, April 25, 2002.

Fred Hutchinson: Mitchell, p. 90.

Zimmer: Rushin, p. 48.

Anderson: interview with author, March 10, 2002.

Kanehl: Golenbock, *Amazin'*, pp. 136-37.

Hook: interview with author, April 13, 2002.

Kanehl: interview with author, April 25, 2002.

Thomas: interview with author, July 3, 2002.

Throneberry: "With 'Marvelous,' Pay's The Thing." *TheNew York Times*, August 11, 1962.

Richie Ashburn: Breslin, *Can't Anybody*, p. 90.

Al Jackson: Weiskopf, "Baseball's Week." *Sports Illustrated*, August 27, 1962, p. 70.

Stengel: Shecter, *Polo Grounds*, p. 93.

Felix Mantilla: Mitchell, p. 124.

George Vecsey: Vecsey, p. 87.

Weiskopf: Weiskopf, "Baseball's Week." *Sports Illustrated*, September 3, 1962, p. 61.

Hook: interview with author, April 13, 2002.

Ashburn: Berkow and Kaplan, p. 124.

Hook: interview with author, April 13, 2002.

Breslin: Breslin, *Can't Anybody*, p. 67.

Stengel: Boyd and Harris, p. 127.

Marv Throneberry: Blake, p. 198.

Nelson: Nelson and Hirshberg, p. 129.

Anderson: interview with author, March 10, 2002.

Anderson: *ibid.*

Anderson: *ibid.*

Anderson: Rushin,

Stengel: Mitchell, p. 154.

Kanehl: Rushin, p. 50; Golenbock, *Amazin'*, p. 137.

Kanehl: Golenbock, *Amazin'*, p. 153.

CHAPTER 13 – JOURNEY'S END

Casey Stengel: Bak, p. 161.

Bob Miller: Allen, *The Incredible Mets*, p. 49.

Maury Allen: *ibid.*

Paul D. Zimmerman: Zimmerman and Schaap, p.

Joe Pignatano: Blake, p. 200-01.

Stengel: Rushin, p. 50.

Stengel: Mitchell, p. 86.

Herman Weiskopf: Weiskopf, "Baseball's Week," *Sports Illustrated*, October 1, 1962.

Allen: Allen, *The Incredible Mets*, p. 50.

Kanehl: Golenbock, *Amazin'*, p. 137.

Don Zimmer: Zimmer and Madden, p. 55.

Jimmy Breslin: Breslin, *Can't Anybody*, p. 86.

Richie Ashburn: Creamer, p. 300.

Ashburn: Rushin, p. 50.

Zimmer: Zimmer and Madden, p. 55.

Frank Thomas: interview with author, July 3, 2002.

Ashburn: Rushin, p. 50.

Stengel: *ibid.*

Thomas: interview with author, July 3, 2002.

Breslin: Breslin, *Can't Anybody*, p. 23.

Walter Pullis: interview with author, July 15, 2002.

Marv Throneberry: *Can't Anybody*, p. 23.

Ashburn: Bak, p. 161; Berkow and Kaplan, p.

Ken MacKenzie: Shecter, *Polo Grounds*, pp. 94-95.

Frank Thomas: Peary, p. 542.

Ed Bouchee: *ibid.*, p. 543.

Throneberry: Breslin, *Can't Anybody*, pp. 23-24.

Dick Schofield: *ibid.*, p. 541.

Jim Brosnan: *ibid.*, p. 547.

Bill Veeck:Jim Bouton, *I Managed Good but Boy Did They Play Bad*, p. 90.

Veeck: Breslin, *Can't Anybody*, p. 91.

Lee Allen: Mitchell, p. 15.

Joan Payson: Breslin, *Can't Anybody*, pp. 52, 65.

Charlie Neal: Shecter, *Polo Grounds*, pp. 101-02.

Kanehl: *ibid.*, p. 102.

Roger Craig: *ibid.*

Zimmerman: Zimmerman and Schaap, p. 143.

Brendan Boyd and Fred Harris: Boyd and Harris, p. 79.

Breslin: Breslin, *Can't Anybody*, pp. 36-37.

Pumpsie Green: Mitchell, p. 152; Howard Blatt, Amazin' Met Memories – Four Decades of Unforgettable Moments, p. 392.

George Weiss: Shaplen, p. 38.

Breslin: Breslin, "Worst Team Ever," p. 53.

The Sporting News: Peter C. Bjarkman, *The New York Mets Encyclopedia*, p. 198.

Stengel: Buk, p. 161.

Stengel: Mitchell, p. 91.

Stengel: Golenbock, *Amazin'*, p. 139.

CHAPTER 14 – THE AFTERMATH

Casey Stengel: Breslin, *Can't Anybody*, p. 109.

Marv Throneberry: Mitchell, p. 107.

Dialogue: Shecter, *Polo Grounds*, p. 101.

George Weiss: Golenbock, *Amazin'*, p. 139.

Craig Anderson: interview with author, March 10, 2002.

Duke Snider: Duke Snider, *The Duke of Flatbush*, p. 250.

Snider: Norman MacLean, *Casey Stengel – A Biography*, p. 157.

Snider: Bak, p. 160.

Anderson: interview with author, March 10, 2002.

Roger Craig: Durso, Casey, p. 156.

Throneberry: Shecter, *Polo Grounds*, p. 106.

Throneberry: *ibid.*

Throneberry: Mitchell, p. 109.

Casey Stengel: Berkow, p. 17.

Kanehl: Golenbock, p. 155.

Tracy Stallard: Vecsey, p. 119.

Kanehl: Golenbock, *Amazin'*, p. 158.

Stengel: Bak, p. 160.

Anderson: interview with author, March 10, 2002.

Kanehl: Golenbock, *Amazin'*, p. 158.

Kanehl: interview with author, April 25, 2002.

Kanehl: *ibid.*

Kanehl: *ibid.*

Kanehl: *ibid.*

Kanehl: Shecter, *The Jocks*, p. 168.

Jay Hook: interview with author, April 13, 2002.

Hook: *ibid.*

Frank Thomas: interview with author, July 3, 2002.

Thomas: *ibid.*

Stengel: Bak, p. 167.

Stengel: *ibid.*, p. 171.

Jim Hickman: Allen, *The Incredible Mets*, p. 74.

Weiss: Vecsey, pp. 138-39.

Anderson: interview with author, March 10, 2002.

Hook: interview with author, April 13, 2002.

Dallas Green: Weaver, p. 426.

Joe Pignatano: interview with Marty Lurie,

www.loveofthegameproductions.com, May 22, 2002.

Bob Miller: Nathan, p. 45.

Bill Shea: Weaver, p. 62.

Jim Murray: Dickson, p. 233.

Bob Case: Cataneo, *Casey Stengel*, p. 211.

CHAPTER 15 – THE LEGEND

Casey Stengel: Rushin, p. 50.

Ed Wolff: interview with author, April 14, 2002.

Jim Fertitta, Sr.: interview with author, June 24, 2002.

Joseph Durso: Durso, *Casey*, pp. 162-63.

Stan Isaacs: e-mail to author, August 7, 2002.

Leonard Koppett: interview with author, August 26, 2002.

Roger Angell: Angell, *The Summer Game*, p. 15.

Craig Anderson: interview with author, March 10, 2002.

George Vecsey: Vecsey, p. 13.

Jay Hook: interview with author, April 13, 2002.

John MacMaster: interview with author, July 15, 2002.

Walter Pullis: interview with author, July 15, 2002.

Stanley Cohen: Cohen, pp. 97-98.

Koppett: Koppett, *New York Mets*, p. 59.

Koppett: interview with author, August 26, 2002.

Brian Heyman: Brian Heyman, e-mail to author, August 14, 2002.

Marv Throneberry: Rushin, p. 51.

Leonard Shecter: Shecter, *Polo Grounds*, p. 14.

Rod Kanehl: Golenbock, *Amazin'*, p. 134.

Dick Schaap: Breslin, *Can't Anybody*, forward by Dick Schaap, pp. 12-13.

Throneberry: Rushin, p. 51.

George Vecsey: Danny Peary, ed., *Cult Baseball Players*, p. 90.

Throneberry: Blake, pp. 198-99.

Anderson: interview with author, March 10, 2002.

Kanehl: interview with author, April 25, 2002.

Throneberry: Rushin, p. 51.

Hook: interview with author, April 13, 2002.

Thomas: interview with author, July 3, 2002.

Anderson: interview with author, March 10, 2002.

Kanehl: interview with author, April 25, 2002.

Hook: interview with author, April 13, 2002.

Anderson: interview with author, March 10, 2002.

Thomas: interview with author, July 3, 2002.

Hook: interview with author, March 10, 2002.

Anderson: Rushin, p. 51.

Gene Woodling: Peary, p. 543; Edward Kiersh, *Where Have You Gone, Vince DiMaggio?* p. 68.

Thomas: interview with author, July 3, 2002.

Joe Ginsberg: Cairns, p. 102.

Al Jackson: Allen, *Baseball*, p. 187.

Roger Craig: Cairns, pp. 179-80.

Ken MacKenzie: Isaacs, September 12

Richie Ashburn: Rushin, p. 51.

Throneberry: Blake, p. 199.

Hook: interview with author, April 13, 2002.

Ashburn: Mitchell, p. 94.

AFTERWARD

Casey Stengel: Weaver, p. 601

Made in the USA
Lexington, KY
06 April 2011